GALATIANS AND EPHESIANS

GALATIANS AND EPHESIANS

by
John M Riddle

40 Beansburn, Kilmarnock, Scotland

ISBN-13: 978 1 912522 89 7

Copyright © 2020 by John Ritchie Ltd.
40 Beansburn, Kilmarnock, Scotland

www.ritchiechristianmedia.co.uk

All rights reserved. No part of this publication may be reproduced, stored in a retrievable system, or transmitted in any form or by any other means – electronic, mechanical, photocopy, recording or otherwise – without prior permission of the copyright owner.

Typeset by John Ritchie Ltd., Kilmarnock
Printed by Bell & Bain Ltd., Glasgow

Contents

Preface	7
The Epistle to the Galatians - Introduction	9
Chapter 1:1-5	18
Chapter 1:6-24	27
Chapter 2:1-10	38
Chapter 2:11-21	47
Chapter 3:1-14	57
Chapter 3:15-29	69
Chapter 4:1-7	79
Chapter 4:8-31	89
Chapter 5:1-12	101
Chapter 5:13-26	113
Chapter 6:1-18	124
The Epistle to the Ephesians - Introduction	139
Chapter 1:1-3	147
Chapter 1:4-8	153
Chapter 1:9-14	161
Chapter 1:15-23	171

Chapter 2:1-10 182

Chapter 2:11-22 192

Chapter 3:1-13 203

Chapter 3:14-21 215

Chapter 4:1-6 227

Chapter 4:7-16 235

Chapter 4:17-19 246

Chapter 4:20-32 252

Chapter 5:1-7 261

Chapter 5:8-21 270

Chapter 5:22-33 280

Chapter 6:1-9 292

Chapter 6:10-17 302

Chapter 6:18-24 314

Preface

This book represents the substance of Bible Class discussions on Friday evenings at Mill Lane Chapel, Cheshunt, between May and December 2016 in the case of Galatians, and January and October 2018 in the case of Ephesians.

While, in introducing earlier publications in this series, it was customary to say that the original notes were prepared and circulated without any expectation of their eventual appearance in the public domain, this not now the case. That is not to say that they are now compiled with one eye on 'assembly opinion', and with a fervent desire not to 'upset the apple-cart'!

One thing that has not changed is that this volume, like its predecessors, does not purport to be a commentary in the usual sense of the word. No attempt is made to be exhaustive.

As time passes by, the personal advice of Mr. Albert McShane increases in relevance: "Don't write a book until you're old – then you haven't got time to change your mind!" What does that tell you?

As before and, again, not as a mere courtesy, the Bible Class at Cheshunt remains genuinely indebted to John Ritchie Ltd for their willingness to publish its notes, something first mooted by Mr. John Grant, and to Mr. Fraser Munro and his colleagues for their invaluable help in editing the material submitted to them. The Bible Class also continues to be grateful to Miss Lesley Prentice for having checked and corrected the original manuscripts, something she continues to do, and to Mr. Eric Browning for his considerable help in continuing to send copies of current studies by Email to a wide readership.

The prayerful desire of the Mill Lane Bible Class is that, in the goodness of God, this volume will prove to be a channel of "edification, and exhortation, and comfort" (1 Cor. 14: 3).

John Riddle
Cheshunt, Hertfordshire
November 2020

THE EPISTLE TO THE GALATIANS

Introduction

Read the whole epistle

Very clearly, a number of New Testament letters were written in connection with early problems in the history of the church. Some of these were internal problems, and we think of 1 & 2 Corinthians particularly here. Paul deals with the rather delicate problem of a fractured relationship in Philippians. Some were external problems, and we think particularly of 1 & 2 Thessalonians, and the severe persecution which faced those believers. But it could be argued that the gravest problem of all is addressed in the Epistle to the Galatians. It is worth noticing that there are no references in the New Testament to either work or assemblies in the northern part of Galatia. Both Acts Chapters 13-14, together with 2 Timothy 3 verse 11, refer only to work in the south of the province: Pisidian Antioch, Iconium, Derbe and Lystra.

Before we examine the problem, we ought to enquire why God permitted such a wide variety of problems to arise so early in the history of the church. To borrow from the world of horticulture, it would surely have been better to allow these young assemblies to 'harden off' a little, before exposing them to such severe pressure. Let us assume that this is what actually did happen. The apostles, with their unique knowledge and authority, would have ultimately passed off the scene, so that when the problems *did* come, there would have been nobody of sufficient spiritual stature to deal with them effectively. The Bible would not have the answers either! An all-wise God therefore allowed the problems to arise when they did, so that His Word would contain all the resources needed to withstand them, not only at the time of writing, but for *all* time. After all, *we* face the same problems in principle, if not in exact detail, and God has given us a book to which *we* can turn with confidence for guidance and help.

1) THE BACKGROUND TO THE EPISTLE

The Epistle to the Galatians deals with an early, if not the earliest, doctrinal problem. We encounter the problem in Acts 15, and this chapter must be read in conjunction with Galatians 2. "And certain men which came down from Judaea taught the brethren (at Antioch in Syria, Acts 14: 26-28), and said, Except ye be circumcised after the manner of Moses, ye cannot be saved" (Acts 15: 1). As a result of this, Paul and Barnabas (Acts 15: 2), together with Titus (Galatians 2: 1), went "up to Jerusalem unto the apostles and elders about this question". As we will see, this was far more than a decision on Paul's part. He "went up by revelation" (Gal. 2: 2). There were at least two reasons for this:

i) **The other apostles were located at Jerusalem,** and it was vital for all the apostles to speak with one voice. Paul could have legislated on the matter at Antioch, but his teaching might then have been dismissed as 'a minority view' or 'a personal view'.

ii) **The problem was taken back to its source.** The false teachers came from Judaea, and it was to Judaea that Paul went. This is a principle worth remembering!

What had happened at Antioch was repeated at Jerusalem once Paul and his party had arrived. "And when they were come to Jerusalem, they were received of the church, and of the apostles and elders, and they declared all things that God had done with them. *But* there rose up certain of the sect of the Pharisees which believed, saying, That it was needful to circumcise them, and to command them to keep the law of Moses" (Acts 15: 4-5). The gravity of this teaching is very clear indeed. The very basis of salvation was under attack. The grand Bible doctrine of justification by faith was discredited. According to these teachers, men and women were not saved by grace, but by works. We must not think for one moment that this was a dispute over a minor surgical operation. These teachers insisted on circumcision, not as a mere *rite,* but as an undertaking to **keep the whole law.**

The Epistle to the Galatians deals with this teaching, and its relevance to the twentieth century is clear. Much of Christendom operates on the principle of faith plus works as the means of salvation, reminding us of the words:

God tells me how I may be saved,
He points to something done,
Accomplished on Mount Calvary
By His beloved Son,
In which no works of mine have place;
For grace with works is no more grace.

We should notice that at the conference in Jerusalem, the apostle Peter asserted that the teaching of these men was in direct conflict with the way in which he had seen Gentiles saved, and that salvation by works was not sustainable by even the Jews themselves: "And God, which knoweth the hearts, bare them witness, giving them the Holy Ghost, even as he did unto us; and put no difference between us and them, purifying their hearts **by faith.** Now therefore why tempt ye God, to put a yoke upon the neck of the disciples, which neither our fathers nor we were able to bear? But we believe that through the grace of the Lord Jesus Christ we shall be saved, even as they" (Acts 15: 8-11). We should note that while the problem at Antioch, which had been dealt with at Jerusalem, had spread to Galatia, it was also threatening the believers at Philippi (Phil. 3: 1-3) and Colosse (Col. 2: 16-17. See also Romans 16: 17-19).

If the Epistle to the Romans deals with justification and **sin,** then the Epistle to the Galatians deals with justification and **the law.** Romans emphasises justification to **life,** and Galatians justification to **liberty.**

2) THE ATMOSPHERE IN THE EPISTLE

The extremely serious nature of the false teaching reflects in the atmosphere of the epistle. For a start, the letter commences without the customary expressions of prayer and praise. There is no reference, for example, to "your faith growth exceedingly" (2 Thess. 1: 3). It also commences with reference to Paul's apostleship in the **strongest terms**: "Paul, an apostle, (not of men, neither by man, but by Jesus Christ, and God the Father, who raised him from the dead)". Paul brings the highest authority to bear upon the situation. We should notice that Paul introduces his letters with reference to the situation in the assemblies to which he is writing.

The letter commences with strong censure of the **Galatian believers themselves,** as well as the **false teachers:**

i) **The Galatians.** "I marvel that ye are so soon removed from him that called you unto (into) the grace of Christ unto another gospel" (1: 6). The false teachers were culpable, but so were the believers in Galatia. Later Paul exclaims, "O ***foolish Galatians***, who hath bewitched you, that ye should not obey the truth, before whose eyes Jesus Christ hath been evidently set forth, crucified among you? ... Are ye ***so foolish?*** having begun in the Spirit, are ye now made perfect by the flesh?" (3: 1-3). The false teachers were wrong in imposing their doctrines on the Galatians, and the Galatians were wrong in accepting them.

But at the same time, we must notice that he employs the term "***brethren***" (1: 11; 3: 15; 4: 12, 28, 31; 5: 11, 13; 6: 1, 18), and addresses them as "***my little children"***, of whom I travail in birth again until Christ be formed in you" (4: 19). It is worth remembering that teaching should never be undertaken, however serious the situation, without affection for the Lord's people. It has been nicely said that "they are deceived, disturbed and defecting in their devotion and duty to Christ. But they are still regarded as brethren: brethren needing Paul's Spirit-inspired counsel!" Paul's deep interest in them (4: 11-13) reminds us of the need for preachers and teachers to have a personal interest in their hearers. He was so concerned about them that he evidently penned the letter personally.

ii) **The false teachers.** "But there be some that trouble you, and would pervert the gospel of Christ. But though we, or an angel from heaven, preach any other gospel unto you than that which we have preached unto you, let him be accursed. As we said before, so say I now again, If any man preach any other gospel unto you than that ye have received, let him be accursed" (1: 7-9). By saying, "let him be accursed", Paul is not stating a wish: he is expressing ***a fact.*** See 1 Corinthians 16 verse 22.

While Paul speaks in affectionate terms to his fellow-believers in Galatia, he does nothing of the sort when speaking of the false teachers. He calls them "***false brethren*** unawares brought in, who came in privily to spy out our liberty which we have in Christ Jesus, that they might bring us into bondage; to whom we gave place by subjection, no, not for an hour; that the truth of the gospel might continue with you" (2: 4-5). He accuses them of attempting to drive a wedge between the Galatians and himself: "They zealously affect you, but not well; yea, they would exclude you, that ye might affect them" (4: 17), or "They are not rightly zealous after you, but desire to shut you out (from us), that ye might be zealous after them" (JND). He says, "I would they were even cut off which trouble you" (5: 12).

Introduction

We should notice that, at least initially, false teachers work **surreptitiously.** "False brethren unawares brought in, who came in privily" 2:4. "Unawares" and "privily" are associated words. "Unawares brought in" *(pareisaktos)* and "came in privily" *(pareiserchomia)* have the literal meaning of 'coming in from the side', that is (quoting W.E.Vine) 'as spies or traitors'. W.E.Vine continues, "Strabo, a Greek historian contemporary with Paul, uses the word of enemies introduced secretly into a city by traitors within". Compare 2 Peter 2 verse 1, "Who privily shall bring in damnable (destructive) heresies", and Jude verse 4, "There are certain men crept in unawares". Here, in Galatians 2 verses 4-5, they were "brought in" and they "came in". They were "brought in" by those who were inclined towards Judaism, and sought help of false brethren to accomplish their ends. The need for care in reception is obvious. The assembly is not a 'free for all'.

3) THE TEACHING OF THE EPISTLE

We have noted the serious nature of the false teaching. The Jewish teachers asserted that Gentile believers must be circumcised, and commanded to keep the law of Moses. See, again Acts 15: 5. In fact, according to them, Gentile believers were not saved until this happened: "Except ye be circumcised after the manner of Moses, ye cannot be saved" (Acts 15: 1). We must now notice the principal arguments against this teaching:

i) **The historical argument.** How had the Jews, the circumcised Jews, been saved? On what basis had they been justified? "**We** who are Jews by nature, and not sinners of the Gentiles, knowing that a man is not justified by the works of the law, but by the faith of Jesus Christ, even **we** have believed in Jesus Christ, that **we** might be justified by the faith of Christ, and not by the works of the law: for by the works of the law shall no flesh be justified" (2: 15-16).

But there is more. The **very** basis of justification, faith in Christ, made clear that "the works of the law" were not involved, and so did the **proof** of justification: "This only would I learn of you, Received ye the Spirit by the works of the law, or by the hearing of faith?" (3: 2).

We might add that if the **basis of salvation** is the work of Christ, and the **proof of salvation** is the possession of the Holy Spirit, then in Chapter 4, the **basis of sonship** is the work of Christ, and the **proof of sonship** is the possession of the Holy Spirit. See 4: 4-7.

*ii) **The Christological argument.*** This is clearly expressed in Chapter 2. "If righteousness come by the law, then Christ is dead in vain" (v.21). Could anything be clearer? If salvation, justification, righteousness, can be obtained through "the works of the law", then why did Christ die? It was not even necessary. Another, chilling, implication is expressed in verse 17, "But, if, while we seek to be justified by Christ, we ourselves also are found sinners, is therefore Christ the minister of sin?" No wonder Paul exclaims, "God forbid". If they had been wrong in abandoning the principle of justification by works in favour of the principle of justification by faith in Christ, then the very Christ in whom they had trusted had led them into sin.

iii) ***The legal argument.*** It was very important indeed to ensure that the Galatians understood that salvation by faith alone rested on a secure legal basis. The Jewish teachers pointed to the law as the established means of acceptance with God. Paul counters this argument by pointing out that it was God's settled purpose to "justify the heathen through faith" (3: 8), and points out that He had announced this to the very man who "believed God, and it was accounted unto him for righteousness" (3: 6), centuries before the law was given: "And the scripture, foreseeing that God would justify the heathen through faith, preached before the gospel unto Abraham, saying, In thee shall all nations be blessed". It was a divinely-ratified covenant that could not be annulled by a subsequent covenant 430 years later. This did not mean that the law had no purpose, but it was not a means to justification, and was only a temporary measure.

All this emphasises the value of Bible history. Paul read his Old Testament with great care. He noticed exactly **what** was said, and **when** it was said. He displayed considerable powers of spiritual observation! But it also underlines the accuracy of the Word of God. There are no 'throw-away lines' in the Bible. Everything is there for a purpose! We have a further illustration in Chapter 4 where Paul describes the two sons, by two mothers, as an "allegory".

Compare the Old Testament references to Melchisedec. Notice how these are expounded in Hebrews Chapters 6-7.

iv) ***The logical argument.*** What had the law accomplished anyway? It brought the most terrible condemnation. "For as many as are of the works of the law are under the curse: for it is written, Cursed is every one that continueth not in all things which are written in the book of the law to do them" (3: 10). Paul calls the precepts of the law, "weak and beggarly elements" (4: 9). The law had no power to strengthen and no power to enrich. It imposed bondage: "But before faith came, we were kept under the law, shut up unto the faith which should afterwards be revealed. Wherefore the law was our schoolmaster to bring us unto Christ ('up to Christ', JND), that we might be justified by faith" (3: 23-24).

The "schoolmaster" was usually a slave, whose duty it was to conduct the boy or youth to and from school, and to superintend his conduct generally. He was often harsh to the point of cruelty, and is usually depicted in ancient drawings with a rod or cane in his hand. The law was just like the "schoolmaster". It imposed **servitude.** It said, "thou shalt" and "thou shalt not", and "every transgression and disobedience received a just recompence of reward" (Heb. 2: 2). At every turn of the way, the law highlighted sin and waywardness, and proclaimed judgment. It buffeted the sinner. Hence the expression "**under** the law" , with all its oppression. It held people tightly in its grip: there was no escape: "shut up ('guarded', Gal. 3:23 JND) unto the faith which should afterwards be revealed".

We should notice the use of the word "**under**" in the epistle: "under the curse...under sin...under the law...under a schoolmaster...under tutors and governors...under the elements of the world". No wonder Paul exclaims, "Stand fast therefore in the **liberty** wherewith Christ hath made us free, and be not entangled again with the yoke of bondage" (5: 1).

*v) **The moral argument.*** But isn't the law essential for moral conduct? It is striking to observe that the law did nothing to control, let alone eliminate, "the lust of the flesh". The law was not a means to **justification,** neither was it a means to **sanctification.** The law served only to reveal the "works of the flesh", and these are enumerated in Chapter 5 verses 19-21. But this does not mean that the Gospel brings a lesser standard, for if "all the law is fulfilled in one word, even in this; Thou shalt love thy neighbour as thyself" (5: 14), then the necessary fulfillment is accomplished, not by human attempts to keep the law, but by the operative power of the Holy Spirit. "But the fruit of the Spirit is **love,** joy, peace, longsuffering, gentleness, goodness, faith, meekness, temperance: against such there is no law" (5:22-23). The Spirit of God produces in our lives what we could never achieve by the "works of the law".

4) THE STRUCTURE OF THE EPISTLE

The epistle divides into three main sections: *(a)* the historical section (chs.1-

2); *(b)* the doctrinal section (chs.3-4); *(c)* the practical section (chs.5-6). In this connection, notice the use of the word "liberty". In treating the subject *historically,* Paul says, "false brethren unawares brought in, who came in privily to spy out our *liberty* which we have in Christ Jesus" (2: 4) Having treated the matter *doctrinally*, Paul exclaims, "Stand fast therefore in the *liberty* wherewith Christ hath made us free" (5: 1). When treating the matter *practically,* Paul cautions, "For brethren, ye have been called unto liberty; only use not *liberty* for an occasion of the flesh" (5: 13). No wonder the epistle has been called the 'Magna Carta of Evangelical Christianity'.

a) The historical section, Chapters 1-2

In this biographical section, Paul emphasises that his authority was imparted to him by Christ Himself (Chapter 1), and that this authority was fully recognised by his fellow-apostles (Chapter 2). It was necessary for Paul to establish his authority in this way before dealing with the error that was sweeping the Galatian assemblies.

b) The doctrinal section, Chapters 3-4

Without any attempt whatsoever to examine the detail, we must notice that the arguments in this section are founded upon the Old Testament scriptures. Paul argues from the very scriptures espoused by the Jewish teachers! In particular, he draws attention to the terms of the covenant-promises made to Abraham, and the way in which the law was given. Not only did the covenant of promise precede the covenant of law, and, since it was ratified, could not be annulled, it was infinitely superior to the covenant of law. The law was inferior to the covenant of promise in view of *(i)* the purpose for which it was given ("It was added because of transgressions"), *(ii)* the period for which it was given ("till the seed should come to whom the promise was made"), and *(iii)* the parties involved when it was given ("it was ordained by angels in the hand of a mediator"). See Chapter 3 verses 19-20. But there is more: if "righteousness should have been by the law", then the covenant made with Abraham would become null and void, and Christ would have become redundant.

c) The practical section, Chapters 5-6

As we have noticed, these chapters present the practical implications for the believer of the gospel of grace. They are also best understood as part of the argument of the epistle. They answer the argument that a gospel of free justification led to loose living, and that the law alone protected the interests of morality. Paul proves that the reverse is true. He emphasises that liberty is not licence to sin. Christian freedom is a freedom from sin, to serve God: it is not freedom to do as we like. See Chapter 5 verse 13, "For, brethren, ye have been called unto liberty; only use not liberty for an occasion to the flesh, but by love serve one another".

We should remember that "justification and practical, progressive sanctification, though distinct, are vitally related. The latter must attend the former. Unless a man is being sanctified, he gives no proof of having been justified. Justification without some measure of growing holiness is a moral absurdity. Equally, practical holiness is a moral impossibility without a secure foundation in acceptance by God on the basis of Christ's work" (Alan Gamble, writing in the *Believer's Magazine*).

In conclusion, we must note that the doctrine of salvation by faith without "the works of the law" was not at all popular. The epistle concludes: "From henceforth let no man trouble me: for I bear in my body the marks of the Lord Jesus" (6: 17). The "allegory" proclaimed this: "But as then he that was born after the flesh persecuted him that was born after the Spirit, even so it is now" (4: 29). See also Chapter 6 verse 12, "As many as desire to make a fair shew in the flesh, they constrain you to be circumcised; only lest they should suffer persecution for the cross of Christ". There is always a cost to preaching and teaching the truth of God.

But bearing in mind the character of the epistle, Paul still desires the blessing of God's people. "Brethren, the grace of our Lord Jesus Christ be with your spirit. Amen" (6: 18).

THE EPISTLE TO THE GALATIANS

The Prologue

Read Chapter 1: 1-5

As we have already noticed in our Introduction, the Epistle to the Galatians comprises three major sections *(i)* the historical section (chs.1-2), *(ii)* the doctrinal section (chs.3-4), *(iii)* the practical section (chs.5-6).

Amongst other things, the historical section emphasises that Paul's authority was directly imparted to him by Christ Himself (1: 1-24), and that his divinely-given authority was fully recognised by his fellow-apostles (2: 1-10) (The balance of Chapter 2 describes the way in which Paul was obliged to confront Peter over his volte-face at Antioch "For before that certain came from James, he did eat with the Gentiles but when they were come, he withdrew and separated himself, fearing them which were of the circumcision", 2: 12).

It was necessary for Paul to establish his authority in this way before dealing with the error that confronted the believers in Galatia. This is emphasised in the introduction, where we should notice *(1)* the authority bestowed upon Paul (v.1), *(2)* the churches addressed by Paul (v.2), *(3)* the deliverance described by Paul (vv.3-5).

As so often in the Bible, 'the key hangs at the door'. Having stated his apostolic authority (v.1), Paul immediately emphasises that salvation, "who gave himself for our sins", and sanctification, "that he might deliver us from this present evil world (age)", rest **solely** upon the death of the Lord Jesus (vv.4-5), reminding us that "not by works of righteousness which we have done, but according to his mercy he saved us ... that being justified by his grace, we should be made heirs according to the hope of eternal life" (Titus 3: 5-7). Neither salvation nor sanctification are accomplished by "the works of the law" (Gal. 2: 16) In Paul's words elsewhere, "now the righteousness of

God without the law is manifested ... even the righteousness of God which is by faith of Jesus Christ unto all and upon all them that believe ..." (Rom. 3: 21-22). Having said this, we must now note:

1) THE AUTHORITY BESTOWED UPON PAUL, v.1

Paul commences by emphasising his apostleship here in the **strongest terms,** something he does nowhere else in his New Testament correspondence: "Paul, an apostle, (not of men, neither by man, but by Jesus Christ, and God the Father, who raised him from the dead)". Compare, for example, Romans 1 verse 1 ("Paul, a servant of Jesus Christ, called to be an apostle"), 1 Corinthians 1 verse 1 ("Paul, called to be an apostle of Jesus Christ through the will of God"), but notice the difference in Philippians 1 verse 1, 1 Thessalonians 1 verse 1 and 2 Thessalonians 1 verse 1 where he does not mention his apostleship at all. Very clearly, Paul introduces his letters with reference to the current situation in the assemblies to which he is writing. He does not deal with everything in the same way. Different situations, and different people, demand a different approach. 'A word to the wise!'

The extremely serious false teaching being perpetrated amongst the assemblies in Galatia meant that Paul was obliged to bring the highest possible authority to bear upon the situation. This accounts for what Alan Gamble (writing in the *Believer's Magazine)* calls "the abrupt beginning of the letter". For a start, the letter commences without the customary expressions of prayer and praise.

It should be noted that what Paul says about himself - "Paul, an apostle, (not of men, neither by man, but by Jesus Christ, and God the Father, who raised him from the dead)" - he also says about his preaching - "But I certify you, brethren, that the gospel which was preached of me is not after man. For I neither received **it** of man, neither was I taught **it,** but by the revelation of Jesus Christ" (1: 11-12).

Paul now emphasises that the authority bestowed upon him was not humanly-imparted, but divinely-imparted.

a) His authority was not humanly-imparted 1:1

"Paul, an apostle **(not of men, neither by man,** but by Jesus Christ and God the Father, who raised him from the dead)."

- "Not of *(apo)* men ('not from men', JND)." We should notice the **plural** here ("men"). That is, not by human appointment. This could refer to the apostles corporately, as in the case of Matthias (Acts 1: 15-26).

- "Neither by *(dia)* man ('nor through man', JND)." That is, not by human mediation. We should now notice the **singular.** This could refer to one prominent man, such as Peter.

His apostleship was not human in origin, and no human channel was used in bestowing it upon him. "The first preposition here *(apo)* denotes the fountain head whence the apostle's authority springs: the second *(dia)* denotes the channel through which it is conveyed" (J. B. Lightfoot). Even the other apostles were not involved.

b) His authority was divinely-imparted

"Paul, an apostle *(not* of men, **neither** by man, but **by Jesus Christ and God the Father, who raised him from the dead)."**

We should remember that on the Damascus Road, the Lord said to Saul, "I am Jesus", to which Paul replied, "Lord, what wilt thou have me to do?" (Acts 9: 5-6). In doing this, Saul (as he was then) confessed with his "mouth Jesus as Lord" (Rom. 10: 9, JND) The answer was not long in coming: having "come again to Jerusalem" and "in a trance" while praying in the temple, he saw the Lord who told him to "get ... quickly out of Jerusalem", adding, "Depart: for I will send thee *(exapostello)* far hence unto the Gentiles" (Acts 22: 17-21). Paul refers to this in Romans 15: 15-16, having previously described himself as the "apostle *(apostolos)* of the Gentiles" (Rom. 11: 13).

His apostleship was divine in origin, and divine in communication. The two statements in verse 1 therefore form a contrast. Paul's authority was *(i)* not **from** men, but from God the Father: *(ii)* not **through** men, but through Jesus Christ. This emphasises that he was not just an apostle in a secondary sense. We should notice that in the words, **"by Jesus Christ and God the Father",** both Christ ("Jesus Christ") and God ("God the Father") are governed by one preposition ("by") and joined by one conjunction ("and"), indicating that they are co-equal and co-eternal. We should notice *(i)* its implications for Paul; *(ii)* its implications for us.

i) Its implications for Paul. He was an apostle "by Jesus Christ, and God the Father, who raised him from the dead":

- **"by Jesus Christ"** This emphasises His humanity: His earthly sojourn. 'Christ Jesus' emphasises His glory. Paul possibly uses the order "Jesus Christ" here to emphasise that he had been appointed by the very Man who was here on earth, and who had appointed 'the twelve'. It has been pointed out that "Christ Jesus" emphasises that He is now in heaven, having been on earth, and that "Jesus Christ" emphasises that He was once on earth, but now in heaven. It is said that Paul usually uses the order "Christ Jesus" since it was from heaven that He revealed Himself to the apostle, whereas Peter uses the order "Jesus Christ" since he was called by the Lord Jesus while He was on earth.

- **"and God the Father"** Not now "our Father" (v.4) We should carefully distinguish between "the Father" in the context of the Godhead, and "our Father" in relationship to ourselves. See John 20 verse 17. The title, "Father", reminds us of plan, purpose and design. For example, "The **Father** sent the Son to be the Saviour of the world" (1 John 4: 14). The purpose of the Father is implemented by the Son in the power of the Holy Spirit

We should notice again that Paul tells us that he was "an apostle by Jesus Christ", that is, by the Lord who had appointed the twelve on **earth.** He was equally "an apostle" by "God the Father, who raised him from the dead" *(ek nekron),* reminding us that "Jesus Christ" is, equally, the **risen and ascended** Lord. This effectively answered his detractors, who denied his apostleship. Compare 1 Corinthians 9: 1 ("Am I not an apostle ... have I not seen Jesus Christ our Lord") and 1 Corinthians 15 verse 8 ("And last of all he was seen of me ..."). He was a true apostle, see Acts 1 verses 21-22: "Wherefore of these men ... must one be ordained to be a witness with us of his resurrection". In resurrection, the Lord Jesus has become "head over all things to the church" (Eph. 1: 22-23). In that capacity, "when he ascended up on high, he led captivity captive, and gave gifts unto men" (Eph. 4: 8). Paul is therefore asserting that his authority was imparted by the risen Christ, in harmony with the purpose of the Father. This has important teaching for us too. So:

ii) Its implications for us. In the first place, we must acknowledge divine sovereignty, and in the second, we must act with due humility.

- **We must acknowledge divine sovereignty.** The Lord Jesus appoints, equips and directs. The church is not an organisation which chooses its officers, and appoints their service. See Ephesians 4 verse 11, "And **he** gave some apostles; and some, prophets; and some, evangelists; and some, pastors and teachers". See 1 Timothy 1 verse 12, "I thank Christ Jesus our Lord, who hath enabled me, for that **he** counted me faithful, putting me into the ministry". See Matthew 9 verse 38, "Pray ye therefore the Lord of the harvest, that **he** will send forth labourers into his harvest" (Compare Acts 13: 4 and 16: 10). See Acts 20 verse 28, "Take heed therefore unto yourselves, and to all the flock, over the which (*'in* the which', RV) the **Holy Ghost** hath made you overseers".

The apostles at Jerusalem recognised Paul's calling: see Chapter 2 verse 9, and the local assembly should be ready to recognise the divine gifts bestowed upon believers in fellowship. See, for example, 1 Thessalonians 5 verse 12, "And we beseech you, brethren, to know them which labour among you, and are over you in the Lord, and admonish you". In this case, Paul refers to the provision of leadership in the local assembly, but the Lord's people are to recognise the sovereignty of the Holy Spirit in "dividing to every man severally as he will" (1 Cor. 12: 11).

- **We must act with due humility.** See, for example, Romans 12 verse 3, "For I say, through the grace given unto me, to every man that is among you, not to think of himself more highly than he ought to think; but to think soberly ('think so as to be wise', JND), according as God hath dealt to every man the measure of faith"; 1 Corinthians 4 verse 7, "What hast thou that thou didst not receive? Now if thou didst receive it, why dost thou glory, as if thou hadst not received it?"

2) THE CHURCHES ADDRESSED BY PAUL, v.2

"Unto the churches of Galatia." The word "churches" translates *ekklesia,* deriving from *ek,* meaning 'out of', and *kaleo,* meaning 'a calling'. A church (or 'the' church) is therefore a 'called out' company of people. In short, the church is a body of people **called out of the world** with its sin and immorality, with its pleasures and pursuits, and with its politics and religion, and **called into sacred fellowship with God** through His Son, the Lord Jesus Christ. Hence the believers at Corinth are described as "the church of God which is at Corinth, to them that are sanctified in Christ Jesus". Corinth was a vile place (see 1 Cor. 6: 9-11), but there was a body of people in the city who were totally different. The words "the church of

God which is at Corinth" describe men and women who had severed their association with the immorality and depravity of Corinth, and who had been brought into fellowship with God. They now belonged to God. They were "God's husbandry ... God's building" (1 Cor. 3: 9) They were "the temple of God" (1 Cor. 3: 16). It might be helpful to add that the expression "church of God" or "churches of God" generally (some say 'always') refers to a local church or local churches, whereas "the church, which is his body" (Eph. 1: 22-23) refers to the church which is above the ages, and above all divisions in the human race.

Paul now writes to "the churches of Galatia". Not, 'the church of the Galatians'. There is no concept in Scripture of an area church, such as the 'Church of England', or the 'Church of Scotland'. There is no concept of church federation. Compare "the churches of Judaea" (1: 22).

Paul is evidently writing to assemblies in those cities visited during his first missionary journey: Pisidian Antioch, Iconium, Lystra, and Derbe. See Acts Chapters 13 & 14.

3) THE DELIVERANCE DESCRIBED BY PAUL, vv.3-5

"Grace be to you and peace from God the Father, and from our Lord Jesus Christ" (v. 3). We have already noted the absence of praise and thanksgiving here. Compare, for example, Ephesians 1 verse 1, "to the saints which are at Ephesus, and to **the faithful** in Christ Jesus", but the believers in Galatia were in danger of relinquishing the essential truths of the gospel of grace, and were going back to the works of the law as a means of justification.

The order is important. Grace is the source of divine blessing: peace is the nature and result of divine blessing. Grace and peace rest on a historical event which exhibited grace, and from which peace is derived. That event is wholly divine: the death of the Lord Jesus Christ. It reminds us that all we possess, grace and peace, flows from the work of the Lord Jesus. Grace is what Christ brought (Titus 2: 11), and peace is what He left (John 14: 27).

Attention is drawn to *(a)* the character of His death (v.4a); *(b)* the purpose of His death (v.4b); *(c)* the predetermining of His death (v.4c); *(d)* the praise resulting from His death (v.5).

a) The character of His death, v.4a

We must not miss the connection with verse 3: "Grace be to you and peace from God the Father, and from our Lord Jesus Christ, **who gave himself for our sins**". The Lord Jesus, co-equal, co-eternal and co-substantial with God the Father, "**gave himself for** our sins". He did so voluntarily. He taught that "no man taketh it (His life) from me" (John 10: 18). He "**gave himself**". Compare Ephesians 5 verse 2, "Christ also hath loved us, and hath **given himself** for us, an offering and a sacrifice to God for a sweet smelling savour"; Ephesians 5 verse 25, "Christ also loved the church, and **gave himself for it**"; 1 Timothy 2 verse 6, "who **gave himself** a ransom for all, to be testified in due time"; Titus 2 verse 14, "who **gave** himself for us, that he might redeem us from all iniquity"; Galatians 2 verse 20, "the Son of God, who loved me, and **gave himself** for me". We must never forget that the "good shepherd **giveth** his life for the sheep" (John 10: 11).

b) The purpose of His death, v.4b

"Who gave himself for **our sins, that he might deliver us from this present evil world"** or "who gave himself for our sins so that he should deliver us out of the present evil world" (JND). He did this to accomplish deliverance *(i)* from the penalty of sin, and *(ii)* from the power of sin.

- **Deliverance from the penalty of sin.** "He gave himself **for our sins.**" He voluntarily and vicariously offered Himself on account of our sins. The preposition *(huper)* speaks of substitution: "Christ gave Himself as a ransom (of a substitutionary character), not instead of all men, but on behalf of all" (W E Vine). See 2 Corinthians 5 verse 21. He took **our** sins and gave us **His** righteousness. He dealt with the underlying problem. There can be no 'deliverance from this present evil world' without a solution to the question of sin.

- **Deliverance from the power of sin.** "He gave himself for our sins, that **he might deliver us from this present evil world.**" The word "deliver" *(exaireo)* indicates a rescue operation. We had been in the grasp of an enemy. Compare Acts 7 verse 34 where, referring to the deliverance from Egypt, Stephen quotes the Lord's words to Moses, "I have heard their groaning, and am come down to **deliver** them *(exaireo)*" or I am "come down to take them out of it", JND). See Acts 12 verse 11, "Now I know of a surety ('certainly', JND) that the Lord hath sent his angel, and hath **delivered** me *(exaireo)* out of the hand of Herod." Acts 23 verse 27, where

Claudius Lysias addresses Felix, "This man was taken of the Jews, and should have been killed of them: then came I with an army ('I came up with the military', JND), and **rescued** him *(exaireo)*".

The words "present evil world" are better translated, "this present evil age". The word "evil" *(poneros)* means not only evil in its nature, but actively and viciously evil in its influence. We should notice that this deliverance is not accomplished through keeping the law, but through the work of Christ.

While some suggest that this refers to 'this present evil **religious** age', this does not seem to be the case. According to W.E.Vine, Paul refers here to "salvation from the evil tendencies and influences which characterise the world *(kosmos),* in this age or period of its history". He also suggests that it might refer "to deliverance out of it (the world) when the saints are caught away at the coming of the Lord Jesus (1 Thess. 4: 17), but this does not appear to fit the context here.

c) The predetermining of His death, v.4c

He "gave himself for our sins, that he might deliver us from this present evil world, **according to the will of God and our Father**" or "the will of our God and Father" (JND). It was His will that the Lord Jesus should give Himself "for our sins, that he might deliver us from this present evil world". As W.E.Vine observes, "Christ did not die in order that God might love men, or that it might become His will to save them. Christ died because God loved men and because it is His will to save them (1 Tim 2: 3, 4)". It also reminds us that the Lord Jesus died according to "the determinate counsel and foreknowledge of God" (Acts 2: 23) in order to secure the purpose of God for His people. Compare the promise made to Abraham (Gal. 3: 8-16).

He is our "God", emphasising His divine power, and our "Father", emphasising His divine love. We therefore approach Him with deepest reverence as God, and with deepest confidence as Father. The words "our Father" must be compared with "God the Father" (v.1). The first ("our Father") refers to our relationship with Him: the second ("God the Father") to the unique relationship enjoyed with Him by the Lord Jesus.

d) The praise resulting from His death, v.5

"To whom be glory for ever and ever. Amen", or "To whom be glory to the ages of the ages. Amen" (JND). As the Psalmist puts it, "Not unto us, O LORD, not unto us, but unto thy name give glory "(Psalm 115: 1).

We should compare the 'ages of the ages' with, "this present evil age" (v.4). We have been delivered from one 'age', in order to enjoy another 'age!' Not "the age to come", that is, the millennium, but the 'ages of the ages', that is, eternity! Compare Philippians 4 verse 20, 1 Timothy 1 verse 17; 2 Timothy 4 verse 18. See also, for example, Hebrews 13 verse 21; 1 Peter 4 verse 11 and 5 verse 11, Revelation 4 verses 9 & 10, 7 verse 12, 10 verse 6 and 15 verse 7. This does not exhaust the list.

Everything in the prologue is divine. Paul's apostleship is "by Jesus Christ, and God the Father": grace and peace are from "God the Father, and from our Lord Jesus Christ": the Lord Jesus gave Himself for us "according to the will of God and our Father". We can write over the prologue, "All things are of God" (2 Cor. 5: 18). Compare Romans 8: 29-30, *"he* did foreknow ... *he* also did predestinate ... *he* also called ... *he* also justified ... *he* also glorified": Romans 11: 36, "For of *him,* and through *him,* and to *him,* are all things: to whom be glory for ever. Amen".

W E Vine points out that "Amen" is a "Hebrew word, the meaning of which may be seen in such passages as Deuteronomy 7 verse 9, 'the faithful *(aman)* God', Isaiah 49 verse 7, 'the LORD that is faithful *(ainan)',* and Isaiah 65 verse 16, 'the God of truth *(amen)'* (margin, 'the God of Amen')". W.E,Vine adds, amongst other things, "once in the New Testament, 'Amen' is a title of Christ ('These things saith the Amen, the faithful and true witness, the beginning of the creation of God', Rev. 3: 14), because through Him the purpose of God are established ('For all the promises of God in him are yea, and in him Amen', 2 Cor. 1: 20)".

The prologue certainly ends on a superlative note!

P.S. No wonder Paul continues: "I marvel that ye are so soon removed from him that called you into the grace of Christ unto another gospel" (v.6). It certainly *is* amazing that they should defect in this way!

THE EPISTLE TO THE GALATIANS

"There be some that trouble you"

Read Chapter 1: 6-24

After his brief introduction, or prologue, (1: 1-5), Paul addresses the serious situation in Galatia. His deep concern is clear: "I marvel that ye are so soon removed from him that called you into the grace of Christ unto another gospel". This section may be divided as follows: *(1)* the perversion of the gospel (vv.6-7); *(2)* the preaching of the gospel (vv.8-10); *(3)* the revelation of the gospel (vv.11-24).

1) THE PERVERSION OF THE GOSPEL, vv.6-7

In this section, Paul addresses both parties involved in the alarming changes which were taking place amongst the believers in Galatia. Firstly, he censures the Galatian believers themselves (v.6), and secondly, he censures the false teachers (v.7).

a) The charge against the Galatians, v.6

"I marvel that ye are so soon removed from him that called you into the grace of Christ unto another gospel". We should carefully notice four things here:

i) "I marvel ('wonder', JND) that ye are **so soon removed** …" The word "marvel" *(thaumazo)* was "often used by Greek orators of surprise at something reprehensible, and can be translated 'amazed … astonished … bewildered'. Paul is painfully surprised and alarmed at the instability of the Galatians". (E.R.Roustio, *Liberty Bible Commentary*). The words, "so soon removed" refer either to the brief time since Paul's visit, or to the speed at which they had defected. The word "removed" *(metatithemi)* was used in classical Greek of a turncoat. The form of the verb is in the 'middle voice': literally, 'I marvel that ye are so soon **removing yourselves** from him that

27

called you into the grace of Christ unto another gospel'. As W.E.Vine points out, this suggests that it was not so much "those who had influenced them but that the Galatians themselves were responsible for their own declension from the faith". They were transferring themselves from grace to law, from liberty to bondage. The solemn lesson here must be noted. False teachers are certainly culpable, but so are the people that *follow them*!

ii) "I marvel that ye are so soon removed *from him that called you* ..." Their defection was not only from the gospel of God: it was from God Himself. If we deny any part of God's Word, we deny God. "This assertion should have startled the Galatians, who probably thought that they were honouring God by trying to keep His law" (E.R.Roustio).

iii) "I marvel that ye are so soon removed from him that *called you into ('in', RV/JND) the grace of Christ*..." Their calling did not rest on their fulfilment of the law, but "in the grace of Christ". If otherwise, "then Christ is dead in vain" (Gal. 2: 21), and "Christ is become of no effect unto you, whosoever of you are justified by the law; ye are fallen from grace" (Gal. 5: 4). Compare Ephesians 2: 8-9, "For by grace are ye saved through faith; and that not of yourselves: it is the gift of God: not of works, lest any man should boast". It was in a Galatian city (Pisidian Antioch) that Paul told the Jews, "through this man is preached unto you the forgiveness of sins: and by him all that believe are justified from all things, from which ye could not be justified by the law of Moses" (Acts 13: 38-39).

iv) "I marvel that ye are so soon removed from him that called you into ('in') the grace of Christ *unto another gospel*..." This is developed in verse 7, which brings us to:

b) The charge against the false teachers, v.7

"I marvel that ye are so soon removed from him that called you into ('in') the grace of Christ unto *another* gospel: which is *not another*, but there be some that trouble you, and would pervert the gospel of Christ." While the word "another" occurs twice here, the underlying words are quite different. The sentence can be translated, "unto *another* gospel (*heteros,* of a different kind): which is not *another* (*allos,* of the same kind)". The false teachers propagated a "gospel that was diametrically opposed to the gospel of God's grace".

The word "trouble" *(tarasso)* means to agitate or to disturb or confuse. False teaching always does this. Compare 2 Peter 2 verse 1 with its reference to "destructive heresies" (JND). (Even Christian teachers can leave the saints disturbed by their attitude and mishandling of the Scriptures.) The word "pervert" (*metastrepho*) means to completely change into something of the opposite nature. See the other two occurrences of the word: one in Acts 2 verse 20, "the sun shall be turned into darkness", and the other in James 4 verse 9, where "laughter be turned to mourning".

> *God tells me how I may be saved,*
> *He points to something done,*
> *Accomplished on Mount Calvary*
> *By His beloved Son,*
> *In which no works of mine have place;*
> *For grace with works is no more grace.*

The false teachers were determined in their work; they "**would** pervert the gospel of Christ". Their activities stirred Paul deeply. Notice what follows:

2) THE PREACHING OF THE GOSPEL, vv.8-10

The gravity of "perverting the gospel of Christ" is now made very clear. Those guilty of such teaching are subject to divine judgment. This is repeated twice for emphasis: "Let him be accursed" (vv.8-9). Paul is not expressing a wish: he is stating a fact. It has been said that "God can do nothing less than put an awful curse on all who reject, pervert and falsify the gospel of His Son". We should notice at least two important things in this section:

a) The finality of the gospel, vv.8-9

"But though we, or an angel from heaven, preach any other gospel unto you **than that which we have preached unto you,** let him be accursed (*anathema*). As we said before (*prolego*: on a former occasion: see 2 Cor. 13: 2), so say I now again, If any man preach any other gospel unto you **than that ye have received,** let him be accursed." The original preaching must never be altered. It is final. This is a vitally important principle. God's Word cannot be amended. We should notice that Paul does not even hint at any mitigating circumstances: no effort is made to disentangle the threads of reasoning in the arguments of the Judaisers, so that parts can be labelled 'true' or 'false'. The whole system is condemned. The strong language here is completely justified when we remember that these false teachers were actually devaluing the work of the Lord Jesus at Calvary. The gospel is not ours to alter. It is the "gospel of God" and the "gospel of Christ". Our approach may require alteration: but never the message.

- **In the first case,** Paul refers to himself and his colleagues, together with "an angel from heaven" (v.8). It has been rightly observed that "Paul does not say that he or a messenger from heaven was likely to preach any other gospel". He simply uses a future hypothetical possibility to illustrate the case.

In this connection, the incident described in 1 Kings 13 makes interesting reading. The "old prophet" said to "the man of God", "I am a prophet also as thou art; and an angel spake unto me by the word of the Lord" (v.18), but if the "old prophet" was to be believed, the "angel" countermanded the original instructions given to "the man of God" by "the word of the LORD". Sadly "the man of God" believed "the old prophet", with disastrous consequences. Incidentally, this passage directly contradicts such claims as those of the Mormons, whose Book of Mormon claims angelic authority as delivered by the Angel Moroni and 'translated' by their founder Joseph Smith!

However, bearing in mind that the law was "ordained by angels in the hand of a mediator" (Gal. 3: 19), Paul may well be saying that if one of the angels associated with the giving of the law were to preach "any other gospel" than "the gospel of the grace of God" (Acts 20: 24) he would fall under divine condemnation.

- **In the second case,** Paul simply says, "If any man", and "hurls the *anathema* directly at the legalists". For *anathema* see 1 Corinthians 16 verse 22. Woe to anyone who dares tamper with the gospel of Christ. It has been said that "Christ supplemented is Christ supplanted".

b) The fidelity to the gospel, v.10

"For do I now persuade men, or God? or do I seek to please men? For if I yet please men, I should not be the servant of Christ." The word "persuade" means 'to win over ... to conciliate ... to render friendly towards'. The word is elsewhere rendered "satisfy" (JND), which seems more satisfactory. The 'gospel" preached by the false teachers certainly 'satisfied' men. Preaching which suggests that we can at least do something towards our salvation, is popular preaching indeed. "Any other gospel" will be well received. Paul certainly did not "please men". Notice the following: "Am I therefore become your enemy, because I tell you the truth?" (4: 16); "And I, brethren, if I yet preach circumcision, why do I yet suffer persecution? then is the offence of the cross ceased" (5: 11); "As many as desire to make a fair show in the flesh, they constrain you to be circumcised; only lest they should suffer persecution for the cross of Christ" (6: 12).

To the contrary, Paul laboured to 'satisfy' God. Compare 1 Thessalonians 2 verse 4, "But as we were allowed of God (approved of God) to be put in trust with the gospel, even so we speak; not as pleasing men, but God, which trieth our hearts". See also 1 Corinthians 4 verses 1-2, "Let a man so account of us, as of the ministers of Christ, and stewards of the mysteries of God. Moreover it is required in stewards, that a man be found faithful". It is impossible to please men, and God. This is emphasised: "Or do I seek to please men? ... for if I yet pleased men, I should not be the servant (*doulos*: referring to the relationship between a man and his master) of Christ" (v.10). How could he be "the servant of Christ" in these circumstances since Christ had revealed the gospel to him? (vv.11-12). There is no better way to please men than to tell them what they want to hear. The gospel tells men what they do *not* want to hear.

3) THE REVELATION OF THE GOSPEL, vv.11-24

Paul now emphasises the divine origin of the message he preached, and the divinely-ordained way in which it was revealed to him. We must therefore give attention *(a)* to the message (vv.11-12), and *(b)* to the messenger (vv.13-24).

a) The divinely-communicated message, vv.11-12

It was: *(i)* divine in its character (v.11) and *(ii)* divinely-communicated to the apostle Paul (v.12.)

i) **It was divine in character, v.11.** "But I certify you ('let you know', JND, or 'I make known to you', RV), brethren, that the gospel which was preached of me is not after man." The introducing word *(gnorizo)* occurs in 1 Corinthians 12 verse 3,"wherefore I give you to **understand**" or "I give you therefore to know", JND). It also occurs in 1 Corinthians 15 verse 1, "Moreover, brethren, I **declare** unto you the gospel which I preached unto you" or "But I **make known** to you, brethren", JND). See also 2 Corinthians 8 verse 1, "Moreover, brethren, we **do you to wit** ('**make known** to you', JND), of the grace of God bestowed on the churches of Macedonia)." The use of the word introduces matters of great importance. It is touching to notice that he addresses them as "brethren". "They are deceived, disturbed and defecting in their devotion and duty to Christ. But they are still regarded as "brethren": brethren needing Paul's Spirit-inspired counsel!"

His preaching was divine in origin. It was not "after man". Compare 1 Corinthians 1 verses 18-21. The statement, "the gospel ... is not after man", reminds us that it is the "gospel of God" (1 Thess. 2: 2). It emanates from the Godhead, and is completely divine in every respect. Note Galatians 4 verses 4-6 in this connection.

ii) It was divinely-communicated, v.12. "For I neither received it of man, neither was I taught it, but by the revelation of Jesus Christ." Paul was taught the principles of Judaism at the feet of Gamaliel (Acts 5: 34; 22: 3), but he received no human instruction, or human interpretation, in connection with the gospel. He received the message directly from the Lord Jesus. Notice the similarity between Paul's apostleship and Paul's gospel preaching:

Paul's gospel preaching, vv.11-12	***Paul's apostleship, v.1***
"The gospel which was preached of me is **not after man**."	"Paul an apostle **(not of men**...)."
"For I neither received it **of man,** neither was I taught it..."	"Neither **by man**..."
"Neither was I taught it, but **by the revelation of Jesus Christ**..."	"But **by Jesus Christ,** and God the Father..."

Paul received the truth of the gospel by **direct** divine revelation, and in this he differed from ourselves. We became acquainted with the gospel through reading the Scriptures and listening to the exposition of the Scriptures. None the less, a most important principle emerges here, namely, that our convictions and doctrine must be formed by divine revelation, and never by human opinion, however well intended. For Paul, this was by direct divine revelation. Those revelations are now part of the Scriptures. For ourselves, those same revelations, though not directly imparted to us, must have the same unchallenged authority as they did for Paul. The Scriptures themselves, rather than comments on them, and exposition of them, should bring conviction to our hearts and minds. The man whose judgment is formed by the Word of

God alone will not be swayed by the winds of doctrinal change which blow across Christendom. Every believer should have good Berean blood in his veins: "they ... searched the scriptures daily, whether these things were so" (Acts 17: 11). The believers at Thessalonica received the word of God, "not as the Word of men, but as it is in truth, the word of God" (1 Thess. 2: 13).

In support of his statement, "I neither received it of men, neither was I taught it, but by the revelation of Jesus Christ", Paul now recounts his spiritual history. He clearly establishes that rather than receiving the truths of the gospel from 'the twelve', making him a 'second hand apostle', he received them directly from the Lord Jesus. So:

b) The divinely-commissioned messenger, vv.13-24

Paul tells us what happened before, when, and after, he was saved. He recounts his pre-conversion activities (vv.13-14), his conversion (vv.15-16a), and his post-conversion movements (vv.16b-24). He refers *(i)* to the persecution of the church (vv.13-14); *(ii)* to intervention by God (vv.15-16a); *(iii)* to preparation for service (vv.16b-24).

i) Persecution of the church, vv.13-14. As noted above, Paul describes here **his pre-conversion activities**: "For ye have heard of my conversation in time past in the Jews' religion, how that beyond measure I persecuted the church of God (meaning, evidently, the local church - at Jerusalem), and wasted it; and profited in the Jews' religion above mine equals in mine own nation, being more exceeding zealous of the traditions of my fathers".

This is quite self-explanatory. The words are interesting and informative: **"beyond measure"** indicates the excessiveness of his zeal in persecuting the church. The imperfect tense of "persecuted" indicates continuous action: literally, 'I kept on persecuting'. The words **"wasted it"** *(portheo)* mean 'to overthrow, destroy, make havoc, lay waste'. Again, the imperfect tense implies that Paul continually, persistently and violently kept on ravaging the church. See Acts 9 verse 13 and 26 verses 10-11. He had been the supreme Judaistic fanatic of his time. **"Profited"** means 'to cut forward', hence, to blaze a trail, or cut a pioneer path. Paul was advancing, pushing forward and outstripping all others in power and prestige. **"Above many mine equals"**: he started out with his fellow classmates, but soon far surpassed them in his zeal and activities for the traditions of Judaism. **"The traditions of my fathers"**: the Lord Jesus distinguished between the written law and man-made traditions,

Galatians

and clearly proclaimed that the traditions of men caused the word of God to be of none effect. See Matthew 15 verses 1-6 and Mark 7 verses 3-13.

ii) Intervention by God, vv.15-16a. As noted above, Paul describes here **his conversion**: "But when it pleased God, who separated me from my mother's womb, and called me by his grace, to reveal his Son in me, that I might preach him among the heathen…" J.Hunter *(What the Bible Teaches - Galatians)* helpfully observes: "We must not isolate Paul's conversion from the context. It is introduced to show that man had nothing to do with it. It was all accomplished by God". No preacher was involved. Hence the words, "But when it pleased God…" He intervened in Paul's life "according to the good pleasure of his will" We should notice four things:

- God "separated" Paul from his "mother's womb". Compare Psalm 58 verse 3, "The wicked are estranged from the womb". Paul evidently alludes here to Jeremiah 1 verse 5, "Before I formed thee in the belly I knew thee; and before thou camest forth out of the womb I sanctified thee, and ordained thee a prophet unto the nations". See also Isaiah 49 verse 1, "The LORD hath called me from the womb; from the bowels of my mother hath he made mention of my name"; Isaiah 49 verse 5, "And now, saith the LORD that formed me from the womb to be his servant". God's plan for Paul's life was determined before he was born. He was "a chosen vessel" (Acts 9: 15). **God's** plan for Paul's life preceded **Paul's** plan for his life!

- God "called" Paul by His grace. This refers to his actual conversion on the road to Damascus. The emphasis on divine grace is most significant in context. The very man who had "persecuted the church of God", and did so "beyond measure", experienced the grace of God. It was totally apart from human merit. Compare 2 Timothy 1 verses 12-14.

- God "revealed" (unveiled) His Son in Paul. This is best understood objectively (W.E.Vine). He continues: "whereas in the case of other Christians, salvation is through the word preached and heard (Rom. 10: 14, 15), in Paul's case, it pleased God to reveal His Son to him". That is, on the road to Damascus, Paul therefore had the necessary qualification for apostolic testimony. See Acts 2 verses 21-22; 9 verse 17; 22 verse 14 and 1 Corinthians 9 verse 1.

- God determined that Paul should "preach" Christ among the heathen. See Acts 9 verse 15: "He is a chosen vessel unto me, to bear my

Chapter 1:6-24

name before the Gentiles, and kings, and the children of Israel". Compare Ephesians 3 verse 8. (See also Acts 22: 21; 26: 12-17.) We must notice that Christ was Paul's message: "that I might **preach him** among the heathen". Christ was the sum total of Paul's message, not the law or ceremonies. He did not proclaim a plan of salvation, but the Person of the Saviour. It was not a matter of one religion against another. Paul had a divine commission to preach Christ. Compare Acts 11 verse 20.

iii) Preparation for service, vv.16b-24. As noted above, Paul describes here ***his post-conversion movements.*** In this section, there are three movements. They all emphasise that Paul's preaching was divinely-revealed to him. It was not "after man" and it was not received "of man" (vv.11-12).

- ***What happened "immediately"***, vv.16b-17. "Immediately, I conferred not with flesh and blood: neither went I up to Jerusalem to them which were apostles before me; but I went into Arabia, and returned again unto Damascus." For "flesh and blood", see Matthew 16 verse 17. Paul is not for one moment disparaging his fellow-apostles, but demonstrating that his ministry was not received from them. No human instrument was involved in his apostleship and ministry. Bearing in mind that after his conversion, Paul "straightway ... preached Christ in the synagogues, that he is the Son of God", and that it was only after "many days" were fulfilled that "the Jews (at Damascus) took counsel to kill him" (Acts 9: 20-23), there can be no doubt that Paul went from Damascus to Arabia, and returned to Damascus during this period. He completely by-passed Jerusalem. The "many days" could have certainly been "three years" (v.18). We cannot assume that he was in Arabia for three years. It is interesting to note that the disciples were with the Lord Jesus for some three years, and that, possibly, Saul of Tarsus (as he was) spent three years with the Lord in Arabia. This is, of course, a little conjectural.

It is significant that Paul went to Arabia ("mount Sinai in Arabia"). See Galatians 4 verses 24-26. He went to the very place where the law was given in order to learn about the relationship between law and grace, between the son of the bondwoman and the son of the freewoman, between Jerusalem beneath and Jerusalem above. We should also notice that whatever the actual period of his stay in Arabia might have been, Paul was alone with God, reminding us that Moses spent forty years in "the backside of the desert" before he became Israel's leader, that Elijah learned to stand in the presence of God in Gilead, before he stood before Ahab and Jezebel, and that John the Baptist was "in the desert until his showing unto Israel". Even the Lord Jesus largely spent the first thirty years of His life on earth in comparative obscurity, before entering His three years' public ministry. As J.Hunter observes, "Being so long away meant that he (Paul) was unknown in Judaea although his story was well known. What a difference in our day! How quickly those with outstanding conversions are made celebrities, made famous as they are called upon to give their testimony, or even to write a book!"

- **What happened "after three years", vv.18-20.** "Then after three years I went up to Jerusalem to see Peter, and abode with him fifteen days. But other of the apostles saw I none, save ('but only', RV margin) James the Lord's brother. Now the things which I write unto you, behold, before God, I lie not." This visit is also described in Acts 9 verses 26-30 and 22 verses 17-21. The fact the Luke tells us that Barnabas "brought him to the apostles" and that Paul was "with them coming in and going out of Jerusalem" does not contradict Galatians 1 verse 19. Paul went to Jerusalem specifically "to see Peter" where the word "see" *(historeo)* means 'to visit in order to become acquainted with'. The purpose of the visit was to become personally acquainted with Peter, not to gain official sanction or recognition. The word *historeo* was "used to express either to learn facts from personal enquiry or observation, or to relate facts as a historian would. There was an interchange of facts between Paul and Peter" (E.R.Roustio, *Liberty Bible Commentary*).

The reference to "James the Lord's brother" has been variously explained. The AV reading suggests that "James the Lord's brother" was an apostle, but this can hardly be true in view of what is said in John 7 verse 5, "neither did his brethren believe in him". It has been suggested that "brother" really means 'kinsman', but perhaps it is best to read "the Lord's brother" in the literal sense (see Matt. 13: 55-56; Mark 6: 3). As Wm.Hendriksen (*Galatians & Ephesians*) observes, "the alternative explanation would appear to be more reasonable, namely, In addition to Cephas, the only apostle whom I saw in Jerusalem, I also saw one other person of special importance, James, the Lord's brother". The important thing is that Paul is emphasising throughout that he was not influenced by 'the twelve', and that his authority was divinely-imparted. The strong affirmation in verse 20 ("Now the things which I write unto you, behold, before God, I lie not") implies that he had been attacked, and that he was only regarded as of secondary importance.

- **What happened "afterwards", vv.21-24.** "Afterwards I came into the regions of Syria and Cilicia; and was unknown by face unto the churches of Judaea which were in Christ: but they had heard only, That he which persecuted us in times past, now preacheth that faith which he once destroyed. And they glorified God in me." See Acts 9 verse 30, "Which when the brethren knew (the plot to kill Paul), they brought him down to Caesrea, and sent him forth to Tarsus". Some years later, Barnabas visited Tarsus, in Cilicia, and brought Paul to Antioch in Syria. See Acts 11 verses 25-26. During this period (in Tarsus), Paul was not in contact with Jerusalem. He remained in comparative obscurity, although the change in his life was the subject of thanksgiving to God: "they glorified God in me". (God is glorified by what He has done *for* us, verse 5: He is glorified by what He has done *in* us, verse 24.) Their recognition of God's intervention in Paul's life stands in direct contrast to the animosity of his opponents. It is deeply significant that this opposition came from Judaea, where Paul's conversion was so gladly recognised. The 'ravening wolf' became a shepherd! "But they heard only, That he which persecuted us in times past now preacheth (*evangeliso,* 'to proclaim good news') the faith which once he destroyed" (v.23). Compare Chapter 2 verse 18.

In summary, Paul establishes that his apostleship and preaching were divinely-given. They originated with God, and were mediated by the Lord Jesus No human instrument was involved. In Chapter 2, Paul establishes the fact that his divinely-given authority was recognised by his fellow-apostles, putting him in a position to deal authoritatively with the error that was sweeping the Galatian churches.

THE EPISTLE TO THE GALATIANS

"I went up again to Jerusalem"

Read Chapter 2: 1-10

Chapters 1 & 2 comprise the historical section of the epistle. Paul establishes that his apostolic authority was divinely-given (Chapter 1), and that his apostolic authority was recognised by his fellow-apostles (Chapter 2). In Chapter 1, apart from Paul's fifteen-day visit, everything takes place apart from Jerusalem. In Chapter 2, a conference takes place at Jerusalem. The context determines the difference in emphasis.

Galatians Chapter 2 clearly divides into two main sections: *(1)* Paul conferring with the apostles at Jerusalem (vv.1-10); *(2)* Paul contending with Peter at Antioch (vv.11-21). It is interesting to compare and contrast the two sections.

a) At Jerusalem, vv.1-10

i) Paul defended the **doctrine or truth** of the gospel. See verse 5, "that the truth of the gospel might continue with you".

ii) It was defended against opposition from "false brethren" (v.4). They insisted on circumcision, **not** as a mere rite, but as an undertaking to keep the whole law.

iii) It was defended by refusal to yield in the slightest way: "To whom we gave place by subjection, no, not for an hour" (v.5).

b) At Antioch, vv.11-21

i) Paul defended a **walk** which was according to the truth of the gospel. See verse 14, "they walked not uprightly according to the truth of the gospel".

ii) It was defended against opposition from Peter (v.11). It was opposition by bad example (vv.12-14). This could have introduced a caste system, by differentiating between Jew and Gentile.

iii) It was defended by refusal to yield in the slightest way: "I withstood him to the face" (v.11).

In the first case, Paul refers to his private visit to Jerusalem, and in the second, to Peter's public visit to Antioch. It has been pointed out that verses 1-10 emphasise preaching, whereas verses 11-21 emphasise practice. It is so necessary for practice to conform to preaching.

1) PAUL CONFERRING WITH THE APOSTLES AT JERUSALEM, vv.1-10

In Acts 15, emphasis is placed on *public* events connected with the conference. In Galatians 2, emphasis is placed upon *private* events connected with the conference. We should now notice here *(A)* the reason for his visit (vv.1-5); *(B)* the result of his visit (vv.6-10).

Alternatively, and perhaps better, the passage may be divided as follows: *(i)* the occasion of the visit (vv.1-2a); *(ii)* the object of the visit (vv.2b-5); *(iii)* the outcome of the visit (vv.6-10).

A) The reason for his visit, vv.1-5

We should notice: *(a)* when Paul went to Jerusalem (v.1a); *(b)* who Paul took to Jerusalem (v.1b); *(c)* how Paul went to Jerusalem (v.2a) *(d)* why Paul went to Jerusalem (vv.2b-5).

a) When Paul went to Jerusalem, v.1a

"Then fourteen years after, I went up again to Jerusalem." The "fourteen years" have been variously interpreted. Some refer this to his visit with Barnabas in Acts 11 verses 27-30, when the church at Antioch sent "relief unto the brethren which dwelt in Judaea" (v.30). This does not agree at all with "fourteen years after". This is made clear by comparing the two passages. The visit in question here (v.1) is evidently described in Acts 15 verses 1-2. The "fourteen years" evidently refers to the period that had elapsed since the visit described in Galatians 1 verse 18 (see Acts 9: 26-29).

We should notice that Paul, Barnabas and the assembly at Antioch dealt with the matter locally, before Paul and Barnabas went to Jerusalem. This reminds us that doctrinal and moral issues must be dealt with expeditiously. "A little leaven leaveneth the whole lump" (1 Cor. 5: 6; Gal. 5: 9).

b) Who Paul took to Jerusalem, v.1b

"I went up again to Jerusalem with Barnabas, and took Titus with me also", reminding us that "in the mouth of two or three witnesses every word may be established" (Matt. 18: 16). Barnabas was Paul's fellow-traveller on the first missionary journey, and could therefore corroborate his description of gospel work amongst the Gentiles. See Acts 15 verses 4 & 12. Barnabas was a Jew, and well-known at Jerusalem. See Acts 9 verse 27 and 11 verse 22 (he had been sent from Jerusalem to Antioch). Titus was a Gentile, and unknown at Jerusalem.

Titus accompanied them for another reason entirely. He was a 'test case'. Titus was uncircumcised and his presence at Jerusalem where "certain of the sect of the Pharisees" asserted that it was "necessary to circumcise them (the Gentile converts), and to command them to keep the law of Moses" (Acts 15: 5), was of great significance. See verse 3. Titus was certainly an example of the power and product of the Gospel!

c) How Paul went to Jerusalem, v.2a

Paul and Barnabas did not hurry to Jerusalem in order to settle a personal grievance! "And I went up by revelation." He did not take the initiative in the matter. He was guided by the Holy Spirit. The divine wisdom in this is most apparent, as we have already noted. Had Paul legislated on the matter at Antioch, he would have given his opponents opportunity to dismiss his teaching as divisive and at variance with the apostles in Jerusalem. As it was, the apostolic band spoke with one voice. See Acts 15 verses 22-27. The principle of united leadership is most important. It reminds us that elders should speak with one voice, and prayerful consultation is necessary to that end.

But we must notice that divinely-imparted conviction about the matter did not constrain Paul to ignore his brethren, or foster an independent spirit. This was true of relationships between the apostles (hence the conferring at Jerusalem), but it was equally true of relationships in the assembly at Antioch. See Acts

15 verses 1-3: "And certain men which came down from Judaea taught the brethren, and said, Except ye be circumcised after the manner of Moses, ye cannot be saved. When therefore Paul and Barnabas had no small dissension and disputation with them, **they** determined that Paul and Barnabas, and certain other of them, should go up to Jerusalem unto the apostles and elders about this question. And being brought on their way by **the church,** they passed through Phenice and Samaria, declaring the conversion of the Gentiles". Paul's deep conviction and divinely-given guidance was shared with the assembly at Antioch. Paul acted in full fellowship with the local assembly. An excellent example to us all! Discord can arise if we act independently, even if we are totally beyond reproach, and absolutely correct in conviction and objective. In Galatians 2, it was a matter of revelation (v.2). In Acts 15, it was a matter of delegation (v.2). The two were mutually complementary.

d) Why Paul went to Jerusalem, vv.2b-5

"I ... communicated unto them that gospel which I preach among the Gentiles, but privately to them which were of reputation, lest by any means I should run, or had run, in vain ... and that because of false brethren unawares brought in ..." The matter was not 'swept under the carpet'. It was dealt with openly. In this connection, we should remember that Paul went to Jerusalem:

- Because, as noted above, it was most important that the apostles should speak with one mind about the matter. We should not forget the general importance of this amongst the Lord's people. See, for example Philippians 1 verse 27: "that ye stand fast in one spirit, with one mind striving together for the faith of the gospel". (See also 1 Corinthians 1: 10; 12: 4-6.)

- Because it was from Judaea that the error had come in the first place. The "apostles and elders" were located at Jerusalem (Acts 15: 2), and the false teachers "came down from Judaea" (Acts 15: 1). The fact that Paul went to Jerusalem does not imply that the church there had jurisdiction over other churches. We should note that Paul, Barnabas and the assembly at Antioch dealt with the matter locally, before Paul and Barnabas went to Jerusalem. We should notice:

i) His attitude to his brethren, v.2b. Paul "communicated" his preaching to the apostles at Jerusalem. The word "communicate" *(anatithemi)* is similar to "conferred" *(prosanatithemi)* in Chapter 1 verse 16. **There** it means 'to place over and toward', that is, to put oneself in communion with another. It has the idea of laying a matter before others so as to seek advice. **Here** it is 'to set up for the consideration of others'. Although Paul went to Jerusalem out of deep conviction, he did not go in a confrontational spirit. He did not go to Jerusalem 'beating the drum'.

- Paul conferred with "the apostles and elders at Jerusalem" (Acts 15: 6), and did so "privately" (*kat' idian:* translated 'when they were alone', Mark 4: 34): "I ... communicated unto them that gospel which I preach among the Gentiles, but privately to them which were of reputation (*dokeo*: held in high esteem)". It seems possible that what was evidently a private meeting preceded a public gathering at which "all the multitude" were present (Acts 15: 12). Whether this was the case or not, it remains that the proceedings closed with complete unanimity between "the apostles and elders with the whole church" (Acts 15: 22).

Speaking generally, and thinking now particularly of local issues, some matters are best dealt with privately. It is not always wise for the whole assembly to be involved, but when this is the case, deliberations should be guided by the elders.

- Paul did this "lest by any means I should run, or had run, in vain". That is, not in case his preaching had been inaccurate or erroneous, but in view of the fact that the results of his preaching were threatened by false teaching. Paul had a deep concern for the welfare of his converts.

- As a result of this, Paul's preaching was vindicated. We should note that verse 3 is a parenthesis: in other words, put verse 3 in brackets: "But neither Titus, who was with me, being a Greek (see Acts 11: 20), was compelled to be circumcised". We should compare this with Acts 16 verse 3: "Him (Timothy) would Paul have to go forth with him; and took and circumcised him, because of the Jews which were in those quarters: for they knew all that his father was a Greek". The circumstances here were totally different to those surrounding Titus. In the case of Timothy, it was a matter of **service:** "because of the Jews". In the case of Titus, it was a matter of **salvation.** While there was no compulsion to circumcise Timothy, it was expedient to do so. But in the case of Titus, compulsion was **urged** by the false teachers. It has been nicely said that the case of Timothy emphasises that Paul was not in bondage to his liberty!

Chapter 2:1-10

ii) His attitude to the false teachers, vv.4-5. Resuming the mainstream of his argument, Paul continues in verse 4: "And that because of false brethren unawares brought in, who came in privily to spy out our liberty which we have in Christ Jesus, that they might bring us into bondage (compare Matthew 23: 4). To whom we gave place by subjection, no, not for an hour; that the truth of the gospel might continue with you". We should notice:

- *"False brethren."* The word *pseudadelphos* occurs only here and in 2 Corinthians 11 verse 26, "in perils from false brethren".

- *"Unawares brought in, who came in privily."* "Unawares" and "privily" are associated words. "Unawares brought in" *(pareisaktos)* and "came in privily" *(pareiserchomia)* have the literal meaning of 'coming in from the side', that is (quoting W.E.Vine) "as spies or traitors". W.E.Vine continues, "Strabo, a Greek historian contemporary with Paul, uses the word of enemies introduced secretly into a city by traitors within". False teachers always act surreptitiously. Compare 2 Peter 2 verse 1, "Who privily shall bring in damnable (destructive) heresies"; Jude v.4, "There are certain men crept in unawares". Here (in our current passage), they were "brought in" and they "came in". They were "brought in" by those who were inclined towards Judaism, and sought help of false brethren to accomplish their ends. The need for care in reception is obvious.

- *"Our liberty which we have in Christ Jesus."* That is, liberty from rites, rules and regulations. It was a question of "liberty" versus "bondage".

- *"To whom we gave subjection, no, not for an hour; that the truth of the gospel might continue with you."* Paul was not concerned with his own position, but for the sake of the gospel. The word "subjection" *(hupotasso)* is a military term, and means to 'rank under'. Paul would countenance no compromise with error, for error is not content to take equal place with truth: it will endeavour to emerge on top! Compare Philippians 4 verse 5, "Let your moderation (yieldingness) be known unto all men". In this case (Phil. 4: 5), it was a matter of *personal interest.* But here, in Galatians 2 verse 5, it was a matter of *divine truth.*

B) The result of his visit, vv.6-10

There are at least three matters for consideration in this paragraph: *(a)* confirmation (v.6); *(b)* commendation (vv.7-9); *(c)* recommendation (v.10).

43

a) Confirmation, v.6

"But of these who seemed to be somewhat, (whatsoever they were, it maketh no difference to me." God accepteth no man's person:) for they who seemed to be somewhat in conference **added nothing to me**". That is, Paul's preaching was recognised and confirmed. Justification by faith alone was acknowledged as the only means of salvation. Hence the fact that Titus was not "compelled to be circumcised". There was no correction of, deletion from, or addition to, Paul's message. There was no deficiency in Paul's gospel. He preached the truth, the whole truth, and nothing but the truth.

We must not conclude that Paul described the apostles at Jerusalem in a derogatory way in saying, "those who seemed to be somewhat (were conspicuous), whatsoever they were, it maketh no difference to me". This is otherwise rendered: "But from those who were reputed to be somewhat (whatsoever they were – or, the margin reading, 'what they once were' – it maketh no matter to me: God accepteth not man's person) – they, I say, who were of repute imparted nothing to me" (RV). Paul is evidently stating that he was not responsible to them, even though they had been chosen by the Lord Jesus whilst here on earth. Personalities should not influence us.

It does seem that the Judaisers were exaggerating the status of the Jewish apostles at the expense of Paul's own position. Paul is not at all depreciatory of the twelve apostles, but rather of the extravagant and exclusive claims made for them by the Judaisers.

b) Commendation, vv.7-9

Attention is drawn to the two expressions, "they added nothing to me" (v.6), and "they gave to me and Barnabas the right hands of fellowship" (v.9). We should notice:

i) The evidence of Paul's calling. "But contrariwise, when they **saw** that the gospel of the circumcision was committed (*pisteuo*: entrusted, as a stewardship) unto me, as the gospel of the circumcision was to Peter ..." The evidence of Paul's calling lay in his ministry. Compare verse 9, where the apostles "perceived the grace that was given unto me". The apostles were not asked to recognise Paul's suggestions about himself, or to accept that he had an exercise of heart about service for God: they were confronted with evidence of his gift and calling. It was not a case of Paul making claims for

Chapter 2:1-10

himself, or of others making claims for him, but recognition of a gift and of ministry which they saw to exist. This is important. Our brethren will recognise our gift as they see it demonstrated, not as we talk about it!

There were obviously not two gospels! The "gospel of the uncircumcision" committed to Paul was precisely the same as the "gospel of the circumcision" committed to Peter. The omission of the italicised words is important. There is no difference in content: only in recipients. The same gospel is for all men. The ministry of Paul was primarily, but not exclusively, to the Gentiles. The ministry of Peter was primarily, but not exclusively, to the Jews. The word "committed" means 'entrusted'.

We should notice in this connection that Paul speaks to a Jewish audience in Acts 13, and Peter speaks to a Gentile audience in Acts 10. Both refer to Old Testament prophets (Acts 10: 43 and 13: 40-41). In passing, do note that Acts 12 commences with Peter, James and John, and concludes with Paul and Barnabas. Acts 12 is a 'transitional chapter'.

ii) The common power enjoyed by both apostles. "For he that wrought effectively in Peter to the apostleship of the circumcision, the same was mighty in me toward the Gentiles" (v.8). We should notice that Paul acknowledged Peter's apostleship here, and that Peter recognised Paul's apostleship in 2 Peter 3 verses 15-16. Both drew on the same resources. The words, "wrought effectively" and "mighty" are the same *(energeo).* The same God gave power and resource to both apostles. See 1 Corinthians 12 verses 4-11. "Now there are diversities of gifts, but the **same Spirit.** And there are differences of administrations, but the **same Lord.** And there are diversities of operations: but it is the **same God** which worketh all in all ... but all these worketh that one and the selfsame Spirit, dividing to every man severally as he will".

iii) The fellowship between fellow-workers. "And when James, Cephas (Aramaic: Peter was his Greek name), and John, who seemed to be pillars, perceived the grace that was given unto me, they gave to me and Barnabas the right hands of fellowship; that we should go unto the heathen, and they unto the circumcision" (v.9). It has been suggested that Paul uses Peter's more intimate Aramaic name (Cephas) as part of his desire to 'break down any barriers' between them.

The apostles are named to emphasise that Paul's ministry was recognised and acknowledged, not by obscure brethren, but by men who were 'conspicuous as being pillars'. The word "seemed", or 'reputed', also occurs in verse 6, and is not used in an ironical sense, but factually. "Pillars" remind us of stability and strength: "pillars" are burden-bearers. Compare Revelation 3 verse 12.

We must notice that the three apostles "perceived the **grace** that was **given** unto me". Compare Romans 12 verse 3. They recognised that God had chosen and equipped Paul for the task of evangelising the Gentiles. See 1 Corinthians 3 verse 5. All service for God can only be undertaken as the Lord gives ability.

The apostles gave to Barnabas and Paul the "right hands (plural) of fellowship". Each of the apostles signified their recognition, and pledged their fellowship with Barnabas and Paul. Here were servants of God, whose ministry lay in different spheres, but who were in full fellowship with each other. There was mutual interest and support. Each apostle expressed their personal fellowship with Paul and Barnabas. Every assembly ought to be marked by the same principle of "right hands of fellowship". We must take care to avoid nominal assent to those activities undertaken by fellow-believers as part of the corporate testimony of the assembly, without personal interest and fellowship on our part.

c) Recommendation, v.10

"Only they would that we should remember the poor; the same which I also was forward to do." This evidently embraced the poor without distinction. Giving lies at the heart of Christianity. "For ye know the grace of our Lord Jesus Christ, that, though he was rich, yet for your sakes he became poor, that ye through his poverty might be rich" (2 Cor. 8: 9). While there is no specific reference here to the "poor saints at Jerusalem", we should note, for example, 1 Corinthians 16 verses 1-3 and Romans 15 verses 26-27. The other matters mentioned in Acts 15 verse 29 are not mentioned here because, presumably, they had already received the letter from Jerusalem.

The next section of the chapter paints an entirely different picture.

THE EPISTLE TO THE GALATIANS

"When Peter was come to Antioch"

Read Chapter 2: 11-21

As we have already noticed, Galatians 2 may be divided as follows: *(1)* Paul conferring with the apostles at Jerusalem (vv.1-10); *(2)* Paul contending with Peter at Antioch (vv.11-21). The unanimity and fellowship resulting from Paul's visit to Jerusalem suffered a serious blow when Peter visited Antioch, reminding us that progress is so often followed by disappointment.

1) PAUL CONFERRING WITH THE APOSTLES AT JERUSALEM, vv.1-10

In this connection, we noticed: *(i) the occasion of the visit* (vv.1-2a): "Then fourteen years after, I went up again to Jerusalem with Barnabas, and took Titus with me also" (v.1); *(ii) the object of the visit* (vv.2b-5): "because of false brethren unawares brought in, who came in privily to spy out our liberty which we have in Christ Jesus, that they might bring us into bondage" (v.4); *(iii) the outcome of the visit* (vv.6-10): "they added nothing to me ... They gave to me and Barnabas the right hands of fellowship; that we should go unto the heathen, and they unto the circumcision" (vv.6, 9). This brings us to:

2) PAUL CONTENDING WITH PETER AT ANTIOCH, vv.11-21

The section commences with a summary of events. "But when Peter was come to Antioch, I withstood him to the face, because he was to be blamed ('was to be condemned', JND)" (v.11). The explanation follows. The words, "he was to be blamed" are explained in verses 12-13, and the words, "I withstood him to the face", are explained in verses 14-21. It can all be summed up in two words: Peter "***withdrew***" from the Gentiles (v.12), and Paul "***withstood***" Peter (v.11). It has been pointed out that while Paul went to Jerusalem "by revelation" (2: 2), no such statement is made concerning Peter's visit to Antioch. However, since the apparent lesson is based on

Galatians

silence we should avoid speaking too dogmatically! We should note that his inconsistent conduct at Antioch in no way cancels the authority of his epistles. "All scripture is given by inspiration of **God**" (2 Tim. 3: 16).

A) Peter withdrew from the Gentiles, vv.12-13

"For before that certain came from James, he did eat with the Gentiles: but when they were come, he withdrew and separated himself, fearing them which were of the circumcision." This explains the statement, "he was to be blamed". The "James" here is, of course, the "James" of Acts 15 verse 13 and 21 verse 18. It should be noted that we are not told that James sent these men with the intent of bringing Gentile believers into bondage to the law. Attention is drawn to the following:

i) Peter was vulnerable to pressure. While, with James and John, Peter was a 'pillar' (v.9), the fact remains that, like us all at times, he succumbed to pressure. The 'pillar' was not as strong as it might have been! The difficulty arose at Antioch from a most unlikely source. The very man who had received the preparatory vision in Acts 10 verses 1-16, who had defended and explained his visit to Caesarea before the church at Jerusalem in Acts 11 verses 4-17, and who had declared that God had justified both Jews and Gentiles on the same basis in Acts 15 verses 7-11, now acted in a way which reversed all that he had previously taught on the subject.

J.Hunter (*What the Bible Teaches - Galatians*), points out that "the first man to learn the truth of Gentile admission to the church is the first to withdraw from it", reminding us that even **great men** are vulnerable. In fact, they can be even more vulnerable than others. The man in the public eye is subject to much more scrutiny and attention! We **all** need to heed the injunction, "Wherefore let him that thinketh he standeth take heed lest he fall" (1 Cor. 10: 12). This leads us to note that:

ii) Peter was influenced by his company. "**Before** that certain came from James, he did eat with the Gentiles: but **when** they were come, he withdrew and separated himself, fearing them which were of the circumcision." The change of company brought a change of position. The change in Peter's behaviour was not engendered by a change in his convictions, but by a change in his company. He became subject to "the fear of man" (Prov. 29: 25). It certainly brought "a snare" in Peter's case! He evidently concluded that it was more important to keep his Jerusalem friends happy than to preserve and protect the position of his Gentile brethren at Antioch. Peter was evidently fearful for his reputation rather than concerned for the welfare of his brethren. We need to remember that truth can be offensive even amongst believers, and so, like Elijah centuries before, "when he saw that, he arose and went for his life" (1 Kings 19. 1-3).

W.E.Vine suggests that the word translated "withdrew" (*hupostello*) is "perhaps metaphor from lowering a sail and so slackening the course, and hence of being remiss in holding the truth". This does seem most appropriate. Peter trimmed the sails of his doctrine to meet different doctrinal breezes. The word "withdrew" could, however, be a military term: a 'drawing back'.

iii) Peter compromised the word of God revealed to him. He failed to take his stand on past teaching. See Acts 10 verses 1-48 with 11 verses 1-18, which describe events leading to his visit to the house of Cornelius at Caesarea. Peter had been charged by the "circumcision" with contact with the "uncircumcised": "Thou wentest in to men uncircumcised, and didst eat with them" (Acts 11: 3). The 'circumcision party' were strongly prejudiced against people outside the covenants with Israel. See Ephesians 2 verses 11-12. Peter answered their charge, first, by describing the vision given him on the housetop at Joppa: "And I heard a voice saying unto me, Arise, Peter; slay and eat. But I said, Not so, Lord: for nothing common or unclean hath at any time entered my mouth. But the voice answered me again from heaven, What God hath cleansed, that call not thou common" (Acts 11: 7-9). This prepared for the visit to Caesarea. Then, having witnessed the Gentiles there receiving the Holy Spirit, he continued, "Forasmuch then as God gave them the like gift as he did unto us, who believed on the Lord Jesus Christ, what was I, that I could withstand God?" (Acts 11: 17). Peter reaffirmed his position at Jerusalem in Acts 15 verses 7-11.

At first, as noted, Peter maintained that position at Antioch: "Before that certain came from James, he did eat with the Gentiles". But he failed to maintain that position: "But when they were come, he withdrew and separated himself" (v.12). In view of the revelation made to him in Acts 10 verses 9-16, and subsequent events, he should have known better. He abandoned what he knew to be right.

This is a solemn lesson to us all. Have **we** abandoned what **we** know to be right? The solemn implications are spelt out line by line by Paul in verses 14-21. Peter began well, but stumbled. What about ***us?***

*iv) **Peter influenced others.*** "And the other Jews dissembled likewise with him: insomuch that Barnabas also was carried away with their dissimulation" (v.13). The words rendered "dissembled" (*sunupokrinomai*) and "dissimulation" (*hupokrisis*) surface in our English word 'hypocrite'. It was a most serious charge. Peter and his fellow Jews were guilty of pretence or playing a part. It looked as if their convictions had changed, but this wasn't the case at all. Although it seemed otherwise, their volte-face was not caused by "loyalty to the law of Moses" (W.E.Vine), but fear of the Jews from Jerusalem. It was this that created the division between Jew and Gentile at Antioch. This was their "dissimulation". They hid their fear of the visitors from Jerusalem under a cloak of loyalty to the law of Moses. The very man who dealt summarily with the hypocrisy of Ananias and Sapphira (Acts 5: 1-11), now became guilty of hypocrisy himself.

Peter was obviously a man of influence. He certainly moved other people. He moved six men in John 21 verses 2-3. Peter having said, "I go a fishing", they responded, "We also go with thee". Then, in visiting the house of Cornelius, he was accompanied by six men: "these six brethren accompanied me" (Acts 11: 12). Now he influences Barnabas, who was "carried away with their dissimulation" (v.13). Barnabas, that "good man, and full of the Holy Ghost and of faith" (Acts 11: 24), who had accompanied Paul on the first missionary journey, and who had accompanied Paul to Jerusalem (Acts 15: 2), was wrongly influenced by Peter. Barnabas above all people! Paul stood alone against the flood-tide of false teaching.

B) Paul withstands Peter, vv.14-21

"But when I saw that they walked not uprightly according to the truth of the gospel, I said unto Peter before them all, If thou, being a Jew, livest after the manner of the Gentiles, why compellest thou the Gentiles to live as do the Jews?" The words, "walked not uprightly" *(orthopodea)* mean, literally, not 'straight-footed, forward, unwavering'. Compare Hebrews 12 verse 13, "make straight (*orthos*) paths for your feet". We should notice that "fear" (v.12) leads to "dissimulation" or hypocrisy (v.13), and hypocrisy leads to conduct which is not "according to the truth of the gospel" (v.14). Fear of brethren can lead us to hypocrisy because we fail to act in accordance with what we know to be true. The "truth of the gospel" should be the rule of our lives. It must, of course, be maintained as the only means of justification (vv.15-16), but it must also shape our conduct. We are to "adorn the doctrine of God our Saviour in all things ..." (Titus 2: 10).

Chapter 2:11-21

We may divide these verses as follows: *(a)* what Paul did: "I said unto Peter before them all"; *(b)* what Paul said: "If thou, being a Jew…"

a) What Paul did, v.14

"But when I saw that they walked not uprightly, according to the truth of the gospel, I said unto Peter **before them all.**" In passing, this does emphasise Paul's independent authority. We should note the following:

i) Paul was not afraid to confront Peter publicly. "I said unto Peter before them *all.*" See also verse 11, "I withstood him to the face", not **behind his back!** All of which reminds us that "Faithful are the wounds of a friend" (Prov. 27: 6) The necessity for public confrontation arose from the public nature of the bad example set by Peter and his associates. The rebuke was as wide as the relapse. Private and personal misdemeanours can and should be adjusted privately, but if the welfare of God's people has been endangered by public teaching and public example, it must be dealt with publicly. The assembly must see and hear the rebuttal of wrong teaching.

In doing this, Paul was acting as a shepherd. He saw "the wolf coming" and acted in the best interests of the flock at Antioch. Saul of Tarsus, like Saul the son of Kish before him, had once demonstrated the character of the tribe to which he belonged, ("Benjamin shall ravin as a wolf", Gen, 49: 27), but the 'wolf' had become a shepherd"!

ii) Paul was not influenced by past friendship with Peter. As J.Hunter observes, Paul "did not oppose Peter because he loved an argument, nor because he wanted to score over Peter, and humiliate him. It was because of 'the truth of the gospel'". He had the purest motives. On the other hand, he did not 'soft-peddle' because of previous fellowship with Peter. See, for example Chapter 1 verse 18. It is all too easy to sacrifice truth on the altar of personal friendship. But we must not think that this led to permanent damage in their relationship.

We should add that although Paul confronted Peter in this way, their mutual regard was not impaired. While we do not know how Peter responded to Paul's public rebuke (we can only assume that it proved effective), we do know that Peter later called him "our beloved brother Paul". Here is the quotation in full: "And account that the longsuffering of our Lord is salvation; even as our beloved brother Paul also according to the wisdom given unto him hath written unto you" (2 Pet. 3: 15). Do notice, incidentally, that Peter's letters, written perhaps something like fifteen years after this incident, were addressed to "the strangers scattered throughout Pontus, **Galatia,** Cappadocia, Asia, and Bythinia" (1 Peter 1:1). But there is more.

iii) Paul did not lose confidence in Barnabas. On the assumption that Peter visited Antioch after the conference at Jerusalem in Acts 15, it is heartening to read: "Paul also and Barnabas continued in Antioch, teaching and preaching the word of the Lord, with many others also. And some days after Paul said unto Barnabas, Let us go again and visit our brethren in every city" (Acts 15: 35-36). See also 1 Corinthians 9 verse 6 (written, according to Scofield, in AD 59, with the Jerusalem conference in AD 52): "Or I only and Barnabas, have not we power to forbear working?" An error of judgment on a previous occasion did not rankle with Paul *ad infinitum.* See also Paul's relationship with Mark. Compare Acts 15 verses 37-39 with 2 Timothy 4 verse 11.

b) What Paul said, vv.14-21

We should notice the stages of his argument. He begins by addressing Peter directly: "thou" (v.14); he continues by including himself: "we" (vv.15-17); he concludes by referring to himself alone: "I" (vv.18-21). As noted above, "this thing was not done in a corner". Paul was not being unkind to Peter. Since the believers at Antioch had seen Peter 'changing horses in mid-stream', it was so important to adjust the matter publicly. It has been suggested that the "we" becomes "I" out of courtesy. Paul does not directly refer to Peter here.

In addressing Peter "before them all", Paul deals with the implications of his actions in altering his stance at Antioch. We should therefore notice:

i)   Its implications for Peter, v.14. "If thou, being a Jew, livest after the manner of Gentiles (that is, as someone justified by faith alone), and not as do the Jews (who strove to keep the law with its ordinances), why compellest thou the Gentiles to live as do the Jews?" To walk "uprightly, according to the truth of the gospel", demanded conduct appropriate to justification by faith. By "eating with the Gentiles" (v.12) he had approved their position, that is, he acted as justified by faith alone. By living "after the manner of the Gentiles" he made it perfectly clear that salvation was not in any way dependent on circumcision or on any other Old Testament requirement. Why then abandon that in view of the fact that even Jews had been justified by faith? By withdrawing from the Gentiles, he had effectively denied that

Chapter 2:11-21

salvation was totally apart from Jewish ordinances. His second stance was totally inconsistent with the first. Hence the question, "why compellest thou the Gentiles to live as do the Jews?" If he had approved their position in the first place, why was he now reversing his judgment?

ii) Its implications for saved Jews, vv.15-16. "*We* who are Jews by nature, and not sinners of the Gentiles, knowing that a man is not justified by the works of the law, but by the faith of Jesus Christ, even *we* have believed in Jesus Christ that *we* might be justified by the faith of Christ, and not by the works of the law: for by the works of the law shall no flesh be justified." Jews had been justified on the basis of faith in Christ alone. So to disapprove the position of the Gentiles (as Peter had done) was to disapprove the position of the Jews as well! It wasn't like that when Peter first arrived at Antioch. By living after the manner of the Gentiles, Peter acknowledged that salvation was by faith alone, and totally apart from Jewish ordinances. Peter acknowledged the "common salvation" (Jude v.3).

It is worth noting that the word "justified" occurs four times in verses 16-17. W.R.Newell *(Romans Verse by Verse)* puts it with crystal clarity. "Justification is not a change wrought by God in us, but a change in our relationship with God." Justification is a judicial act. It must not be confused with pardon. They are quite different. Under law, we are condemned by God. Justification is the reverse: it means that we are pronounced righteous by God.

We should notice the words, "knowing that a *man* is not justified by the works of the law, but by the faith of Jesus Christ" (v.16) or "saved through faith in Jesus Christ" (RV). The "man" here is any man. Grace eliminates the difference between Jew and Gentile when it comes to justification. This is emphasised by the words, "for by the works of the law shall *no flesh* be justified" (v.16). See also Romans 3 verse 20, "Therefore by the deeds of the law there shall no flesh be justified in his sight ..." As noted above, the words "by the faith of Jesus Christ" (AV) mean "through faith *in* Jesus Christ" (RV). (For the record, this is what the grammarians call a case of the 'objective genitive'. See also v.20.)

By acting as he did when "certain came from James", Peter effectively misrepresented and denied his own justification! He undermined the basis of justification for Jews as well as Gentiles.

iii) The implications for Christ, v.17. "But if, while we seek to be justified by Christ (or "*in* Christ", JND: not in the law) we ourselves also are found sinners, is therefore Christ the minister of sin? (that is, by making them forsake the law and causing them to trust in Him alone) God forbid." If they had been wrong in abandoning the principle of justification by works in favour of the principle of justification by faith in Christ alone, then the very Christ in whom they had trusted had led them into sin. No wonder Paul says, "God forbid!", or, "Far be the thought" (JND). We would say 'Perish the thought'. It is unthinkable that Christ should be "the minister of sin" by causing men to abandon the law as a means of justification. But Peter had implied this by his conduct.

iv) The implications for the Gospel preacher, v.18. "For if I build again the things which I destroyed (*kataluo*, to destroy utterly: as Matthew 24 verse 2, "thrown down") I make myself a transgressor." Peter had actually done this by refusing to eat with the Gentiles. Paul now puts himself in the same position, and discusses its implications. Peter had implied that he had been originally wrong to abandon keeping the law as the means of justification, and Paul agrees that if salvation really was by "the works of the law", then he too was a transgressor. In the words of Wm.Trew (*Galatians*, Precious Seed Publications), "To build again the things that they had so deliberately destroyed was to make themselves transgressors in having destroyed them".

But the answer is a resounding 'No'. The Lord Jesus was not "the minister of sin" (v.17) and Paul was not "a transgressor" (v.18). Paul explains why in verses 19-21.

- ***Law works and Paul personally.*** Paul had not destroyed the claims of the law: they had been fulfilled in him! He had not acted in opposition to the law. The claims of the law had been fully met. "For I through the law am dead to the law (how? see v.20 "crucified"), that I might live unto God" (how? see v.20: "by faith") (v.19). The law had nothing to say to a dead man. It condemned Paul to death, and the sentence had been carried out. After all, the law demanded entire obedience, or death. It was a case of 'do or die'. Since the claims of the law had been fully met and there was now no outstanding claim against him, Paul could now live for God's pleasure and do God's will. This is the fountain-head from which later teaching in the epistle flows: see Chapters 5-6.

But *how* had the claims of the law been satisfied? The answer follows in verse 20: "I am crucified with Christ: nevertheless I live; yet not I, but Christ liveth in me: and the life which I now live in the flesh I live by the faith of the Son of God ('the faith which is in the Son of God', RV), who loved me, and gave himself for me". The Lord Jesus *actually* met the claims of the law. See Chapter 3 verse 13, "Christ hath redeemed us from the curse of the law, being made a curse for us: for it is written, Cursed is every one that hangeth on a tree". By trusting in Christ, the claims of the law were *figuratively* carried out on us too. Crucifixion was an act of judgment. The cross means the end of us as sinners. It was a judicial act. The man himself is removed. The verse emphasises *identification* rather than substitution. It is, metaphorically, 'co-crucifixion with Christ'. The sentence pronounced on *us* has been executed on *Christ.*

But *how* does Paul "live unto God?" This follows: "nevertheless I live; yet not I, but Christ liveth in me". The life of Christ was manifest in him. This is the basis of teaching in Chapter 5. The power of Paul's new life is the indwelling Christ. Whereas before, Paul endeavoured to live by keeping the law, now he lives by the power of the Lord Jesus, and that power is made good by faith. "The life that I now live in the flesh, I live by the faith of (in) the Son of God, who loved me, and gave himself for me." Life for Paul did not consist of law-keeping, but the outworking of the life of Christ in him.

Paul's contemplation of this leads to praise and thankfulness: "The Son of God, who loved me, and gave himself for me". The title, "Son of God", emphasises the power of Christ in Paul's life. But it also stresses the eternity of His love. It was "the Son of God" who "loved me, and gave himself for me". This underlines the greatness of Paul's Saviour. To think that One so great, should love him so much as to give Himself in order to save him, the 'chief of sinners' (1 Tim. 1:15)! Paul did not preach justification by faith alone in a cold mechanical way: he preached it with a deep, deep appreciation of the love of Christ. His doctrine and his preaching were suffused by divine love

- *Law works and God's grace.* "I do not frustrate the grace of God: for if righteousness came by the law, then Christ is dead in vain." Paul's ministry as a preacher of justification by faith did not "frustrate (*athateo*, disannul) the grace of God". Others were setting aside (make void, RV) the grace of God, by returning to law-keeping, causing Paul to observe that if that was the way in which men could be justified, then Christ died needlessly. His death was "in vain" *(dorean):* it was 'without a cause' and 'for nothing'. What a chilling conclusion!

Galatians

When Paul preached at Antioch in Pisidia there was no question of Christ being "dead in vain": "Be it known unto you therefore, men and brethren, that through this man is preached unto you the forgiveness of sins: and by him all that believe are justified from all things, from which ye could not be justified by the law of Moses" (Acts 13: 38-39).

THE EPISTLE TO THE GALATIANS

"The just shall live by faith"

Read Chapter 3: 1-14

Chapters 3 & 4 represent the second of the three major divisions of the epistle. As we have already noted, Chapters 1 & 2 can be called the **historical** section, Chapters 3 & 4 the **doctrinal** section, and Chapters 5 & 6 the **practical** section. In Chapter 1, Paul presents his **divinely-given credentials**, and in Chapter 2 his **humanly-given credentials.** His apostolic authority was bestowed upon him by the Lord Jesus (Chapter 1), and this was fully recognised by his fellow-apostles (Chapter 2).

The transition from the historical to the doctrinal section of the epistle lies in Paul's censure of Peter at Antioch. See Chapter 2 verses 14-21. By withdrawing from the Gentile believers at Antioch, Peter had contradicted his own teaching in Acts 15: "God made choice among us, that the Gentiles by my mouth should hear the word of the gospel, and believe. And God, which knoweth the hearts, bare them witness, giving them the Holy Ghost, even as he did unto us; and put no difference between us and them, purifying their hearts by faith" (Acts 15: 7-9) . Paul reminded Peter of this at Antioch: "**We** who are Jews by nature, and not sinners of the Gentiles, knowing that a man is not justified by the works of the law, but by the faith of Jesus Christ, even **we** have believed in Jesus Christ, that **we** might be justified by the faith of Christ, and not by the works of the law: for by the works of the law shall no flesh be justified" (Gal. 2: 15-16). The implications of reverting to "the works of the law" for salvation and justification are most solemn. Hence Paul reminded his Galatian brethren that he gave place to the false teachers "no, not for an hour" (Gal 2: 5, 5). In fact he went as far as to say "let him be accursed" of anyone who "preached any other gospel" (Gal 1: 8-9). This was certainly not 'over the top'. Look at the implications if the false teachers were right:

- ***Its implications for Christ, 2: 17.*** It meant that Christ had led believers into sin: "But if, while we seek to be justified by Christ, we ourselves also are found sinners, is therefore Christ the minister of sin? God forbid". If they had been wrong in abandoning the principle of justification by works in favour of the principle of justification by faith, then the very Christ in whom they had trusted had led them into sin! That is, the sin of abrogating/breaking the law. No wonder Paul says, "God forbid". Further, if justification was by works and not faith, then "Christ is dead in vain" (2: 21). Law and faith are mutually exclusive: you cannot have both.

- ***Its implications for Paul, 2:18.*** It meant that he was guilty of transgressing the law of God. "For if I build again the things which I destroyed, I make myself a transgressor." Wm.Trew (*Galatians*, Precious Seed Publications) states the matter clearly: "To build again the things that they had so deliberately destroyed was to make themselves transgressors in having destroyed them".

But Christ was not "the minister of sin", and Paul was not "a transgressor", because the claims of the law had been fully met, "For I through the law am dead to the law, that I might live unto God" (2: 19).

In view of these statements, Paul censures the Galatians: "O foolish Galatians, who hath bewitched you, that ye should not obey the truth, before whose eyes, Jesus Christ hath been evidently set forth crucified among you?" (3: 1) or "O senseless Galatians, who has bewitched you; to whom, as before your very eyes, Jesus Christ has been portrayed, crucified [among you]?" (JND).

Galatians 3 divides into two main sections: *(1)* faith and works (vv.1-14); *(2)* promise and law (vv.15-29):

- ***Faith and works (vv.1-14)***, where faith is broadly contrasted with works, and where we should notice reference to "the **works** of the law ... the hearing of **faith**" (vv.2, 5) and the contrast, "So then they which be of **faith** ... as are of the **works** of the **law**" (vv.9-10).

- ***Promise and law (vv.15-29)***, where promise is broadly contrasted with law, and where we should notice the statements "the **law** ... cannot ... make the **promise** of none effect" (v.17); "For if the inheritance be of the **law**, it is no more of **promise**"(v.18); "Wherefore then serveth the **law?** It was added

... till the seed should come to whom the *promise* was made" (v.19); "Is the *law* then against the *promises* of God?" (v.21).

1) FAITH AND WORKS, vv.1-14

In this section, Paul appeals firstly to their experience (vv.1-5) and, secondly, to the Scriptures (vv.6-14). It has been observed that in appealing to their experience in these verses, he asks six questions, and that in appealing to the Scriptures, he gives six quotations. The double appeal is most significant. Their experience told them that not one shred of law-keeping was involved in their salvation, and, of great importance, that this was entirely consistent with the Scriptures.

A) *His appeal to their experience, vv.1-5*

As noted above, Paul asks six questions. The first refers to the basis of their justification (v.1), and the following five refer to the proof of their justification (vv.2-5). In both cases, Paul charged the Galatians with foolishness. "O foolish ('senseless, JND) Galatians" (v.1); "Are ye so foolish ('senseless', JND)?" (v.3).

a) *The basis of justification, v.1*

The basis of their salvation or justification was the death of the Lord Jesus. Paul refers to the original preaching with its emphasis on the cross, and therefore upon divine judgment. He bore the curse. In view of the fact that "if righteousness come by the law, then Christ is dead in vain" (2: 21), how could they be so senseless as to think that salvation depended on law-works, when Christ, who had borne divine judgment upon the cross, had been preached unto them? Did not His very death proclaim the insufficiency of law-works? We should notice:

- *The importance of careful thinking.* "O foolish (*anoetos*) Galatians, who hath bewitched you....?" Paul speaks here out of deep feeling. Compare 2 Corinthians 6 verse 11, "O ye Corinthians", and Philippians 4 verse 15, "And know also ye, O Philippians" (JND). See also Luke 24 verse 25, "O fools (*anoetos*), and slow of heart to believe all that the prophets have spoken". The word "foolish" here ('senseless', JND) means 'not understanding ... an unworthy lack of understanding" (W.E.Vine), reminding us of the necessity to heed the injunction given to Timothy: "Meditate upon these things; give thyself wholly to them; that thy profiting (progress) may appear to all. Take heed unto thyself, and unto the doctrine" (1 Tim. 4: 15-16). In the words of Jeffrey Harrison, "We all need good Berean blood in our veins" (Acts 17: 11).

Where will thoughtlessness lead? What will be its effect? "O foolish Galatians, **who hath bewitched you?**" (The words, "that ye should not obey the truth" are omitted on textual grounds by RV/JND). The word "bewitched" (*baskaino*) means 'to charm' and in this case, to lead "into evil doctrine" (W.E.Vine) or, to bring under the power of evil doctrine. While it is a rhetorical question ("who hath bewitched you?") the word "who" is in the singular, which may suggest that this is a reference to Satan himself. Compare Chapter 5 verses 7-8. See John 8 verse 44, "When he (the devil) speaketh a lie, he speaketh of his own: for he is a liar, and the father of it".

- The importance of careful preaching. We know what Paul and his colleagues preached about in Galatia: "Before whose eyes Jesus Christ hath been evidently set forth, crucified among you". Compare 1 Corinthians 1 verses 23-24, "But we preach Christ crucified ..." See also 1 Corinthians 2 verses 1-2. The word "evidently" means, in this context, 'openly' or 'graphically'. The underlying word *(prographo)* means, literally, 'to write before'. It is used in Ephesians 3 verse 3 ("as I wrote afore in a few words"), in Romans 15 verse 4 ("whatsoever things were written aforetime"), and Jude verse 4 ("who were before of old ordained to this condemnation").

According to W.E.Vine, in all probability the word is used here in its sense in contemporary literature, where it meant to 'proclaim' or 'placard'. A judge would 'placard' his proclamation in a public place. It was used of edicts and laws put up in some public place for all to read. Similarly, Paul and his colleagues had visited Galatia and publicly preached the Gospel there, but now the eyes of the converts, previously fixed on Christ alone for salvation, had been turned in another direction. They had allowed themselves to be fascinated (or charmed) by "the enemies of the Cross of Christ" (W.E.Vine) instead continuing to look only to Him for salvation. See W.E.Vine's *Expository Dictionary of New Testament Words*. W.E.Vine suggests the possibility of reference here to Numbers 21 verses 8-9 and the necessity to "look" solely towards the 'brazen serpent' for salvation.

This serves to emphasise that Gospel preaching must set Christ before men and women. Our preaching must publicly present Christ crucified, and nothing must be allowed to deflect attention from His finished work as the basis of salvation.

Chapter 3:1-14

In passing, we should notice that this epistle applies the crucifixion of the Lord Jesus in four ways: legally (2: 20); historically (3: 1); morally (5: 24); socially (6: 14).

b) The evidence of justification, vv.2-5

"This only would I learn of you, received ye the Spirit (the first mention of the Holy Spirit in the epistle) by the works of the law, or by the hearing of faith?" The reception of the Holy Spirit was proof of justification. See Acts 15 verse 8, "And God, which knoweth the hearts (that is knowing the reality of their faith), **bare them witness,** giving them the Holy Ghost, even as he did unto us". Compare Acts 10 verses 43-44, "While Peter yet spoke these words, the Holy Ghost fell on all them which heard the word". The "word" in question was Peter's preaching that "whosoever believeth in him shall receive remission of sins". We should notice that justification by faith and the reception of the Holy Spirit are simultaneous. See Chapter 2 verse 16 and Chapter 3 verse 2. Compare Ephesians 1 verse 13.

Paul is not emphasising here so much the **fact** that they had received the Holy Spirit, but the **way** in which they had done so. It was not by "the works of the law", but by the "hearing of faith". They had not been justified "by the works of the law, but by the faith of (in) Jesus Christ" (2: 16). The very fact that they had received the Holy Spirit without any contribution on their part should have been further evidence of the futility of reverting to "the works of the law". No wonder Paul says, "Are ye so foolish ...?" We should notice three things:

- **Receiving the Spirit, v.2.** "**Received** ye the Spirit by the works of the law, or by the hearing of faith?" Compare Chapter 4 verse 6, "And because ye are sons, God hath sent forth the Spirit of his Son into your hearts ..." The reception of the Holy Spirit is evidence of justification. See Chapter 5 verse 18. It is evidence of sonship. See Chapter 4 verse 6. This is but one of the implications of the reception and indwelling of the Holy Spirit, some of which are mentioned in 2 Corinthians 1 verses 21-22, "Now he which stablisheth us with you in Christ, and hath anointed us, is God; who hath also sealed us, and given the earnest of the Spirit in our hearts". Another aspect of the reception and indwelling of the Holy Spirit is the fact that His coming is evidence of the exaltation of the Lord Jesus. See Acts 2 verses 32-33.

- **Beginning in the Spirit, v.3-4.** "Are ye so foolish? having **begun** in the Spirit, are ye now made perfect by the flesh?" Compare Philippians 1 verse 6,

"He which hath **begun** a good work in you ..." In passing, it might be helpful to say that whereas Paul refers to the "**works** of the flesh" in connection with unregenerate men and women, he refers to the "the **fruit** of the Spirit" in connection with saved men and women (Gal. 5: 19-23). Compare Chapter 5 verse 25, "If we live in the Spirit, let us also walk in the Spirit".

The argument is clear: "having begun in the Spirit (something divinely and inwardly accomplished), are ye now made perfect (Greek *epiteleo:* to bring through to the end) by the flesh (something humanly and outwardly accomplished)?" It is, literally, 'are ye now perfecting yourselves?' Since the law made demands on human nature, which human nature cannot meet, this is another way of saying: 'are ye now made perfect by the law?' The Judaisers were therefore implying that the work of Christ and the work of the Holy Spirit were alike insufficient. As already noted, the practical implications of "begun in the Spirit", are discussed later in the epistle. See Chapter 5 verses 22-25. However, we must notice that **spiritual life can only be maintained by spiritual means.**

It is not without significance that having referred to the beginning of spiritual life, Paul continues with reference to their suffering: "Have ye suffered so many things in vain (*eike,* 'without a cause')? If it be yet in vain (*eike*)" (v.4). See also Chapter 4 verse 11. A different word is used in Chapter 2 verse 2 (*kenos*), meaning "empty", and in Chapter 2 verse 21 (*dorean*), meanng 'uselessly' or 'for nought'.

This is an eloquent reminder of the sequel to new life in Christ. The gospel brings suffering to those who respond by "the hearing of faith". Compare Galatians 4 verse 29, "But as then he that was born after the flesh persecuted (persecuted by mockery, Gen. 21: 9) him that was born after the Spirit, even so it is now"; Galatians 6 verse 12, "As many as desire to make a fair show in the flesh, they constrain you to be circumcised; only lest they should suffer persecution for the cross of Christ". As J.Hunter (*What the Bible Teaches - Galatians*) observes, "In those early days, suffering was the common lot of Christians, but it would all be for nothing if they went on to embrace the Law".

- Serving in the Spirit, v.5. "He therefore that ministereth to you the Spirit, and worketh miracles among you, doeth he it by the works of the law, or by the hearing of faith?", or "He therefore who ministers to you the Spirit, and works miracles among you, [is it] on the principle of works of law, or of [the] report of faith?" (JND). In verse 3, they "**received**" the Spirit through faith. But here (v.5) it is *power* of the Spirit amongst them. "He (that is, God) therefore that ministereth to you the Spirit ..." On what basis do they enter into the blessings of God working amongst them? It is by *faith*. The word "ministereth" (*epichoregeo*) means 'supplieth', abundantly supplieth, and occurs in 2 Corinthians 9 verse 10 ("Now he that *ministereth* seed to the sower"); Colossians 2 verse 19 ("having nourishment *ministered*"); 2 Peter 1 verse 11 ("for so an entrance shall be *ministered* unto you"); 2 Peter 1 verse 5, ("*add* to your faith").

The "hearing of faith" (v.2 & v.5) connects both aspects of their experience of the Holy Spirit. He is possessed by faith, and His power is known by faith. For the expression, "and worketh miracles among you", see 2 Corinthians 12 verse 12, "Truly the signs of an apostle were wrought among you in all patience, in signs, and wonders, and mighty deeds".

In the words of J.Hunter: "It was God who had given them the Spirit: it was God who had performed miracles among them. Paul does not indicate whether the miracles were performed by himself or others, but he does state that the power of God was present among them. It was not present by the works of the law, but by the hearing of faith". In the words of the Amplified Version: "Then does He who supplies you with His marvellous (Holy) Spirit, and works powerfully and miraculously among you, [do so on the grounds of your doing] what the law demands, or because of your believing in and adhering to and trusting in and relying on the message that you heard?"

In summary: we have received the Spirit, we have begun in the Spirit, we serve in the Spirit. Not by the law of Moses, but by the Spirit of God.

The expression, "hearing of faith" (v.5) introduces the man in the Old Testament of whom this was pre-eminently true. Paul therefore continues, "Even as Abraham believed God, and it was accounted to him for righteousness". This brings us to:

A) His appeal to the Scriptures, vv.6-14

We have noticed that this section includes six quotations from the Old Testament: *(i)* Genesis 15 verse 6, see verse 6; *(ii)* Genesis 12 verse 3, see verse 8; *(iii)* Deuteronomy 27 verse 26, see verse 19; *(iv)* Habakkuk 2 verse 4, see verse 11; *(v)* Leviticus 18 verse 5, see verse 12; *(vi)* Deuteronomy 21 verse 23, see verse 13. These passages are cited in connection with four major points: *(a)* the position of Abraham (vv.6-7); *(b)* the promise of blessing (vv.8-9); *(c)* the problem of law (vv.10-12); *(d)* the provision through Christ (vv.13-14).

a) The position of Abraham, vv.6-7

Salvation was accounted to Abraham on the ground of faith. With this in mind, Paul states a fact (v.6), and draws a conclusion (v.7)

i) Paul states a fact, v.6. He appeals to Genesis 15 verse 6 in this connection: "Even as Abraham believed God, and it was accounted unto him for righteousness". The word "accounted" means 'reckoned'. We have three key words in the statement: "believed … accounted … righteousness". Abraham's part was to simply accept the word of God. He "believed". God's part was to reckon Abraham's faith for righteousness. The passage does not say that 'it was accounted unto him *instead* of righteousness'. Faith is not meritorious. It was not Abraham's righteousness, but God's righteousness reckoned to him.

ii) Paul draws a conclusion, v.7. "Know ye **therefore** that they which are of faith, the same are the children ('sons', JND/RV) of Abraham." That is, there is a family likeness, a spiritual family likeness. Compare John 8 where the Jews said, "We be Abraham's **seed**" (v.33), to be told by the Lord Jesus, "I know that ye are Abraham's **seed**" (v.37) but "If ye were Abraham's **children**, ye would do the works of Abraham" (v.39). Compare Romans 4: "Abraham believed God, and it was counted unto him for righteousness" (v.3). This took place when he was "in uncircumcision". Hence verses 11-12, "And he received the sign of circumcision, a seal of the righteousness of the faith which he had being yet uncircumcised: that he might be the father of all them that believe, though they be not circumcised; that righteousness might be imparted to them also: and the father of circumcision to them, who are not of the circumcision only, but who also walk in the steps of that faith of our father Abraham, which he had being yet uncircumcised".

b) The promise of blessing, vv.8-9

Salvation is not for the Jews only, but equally for the Gentiles. With this in mind, Paul states a fact (v.8), and draws a conclusion (v.9)

i) Paul states a fact, v.8. He appeals to Genesis 12 verse 3: "And the scripture foreseeing that God would justify the heathen through faith, preached before the gospel unto Abraham, saying, In thee shall all nations be blessed". We should not overlook the significance of the chronological order of the statements. Genesis 12 verse 3 precedes Genesis 15 verse 6 ("And he believed in the LORD; and he counted it to him for righteousness"). God's purpose existed even before the date of Abraham's justification. We should observe the following.

- "The **scripture,** foreseeing ..." God and His Word cannot be separated. What is predicted of one, is predicted of the other. The inspiration of Scripture is emphasised here. See also Romans 9 verse 17. Compare Galatians 1 verse 6. See also Galatians 3 verse 22, "But the **scripture** hath concluded ..."

- "That **God** would justify the heathen through faith." Compare Romans 8 verses 30-33, "And whom he called, them **he** also justified ... Who shall lay anything to the charge of God's elect? It is **God** that justifieth". See also Romans 3 verse 30.

- "That God would justify the **heathen** through faith." That is, "all the families of the earth" (Gen. 12: 3). The word "heathen" (*ethnos*) means a nation or people. It is rendered "Gentiles" in Galatians 2 verses 12 and 14. God had Gentiles in mind as well as Jews.

- "Preached **before** the gospel (good news) unto Abraham." God announced the terms of the gospel beforehand. The 'good news' did not involve the "works of the law". "By him **all that believe** are justified from all things, from which ye could not be justified by the law of Moses" (Acts 13: 39). It has also been suggested that the word "before" could mean 'before the law existed'.

- "In thee shall all nations be **blessed.**" The blessing here is the blessing of justification by faith in Christ.

ii) Paul draws a conclusion, v.9. "So then they which be of faith are blessed with faithful Abraham." The Christian position is in fulfilment of the divine promise announced to Abraham.

We should notice that the blessing of justification by faith was purposed by God before the law was given. Abraham was justified by faith, and the promise of justification by faith for all men, was made before the law was given. **Blessing through faith was God's settled purpose.**

But now the word "blessed" (vv.8-9) gives place to the word "cursed" (v.10). We learn that while faith brings blessing, law brings cursing. So, "they which be of faith are **blessed**" (v.9), but "as many as are of the works of the law are under the **curse**" (v.10). So far as the former is concerned, everything depends upon God: "By myself *I* have sworn … *I* will bless thee … *I* will multiply thy seed …" (Gen. 22: 15-17). So far as the latter is concerned, everything depends on us: "***thou*** shalt … ***thou*** shalt not". This is now emphasised:

c) The problem of law, vv.10-12

Salvation is by faith, not by works. With this in mind, Paul states two facts (v.10-11), and draws a conclusion (v.12)

i) Paul states two facts, v.10-11. First of all, he appeals to Deuteronomy 27 verse 26, and then he appeals to Habakkuk 2 verse 4.

- He appeals to Deuteronomy 27 verse 26. Salvation is not by works. "For as many as are of the works of the law are under the curse: for it is written, Cursed is every one that continueth not in all things which are written in the book of the law to do them" (v.10). The word "curse" here (*katara*) differs from Chapter 1 verses 8-9 (*anathema*) where it means 'devoted to destruction'. Here it denotes the righteous judgment of God. We should notice the word "under". Compare "under the curse … under sin … under the law … under a schoolmaster … under tutors and governors … under the elements of the world". The "curse" is death. Not just physical death, but the "second death". It has been pointed out that verses 10-14 include five references to "curse", whereas verses 26-29 include five references to Christ. Now that's worth thinking about!

In Deuteronomy 27 verse 26, we stand, as it were, on Mount Ebal. We must not overlook the comprehensive nature of the statement: "Cursed is ***every one*** (so it involves all people) that ***continueth not*** (so it involves all times) in ***all things*** (so it involves all commandments: see James 2: 10) which are written in the book of the law to do them".

- *He appeals to Habakkuk 2 verse 4.* Salvation is by faith. "But that no man is justified by the law in the sight of God, it is evident: for, the just shall live by faith" (v.11). This brings hope into the unrelieved gloom of the preceding verse. If the situation in verse 10 is hopeless, we must remember that God never purposed that justification should be on the basis of law. He had said so categorically: "The just shall live ***by faith***".

ii) Paul draws a conclusion, v.12. He states that works and faith are mutually exclusive. He appeals to Leviticus 18 verse 5, which made a promise on impossible terms. "And the law is not of faith; but, The man that doeth them shall live in them ('in virtue of them', JND margin)". There are two alternatives: in verse 11 the words "shall live" indicate that life is promised to the *believer,* and in verse 12 the words "shall live" indicate that life is promised to the *doer.* But justification by law was impossible: none could comply with its terms. The law is a matter of *doing*: hence the expression, "the *works* of the law" (v.10). Faith is a matter of *believing*: hence the expression, "the hearing of *faith*" (v.2).

We should remember, of course, that there was only one Man of whom it could be said, "shall live in them".

But this leaves a problem. God had said that justification is by faith: "The just shall live by faith". But at the same time, God had said, "Cursed is every one that continueth not in all things that are written in the book of the law to do them". How, therefore, can one scripture be fulfilled without violating the other? The answer follows:

d) The provision through Christ, vv.13-14

Salvation is through the death of Christ. With this in mind, Paul states a fact (v.13), what Christ *has done*, and draws a conclusion (v.14), what Christ *has secured.*

i) Paul states a fact, v.13. He appeals to Deuteronomy 21 verse 23, "Christ hath redeemed us from the curse of the law, being made a curse for us: for it is written, Cursed is every one that hangeth on a tree". The king of Ai, the Canaanite kings, Absalom and Haman were all hanged, but the Lord Jesus was not worthy of death. Although He 'did no sin", He stood in the place of a disobedient son (Deut. 21: 18-21). His finished work removes for ever the claims of law upon us. For us, there is "no more curse" (Rev. 22: 3)

So Deuteronomy 27 verse 26 and Habakkuk 2 verse 4 are not mutually exclusive. This would have been the case had Christ not died, "being made a curse for us". He has "redeemed" us. The Greek word (*exagorazo*, as in 4: 5) means deliverance with a view to freedom: delivered out of the slave market, and never ever again to be re-exposed to sale. He "redeemed" us from the curse of the law by "being made a curse for us". If the "curse" was the "second death" (Rev. 20: 14), then the Lord Jesus experienced that *very same death* on the cross, causing Him to cry, "My God, my God, Why hast thou forsaken me?" It was an eternity of death concentrated in three hours. He has fully met the claims of the law, which otherwise would have been at variance with God's purpose of justification by faith, enabling God to fulfil His promise to Abraham. To secure our salvation and justification the Lord Jesus, "the son of man", "must ... be lifted up", that is, 'hanged on a tree'. Not on a living, growing tree (*dendron*), but on a piece of wood (*xulon*). The sense is not that a person was cursed because hanged, but hanged because cursed. The law, which demanded the death of the sinner, has been satisfied in the death of Christ. On this basis, we must notice:

ii) **Paul draws a conclusion, v.14.** Christ died on the cross (He died hanging on a tree*)* "that the blessing of Abraham (justification by faith) might come on the Gentiles ... that we (Jew and Gentile) might receive the promise of the Spirit through faith". What wonderful provision for us, and all resulting from the redemptive work of Christ!

Thus, what the Galatian believers, with all believers, had experienced (vv.1-5), rested upon a scriptural basis (vv.6-14). To teach otherwise would detract from Christ's finished work, and reopen a question that God closed at Calvary. Verse 14 completes the argument: it explains *how* we have become "the children of Abraham" (v.7).

Addendum

According to the late E.W.Rogers, a judge must do three things: *(i)* he must consider the law: common law: hence Deuteronomy 27: 26; *(ii)* he must consider precedence: case law: hence Deuteronomy 21: 23; *(iii)* he must consider the actual case.

THE EPISTLE TO THE GALATIANS

"The law was our school-master ... unto Christ

Read Chapter 3: 15-29

We have already noticed that Galatians 3 divides into two main sections: *(1)* faith and works (vv.1-14); *(2)* promise and law (vv.15-29).

- *Faith and works (vv.1-14)*, where faith is broadly contrasted with works, and where we should notice reference to "the **works** of the law ... the hearing of **faith**" (vv.2, 5) and the contrast, "So then they which be of **faith** ... as many as are under the **works** of the **law**" (vv.9-10).

- *Promise and law (vv.15-29)*, where promise is broadly contrasted with law, and where we should notice the statements "the **law** ... cannot ... make the **promise** of none effect" (v.17); "For if the inheritance be of **law**, it is no more of **promise**"(v.18); "Wherefore then serveth the **law?** It was added ... till the seed should come to whom the **promise** was made" (v.19); "Is the **law** then against the **promises** of God?" (v.21).

1) FAITH AND WORKS, vv.1-14

In our previous study, we noticed that Paul appeals, firstly, to their experience (vv.1-5) and, secondly, to the Scriptures (vv.6-14). In appealing to their experience in these verses, he asks six questions, and in appealing to the Scriptures, he gives six quotations. The double appeal is most significant. Their experience told them that not one shred of law-keeping was involved in their salvation, and, of great importance, that this was entirely consistent with the Scriptures.

- *In appealing to their experience (vv.1-5),* Paul refers to the basis of their justification (v.1) and the proof of their justification (vv.2-5).

- *In appealing to the Scriptures (vv.6-14),* Paul, having asked the question "he therefore that ministereth to you the Spirit, and worketh miracles among you, doeth he it by the works of the law, or by the hearing of faith?" (v.5), then draws attention to the man in the Old Testament of whom this was pre-eminently true: "Even as **Abraham** believed God, and it was accounted to him for righteousness" (v.6). This is the first of six quotations from the Old Testament cited in connection with four major points: *(a)* the position of Abraham (vv.6-7); *(b)* the promise of blessing (vv.8-9); *(c)* the problem of law (vv.10-12*); (d)* the provision through Christ (vv.13-14).

2) PROMISE AND LAW, vv.15-29

In this section, Paul deals with a possible objection to his conclusions in the preceding verses. In effect, he now asks, 'But is this really right?' It could be argued that his reasoning did not take into account the fact that law came after promise, and therefore nullified and overrode, or at least modified, promise. We should therefore notice the way in which the apostle deals with this objection. The passage may be divided as follows: *(A)* the law cannot invalidate promise (vv.15-18); *(B)* the law is inferior to promise (vv.19-20); *(C)* the law is not irreconcilable with promise (vv.21-26); *(D)* the law cannot impart the blessings of promise (vv.27-29). (Alternatively: the relationship of promise and law, vv.15-18; the reason the law was given, vv.19-24; the release from law, vv.25-29.)

A) THE LAW CANNOT INVALIDATE PROMISE, vv.15-18

Paul deals with this by referring, first of all to "a man's covenant" (v.15), and then to God's covenant (v.17).

a) Man's covenant, v.15

"Brethren, I speak after the manner of men: Though it be but a man's covenant (a promise or undertaking; not necessarily between two parties), yet if it be confirmed (ratified), no man disannulleth (*akuroo*, to deprive of authority), or addeth thereto." Do notice that Paul addresses them as "Brethren". It has been nicely said that "this reveals Paul's compassionate love for the Galatians who may have begun to question this in the light of the stern rebuke in verses 1 and 3." (supplied by Justin Waldron).

In referring to a "man's covenant", Paul uses language his readers can

Chapter 3:15-29

well understand, and does not apologise for doing so. Once a man has validated a covenant or testament by his hand, it is legally established. It was a principle in law. The argument is clear: if this is applicable to a human covenant, how much more to a divine covenant! So:

b) God's covenant, vv.16-18

"Now to Abraham and his seed were the promises made. He saith not, And to seeds (Ishmael was set aside: "In Isaac shall thy seed be called"), as of many; but as of one. And to thy seed, which is Christ. And this I say, that the covenant, that was confirmed before of God in Christ, the law, which was four hundred and thirty years after, cannot disannul, that it should make the promise of none effect. For if the inheritance be of the law, it is no more of promise: but God gave it to Abraham by promise." If it is true to say of a man's covenant that "no man disannulleth or addeth thereto", it is equally true of God's covenant. We should notice the following:

i) ***God's covenant is not subject to annulment, vv.16-17.*** As noted above, the principle is established in verse 15. God's covenant is not subject to annulment for the following reasons:

- ***The parties involved in the covenant, v.16.*** The covenant was made with **Christ.** "Now to Abraham and his seed were the promises made. He saith not, And to seeds, as of many; but as of one. And to thy seed, which is Christ." There could never be any thought of annulment here! The covenant did not depend on Abraham for its enactment. Paul has already referred to Genesis 12 verse 3 (see v.8) and Genesis 15 verse 6. Now he refers to Genesis 22 verses 17-18, "In blessing I will bless thee ... and thy seed shall possess the gate of his enemies; and in thy seed shall all the nations of the earth be blessed". The promises were made to Abraham and Christ. Even if the words "in Christ" (v.17) are omitted (see JND), the statement in verse 16 is perfectly clear. This reminds us that "all the promises of God" are "in him (Christ) ... yea, and in him, Amen" (2 Cor. 1: 20). We should remember that the promise was made ***unconditionally.*** We should also remember the necessity to read our Bible ***carefully***: "He saith ***not***, And to seeds, as of many, ***but*** as of one, And to thy seed, which is Christ". This illustrates that the Scriptures have been verbally and literally inspired. (2 Tim. 3: 16; 2 Pet. 1: 20)

- ***The promises of the covenant were ratified, v.17.*** "And this I say, that the covenant, that was **confirmed** before of God ..." The confirmation of the covenant actually took place in Genesis 15 verses 6-18. The passage commences; "And he (Abram, as he was then) believed in the LORD, and he accounted it to him for righteousness" (v.6) and continues, "And he (the Lord GOD) said unto him, Take me an heifer of three years old, and a she goat ... and a ram ... a turtle dove ... a young pigeon. And he took unto him all these, and divided them in the midst, and laid each piece one against another ... And it came to pass, that, when the sun went down, and it was dark, behold a smoking furnace, and a burning lamp that passed between those pieces" (vv.9, 10, 17). It was the Lord Himself. "Our God is a consuming fire" (Heb. 12: 29). We then read, "In the same day the LORD made a covenant with Abram ..." (v.18). Jeremiah 34 verses 18-19 explains why the parts of the animals were placed "each piece against another". It was to enable the person making the covenant to walk between them, and say, in effect, that it would be as impossible for them to break their pledges it was to rejoin the divided animals. God's promises rest on the work of Christ, and these sacrifices remind us that this can never be reversed.

- The precedence of the covenant in time, v.17. "And this I say that ... the law, which was four hundred and thirty years after, cannot disannul, that it should make the promise of none effect". See Exodus 12 verses 40-41, "Now the sojourning of the children of Israel, who dwelt in Egypt, was four hundred and thirty years. And it came to pass at the end of the four hundred and thirty years, even the selfsame day it came to pass, that all the hosts of the LORD went out from the land of Egypt".

But when, exactly, did the period of 430 years commence? A period of "four hundred years" is mentioned in Acts 7 verse 6 and in Genesis 15 verse 13, whereas, as noted above, Exodus 12 verses 40-41 give a period of "four hundred and thirty years", which is confirmed in our current passage. To say that "four hundred years" is expressing "four hundred and thirty years" in round figures is not acceptable! The period of "four hundred years" evidently includes the period in Canaan as well as Egypt, and dates from the birth of Isaac, the "seed" from which the nation sprang. A glance at the dates at the top of many Bibles will show that Israel was in Egypt for something like two hundred years. The period of "four hundred and thirty years" evidently commences with the call of Abraham, twenty-five of the thirty years being accounted for by the difference in his age between entering Canaan (at age 75) and the birth of Isaac (at age 100). The balance of five years can be accounted for by the years spent in Haran. For fuller details see the *Writings of Albert McShane*.

ii) God's covenant is not subject to amendment, v.18. "For if the inheritance be of the law, it is no more of promise: but God gave it Abraham by promise." If "works of the law" (v.5) are added, it ceases to be promise. The word "gave" emphasises that it was a free gift. The perfect tense is used here: it was given for good! This has been nicely illustrated by Richard Catchpole (Eastbourne Bible Readings, 2004): "If I say, 'I promise you £100, come over and collect it', but on arriving, I say 'dig the garden and then collect the money', you will get your money alright, but not on the ground of promise!" It is "no more of promise: but God gave it to Abraham by promise".

B) THE LAW IS INFERIOR TO PROMISE, vv.19-20

"Wherefore then serveth the law?" If the law did not revise the promise, what was its purpose? "It was added because of transgressions, till the seed should come to whom the promise was made: and it was ordained by angels in the hand of a mediator. Now a mediator is not a mediator of one, but God is one." The inferiority of the law is emphasised in three ways. It was inferior, though necessary, in view of:

a) The purpose for which it was given, v.19

"It was added because of transgressions." Not 'because of *sins*', but "because of *transgressions*". It was given to expose the *nature* of sin. Not because knowledge of sin was unknown, but to show what sin is: it is seen to be rebellion against God. See Romans 3 verse 20, "For by the law is the knowledge of sin"; Romans 5 verse 13, "But sin is not imputed when there is no law"; Romans 7 verse 7, "I had not known sin, but by the law". (See also Romans 7: 13.) We should notice that in verse 15, the word "addeth" (*epidiatasso*) means to supplement an agreement made, but here, in verse 19, the word (*prostithemi*) means something given in addition to the promise. The law was given to emphasise transgressions. It was *not* a means of justification.

b) The period for which it was given, v.19

"Till the seed should come to whom the promise was made." It was instituted for a limited duration. As opposed to the "everlasting covenant" (Heb. 13: 20).

c) The parties involved when it was given, v.19

"It was ordained (appointed or administered) by angels in the hand of a mediator (the Septuagint Version has 'daysman'). Now a mediator is not a mediator of one, but God is one." For the role of the angels, see Hebrews 2 verses 1-2, Acts 7 verse 53. The reference to the angels helps us to understand Paul's earlier statement, "But though we, or an angel from heaven, preach any other gospel unto you ..." (1: 8).

There were two parties involved: God and man. Hence the need for a mediator. The mediator was Moses. We know, of course, that the law was a **conditional** covenant: "Now therefore, **if** ye will obey my voice indeed, and keep my covenant, **then** ..." (Ex. 19: 5). The covenant of law made demands on human nature, and was therefore "weak through the flesh" (Rom. 8: 3). Not so the covenant made with Abraham. It was **unconditional.** Hence we read, in a different but associated connection, "For when God made promise to Abraham, because he could swear by no greater, **he sware by himself**, saying, Surely blessing I will bless thee ..." (Heb. 6: 13). The same idea is expressed here: "Now a mediator is not a mediator of one, **but God is one**". In other words, it was a unilateral covenant. Everything depended on God. The covenant with Abraham was in effect between divine Persons: "Till the seed (Christ) should come to whom the promise was made". There could be no failure between divine Persons! God fulfils the obligations of the covenant Himself. The Lord Jesus said, "I and my Father are one" (John 10: 30).

C) THE LAW IS NOT IRRECONCILABLE WITH PROMISE, vv.21-26

"Is the law then (inferior though it is for the reasons given) against the promises of God? (is it contrary to promise?) God forbid." While the law cannot give life (v.21) it was given for a purpose wholly consistent with divine promise (v.22-26).

a) The purpose of the law was not to give life, v.21

It was not given to cancel promise. The law could not impart life. That was impossible. Human nature made it impossible. Although in itself the law was "holy, just and good" (Rom. 7: 12) it was, as already noted, "weak through the flesh" (Rom. 8: 3). We therefore read here, "if there had been a law which could have given life, verily righteousness should have been by the law".

b) The purpose of the law was to make promise desirable, vv.22-26

Chapter 3:15-29

Someone has said that the law took mankind by the hand and led him to the cross of Christ and said, 'You need a Saviour' (supplied by Justin Waldron).

To this end, "the scripture (see, for example, Deuteronomy 27: 26) hath concluded all under sin, that the promise (of justification by faith) by faith of Jesus Christ might be **given** (not earned) to them that believe" (v.22). The law was given to facilitate promise. It "concluded all under sin". The word "concluded" (*sunkleio*) means to 'shut up' or 'inclose' as in verse 23 ("before faith came, we were kept under the law, shut up unto the faith which should afterwards be revealed"). See also Romans 11 verse 32 ("For God hath concluded them all – shut up them all - in unbelief, that he might have mercy upon all"). It is used literally in Luke 5 verse 6, "they inclosed a great multitude of fishes". But how did this work? Paul explains:

"But before faith came, we were kept under the law, shut up unto the faith which should afterwards be revealed" (v.23). The words "before faith came" should be understood as 'before **the** faith came'. Jude refers to "the faith which was once delivered unto the saints" (v.3) It is not that there was no faith in the Old Testament days! But now it is 'the faith' with Christ as its object. Hence "the word of faith, which we preach; that if thou shalt confess with thy mouth the Lord Jesus, and shalt believe in thine heart ..." (Rom 10: 8-10).

The word "kept" (*phroureo*) is elsewhere rendered, "kept in ward" (RV). It is a military term deriving from a guard or garrison. See 2 Corinthians 11 verse 32, "In Damascus the governor under Aretas the king kept (*phroureo*) the city of the Damascenes with a garrison". However, Paul illustrates the way in which the law functioned, not with reference to a prison or to confinement, but with reference to "a schoolmaster".

We must notice Paul's new word - "schoolmaster" (*paidagogos*). The 'new word' is used in connection with a new direction leading to release from bondge, to liberty. The word rendered "schoolmaster" refers to "a guide, or guardian, or trainer of boys" (W.E.Vine). His function was not to impart knowledge, but to undertake training and discipline. See 1 Corinthians 4 verse 15, "For though ye have ten thousand **instructors** (*paidagogos*) in Christ, yet have ye not many fathers". The "schoolmaster" was usually a slave, whose duty it was to conduct the boy or youth (said to be between the ages of five and sixteen approximately) to and from school, and to superintend his conduct generally. He was often harsh to the point of cruelty, and is usually depicted in ancient drawings with a rod or cane in his hand.

Galatians

The illustration is accompanied by explanation in verses 23-26 as follows.

i) The duration of his role, vv.23-24. The "schoolmaster" functioned during the ***early life*** of the child. "But ***before*** faith came, we were kept under the law, shut up to the faith which should afterwards be revealed. Wherefore the law was our schoolmaster (to bring us) unto Christ, that we might be justified by faith." The "schoolmaster" functioned "***before faith came***".

This is the first of two named periods: "before faith came" (v.23) and "after that faith is come" (v.25). The law imposed ***servitude.*** It said, "thou shalt" and "thou shalt not", and "every transgression and disobedience received a just recompence of reward" (Heb. 2: 2). At every turn of the way, the law highlighted sin and waywardness, and proclaimed judgment. It buffeted the sinner. Hence the expression "***under*** the law", with all its oppression. It held people tightly in its grip: there was no escape: "shut up ('guarded', JND) unto the faith which should afterwards be revealed". Here is its duration: it "shut up" people "unto the faith ('to faith', JND) which should afterwards be revealed". It was "our schoolmaster ... unto Christ".

ii) The cessation of his role, vv.25-26. The "schoolmaster" ceased to function on the ***maturity*** of the child. That is, when he was recognised as a son, or, to put it differently, when he became an adult. "But ***after that faith is come*** (the second of the two periods noted: see v.23)***, we*** are no longer under a schoolmaster. For ***ye*** are all the children ***(sons)*** of God by faith in Christ Jesus." The "schoolmaster" became redundant "after faith came". That is, when then the present dispensation began, and men and women, through faith, enjoyed the forgiveness of sins and justification by faith. The "schoolmaster" has nothing to say to those who are right with God, and therefore "sons of God", that is, having His character. When a boy reached manhood, he put on the white toga of an adult citizen.

We should notice the use of "we" and "ye" in the passage. Paul argues from the Jewish standpoint. Hence, "***we*** were kept under law ... wherefore the law was ***our*** schoolmaster ... ***we*** are no longer under a schoolmaster". But what was true of the Jews is equally true of the Gentiles: "for ***ye*** are all the children of God through faith in Christ Jesus". The argument is clear: if Jews had been delivered from servitude to the law into the liberty of sonship, it was quite futile to impose Jewish ordinances on people who had never been subject to the law in the same way at all! This leads to:

Chapter 3:15-29

D) THE LAW CANNOT IMPART THE BLESSINGS OF PROMISE, vv.27-29

The achievements of promise are set out in the concluding verses of the chapter: *(a)* "ye are all the children (*huioi,* sons) of God (v.26); (b) "you ... have put on Christ" (v.27); *(c)* "ye are all one in Christ Jesus" (v.28); *(d)* ye are "Abraham's seed, and heirs according to the promise".

a) "Ye are all the children (sons) of God", v.26

We have already commented on the above. The expression 'sons of God' involves character and dignity.

b) "You ... have put on Christ", v.27

Believers today have a new place in relation to Christ. Paul refers to their baptism in this connection. "For as many of you (compare v.10, "as many as are of the works of the law") as have been baptized into Christ have put on Christ" or "For ye, as many as have been baptised *unto* Christ, have put on Christ" (JND). (So, today, for believers, there is no longer Jew and Gentile! See v.28.) This does not imply that some had been baptized, and some had not been baptized, but that the ordinance of baptism taught their identification with the Lord Jesus. The words "have put on Christ" refers to our standing in Christ. It is not now, "But put ye on the Lord Jesus Christ, and make not provision for the flesh" (Rom. 13: 14), but our identification with Him. As the sons of God, we are identified with *the* Son of God. The law could not do this.

c) "Ye are all one in Christ Jesus", v.28

Believers today have a new place in relation to society. "There is neither Jew nor Greek, there is neither bond nor free, there is neither male nor female." Faith unites believers in a common standing before God. The distinctions exist elsewhere. God still recognises Jew and Gentile nationally, master and servant in society, and men and women in the assembly, but "all are accepted before God in Christ on the same ground, no matter who they are or what they are" (J.Hunter, *What the Bible Teaches – Galatians*). He continues, "Being a Jew did not give one priority before God; being a free man did not give one favour with God; and being a male did not assure privileged treatment from God". There are no national, social, or sexual distinctions in connection with our standing before God in Christ. The law certainly could not do this!

d) "Ye are Abraham's seed, and heirs according to the promise", v.29

Believers today have a new place in relation to eternity. "And if ye be Christ's, then are ye Abraham's seed, and heirs according to the promise." This completes the argument. All believers, without national, social or sexual distinctions, are "heirs according to the promise". Hence, "And if *ye* be Christ's, then are *ye* Abraham's seed, and heirs according to the promise". The words "Abraham's seed" refers to our identification with him as men and women justified by faith. See verse 7, "Know ye therefore that they which are of faith, the same are the children of Abraham". The relationship is spiritual, not natural. Faith in Christ puts us on the same basis before God as Abraham: we have therefore become the spiritual children of Abraham, and gained the promised blessing. The words, "heirs according to the promise", refers to our position as sons of God with all the attendant prospects. Every believer is an "heir of God through Christ" (4: 7).

This reminds us, firstly, of the promise made to Abraham that he should be "heir of the world" (Rom. 4: 12-26), and, secondly, of our position as "heirs of God and joint-heirs with Christ" (Rom. 8: 17).

The implications of relinquishing the "hearing of faith" (vv.2, 5) in favour of "the works of the law" (v.5) are catastrophic. It means, as noted above, *(i)* denial of their relationship with God; *(ii)* denial of their identification with Christ; *(iii)* denial of their common standing before God; *(iv)* denial of future prospects. The law promises nothing!

Looking back over the passage, we may say that to revert to the law was *(i)* to lose a position originally intended by God for His children; *(ii)* to re-open a question that God had closed at Calvary; *(iii)* to participate in an inferior covenant; *(iv)* to return to spiritual infancy.

Whereas, to maintain the truth of the gospel was *(i)* to take the ground of divine promise; *(ii)* to take the ground of the finished work of Christ; *(iii)* to take the ground of a better covenant; *(iv)* to take the ground of sonship.

THE EPISTLE TO THE GALATIANS

"When the fulness of the time was come"

Read Chapter 4: 1-7

In Galatians 4, Paul develops the subject of sonship and heirship, with which Chapter 3 concludes: "For ye are all the children (*huios,* sons) of God by faith in Christ Jesus … and if ye be Christ's, then are ye Abraham's seed, and heirs according to the promise" (3: 26, 29). Hence, Paul now says, "because ye are **sons**, God hath sent forth the Spirit of his Son into your hearts, crying, Abba, Father. Wherefore thou art no more a servant, but a son; and if a son, then an **heir** of God through Christ" (vv.6-7); "Nevertheless what saith the scripture? Cast out the bondwoman and her son: for the son of the bondwoman shall not be **heir** with the son of the freewoman" (v.30).

The subject is introduced in Chapter 3, where Paul contrasts the blessings of faith and the curse of the law: "And the scripture, foreseeing that God would justify the heathen through faith, preached before the gospel unto Abraham, saying, In thee shall all nations be blessed. So then they which be of **faith are blessed** with faithful Abraham. For as many as are of **the works of the law are under the curse:** for it is written, Cursed is every one that continueth not in all things which are written in the book of the law to do them" (3: 8-10).

As we have already noticed, Chapter 3 emphasises the immense blessing of justification by faith:

- ***It fulfils the unconditional promises of God, vv.6-9***. "And the scripture, foreseeing that God would justify the heathen through faith, preached before the gospel unto Abraham, saying, In thee shall all nations be blessed."

- ***It rests on the finished work of Christ, vv.10-14.*** "Christ hath redeemed us from the curse of the law, being made a curse for us: for it is written, Cursed is every one that hangeth on a tree."

- *It arises from a superior covenant, vv.15-20.* "Wherefore then serveth the law? It was added because of transgressions, till the seed should come to whom the promise was made; and it was ordained by angels in the hand of a mediator. Now a mediator is not a mediator of one, but God is one."

- *It provides sonship for the believer, vv.21-29.* "Wherefore the law was our schoolmaster (to bring us) to Christ, that we might be justified by faith. But after that faith is come, we are no longer under a schoolmaster. For ye are all the children *(sons)* of God by faith in Christ Jesus."

The concluding verses of Chapter 3 therefore emphasise that faith in Christ brings deliverance from **servitude to sonship.** Once "kept under the law, shut up unto the faith which should afterwards be revealed", believers are no longer "under a schoolmaster" (3: 23-25), but "God's sons by faith in Christ Jesus" (3: 26, JND). The connection between Chapter 3 verse 29 and Chapter 4 verse 3: "And if ye be Christ's, then are ye Abraham's seed, and heirs according to the promise. Now I say, That the heir, as long as he is a child, differeth nothing from a servant, though he be lord of all; but is under tutors and governors until the time appointed of the father". As noted above, Paul now expands the closing statement in Chapter 3, "And if ye are Christ's, then are ye Abraham's seed, and heirs according to the promise (v.29).

In this connection, we should note that Paul uses three figures to describe the law between Chapter 3 verse 22 and Chapter 4 verse 3: a jailor, a schoolmaster and tutors and governors. **See addenda.**

The late Harold St.John divided Galatians 4 as follows (quoted by Richard Catchpole, *Eastbourne Bible Readings 2004*): *(1) the adoption (vv.1-7):* "but when the fulness of the time was come, God sent forth his Son ... to redeem them that were under the law, that we might receive **the adoption of sons**" (vv.3-5); *(2) the anxiety (vv.8-11):* "I am **afraid** of you, lest I have bestowed upon you labour in vain" (v.11); *(3) the appeal (vv.12-20):* "Brethren, I *beseech you* ..." (v.12); *(4) the allegory (vv.21-31):* "which things are an allegory: for these are the two covenants ..." (v.24).

1) THE ADOPTION, vv.1-7

Or, 'Their deliverance from bondage to liberty described'. In dealing with their transition from servants to sons, we should notice: *(a)* preparation for sonship (vv.1-3); *(b)* provision for sonship (vv.4-5); *(c)* proof of sonship (v.6).

Paul then states his conclusion: "Wherefore thou art no more a servant, but a son; and if a son, then an heir of God through Christ" (v.7).

In this connection, it is nothing short of amazing, and wonderful, to remember that in order to accomplish our sonship, **the Lord Jesus became a servant**: He "took upon him the form of a servant, and was made in the likeness of men" (Phil. 2: 7).

a) Preparation for sonship, vv.1-3

i)   Paul states a fact, vv.1-2. "Now I say, That the heir, as long as he is a child, differeth nothing from a servant, though he be lord of all; but is under tutors and governors until the time appointed of the father." Paul uses an illustration well known to his readers. In the words of J.Hunter (*What the Bible Teaches - Galatians*): "A child or minor is heir to a large and prosperous estate, but while he is so young and immature, he is not capable of administering it, so his position is no different from that of a servant or slave. He is continually under orders to do one thing or another. He is under the control of "tutors" (*epitropos,* not teachers, but 'guardians', JND/RV: 'stewards', Matt. 20: 8; Luke 8: 3), who look after his *person,* and "governors" (*oikonomos,* 'one who rules a house'), who look after his *property.* He is under care and discipline ... This will be his status until he reaches his majority, the date of which was stipulated by his father".

ii) Paul makes an application, v.3. "Even so we, when we were children, were in bondage under the elements ('rudiments' or 'principles', JND: or 'first step', Young's *Concordance*) of the world." While some consider that the expression "elements of the world", elsewhere translated "the elemental spirits of the universe" (RSV: NEB), refers to the demons and evil spirits in verse 8, the context suggests that Paul refers here to what J.R.Stott (*The Message of Galatians*) calls "the rudimentary education of the people of God, which was completed by further education when Christ came". The word "elements" (*stoicheia*: defined in vv.9-10) means elementary things: it refers to the substance from which a finished article is made. For example, the letters of the alphabet, which are the elements of speech. As letters ultimately become words, so the ordinances and procedures of the Old Testament pointed on to Christ - "the shadow of good things to come" (Heb. 10: 1). We have the same idea in the expressions "a worldly sanctuary" and "carnal ordinances" (Heb. 9: 1, 10), where neither "worldly" nor "carnal" are used in a derogatory way. They existed only "until the time of reformation" ('the time of setting things right', JND).

But why does Paul call this, "the elements of the *world*"? They are called "the elements of the world" because they reflect the universal idea that mankind is bound by an obligation to *earn* divine favour. This was certainly in Israel's case: "If ye will *obey* my voice indeed, and keep my covenant, *then* ..." (Exodus 19: 5). Paul describes these "elements" as "weak (because they provided no power to strengthen) and beggarly (because they provided no power to enrich)" (v.9). These "elements" comprised "days, and months, and times, and years" (v.10). But, as William Trew (writing in *Precious Seed)* points out, "The idea that the natural man should devote himself to the externals of religious rites in order to acquire merit, in the value of which to make himself acceptable to God, is **the basic, elemental idea in every kind of human religion today**". W.E.Vine concurs in saying that "the elements of the world" are "the elementary principles of religion, whether Jewish, here, or Gentile (Col. 2: 8, 20), or both (v.9)." An additional note is given in the addendum.

But with the coming and work of the Lord Jesus, freedom from "bondage under the elements of the world" became available to men and women. This was "the time appointed by the father". That is, "the fulness of the time" (v.4).

b) Provision for sonship, vv.4-5

"But when the fulness of the time was come, God sent forth his Son, made of a woman, made under the law, to redeem them that were under the law, that we might receive the adoption of sons." Without Christ, men could only anticipate a hopeless end. But with Christ, men can anticipate an endless hope.

We should notice the parallel between Chapters 3 verses 1-5 and Chapter 4 verses 4-6. In Chapter 3 verses 1-5, we have the work of Christ as the basis of *justification,* and the reception of the Spirit as the proof of *justification.* In Chapter 4 verses 4-6, we have the work of Christ as the basis of **sonship,** and the reception of the Spirit as the proof of **sonship.**

We should notice the following: *(i)* the time at which He came; *(ii)* the identity in which He came; *(iii)* the way in which He came; *(iv)* the purpose for which He came.

i) **The time at which He came, v.4.** "But when the fulness of the time (not in 'the fullness of time') was come ..." He came at the time appointed by God. The appointed time of infancy and bondage had run its course.

Compare Mark 1 verse 15, "The time is fulfilled, and the kingdom of God is at hand: repent ye, and believe the gospel". Compare 1 Peter 1 verses 10-11, "Of which salvation the prophets have inquired and searched diligently ... searching what, or what manner **of time** the Spirit of Christ which was in them did signify ..." Certain historical features must be born in mind:

- The excellent communications of the Roman Empire facilitated the spread of the gospel. The preachers used the famous Roman roads as they proclaimed the message of salvation.

- The common language of the Roman Empire facilitated the spread of the gospel. Greek was the language of the Empire.

- The synagogue system was everywhere in the Roman Empire, and this gave the early preachers an immediate 'platform'.

- The conditions prevailing in Jewry must be considered. The law had been in existence for 1,300 years, but in addition to this, the scribes and Pharisees had imposed innumerable burdens upon men and women. This made the message of divine grace still more acceptable. "All bore him witness, and **wondered at the gracious words** which proceeded out of his mouth" (Luke 4: 22).

- The coming of the Lord Jesus marked the commencement of the fulfilment of the 'seventy weeks' prophecy (Daniel 9: 24-27), particularly verse 26, "And after threescore and two weeks shall Messiah be cut off, but not for himself ..."

But over and above all this, the "time appointed of the father" - verse 2, quoted out of context! - had come, reminding us that the precise time and circumstances (see above) of His advent were predetermined. How glad we are that this is always the case, and that we can therefore rest in the Father's perfect timing and absolute control of all future events. Compare Titus 1 verses 2-3. See Acts 1 verse 7. In this connection, do notice what Paul said in Athens. See Acts 17 verse 31.

*ii) **The identity in which He came.*** "God sent forth his Son." The promise made to Abraham depended for its fulfilment on Abraham's "seed": "Now to Abraham and his seed were the promises made. He saith not, And to seeds, as of many; but as of one, and to thy seed, which is Christ" (3: 16). The law was "added ... till the seed should come to whom the promise was made" (3: 19). Abraham's "seed" was none other than the Son of God. We should notice:

- "***God*** sent forth his Son." Compare other passages: "For God so loved the world that he gave his only begotten Son" (John 3: 16); "The Father sent the Son to be the Saviour of the world" (1 John 4: 14); "I proceeded forth and came from God; neither came I of myself, but he sent me" (John 8: 42). We should, at this point, discuss the respective and relative roles of the divine Persons, but it is a vast and profound subject, far beyond our present study.

- "God ***sent forth*** his Son." This implies pre-existence. Scripture speaks of the "days of his flesh" (Heb. 5: 7), but also of "the days of eternity" (Micah 5: 2 JND). The Lord Jesus lived before He was born. As to His deity, He is "without ... beginning of days, nor end of life" (Heb. 7: 3).

- "God sent forth his ***Son***." This emphasises His absolute deity and His eternal sonship. Melchisedec was "made like unto the Son of God" (Heb. 7: 3).

iii) The way in which He came. "Made of a woman, made under the law" or "Come of woman, come under law" (JND).

- ***"Come of woman"*** (JND). Note, not 'come of a virgin', but "come of woman", emphasising His humanity, as opposed to His deity. But the expression is none the less significant: after all, all men "come of woman"! But He is the 'seed of the woman'. It has been pointed out that whenever "seed" is mentioned in the Old Testament, whether of man or beast, the progenitor, with one exception, is always male. Here is the exception! The doctrine of the incarnation is taught here. His incarnation was not natural, and it was not supernatural: it was ***divine.*** It was without precedent.

Man's sin can only be put away in man. So Hebrews 10 verses 4-5, "For it is not possible that the blood of bulls and of goats should take away sins. Wherefore, when he cometh into the world, he saith, Sacrifice and offering thou wouldest not, but a body hast thou prepared me"

- ***"Come under law."*** That is, the very law advocated by the Judaisers. The Lord Jesus assumed the obligations of the law, and fulfilled them. His life was perfect: it was utterly beyond the claims of the law. He "offered himself without spot to God" (Heb. 9: 14). He took the very place of those in bondage to the law, demonstrated His ability to meet its claims, and offered Himself as the perfect sacrifice. He said, "Think not that I am come to destroy the law, or the prophets: I am not come to destroy, but to fulfil" (Matt. 5: 17).

*iv) **The purpose for which He came.*** "To redeem them that were under the law, that we might receive the adoption of sons." He came to "**redeem** them that were under the law". The Greek word "redeem" (*exagorazo)* means 'to buy out of the market'. He did this by bearing the curse of the law: "Christ hath **redeemed** (*exagorazo)* us from the curse of the law, being made a curse for us: for it is written, cursed is every one that hangeth on a tree" (3: 13). Christ has delivered us from the **curse**, that is, the penalty, of the law. Here, in verse 5, He has delivered us from the **bondage** of the law with this in view: "that we might receive the adoption of sons" or "that we might receive sonship" (JND).

The Lord Jesus paid in full the price of our deliverance from bondage to the law. In the place of bondage to the law, which controlled and punished men, the believer enjoys liberty from its claims, in just the same way as the child, having attained his majority, is no longer subject to "tutors and governors". The law now has nothing more to say to us: we are beyond its claims and demands.

*c) **Proof of sonship, v.6***

"And because ye are sons, God hath sent forth the Spirit of his Son into your hearts, crying, Abba, Father." Ephesians 1 verse 5 (see JND) refers to sonship as determined in the past, Galatians 4 verse 6 as now, and Romans 8 verse 19 in the future.

We should notice the progression here. In the first place, "God sent forth his Son": the result is sonship. In the second place, God "sent forth the Spirit of his Son": the result is assurance of sonship. The Godhead is marvellously involved in this: "***God*** hath sent forth the ***Spirit*** of his ***Son***". Compare John 14 verse 16. Just think – two divine Persons have come out of heaven for our eternal blessing!

Having been made sons of God by identification with the Lord Jesus, the reality of that sonship is made good by the indwelling of the same Holy Spirit who indwelt Him. See Romans 8 verse 11, "But if the Spirit of him that raised up Jesus from the dead dwell in you, he that raised up Christ from the dead shall also quicken your mortal bodies by his Spirit that dwelleth in you". Romans 8 verses 11-17 should be read in conjunction with Galatians 4 verse 6. In particular, notice Romans 8 verses 14-16, "For as many as are led by the Spirit of God, they are the sons of God. For ye have not received the spirit of bondage again to fear; but ye have received the Spirit of adoption, whereby we cry, Abba, Father. The Spirit itself beareth witness with our spirit, that we are the children of God." To be a son of God means of necessity that we do not live by the "works of the law", but by the power of the Holy Spirit.

On the day of Pentecost, the anointing received by the Head became the anointing received by the body. The indwelling of the Holy Spirit secured the union of the Head of the body and the body itself. The Spirit with whom the Lord Jesus was anointed (Acts 10: 38) is the same Spirit with which the body has been anointed. See 2 Corinthians 1 verses 21-22, "Now he which stablisheth us with you in Christ, and hath anointed us, is God; who hath also sealed us, and the earnest of the Spirit in our hearts". See also Psalm 133 verse 2, where the anointing of the head flows down to the garments.

We should notice the words, "Crying, Abba, Father". The combination of Aramaic ("Abba") and Greek ("Father") may suggest the impartiality of the Holy Spirit. He has been received by both Jews and Greeks. The untranslated Aramaic is used in situations of deep pathos. See, for example, Mark 5 verse 41, "he ... said unto her, Talitha cumi; which is, being interpreted, Damsel, I say unto thee, arise"; Mark 15 verse 34, "And at the ninth hour Jesus cried with a loud voice, saying Eloi, Eloi, lama sabachthani? which is, being interpreted, My God, my God, why hast thou forsaken me?" Matthew actually recorded the Lord's words in Hebrew ("Eli, Eli, lama sabachthani") but Mark in Aramaic, the actual language used by the Lord.

It is the Holy Spirit who cries "Abba, Father". Compare, again, Romans 8 verse 15, "ye have received the Spirit of adoption (sonship), whereby **we** cry, Abba, Father". Together, the passages teach us that our enjoyment of filial relationship with God is the work of the Holy Spirit. Since the Holy Spirit is "the Spirit of his Son", it is not therefore surprising to observe that the same filial relationship, but utterly perfect in His case, was enjoyed by the Son of God. See Mark 14 verse 36, "And he said, Abba, Father, all things are possible unto thee; take away this cup from me: nevertheless not what I will, but what thou wilt".

We are told that "Abba" was a word that slaves were not permitted to use! "Abba", the language of an infant, conveys unreasoning trust, with all the love and devotion implicit in this. "Father" is the language of intelligent relationship. Thus, "thou art no more a servant, but a son" (v.7). The Son of God is the "heir of all things" (Heb. 1: 2), and therefore, in keeping with the overall teaching of this passage, the sons of God are heirs too! "And if a son, then an heir of God through Christ" or "So thou art no longer bondman, but

Chapter 4:1-7

son; but if son, heir also through God" (JND). While as "the Son of God", the Lord Jesus has, to perfection, the very nature, character, and identity of God, nevertheless, as 'sons of God' we display divine character in our lives. Amongst other things, "sons of God" conveys the dignity of our calling.

ADDENDA

1) The three figures used to describe the law.

i) A jailor, 3: 22-23. Paul describes a man in prison: "the scripture hath **concluded** all under sin, that the promise by faith of Jesus Christ might be given to them that believe" (v.22). The word "concluded" (*sunkleio*) means to 'shut up' or 'inclose' as in verse 23.

But there is more, and Paul continues, "But before faith came, we were **kept** under the law, shut up unto the faith which should afterwards be revealed" (v.23). The word "kept" (*phroureo*) is elsewhere rendered, "kept in ward" (RV). As previously noted, it is a military term deriving from a guard or garrison. See 2 Corinthians 11 verse 32, "In Damascus the governor under Aretas the king kept (*phroureo*) the city of the Damascenes with a garrison". People under law are prisoners! Notice the word ***"under"*** (v.22, 23).

ii) A Schoolmaster, 3: 24-25. "Wherefore the law was our schoolmaster (to bring us) unto Christ, that we might be justified by faith." As we have already noted, the word (*paidagogos*) is used in connection with a new direction leading to release from bondage, to the enjoyment of liberty. The word rendered "schoolmaster" refers to "a guide, or guardian, or trainer of boys" (W.E.Vine). His function was not to impart knowledge, but to undertake training and discipline. See 1 Corinthians 4 verse 15, "For though ye have ten thousand **instructors** (*paidagogos*) in Christ, yet have ye not many fathers". The "schoolmaster" was usually a slave, whose duty it was to conduct the boy or youth (said to be between the ages of five and sixteen approximately) to and from school, and to superintend his conduct generally. He was often harsh to the point of cruelty, and is usually depicted in ancient drawings with a rod or cane in his hand. He had a limited term of office. Hence the change of figure in verses 25-26. "But after that faith is come, we are no longer under a schoolmaster. For ye are all the **children (sons) of God** by faith in Christ Jesus". But do notice, again, the word ***"under"*** (v.25).

iii)   Tutors and governors, 4: 2. Or, as noted above, "guardians and stewards" (JND). In life, these roles were undertaken in view of the future, that is, the child's future possession of the inheritance. "Tutors and governors" cared for the child in his younger years with the future in view. Notice, yet again, the word ***"under".*** It occurs again in verse 3.

2) The use of "we".

"Even so we, when we were children, were in bondage under the elements of the world" (v.3). Notice, the use of the word "bondage" (vv.3, 9, 24, 25).

The reference here to the Jews is emphasised by the use of "we": even so **we**, when **we** were children". Compare Chapter 3 verses 23-25 ("**we** were kept under the law ... that **we** might be justified by faith ... **we** are no longer under a schoolmaster), followed by "ye" and "you" (the Galatians themselves, being Gentiles) in verses 26-29. The use of these pronouns emphasises that Paul is arguing his case on Jewish ground, and if the law was no longer binding as a covenant on the believing Jew, how much less so on a Gentile! Compare Ephesians 1 verses 12-13, "That **we** should be to the praise of his glory, who first trusted in Christ. In whom **ye** also trusted ..."

As a nation, the Jews ("we") were in bondage, like an infant or minor under "tutors and governors". The 'child' ("when we were children", v.3) here is the Jew under law, in his minority. The "son" ("ye", v.6) is the Christian under grace, in his majority. The word "child" *(nepios)* means "a babe" and is used here in a legal sense, much as the word 'minor' is used in English law. The word "child" is used here in a ***dispensational*** sense. See Hebrews 5 verse 13 where the Jew was "unskilful in ***the*** word of righteousness (that is, the law): for he is a ***babe*** *(nepios)*". The Jew was "unskilful in the word of righteousness", because he failed to understand the purpose of the law: "For when for the time ye ought to be teachers, ye have need that one teach you again which be the first principles (elements: *stoicheion*) of the oracles of God" (Heb. 5: 12). That is, he failed to understand that the law ("the oracles of God") was 'the first step' (Young's *Concordance*) in God's purpose to bless men and women.

THE EPISTLE TO THE GALATIANS

"Where is the blessedness ye spake of?"

Read Chapter 4: 8-31

We have already noticed that Galatians 4 develops the closing statements of the previous chapter: "For ye are all the ***children (sons)*** of God by faith in Christ Jesus ... And if ye be Christ's, then are ye Abraham's seed, and ***heirs*** according to the promise" (3:26-29). Hence we read in Chapter 4, for example, "because ye are ***sons***, God hath sent forth the Spirit of his Son into your hearts, crying, Abba, Father. Wherefore thou art no more a servant, but ***a son***; and if a son, then ***an heir*** of God through Christ" (vv.6-7).

In our previous study we 'adopted' (no pun intended) the chapter divisions suggested by Harold St.John: ***(1) the adoption (vv.1-7):*** "but when the fulness of the time was come, God sent forth his Son ... to redeem them that were under the law, that we might receive ***the adoption of sons***" (vv.3-5); ***(2) the anxiety (vv.8-11):*** "I am ***afraid*** of you, lest I have bestowed upon you labour in vain" (v.11); ***(3) the appeal (vv.12-20):*** "Brethren, I ***beseech you***..." (v.12); ***(4) the allegory (vv.21-31):*** "which things are an allegory: for these are the two covenants..." (v.24). Notice the use of the word "bondage" in the chapter (vv.3, 9, 24, 25).

1) THE ADOPTION, vv.1-7

Or, 'Their deliverance from bondage to liberty described'. We have already dealt with this, and noticed ***(a)*** preparation for sonship (vv.1-3); ***(b)*** provision for sonship (vv.4-5); ***(c)*** proof of sonship (v.6). This brings us to:

2) THE ANXIETY, vv.8-11

Or, 'Their return from liberty to bondage censured'. If verses 1-7 describe the transition from servants to sons, then verses 8-20 refer to a reversal, from liberty to law. Hence the question: "How turn ye again to the weak and beggarly elements, whereunto ye desire again to be in bondage?" We should notice here (vv.8-11) a change of position, and in the next section (vv.12-20) a change of attitude (vv.12-18) and a change of voice (vv.19-20).

In dealing with their change of position, Paul demonstrates that by submitting to "the works of the law", they were relinquishing the exalted position described in verse 7 for nothing less than spiritual poverty. He reviews their spiritual history:

a) Their previous idolatry, v.8

This was "***when***" they "knew not God". "Howbeit then, when ye knew not God, ye did service unto them which by nature are no gods" or "ye were ***in bondage*** to those who by nature are not gods" (JND). It is "ye" Gentiles. Various Old Testament passages amplify the words "no gods". For example, "Thy children have forsaken me, and sworn by them that are ***no gods***" (Jer. 5: 7); "They have moved me to jealousy with that which is ***not god***" (Deut. 32: 21); "Whosoever cometh to consecrate himself with a young bullock and seven rams, the same may be a priest of them that are ***no gods***" (2 Chron. 13: 9). See also 1 Corinthians 8 verses 4-6, "As concerning therefore the eating of those things that are offered in sacrifice unto idols, we know that an idol is nothing in this world, and that there is none other God but one. For though there be that are ***called gods***, whether in heaven or in earth, (as there be gods many and lords many), but to us there is but one God, the Father, of whom are all things; and one Lord Jesus Christ, by whom are all things, and we by him". We should notice that if there is no knowledge of the true God, men are vulnerable to the influence of false gods. Paul explains this in 1 Corinthians 10 verses 19-20, "What say I then? that the idol is any thing, or that which is offered in sacrifice to idols is any thing? But I say, that the things which the Gentiles sacrifice, they sacrifice to devils, and not to God".

b) Their conversion, v.9a

It is no longer "when" (v.8), but "***now***". "But now, after that ye have known God, or rather are known of God ..." Paul emphasises that the work of salvation was divine! "Ye ... are known of God". "Salvation is of the Lord!" (Jonah 2: 9).

c) Their current danger, vv.9b-10

"How turn ye again to the weak and beggarly elements, whereunto ye desire again to be in bondage? Ye observe days, and months, and times, and years." They had "turned to God from idols": now they were making a second turn - to bondage. The word "turn" is in the present tense: they were in the process of turning. "Ye desire again to be *in bondage*" (v.9). It was absurd to want to be slaves again! Would a son want to be a slave once more?

The force of this is most striking. "Ye desire *again* to be in bondage." But the Galatian believers were not reverting to idolatry with its "no gods": they were placing themselves under law. It was a different kind of bondage - but *bondage no less.* It was bondage to "weak and beggarly elements". They were "*weak*" because they had no power to bless. They were "*beggarly*" because they had no power to enrich. The description "*weak*" (*asthenes*) reminds us that the law was "weak through the flesh" (Rom. 8: 3). The word "beggarly" means 'poverty stricken'. The underlying Greek word (*ptochos*) means 'to cower down and hide oneself from fear'. The "weak and beggarly elements" are now described: "Ye observe days, and months, and times, and years". The "days" were the Jewish sabbaths: the "months" were the new moons: the "times" were "the feasts of the Lord": the "years" were the sabbatical years. While we greatly appreciate their typical teaching, the fact remains, as we have said, that in themselves they had no power to bless or power to enrich.

There is nothing "*weak*" about the position and blessings of the believer. Paul prayed that the saints at Ephesus might know "what is the *exceeding greatness of his power* to us-ward who believe, according to the working of his *mighty power*, which he wrought in Christ, when he raised him from the dead" (Eph. 1: 19-20). Paul could say, "Our sufficiency is of God" (2 Cor. 3: 5). There is nothing "*beggarly*" either: see, for example, 2 Corinthians 8 verse 9, "For ye know the grace of our Lord Jesus Christ, that, though he was rich (*plousios*), yet for your sakes he became poor, that ye through his poverty might be *rich* (*ploutos*)". Paul speaks of "the *riches* (*ploutos*) of his grace" (Eph. 1: 7), and "the *exceeding riches* (*ploutos*) of his grace in his kindness toward us through Christ Jesus" (Eph. 2: 7). The assembly at Corinth was "*enriched* (*ploutizo*) by him, in all utterance, and in all knowledge" (1 Cor.1: 5).

The danger of defection by the Galatian believers made Paul apprehensive: "I am afraid of you, lest I have bestowed upon you labour in vain" (v.11).

J.Hunter comments, "He had expended prodigious effort in bring the gospel to them". The "labour" (*kopiao*) involved toil to the point of exhaustion. The word "vain" *(eike)* means 'without cause'. It seemed as if Paul need not have expended such energy in the first place. How often servants of God feel just like that! This brings us to:

3) THE APPEAL, vv.12-20

In this paragraph, we should notice *(a)* a change of attitude on their part (vv.12-18) and *(b)* a change of voice on his part (vv.19-20).

a) A change of attitude on their part, vv.12-18

In this connection we should note *(i)* their original attitude to Paul (vv.12-15); *(ii)* their current attitude to Paul (vv.16-18). They had changed their attitude to Paul, but Paul had not changed his attitude to them! He describes them as "brethren" (v.12), 'sons' (v.6), "my little children" (v.19). We can only help the saints if we love them.

i) Their original attitude to Paul, vv.12-15. Paul begins with a strong plea: "Brethren, I beseech you, be as I am; for I am as ye are: ye have not injured me at all".

- The ground of the appeal, v.12a. He addresses them as "brethren" (*adelphos*), that is, without distinguishing between Jew and Gentile. Later he calls them "my little children" (v.19). There he uses the word *teknion,* a term of affection. The term "brethren" indicates "persons united by a common calling" (W.E.Vine). The word "beseech" *(deomai)* means 'to desire ... to long for'. Paul's emphasis on his apostleship in commencing the epistle (1:1) did not diminish his affection and love for these believers.

- The nature of his appeal, vv.12b-15. "Be as I am; for I am as ye are: ye have not injured me at all." The words, "**be as I am**", are an appeal to them to take exactly the same ground as he had taken: Paul, the Jew, had been justified by faith alone, totally without the "works of the law". See Galatians 2 verses 15-16 and Acts 15 verses 8-9. He had been justified apart from Jewish ritual and ceremony. "Paul longed for them to become like him in his Christian faith and life, to be delivered from the evil influence of false teachers, and to share his convictions about the truth as it is in Jesus, about the liberty wherewith Christ has made us free. He wanted them to become like himself in his Christian freedom" (J.R.W.Stott). The words, "**for I am as ye are**", mean that Paul had "become like them in non-observance of legal ordinances" (Wm.Trew)

The words, "ye have not injured me at all" (v.12) or "ye have not at all wronged me" (JND), or "ye did me no wrong" (RV), evidently refer to his visit to Galatia (v.13), that is, when he was there they 'did him no wrong'. However, not all understand it that way, suggesting that their defection did not injure his attitude towards them. (In passing, compare 2 Timothy 3 verse 11 where Paul refers to the severe opposition he encountered in the area.)

Following our suggested meaning here, rather than 'doing him wrong' while in Galatia, they gladly received him: "Ye know how through infirmity of the flesh I preached the gospel unto you at the first. And my temptation which was in my flesh ye despised not, nor rejected; but received me as an angel of God, even as Christ Jesus. Where is then the blessedness ye spake of? for I bear you record that, if it had been possible, ye would have plucked out your own eyes, and have given them to me" (vv.13-15). It has been pointed out that Paul's "infirmity", whatever it might have been, was a **trial to him** (he calls it "my temptation" or 'my trial', v.14), but this was not a stumbling-block to the Galatians: "my temptation ... ye despised not, nor rejected" (v.14). The word "despise" means to 'treat with contempt' and "reject" means 'to loathe' or 'to spit out'. According to Hogg and Vine, cited by J.Hunter, "The sentence is elliptical: although my disease repelled you, ye did not on that account refuse to hear my message". Jack Hunter continues: "Clearly, Paul's physical condition was such as to make them want to turn away in disgust. Yet he was so absorbed in his message, so taken up with Christ, the treasure so shining through the earthen vessel, that the excellency and exceeding greatness of the power was seen to be of God. See 2 Corinthians 4 verses 7-11. The physical was forgotten as Paul declared the glorious message of the gospel, and they received him as a messenger from another world and accorded to him a welcome worthy of the Lord Himself ... The words of the Lord Jesus come to mind, 'he that heareth you, heareth me: and he that despiseth you despiseth me' (Luke 10: 16)".

But this had changed, and Paul was obliged to say, "Where is then the blessedness ye spake of?" They were no longer willing to 'pluck out their own eyes, and give them to him' (v.15). The reference to his eyes here could explain Chapter 6 verse 11 ("Ye see how large a letter – or 'with how large letters' – I have written unto you with mine own hand"), and to the possibility that Paul was afflicted with ophthalmia which, according to C.I.Scofield, was "a common disease in the Middle East, to the point of almost total blindness". This brings us to:

ii) Their current attitude to Paul, vv.16-18. "Am I therefore become your enemy, because I tell you the truth? They zealously affect you, but not well; yea, they would exclude you, that ye might affect them. But it is good to be zealously affected always in a good thing, and not only when I am present with you." This contrasts sharply with the preceding paragraph: "Ye did me no wrong" (RV) or "ye have not injured me at all" (v.12); "ye ... received me as an angel of God, even as Christ Jesus" (v.14). But now, "Am I therefore become your enemy ...?" These verses describe the wreckage caused by false teaching:

- **It ruins former blessing.** "Where is then the blessedness ye spake of?" (v.15). The Greek word *(makarismos)* denotes happiness. The Galatian believers had counted themselves happy when they heard and received the gospel. False teaching kills spiritual enthusiasm.

- **It creates resentment of the truth.** "Am I therefore become your enemy, because I tell you the truth?" (v.16). The present tense is used here: "because I **tell** you the truth". Sadly, this is repeated so often. The teaching of God's Word is resented when it is brought to bear upon people's corporate and individual lives, especially in the area of church practice.

- **It brings division.** "They zealously affect you, but not well; yea, they would exclude you, that ye might affect them" (v.17), or "They are not rightly zealous after you, but desire to shut you out (from us), that ye might be zealous after them" (JND). Notice the words, "after **them**". Not 'after the truth', but "after them". The false teachers were intent on winning them for a religion or sect. False teachers will do all they can to ensure that their followers have nothing to do with faithful men and women of God. False teaching divides God's people: truth binds the people of God together.

Paul adds, "But it is good to be zealously affected always in a good thing, and not only when I am present with you" (v.18), or "But it is right to be zealous at all times in what is right, and not only when I am present with you" (JND). Spiritual zeal is commendable, always provided that it is exercised in the right direction. There are worthy things to be zealously pursued. But notice the 'sting in the tail' here: the Galatians had defected in Paul's absence.

We must not miss the lesson: we can all be good Bible-loving, Bible-based, Bible-practising Christians, as long as the truth is championed by strong leaders. But what happens when those strong leaders are no longer with us? The lessons from the book of Judges are relevant here. Notice Judges 2 verses 7-11 in this connection.

b) A change of voice on his part, vv.19-20

"My little children (only here in Paul's writings, but see John 13: 33 and occurrences in 1 John: all references against background of problems and difficulties), of whom I travail in birth *again* until Christ be formed in you, I desire to be present with you now, and to change my voice; for I stand in doubt of you." As J.Hunter observes, "Very tenderly he addresses them as 'my little children'. They were his for he had brought them to Christ. He had brought them to birth, so to speak. Paul is deeply moved; his emotions are rising. His expression now goes beyond 'brethren': they were his own children. He felt for them as only one can who had brought others to Christ, as he now sees them in very real danger. He says he is travailing in birth-pangs again. The first time was to bring them to Christ: now it was that Christ should be formed in them. The first was to free them from idolatry (v.8): the second to free them from law-keeping. The first was the agony of the evangelist: the second the agony of the pastor-teacher (Eph. 4: 11). His ardent desire was to see Christ formed in their lives". (It has been said that in Gospel work, it is a case of prayer and preaching, but in Bible teaching, it is a case of prayer and weeping.) Instead of occupation with "the works of the law", Paul desired they should be occupied with Christ. W.E.Vine explains that the word "formed" (*morphoo*) "refers, not to the external and transient, but to the inward and real; it is used in Galatians 4 verse 19, expressing the necessity of a change in character and conduct to correspond with inward spiritual condition, so that there may be moral conformity to Christ". For example, "Let this mind be in you, which was also in Christ Jesus ..." (Phil. 2: 5)

Paul's great desire was to be with them, and thus be in a position to assess the situation accurately. He would then "be able to adjust his speech to their state. He could be more tender or more stern as the situation demanded. In either case, with more understanding, he could expound in detail what was necessary to help them in their spiritual crisis. He obviously preferred to speak than to write, for the voice is usually more effective than the pen" (J.Hunter). Compare 2 Corinthians 1 verse 23 to 2 verse 3. As it was, he 'stood in doubt of them' or "I am perplexed as to you" (JND). It was almost beyond belief that they were in process of abandoning the liberty of the Christian gospel for the bondage of Judaism. This brings us to

3) THE ALLEGORY, vv.21-31

Or, 'The relationship between bondage and liberty illustrated'. The closing section of the chapter gives further consideration to Abraham. The 'father of the faithful' is reintroduced, not, as before, to show the precedence of the covenant made with him over law, but to illustrate from an event in his life, the relationship between law and promise. We must therefore notice two mothers, two sons, two cities, and two covenants. The section may be analysed as follows: *(a)* The historical facts (vv.21-23), where verse 22 emphasises the mothers and verse 23 emphasises the sons; *(b)* the allegorical lessons, (vv.24-31), where verses 24-27 emphasise the mothers and verses 28-31 emphasise the sons.

a) The historical facts, vv.21-23

"Tell me, ye that desire to be under the law, do ye not hear the law?" Let's stop there for a moment, and remind ourselves, firstly, that this illustrates Romans 15 verse 4, "whatsoever things were written aforetime were written for our learning" and, secondly, that the Word of God is a voice to us - His voice!

Now let's start again: "Tell me, ye that desire to be under the law, do ye not hear the law? For it is written, that Abraham had two sons; the one by a bondmaid, the other by a freewoman. But he who was of the bondwoman was born after the flesh; but he of the freewoman was by promise". The word "law" ("do ye not hear the law") is used here in connection with the Pentateuch, the first five books of the Bible. The "law" in this sense pointed them in the opposite direction to the one they were taking! The **bondwoman** was, of course, Hagar. The **freewoman** was, of course, Sarah. Sarah was chronologically **first,** but her promised son was **second.** Hagar was chronologically **second,** but her son was **first.** Ishmael represents the fruit of nature, while Isaac represents the fruit of God's promise. We should notice the references to this in the New Testament. See Romans 4 verses 19-20, Hebrews 11 verse 11. The important thing here is not physical descent, but different mothers.

Looking again at verse 23, we must notice that Isaac is described as follows: "he of the freewoman was by promise". But Hagar stands between the promise and its fulfilment. She therefore represents the covenant of law, and her son, Ishmael, is described as follows: "he who was born of the bondwoman was born after the flesh". Compare the expressions:

- **"But he who was of the bondwoman was born after the flesh."** As noted above, Ishmael was, solely, the fruit of nature, reminding us that the law demands human power for its fulfilment. The words "after the flesh" might also remind us that Ishmael was born as a result of human scheming. See Genesis 16 verses 1-5. Like lots of human schemes, it 'back-fired'.

- **"But he of the freewoman was by promise".** Isaac was born out of divine power or, as stated in verse 29, "born after the Spirit". It was God's power. The promise of God required His power for its fulfilment.

b) The allegorical lessons, vv.24-27

An allegory is 'a figurative way of speaking or writing in which a subject of higher order is described in terms of that of a lower' or, to quote W.E.Vine, an allegory (*allegoreo*) came to signify speaking, "not according to the primary sense of the word, but so that the facts stated are applied to illustrate principles. The allegorical meaning does not do away with the literal meaning of the narrative". So, having noted the historical facts, Paul continues, "Which things are an allegory: for these are the two covenants: the one is from mount Sinai, which gendereth to bondage, which is Agar. For this Agar is mount Sinai in Arabia, and answereth to Jerusalem which now is, and is in bondage with her children. But Jerusalem which is above is free, which is the mother of us all" (vv.24-26). The two mothers, Hagar and Sarah represent the old and new covenants.

- *Hagar* represents the covenant given at mount Sinai, where the law was given. The law "gendereth to bondage" (v.24): it begets children to slavery. People under law are in bondage. Paul extends this with the words, "and answereth to Jerusalem which now is, and is in bondage with her children". J.Hunter sets out the reasoning very clearly: "This extension to Jerusalem was brilliant, but only too true, for Jerusalem was the true home of Judaism. It was from there that the principle of law-keeping was being sent forth, that circumcision and the observance of the legal code were necessary to be saved".

- ***Sarah*** represents the new covenant or, better, the covenant of promise. Again, J.Hunter deals with the matter most helpfully. "Paul does not tabulate all that stands in antithesis. *This can nevertheless be stated as follows* (our words): Hagar and Sarah; Ishmael and Isaac; Sinai and Zion; earthly Jerusalem and heavenly Jerusalem; Jews and others under law, and the Christian believers; bondage and freedom".

Jack Hunter continues: "'Jerusalem above' is the system of grace, for the true gospel comes from heaven, from God. It is "free", since it is not subject to legal ordinances. And it is the mother of all Christians, for that "mother" gave us both origin and formation of character. How true this is! We were born from above. Our citizenship is there. Our names are written there. Our lives are governed and character formed by heaven's standards. Our prayers ascend there, our hope is centred there. One day soon we hope to be there". Compare Hebrews 12 verses 18-22, "For ye are not come unto the mount that might be touched ... But ye are come unto mount Sion, and unto the city of the living God, the heavenly Jerusalem ..." For those who have *The Epistle of Paul to the Churches of Galatia* (Herman N. Ridderbos), pages 178-179 make very good reading here.

- ***Hagar*** represents the law: her son, Ishmael, was born under the law: his birth resulted from the laws of nature and can be said to have been entirely earthly.

- ***Sarah*** represents the promises of God: her son, Isaac, was the son of promise: his birth resulted from the exercise of divine power, that is, not earthly but heavenly power.

In support of his argument, Paul quotes Isaiah 54 verse 1, "Rejoice, thou barren that bearest not; break forth and cry, thou that travailest not; for the desolate hath many more children than she which hath an husband". The passage emphasises joy brought through promise. This verse does not, in context, refer to Sarah and Hagar, but it is **applied** to Sarah and Hagar. The verse refers to the joy of the earthly Jerusalem in the millennium. Israel, desolate because of unbelief, will ultimately be even more fruitful than she was as "the married wife" (in New Testament words, here in verse 27: "she which hath an husband") prior to her captivity and desolation. Paul applies it with reference to Sarah's former barrenness and desolation. "Sarah was the barren and desolate who cried for children, and Hagar is regarded as the woman who had an husband. But in due time the position was reversed.

Thus, although the law had been prominent in the past, grace had now come into prominence, and the vast multitude saved through the gospel would far exceed those under law" (J.Hunter).

Paul now applies the allegory: "Now we, brethren, as Isaac was, are the children of promise". Not children of 'the bondwoman'. Not under the covenant of law. Not connected with "Jerusalem which now is, and is in bondage with her children". The allegory yields two further considerations:

- **The persecution by Ishmael.** "But as then he that was born after the flesh persecuted him that was born after the Spirit, even so it is now" (v.29). Do notice that Isaac is named in verse 28, but Ishmael is not named in verse 29: he is set aside! The persecution to which Paul refers occurred in Genesis 21 verse 9 ("And Sarah saw the son of Hagar the Egyptian, which she had born unto Abraham, mocking"). It is worth noticing that this happened when Isaac was weaned. He was making progress and then came mockery. It still happens, a young believer starts to make good progress, and then people start to laugh at him, and worse. Paul refers to 'persecution' later in the epistle: see Chapter 5 verse 11 ("And I, brethren, if I yet preach circumcision, why do I yet suffer persecution? then is the offence of the cross ceased"); 6 verse 12 ("As many as desire to make a fair show in the flesh, they constrain you to be circumcised; only lest they should suffer persecution for the cross of Christ"). Men of the flesh detest men of the Spirit. No one despises grace like the man who is trying to save himself by his own merit.

- **The exclusion of Ishmael.** "Nevertheless what saith the scripture? Cast out the bondwoman and her son: for the son of the bondwoman shall not be heir with the son of the freewoman." This refers to Genesis 21 verse 10. In the words of J.Hunter, "The issue of this stormy scene in Abraham's household was that at the request of Sarah (supported by the divine decree, verse 12) Hagar and Ishmael were cast out and disowned". There was only room for Isaac. Jack Hunter continues: "Clearly Paul is calling on the Galatians to adopt the same tactics and be finished with the false teaching of works. Let them take decisive, urgent and permanent action to rid themselves of that which God had disowned". This is akin to the command, "purge out therefore the old leaven ..." (1 Cor. 5: 7).

We should notice that Hagar had a *temporary* place in the house, but Sarah had a *permanent* place in the house. This serves to emphasise still further the respective place of law and promise.

The conclusion is given in verse 31: having said "***now we, brethren,*** as Isaac was, are the children of promise" (v.28), Paul now says "***So then, brethren***, we are not children of the bondwoman, but of the free", or "So then, brethren, we are not maid-servant's children, but [children] of the free woman" (JND). The allegory is perfect! It should be noted that the definite article is omitted by the RV - "we are not children of ***a*** handmaid, but of ***the*** freewoman". That is, while we are not subject to ***any*** system imposing bondage, we are children of the freewoman, the ***one and only*** divine means of blessing.

No wonder that in referring to "false brethren unawares brought in" with the object of bringing us "into bondage", Paul said "to whom we gave place by subjection, no, not for an hour; that the truth of the gospel might continue with you" (Gal. 2: 4-5).

THE EPISTLE TO THE GALATIANS

"Stand fast"

Read Chapter 5: 1-12

Galatians 5 commences with the injunction, "Stand fast **therefore** in the liberty wherewith Christ hath made us free, and be not entangled again with the yoke of bondage". The "therefore" refers to the allegory at the end of the previous chapter (although it could be said to embrace the whole of the doctrinal section), in which Paul contrasts Hagar and Sarah (4: 21-31). The passage makes two major points in connection with their respective sons, and both are developed in Chapter 5 where Paul describes the conflict between "the flesh" and "the Spirit" (see vv.16-26). In referring, in his allegory, to Hagar and Sarah, Paul emphasises the following:

- That Ishmael was "the son of the bondwoman" (4: 30), and that he was "born after the flesh" (4: 23).

- That Isaac was "the son of the freewoman" (4: 30), and that he was "born after the Spirit" (4: 29).

Hagar, the bondwoman, is likened to mount Sinai ("which gendereth to bondage", 4: 24), and to "Jerusalem which now is, and is in bondage with her children" (4: 25). Sarah stands for "Jerusalem which is above" and "free" (4: 26). The first city is earthly: the second city is heavenly. The first directs us to earth: "mount Sinai which is *in Arabia*" (4: 25): the second directs us to heaven: "Jerusalem which is above" (4: 26). The first implies human merit: the second implies divine grace.

We have noticed that Isaac is described as follows: "he of the freewoman was by promise" (4: 23). But Hagar stands between the promise and its fulfilment. She therefore represents the covenant of law, and her son, Ishmael is described, as already noted, as "he who was of the bondwoman was born after the flesh" (4: 23). In this connection we should re-compare the statements (see our previous study):

- *"He of the freewoman was by promise".* Isaac was born by divine grace and power, or, as verse 29 states, he was "born after the Spirit". He was born as the result of divine intervention. The promise of God required His power for its fulfilment.

- *"He who was of the bondwoman was born after the flesh".* Ishmael was, solely, the fruit of nature, reminding us that the law demands human power for its fulfilment.

We may summarise as follows:

- **Hagar represents the law.** Her son, Ishmael, was, so to speak, born under law: his birth resulted solely from earthly and human activity.

- **Sarah represents the promises of God.** Her son, Isaac, was the son of promise: his birth resulted from divine power: the source of that power was heaven.

Paul uses this part of Old Testament history to illustrate the position of believers today. Isaac was never a servant. He was not born into servitude. He was the son of promise. He was born into liberty. That is exactly the position of every believer in the Lord Jesus. We are not subject to the bondage, and punishment of the law. We do not spend our lives endeavouring, as best we can, to keep the law. We live in another sphere entirely. The law has nothing to say to us at all: we are beyond its dictates and its commands. God intended this for us long before the law was ever given. "Now **we**, brethren, as Isaac was, are the children of promise ... So then, brethren, **we** are not children of the bondwoman, but of the free" (4: 28, 31).

Hence the injunction, "Stand fast therefore in the liberty wherewith Christ hath made us free, and be not entangled again with the yoke of bondage" (v.1). Do notice that this is exactly what Paul did at Antioch. He went "up again to Jerusalem ... because of false brethren unawares brought in, who came in privily to spy out our liberty which we have in Christ Jesus, that they might bring us into bondage: to whom we gave place by subjection, no, not for an hour; that the truth of the gospel might continue with you" (2:1, vv.4-5). He was obliged to "stand fast" at Antioch again, this time in confronting

Chapter 5:1-12

Peter on the same subject (2: 11-21). We should also notice that Paul did not change his mind as the years went. On the assumption that Galatians was written circa AD 58 (perhaps a few years earlier) and 1 Timothy in AD 65 (according to the Scofield Bible), he certainly hadn't amended his view of the Judaisers in the interim years. See 1 Timothy 1 verses 3-7.

To become subject again to "the works of the law" was like turning back the pages of history. It was inconceivable that Isaac would ever wish to be like Ishmael, born into slavery. It should be equally inconceivable that any believer should wish to relinquish the blessings of faith, for the "works of the law". But this was infinitely more serious than just going back in history. To become "entangled again with the yoke of bondage" was to deny the efficacy of the work of Christ. We must remember the seriousness of the false teaching: "Except ye be circumcised after the manner of Moses, ye cannot be saved ... it was needful to circumcise them, and to command them to keep the law of Moses" (Acts 15: 1, 5).

Galatians 5 divides into two major sections, both of which are governed by the word "liberty": *(1)* Christian liberty is freedom from the claims of the law (vv.1-12): "Stand fast therefore in the *liberty* wherewith Christ hath made us free" (v.1). *(2)* Christian liberty is freedom to fulfil the requirements of the law (vv.13-26). "For, brethren, ye have been called unto *liberty;* only use not *liberty* for an occasion to the flesh, but by love serve one another" (v.13). We learn:

- That "liberty" is freedom from the law as a means of justification (vv.1-12), and

- That "liberty" is not freedom to act as we please once we are justified (vv.13-26).

The ground of the former is the work of Christ: the ground of the latter is the power of the Holy Spirit. We should notice that Paul uses the word "liberty" in connection with the historical (or, biographical) section of the epistle (2: 4), the doctrinal section (5: 1) and the practical section (5: 13).

1) FREEDOM FROM THE CLAIMS OF THE LAW, vv.1-12

The three paragraphs in this section of the chapter may be summarised as follows: *(a)* the implications of circumcision, (vv.1-4): "Christ shall profit you nothing ... Christ is become of no effect unto you"; *(b)* the expectation of faith (vv.5-6): "we through the Spirit wait for the hope of righteousness"; *(c)* the effects of false teaching (vv.7-12): "Ye did run well; who did hinder you that ye should not obey the truth?"

a) The implications of circumcision, vv.1-4

It has been suggested that verses 1-4 maintain the character of a son of the freewomen, and verse 5 maintains the hope of a son of the freewoman. In these verses we have *(i)* an exhortation (v.1): "Stand fast in the liberty ..."; *(ii)* an explanation (vv.2-4): "Behold, I Paul say unto you ..."

i) The exhortation, v.1

"Stand fast therefore in the liberty wherewith Christ hath made us free, and be not entangled again with the yoke of bondage." We should notice that Paul's exhortation is both positive and negative:

- **It is positive**. **"Stand fast therefore in the liberty wherewith Christ hath made us free."** The words "Stand fast (*steko*) therefore ..." remind us of other passages employing the same word (*steko*): 1 Corinthians 16 verse 13, "Watch ye, **stand fast in the faith,** quit you like men, be strong" (1 Cor. 16: 13); That "I may hear of your affairs, that ye **stand fast** in one spirit" (Phil. 1: 27); "So **stand fast** in the Lord" (Phil. 4: 1); "For now we live, if ye **stand fast** in the Lord" (1 Thess. 3: 8); "Therefore brethren **stand fast,** and hold the traditions (what has been handed down) which ye have been taught" (2 Thess. 2: 15).

The verse continues, "Stand fast therefore *in the liberty* wherewith Christ hath made us free" or, as it has been rendered, "the liberty for which Christ hath made us free". "Liberty" is, of course, freedom. But freedom from what? See, particularly, Chapter 4 verses 21-26. It is a liberty that is intended to be permanent ("cast out the bondwoman ... the son of the bondwoman shall not be heir ...", 4: 30). It is "liberty" from the law which demanded something of us that we could not supply. It was "liberty" of conscience: the dreadful struggle to keep the law.

This part of the verse concludes with "Stand fast therefore in the liberty **wherewith Christ hath made us free"**. That "liberty" was accomplished for us by Christ. He has "redeemed us from the curse of the law" (3: 13).

- *It is negative*. *"Be not entangled again with the yoke of bondage."*
We should notice the following: "Be not entangled (literally, 'be held in') again". Do note the word "again". Compare Chapter 4 verse 9, "But now, after that ye have known God ... how turn ye *again* to the weak and beggarly elements, whereunto ye desire again to be in bondage?" Paul employs a passive verb here: 'Be not loaded down' ("Be not entangled", AV 5:1). Behind it stands the picture of an ox bowed down with a heavy yoke. Compare Acts 15 verse 10, "Now therefore why tempt ye God, to put a yoke upon the neck of the disciples, which neither our fathers nor we were able to bear?" Since the law demanded something from men which they could not supply, the law became "a yoke of bondage". None could break free from it. Note that the word *enecho* ("entangled") is elsewhere rendered "quarrel ('set herself against', RV)" (Mark 6: 19), and "urge him" (Luke 11: 53, "urge him vehemently"). All three occurrences of the word have an evil background.

The verse continues: "Be not entangled again *with the yoke of bondage"*. This is a good description of the law. The allegory in Chapter 4 stresses this: "Mount Sinai which gendereth to bondage" (v.24). See also Chapter 4 verse 9, "How turn ye again to the weak and beggarly elements, whereunto ye desire again to be in bondage?" This is exactly what the law did; it bound people. It accused them, convicted them of their sin, promised them nothing but judgment, and gave no promise of assistance in deliverance. It pinpointed man's guilt, but gave no deliverance from that guilt. It kept man where he was. That yoke crushed: it did not elevate. The Galatians were going back *to that!*

Compare another yoke. "Take my yoke upon you, and learn of me ... for my yoke is easy, and my burden is light" (Matt. 11: 28-30). This is the only place in which "yoke" has a good sense. It should be contrasted with the cumbersome requirements of the law as interpreted and applied by the scribes and Pharisees.

ii) The explanation, vv.2-4

Why they were to "stand fast". Paul makes a *general statement* in verse 2, and *expands this* in verses 3-4:

- *A general statement, v.2.* "Behold, I Paul say unto you, that if ye be circumcised, Christ shall profit you nothing." We should notice: "Behold, *I Paul* say unto you". It is said that the word "Behold" is an imperative. The words, "I Paul say unto you" may well refer to Philippians 3 verse 4, "If any other man thinketh that he hath whereof he might trust in the flesh, I more: circumcised the eighth day ..." Paul, a circumcised man, as circumcised as the false teachers were, categorically states that circumcision was no longer necessary.

In saying, "If ye be circumcised, Christ shall profit you nothing" or "If ye **receive** circumcision ..." (RV), Paul refers not only to the actual rite of circumcision, but to the doctrine of circumcision. The word "profit" (*opheleo*) means "advantaged" or 'bettered'. Why does Paul say, "Christ shall profit you nothing"? Because if, having received Christ, so acknowledging that you **cannot** save yourself, you **then** receive circumcision, so acknowledging that you **can** save yourself, you are then saying that receiving Christ was to no avail. We must remember that the false teachers were not simply urging circumcision as a rite, but stating that it was essential to salvation. See Acts 15 verse 1, "Except ye be circumcised after the manner of Moses, ye cannot be saved".

This is explained in the following verse (v.3). To be circumcised was an admission that there was no finished work: that the claims of the law were not satisfied at Calvary, and therefore the requirements of the law must still be met. So "Christ shall profit you nothing". No wonder Peter said, "Now therefore why tempt ye God, to put a yoke upon the neck of the disciples" (Acts 15: 10). This brings us to:

- The statement expanded, vv.3-4. "For I testify again to every man that is circumcised, that he is a debtor to do the whole law. Christ is become of no effect unto you, whosoever of you are justified by the law; ye are fallen from grace."

We should notice, firstly, that **to be circumcised signified total indebtedness to the law.** "For I testify again (I bear witness again: a solemn protestation) to every man that is circumcised, that he is a debtor to do the **whole law**" (v.3). Why? Because circumcision was more than a rite, or minor operation. It was an admission of an obligation to "do the whole law". It was an undertaking with this in mind. Why? While circumcision was, for Abraham, "a seal of the righteousness of faith which he had being uncircumcised", that is, a covenant sign signifying that he had no confidence in himself but absolute faith in God (see Philippians. 3: 3; Col. 2: 11 for our position in this connection), it **became** the sign of membership of a nation which said,

Chapter 5:1-12

"***All that the Lord hath spoken we will do***". So, "Cursed is everyone that continueth not in ***all*** things which are written in the book of the law ***to do them***" (3: 10). Therefore to be circumcised was to identify oneself with a people obliged to keep the law – that is, to become a Jew. The law was a unified system: the separate commands were each essential to the whole. Circumcision had doctrinal implications: it was a theological symbol. See again Acts 15 verses 1-5.

We should notice, secondly, that ***to be circumcised signified their independence of Christ.*** "Christ is become of no effect unto you, whosoever of you are justified by the law" (v.4), or, "Ye are severed from Christ" (RV) with marginal note, 'brought to nought from Christ'. It has been elsewhere traslated, 'rendered inactive in relation to him'. The words "no effect" (*katargeo*) mean 'rendered inoperative'.

This leads to a conclusion: "Ye are fallen from grace" or "Ye have fallen away from grace" (JND). The word "fallen" (*ekpipto*) means 'to fall out'. Compare 2 Peter 3 verse 17, "Ye therefore, beloved, seeing ye know these things before, beware lest ye also, being led away with the error of the wicked, ***fall*** from your own steadfastness". It has been suggested that the words, "whosoever of you are justified by the law; ye are fallen from grace", refer to the unbelieving Jew, but this seems unlikely in the context. The meaning of "Ye are fallen from grace" is made very clear by Wesley Ferguson (writing in *Precious Seed*, November 2006): "The issue is whether a person can depend on an ordinance or a system on the one hand and at the same time also be depending on the work of Christ. Paul says that if we refuse the liberty of justification through grace, by Christ's blood, to go back to ordinances for our justification, this is to deny in the most fundamental way possible our place in Christ. We simply cannot have both works of law and salvation by grace together. When we examine our verse in its context, we see that it has nothing to do with a person ceasing to be a believer because he or she has failed the Lord or grown slack in spiritual exercises. It is a statement of the impossibility of depending on the work of Christ while also depending on one's own efforts".

> *God tells me how I may be saved*
> *He points to something done,*
> *Accomplished on Mount Calvary*
> *By His beloved Son,*
> *In which no works of mine have place;*
> *For grace with works is no more grace.*

> *Ah, yes; it is His finished work*
> *On which my soul relies;*
> *And if my unbelieving heart*
> *Its preciousness denies,*
> *That works of mine might have a place;*
> *Then grace, indeed, is no more grace.*

In Paul's words elsewhere: "if Abraham were justified by works, he hath whereof to glory; but not before God. For what saith the scripture? Abraham believed God, and it was counted unto him for righteousness" (Rom. 4: 2-3).

To sum up *(i)* Circumcision is an admission of liability to meet the requirements of the whole law, and therefore to say that justification is by the law. *(ii)* Circumcision is a denial that there is benefit from the work of Christ, and a denial of the grace of God. *(iii)* Circumcision stood for the law. Christ stands for grace. This brings us to:

b) The expectation of faith, vv.5-6

"For we through the Spirit wait for the hope of righteousness by faith. For in Jesus Christ neither circumcision availeth any thing, nor uncircumcision; but faith which worketh by love." It can be said that Paul refers here to *(i)* the anticipation of faith (v.5); *(ii)* the expression of faith (v.6).

i) The anticipation of faith, v.5

"For we through the Spirit wait for the hope of righteousness by faith." We should notice that Paul now uses "**we**" as opposed to "**ye**" ("ye are fallen from grace", v.4). It is "through the Spirit" as opposed to the 'flesh'. It is "wait" as opposed to 'work'. It is "by faith" as opposed to the law.

Paul does not say 'we ... wait for righteousness', but "we ... wait for the **hope** of righteousness". That is, we wait for all that will be ours because of righteousness. In the New Testament, we have "the hope of **his calling**" (Eph. 1: 18), "the hope of **the gospel**" (Col. 1: 23), and "the hope **of righteousness**" (here). The "hope of righteousness" includes all that lies ahead: the Lord's coming, our eternal inheritance: in fact, all that belongs to justified people. It is not only that we **are** "righteous" - that is marvellous in itself - but that righteousness brings a wonderful "hope".

Paul says, in effect, through 'receiving circumcision' you surrender your position as a "son of the freewoman": you are no longer an heir. But, to the glory of the grace of God, **we** retain the blessings of the "son of the freewoman". That is, we enjoy "the hope of righteousness" because, like Isaac, we are heirs, See Chapter 4 verse 30. Compare Chapter 4 verse 7: "Wherefore thou art no more a servant, but a son: and if a son, then an heir of God through Christ".

The word "wait" (*apekdekomai*) means to wait and expect eagerly. See also Philippians 3 verse 20, "***look for***"; Romans 8 verse 19, "The earnest expectation of the creature **waiteth** for the manifestation of the sons of God". See also Romans 8 verses 23 & 25 and 1 Corinthians 1 verse 7. It is "wait", not 'work', reminding us again that "the son of the bondwoman shall not be heir with the son of the freewoman" (4: 30). Paul tells us that our enjoyment of "the hope of righteousness" is "through the Spirit", reminding us that "because ye are sons, God hath sent forth **the Spirit of his Son** into your hearts, crying, Abba, Father" (Gal. 4: 6). We do not strive to obtain "the hope of righteousness". We are heirs of that hope by faith alone.

ii) The expression of faith, v.6

"For in **Christ Jesus** neither circumcision availeth anything, nor uncircumcision", that is, as to justification, circumcision brings no national advantage, nationality does not confer any religious privilege upon men" (W.E.Vine). Compare Acts 15 verses 8-9, "And God ... bare them witness, giving them the Holy Ghost, even as he did unto us; and put no difference between us, and them purifying their hearts by faith". Whereas circumcision and uncircumcision have no moral or doctrinal effect, "faith ... worketh by love". Faith is a living and active power expressing itself in love, for "the love of God is shed abroad in our hearts by the Holy Ghost which is given unto us" (Rom. 5: 5). W.E.Vine points out that the words "faith working through love" (RV) are in the middle voice with the meaning, faith 'exerts itself in, or producing, love'. This is developed in verses 13-14.

The words "faith which worketh by love" might imply that the Judaisers were saying that by preaching faith, Paul was minimising love as the fulfilment of the law. We should note the implications of "in Christ Jesus" (AV margin: JND). That is, in the Lord Jesus, now glorified in heaven ("Christ") but who was once here as a man on earth ("Jesus"). This implies our heavenly relationship with Him. Our relationship with Him is heavenly, not earthly.

Hence, earthly distinctions are removed in that 'the circumcision' (believing Jews) and 'the uncircumcision' (believing Gentiles) are in Him on the basis of faith, and that faith exhibits its energy in love.

We should therefore notice two things which mark God's people today. "We through the Spirit **wait**..." That is **now.** "Faith which **worketh** by love". That is **now.** We wait and we work. So faith **works!**

c) The effects of false teaching, vv.7-12

These verses emphasise the dangers of false teaching. They are many and varied.

i) **False teaching interrupts progress, v.7.** "Ye did run well; who did hinder you that ye should not obey the truth?" 'Ye were running well'. That is, in a right way. We must never forget, speaking now generally, that we can all stumble after a good start.

The word "**hinder**" (*enkopto*) means, literally, 'to cut into'. It was used of impeding persons by breaking up the path; or by placing an obstacle sharply in the path, thus to detain a person unncessarily. It is rendered "tedious" in Acts 24 verse 4 (Tertullus before Felix), and "hinder" in Romans 15 verse 22 ("much hindered from coming to you") and in 1 Thessalonians 2 verse 18. The words, "that ye should not **obey** *(peitho)* the truth" have been rendered, 'should not be won over by the truth'. So false teachers were breaking up the path established by Paul.

ii) **False teaching is inconsistent with our calling, v.8.** "This persuasion *(peismone)* cometh not of him that calleth you." Literally, 'this persuasion that has won you over'. There is a play on words here (*peitho,* v.7, and *peismone,* v.8). God had called them "in grace" (1: 6). He does not call - and then amend His terms!

iii) **False teaching is invasive, v.9.** It infiltrates. In 1 Corinthians 5 verse 6, it is the "whole lump" of the gospel. In 1 Corinthians 5 verse 7 the saints are urged to "purge out" the leaven, that is, the man in fellowship with his guilt. There is no such exhortation here. It was from without. We must notice that false teaching is likened to leaven in another way: it is **evil.** (See, for example, the Lord's teaching in Matthew 16 verses 6, 11 and 12). We should also note that false teaching both spreads, and invades and corrupts.

iv) False teaching incurs divine judgment, v.10. "I have confidence (*peitho*) in you through the Lord ('I have confidence towards you in the Lord'), that ye will be none otherwise minded: but he that troubleth you shall bear his judgment (*krima*, meaning 'condemnation'), whosoever he be." See Chapter 1 verses 8-9. We should notice the contrast between Paul's expectation of the Galatians ("I have confidence in you through *the Lord*") and his opinion of the false teachers ("he that troubleth you"). The word "troubleth" (*tarraso*) means 'disturb'. It is used in John 14 verse 1. False teaching disturbs the saints.

v) False teaching invites popularity, v.11. "And I, brethren, if I yet preach circumcision (i.e. if I actually *do preach* circumcision), why do I yet suffer persecution? then is the offence of the cross ceased." Some suggest that there were people who asserted that Paul taught exactly the same thing as the false teachers, perhaps because of the circumcision of Timothy (Acts 16: 3). If there were such people then this highlights the danger of false impressions. But the fact that Paul was persecuted proves the contrary: he was *not* one of the false teachers. After all, those who teach and preach the truth usually attract animosity. For example, anyone today who believes in creation as opposed to evolution is likely to have 'a rough ride' in religious circles, let alone in secular circles. False teaching is far more palatable to unsaved men and women than the Word of God, and 'do it yourself' religion, which enables people to congratulate themselves, beats the Gospel hands down.

The word "offence" (*skandalon*) means a snare or trap. The RV has 'stumblingblock' here. See, for example, 1 Corinthians 1 verse 23, "But we preach Christ crucified, unto the Jews a stumblingblock ..." How was the cross a 'stumblingblock'? It was a 'stumblingblock' in the way that it displayed the utter ruin of human nature. Circumcision proclaimed that something could be done with the human nature ('the flesh), but the death of the Lord Jesus on the cross taught the contrary. The cross is an offence to man.

vi) False teaching should incite our abhorrence, v.12. "I would they were even cut off (*apokopto*, to amputate) which trouble you" or 'cut themselves off' (RV with margin 'mutilate themselves'). As W.E.Vine points out, "The Judaizers attempted to excommunicate the Galatian believers (4: 17), the apostle desired that they would excommunicate themselves, and so relieve the troubled churches of their presence altogether. We should carefully note this. False teaching should elicit our strong censure. The word "trouble" (*anastatoo*) is elsewhere translated "turned ... upside down" (Acts 17: 6) and "madest an uproar" or "stirred up to sedition", RV (Acts 21: 38).

Galatians

With verse 13, we come to a pivotal point in the argument. Paul says, "For, brethren, ye have been called unto liberty", completing the doctrinal section of the epistle, and continues, "only use not liberty for an occasion to the flesh, but by love serve one another", commencing the practical section of the epistle, and expanding verse 6. "For in Christ Jesus neither circumcision availeth any thing, nor uncircumcision; but **faith which worketh by love**", RV/JND.

This brings us to:

2) *FREEDOM TO FULFIL THE REQUIREMENTS OF THE LAW, vv.13-26*

In our next study, we will notice that this part of the chapter may be divided into two sections: *(a)* the relationship between justified people (vv.13-15); *(b)* the resources of justified people (vv.16-26). In the first case, the apostle emphasises the presence of love, and in the second the power of the Holy Spirit.

THE EPISTLE TO THE GALATIANS

"Walk in the Spirit"

Read Chapter 5: 13-26

We have already noticed that Galatians 5 may be divided into two major sections, both of which are shaped by the word "liberty": *(1)* Christian liberty is freedom from the claims of the law (vv.1-12): "Stand fast therefore in the *liberty* wherewith Christ hath made us free" (v.1); *(2)* Christian liberty is freedom to fulfil the requirements of the law (vv.13-26): "For, brethren, ye have been called unto *liberty;* only use not *liberty* for an occasion to the flesh, but by love serve one another" (v.13). We can therefore say, firstly, that "liberty" is freedom from the law as a means of justification (vv.1-12) and, secondly, that "liberty" is not freedom to act as we please once we are justified (vv.13-26). The ground of the former is the work of Christ: the ground of the latter is the power of the Holy Spirit.

1) FREEDOM FROM THE CLAIMS OF THE LAW, vv.1-12

In considering this, we noticed *(a)* the implications of circumcision, (vv.1-4): "if ye be circumcised, Christ shall profit you nothing … Christ is become of no effect unto you, whosoever of you are justified by the law" (vv.2, 4); *(b)* the expectation of faith (vv.5-6): "we through the Spirit wait for the hope of righteousness"; *(c)* the effects of false teaching (vv.7-12): "Ye did run well; who did hinder you that ye should not obey the truth?"

2) FREEDOM TO FULFIL THE REQUIREMENTS OF THE LAW, vv.13-26

There is a change of emphasis on the word liberty in verse 13, "For, brethren, ye have been called unto liberty; only use not liberty for an occasion to the flesh, but by love serve one another". Christian liberty is twofold:

- We "have been called unto liberty". We are not required to accomplish our own justification. In Christ, we *are* justified. It is freedom from the bondage of working to merit divine favour, something quite impossible since the law only condemns us.

- "Only use not liberty for an occasion to the flesh." As already noted, we are required to live in a manner befitting justified people. Liberty is not freedom to act as we please.

This passage may be divided into two main sections: *(A)* the relationship between justified people (vv.13-15); *(B)* the resources of justified people (vv.16-26). The relationship is one of *love*, and the resources lie in the *Holy Spirit*. It is by the Holy Spirit that our relationships are maintained. In the first case, relationships between believers are emphasised. Hence the expression "by love serve *one another* ... take heed that ye be not consumed *one of another*" (vv.13, 15). In the second case, the overall life of the believer is embraced, hence the exhortation "walk in the Spirit (v.16), and the blessings of being "led of the Spirit" (v.18) and displaying "the fruit of the Spirit" (v.22).

A) *The relationship between justified people, vv.13-15*

"For, brethren, ye have been called unto liberty; only use not liberty for an occasion to the flesh, but by love serve one another." This can be beautifully illustrated from the attitude of the Hebrew servant (Ex. 21: 1-6; Deut. 15: 12-17). If, when the time came for his release, instead of selfishly pleasing himself, he said "I love my master, my wife, and my children: I will not go out free", then "his master shall bore his ear through with an aul; and he shall serve him for ever" (Ex. 21: 5-6). We too have been set free, but love for our Divine Master, who set us free, precludes us from pleasing ourselves, and promotes ongoing devotion to Him and to every member of the spiritual family. We gladly say, "I will not go out free".

Once we were "the servants of sin", but we have now been "made free from sin, and become servants to God" with "fruit unto holiness, and the end everlasting life" (Rom. 6: 20-22). In consequence, Peter reminds us that although we are "free", we must not use our "liberty for a cloak of maliciousness, but as the servants of God" (1 Pet. 2: 16).

Our relationships with fellow-believers can be exhibited in one of two ways: either by indulging 'the flesh' in self-promotion and self-assertion among them, or by expressing our love for them.

- *In the first case*, Paul says, "use not liberty for an occasion to the flesh". The word 'flesh' (*sarx*) is easily defined if we omit the last letter and then spell it backwards - self. The word "occasion" (*aphorme*) means a "starting point" and "was used to denote a base of operations in war" (W.E.Vine). Compare the following: "Give none *occasion* to the adversary to speak reproachfully" (1 Tim. 5: 14); "For we commend not ourselves again unto you, but give you *occasion* to glory on our behalf" (2 Cor. 5: 12); "But what I do, that I will do, that I may cut off *occasion* from them which desire occasion" (2 Cor. 11: 12); "But sin, taking *occasion* by the commandment, wrought in me all manner of concupiscence" (Rom. 7: 8). See also Romans 7 verse 11.

Looking at these verses, we are warned against the activities of the flesh. It will use every opportunity to exert its claims. In this case, it can use a doctrinal position to achieve its ends, namely in the attitude which says, 'Well, since I am saved, I can do what I like, it doesn't matter now', a case of "turning the grace of our God into lasciviousness" (Jude v.4). But we need to carefully monitor *every* aspect of our lives, including what we read, what we listen to and what we watch, to ensure that we do not give "occasion to the flesh". The words "use not liberty for an occasion to the flesh, but by love serve one another" are amplified in the reverse order in vv.14-15. Relationships can be either constructive ("by love serve one another", v.13) or destructive ("take heed that ye be not consumed one of another", v.15).

- *In the second case,* "by love serve one another" flows, not from "the flesh" but from the new nature imparted to us at conversion: "We know that we have passed from death unto life, because we love the brethren ... If we love one another, God dwelleth in us, and his love is perfected in us" (1 John 3: 14; 4: 12). In Paul's words, "the love of God is shed abroad in our hearts by the Holy Ghost which is given unto us" (Rom. 5: 5).

This leads us to compare *(a)* the service of love (vv.13-14) with *(b)* the savagery of the flesh (v.15)

a) The service of love, vv.13-14

"But by love serve (*douleuo*, a verb) one another." The word "serve" means to serve as bond-servants. Paul refers to "the yoke of bondage (*douleia*, a noun)" (v.1), but refers here to something very different indeed. We may call it the bond-service of love. So "liberty" is not liberty to be **selfish**, but liberty to **serve.** Do notice that "an occasion to the flesh" is certainly **not** an occasion to "serve one another"! That is the last thing envisaged in an "occasion to the flesh". It is, rather, an occasion to attack one another - and worse (v.13).

Paul continues: "For all the law ('the whole law', RV) is fulfilled (past tense, 'has been fulfilled') in one word, even in this; Thou shalt love thy neighbour as thyself" (v.14). See also Romans 13 verses 8-10. In saying, "For all the law is fulfilled in one word, even in this; Thou shalt love thy neighbour as thyself", Paul is quoting Leviticus 19 verse 18, "Thou shalt not hate thy brother ... Thou shalt not avenge, nor bear any grudge against the children of thy people, but thou shalt love thy neighbour as thyself". This is **constructive.** If we use liberty to "by love serve **one another**", we will be constructive. We should note the context of the quotation: "one another". So that the words "all the law is fulfilled in one word" (v.14), mean all the law relating to relationships between men and women. The Lord Jesus called this, the 'second commandment' (Matt. 22: 39; Mark 12: 31). The power to keep the second commandment lies in keeping the first: "Thou shalt love the Lord thy God with all thy heart ... soul ... mind. This is the first and great commandment. and the second is like unto it, Thou shalt love thy neighbour as thyself. On these **two** commandments hang all the law and the prophets". Compare 1 John 5 verse 1, "every one that loveth him that begat loveth him also that is begotten of him".

In passing, it is well worth noting that grace provides better things than law: "But in lowliness of mind let each esteem other **better** than themselves" (Phil. 2: 3). The law said, "Thou shalt not steal", but grace says, "Let him that stole steal no more: but rather let him labour, working with his hands the thing which is good, that he may have **to give** to him that needeth" (Eph. 4: 28).

b) The savagery of the flesh, v.15

"But if ye bite and devour one another, take heed that ye be not consumed **one of another.**" There are 'no winners' here!

We should notice the words: **"bite"** (*dakno*): see Micah 3 verse 5, "The prophets that make my people err, that bite with their teeth, and cry, Peace"; **"devour"** (*katesthio*): "to consume by eating" (W.E.Vine); **"consume"** (*analisko*): "to use up, send up, especially in a bad sense, to destroy" (W.E.Vine). Compare Luke 9 verse 54 where the word is used literally: "Lord, wilt thou that we command fire to come down from heaven, and consume them?"

W.E.Vine draws attention to the progression here, "bite ... devour ...

consume": he writes, "the first two describing a process, the last the act of swallowing down". It is spiritual cannibalism. The language is descriptive of wild animals, rather than brethren. We must therefore studiously avoid involvement in such things as back-biting, slander-mongering, character assassination and tale-bearing, things dealt with extensively in the book of Proverbs. No wonder Paul concludes the chapter by saying, "Let us not be desirous of vain glory, provoking **one another,** envying **one another**" (v.26). The antidote to such poison lies, as noted above, in Philippians 2 verse 3, "But in lowliness of mind let each esteem other **better** than themselves".

So we can have either a 'blessed' or a 'baneful' effect on "one another". The overall point to note is this: "For all **the law** is fufilled in one word, even in this; Thou shalt love thy neighbour as thyself". Justified people are in a position to fulfil the law. They enjoy a liberty to do this, something that never existed before. Their standard of life is not below the standard required by law. To the contrary, the standard of life is higher than the requirements of the law

B) The resources available to justified people, vv.16-26

This section answers the question of the power necessary to fulfil the law. "This I say then, Walk in the Spirit, and ye shall not fulfil the lust of the flesh." If the demands of the law can be fulfilled in us (vv.13-14), then the demands of the flesh need **not** (note this) be fulfilled in us (v.16).

In this section, we should notice: *(a)* "Walk in the Spirit" (vv.16-17); *(b)* "led of the Spirit (v.18); *(c)* "the fruit of the Spirit" as opposed to "the works of the flesh" (vv.19-23). The section ends with a summary: "And they that are Christ's have crucified the flesh with the affections and lusts. If we live in the Spirit, let us also walk in the Spirit. Let us not be desirous of vainglory, provoking one another, envying one another" (vv.24-26). The law was not the means of **justification.** We "**live** in the Spirit". The law was not the means of **sanctification.** We are to "**walk** in the Spirit". The work of Christ is the basis of sanctification. The power of the Holy Spirit is the means of sanctification. Faith brings us into the good of the first: the reception of the Holy Spirit brings us into the good of the second.

a) "Walk in the Spirit", vv.16-17

It has been nicely said that to "walk in the Spirit" will **provoke conflict**

Galatians

(vv.17), **provide guidance** (v.18); **produce fruit** (vv.21-24) and **promote unity** (vv.25-26).

This emphasises what **we** must do. (The expression "led of the Spirit" emphasises what **He** does.) "This I say then, Walk in the Spirit, and ye shall not fulfil the lust of the flesh." The idea of "walk" *(peripateo)* is "habitual conduct" (M.R.Vincent), or "the whole round of activites of the individual life" (W.E.Vine). (A different word – *stoicheo* - is used in v.25.) Hence the word "walk" in the expressions, "**walk** in newness of life" (Rom. 6: 4); "**walk** in love" (Eph. 5: 2); "good works, which God hath before ordained that we should **walk** in them" (Eph. 2: 10); "**walk** in wisdom" (Col. 4: 5).

We should notice 'the cause and effect' situation in the words, "Walk in the Spirit, and ye shall not fulfil the lust of the flesh".

- **The cause: "Walk in the Spirit"**. This is positive and active, whereas "led" (v.18) is passive. So it is a deliberate policy. See Romans 8 verse 5, "They that are after the flesh do mind the things of the flesh; but they that are after the Spirit the things of the Spirit". To "walk in the Spirit" means that we actively pursue the desires and will of the Holy Spirit, that is, the mind and will of God as expressed in His Word. Compare Romans 13 verse 14, "put on the Lord Jesus Christ, and do not take forethought for the flesh to [fulfil its] lusts" (JND).

- **The effect: "and ye shall not fulfil the lust of the flesh".** The word "lust" means, basically 'strong desire'. It refers to the sinful desires of fallen nature, whether **crude** or **refined.** We should notice the certainty of victory here: "And ye shall **by no means** fulfil the lust of the flesh" (Newberry margin).

Paul refers here to two opposing forces: **"For** the flesh lusteth against the Spirit (this is mentioned first, perhaps because we were originally "in the flesh", Rom. 7: 5), and the Spirit against the flesh: and these are contrary (*antikeimai*, meaning 'to lie against' or 'opposite to') the one to the other: so that ye cannot do the things that ye would" (that is, evil things). While this may be understood differently, it does seem, in the words of W.E.Vine, that "the object of the striving of the Spirit in the believer is that he may be saved from yielding to the evil tendencies of his own nature". It should be carefully noted that the words "ye cannot do" are elsewhere translated "that ye **should** not do those things which ye desire" (JND), or "so that ye **may** not do the things that ye would" (RV). It is not, alas, a case of finding it impossible to do "the things that ye would", that is, yield to the "lust of the flesh", but that in the power of the Holy Spirit provision is made for us not to do so.

b) "Led of the Spirit", v.18

"But if ye be led of the Spirit, ye are not under (the) law." As noted above, this emphasises what *He* does. We are not "under the law" as a principle of life. If we are led of the Spirit, then the law can have nothing to say by way of condemnation. Hence the words, "against such there is no law" (v.23). To cite verse 14 again, "For all the law is fulfilled in one word, even in this; Thou shalt love thy neighbour as thyself". We are "not under the law" because "the righteousness of the law is fulfilled in us, who walk not after the flesh, but after the Spirit" (Rom. 8: 4). We must remember that the words, "led of the Spirit", refer, not to audible participation at the Lord's Supper or a strong desire to do something or go somewhere, but to a life directed by the Holy Spirit. People often say, 'the Lord led me to do or say this or that", but "led of the Spirit" refers to our *entire* lives.

c) "The fruit of the Spirit", vv.22-23

The expression "works of the flesh" emphasises **human effort.** The expression "fruit of the Spirit" emphasises **divine power**, which enables us, like the godly man in Psalm 1, who is "planted by the rivers of water", to bring "forth his fruit in his season" (v.3). The believer does not work to produce fruit. The "fruit" in his life is "the fruit of the Spirit".

The section contrasts *(i)* "the **works** of the flesh" (vv.19-21) and *(ii)* "the **fruit** of the Spirit" (vv.22-23), with *(iii)* a summary (vv.24-26).

i) "The works of the flesh", vv.19-21

"Now the works of the flesh are manifest, which are these; Adultery, fornication, uncleanness, lasciviousness, idolatry, witchcraft, hatred, variance, emulations, wrath, strife, seditions, heresies, envyings, murders, drunkenness, revellings, and such like (so it is not an exhaustive list)." The "works of the flesh" may be classified as follows:

- **Sensual sins, v.19.** "Adultery (omitted by JND/RV), fornication, uncleanness, lasciviousness." "**Fornication**" *(porneia)* and "**uncleanness**" (meaning 'impurity') are linked in Ephesians. 5 verse 3, "But fornication, and all uncleanness, or covetousness, let it not be once named among you, as becometh saints". "***Uncleanness***" and "***lasciviousness***" are linked in Ephesians 4 verse 19, "who being past feeling have given themselves over unto lasciviousness, to work all uncleanness with greediness". "Lasciviousness" is excess or freedom from restraint. It is rendered "wantonness" in Romans 13 verse 13, where it is linked with "chambering", meaning 'a place to lie down in' or 'bed', meaning illicit intercourse.

- ***Religious sins, v.20a.*** "Idolatry, witchcraft". "***Idolatry***" is public: "***witchcraft***" is private. The Greek word for "witchcraft" is *pharmakia* (English 'pharmacy'), meaning 'sorcery'. The word is associated with drug-taking. W.E.Vine explains: against *pharmakos* he writes: "An adjective signifying 'devoted to magical arts', is used as a noun, a sorcerer, especially one who uses drugs, potions, spells, enchantments, Revelation 21 verse 8". Here is the verse in question: "But the fearful, and unbelieving, and the abominable, and murderers, and whoremongers, and ***sorcerers***, and idolaters, and all liars, shall have their part in the lake which burneth with fire and brimstone: which is the second death". See also Revelation 9 verse 21, "Neither repented they of their murders, nor of their ***sorceries,*** nor of their fornication, nor of their thefts".

- ***Social sins, v.20b.*** There is "***hatred***" (*echthra*) meaning 'enmity'. The root word is 'enemy' (*echthros*). It is the opposite of love. "***Variance***" (*eris*, meaning strife or contention). It is the product of hatred. The word is rendered "contentions" in 1 Corinthians 1 verse 11 ("there are contentions among you"). It means wrangling or quarrelling. "***Emulations***" (*zelos*): that is, 'jealousies'. "***Wrath***" (*thumos)* meaning hot anger or passion. The product of "emulations". "***Strife***", or 'strifes' *(erithia)* meaning party-making or factions. It derives from *erithos*, meaning 'hireling', referring to someone seeking to win followers. Notice the same order as 2 Corinthians 12 verse 20, "envyings ... wraths ... strifes". Then "***Seditions***" (*dichostasia*), meaning, literally, 'divisions' or ' standing apart'. See Romans 16 verse 17, "mark them which cause divisions". "***Heresies***" (*hairesis*), that is, parties. The word is rendered "sects" elsewhere: see, for example, Acts 5 verse 17, 1 Corinthians 11 verse 19, 2 Peter 2 verse 1. "***Envyings***" (*phthonos*). It has been said that envy is displeasure at the prosperity of others: we begrudge them that, while jealousy is the desire for what others have for ourselves. "***Murders***". No explanation required.

- ***Personal sins, v.21.*** "***Drunkenness***". No explanation required. "***Revelling***" (*komos*), meaning a carousal. The consequence of drunkenness. See also Romans 13 verse 13, where "rioting" (*komos*) is associated with drunkenness.

Chapter 5:13-26

Paul summarises: "of the which I tell you before, as I have told you in time past, that they which do such things shall not inherit the kingdom of God". That is, they will be subject to eternal judgment. The words "*do* (*prasso*) such things" mean 'practise such things'.

ii) "The fruit of the Spirit", vv.22-23

"But the fruit of the Spirit is love, joy, peace, longsuffering, gentleness, goodness, faith, meekness, temperance: against such there is no law." It is "the fruit of the Spirit", that is, what the Spirit produces. All are seen perfectly in the life of the Lord Jesus. He was "full of the "Holy Ghost" (Luke 4: 1). The "fruit of the Spirit" is therefore the reproduction of the character of Christ in His people. It reminds us of Paul's deep desire for the Galatians, "I travail in birth again until Christ be formed in you" (4: 19).

So much has been said and written about these two verses, and you are heartily recommended, amongst other things, to purse the subject in the delightful series of articles entitled 'The Fruit of the Spirit in the Life of Christ' by J.M.Flanigan, published in *Counsel*. That is, if you can get hold of the 'back numbers' from 1997-1998!

It has been suggested that "love, joy, peace" are *inward*: "longsuffering, gentleness, goodness" are *manward*: "faith, meekness, temperance" are *selfward*. However, the context does suggest that in context "the fruit of the Spirit" is something that should mark relationships between believers. The local assembly should be a spiritual vineyard!

The first three are the source of the remaining six. They were 'left' by the Lord Jesus. For "*love*", see John 17 verse 26 where the Lord prays that "the love wherewith thou hast loved me may be in them, and I in them"; for "*joy*", see John 15 verse 11 where the Lord said to His disciples, "These things have I spoken unto you, that my joy might remain in you, and that your joy might be full"; for "*peace*", see John 14 verse 27 where the Lord said to His disciples, "Peace I leave with you, my peace I give unto you: not as the world giveth, give I unto you. Let not your heart be troubled, neither let it be afraid". It had been said that the remaining six are all seen in our Lord's life between the garden and the cross. He was "led of the Spirit".

All we can do at present is to append some brief notes on the meanings of the remaining six words used by the apostle Paul. "***Longsuffering***" (*makrothumia*), meaning, literally, 'long-tempered'. It is rendered "patience" in Hebrews 6 verse 12 and James 5 verse 10. "**Gentleness**" (*chrestotes*) means 'kindness': it has been defined as 'goodness in deed'. The adjective (*chrestos*) is rendered "gracious" in 1 Peter 2 verse 3. "**Goodness**" (*agathosune*) here means 'good in character'. "**Faith**": no comment required. **"Meekness**" (*praotes*) is the exact opposite of self-assertiveness and self-interest. It does not mean powerlessness, but rather, 'power under control' (E.W.Rogers). "**Temperance**" (*enkrateia*) comes from a root meaning 'strength', and signifies 'self-control' or, better, "the will under the operation of the Spirit of God" (W.E.Vine).

"Against such there is no law." The law has nothing to say when these features are present. The Gospel does not only give men a righteous standing before God, it brings righteousness of life.

c) The summary, vv.24-26

In concluding this part of the epistle, Paul refers again to the believer and "the flesh" (v.24), and to the believer and "the Spirit" (vv.25-26).

i) The believer and the flesh, v.24

"And they that are Christ's (RV 'of Christ Jesus') have crucified the flesh with its affections and lusts." Paul uses the aorist tense here. They have "crucified the flesh" once for all. We *have* done it: not, we are to do it. We must not forget that in coming to Christ, we passed a judicial sentence on "the flesh". We must leave the flesh where it is; we must not take it down and pamper it. The word "affections" *(pathema)* means passions (RV). See Romans 7 verse 5, "For when we were in the flesh, the *motions* (*pathema*) of sins, which were by the law, did work in our members to bring forth fruit unto death". Compare Chapter 2 verse 20 where Paul describes *himself* as "crucified with Christ".

ii) The believer and the Spirit", vv.25-26

"If we live in the Spirit, let us also walk in the Spirit. Let us not be desirous of vain glory, provoking one another, envying one another." The words, "If we live in the Spirit", may be rendered (the dative) "If we live by the power of the Spirit". We must notice the contrast between "have crucified" and "live. (See, again, Galatians 2: 20.)

Chapter 5:13-26

The words "let us walk in the Spirit" mean 'let us walk in line' (*stoicheo*)'. So, in keeping with the context ("one another"), "Let us keep step (walk in line) with one another in submission of heart to the Holy Spirit" (W.E.Vine). Compare 1 Chronicles 12 verse 38, "All these men of war, that could keep rank". (We should now read Psalm 133: 1.) This will enable us to avoid the pitfalls in verse 13. "Let us not be desirous of vain glory (*kenodoxos*), provoking (*prokaleomia*) one another, envying one another". The word *kenodoxos* comes from *kenos* meaning 'vain', and *doxa* meaning 'glory': *prokaleomia* means 'to call forth', as to a contest. So, "to stir up evil in another" (W.E.Vine). Then there is a third warning, against "envying one another". The three are connected: the first will produce the second and third, but not in the lives of those "walk in the Spirit".

THE EPISTLE TO THE GALATIANS

"Whatsoever a man soweth, that shall he also reap"

Read Chapter 6: 1-18

Galatians 6 is a continuation of the previous chapter, and describes "the distinguishing features of a Christian who is walking by the Spirit of God, both in relation to the assembly of the saints (vv.1-10), and in relation to the world (vv.11-18)" (Wm.Trew) . The first section further amplifies Chapter 5 verse 13, "For, brethren, ye have been called unto liberty; only use not liberty for an occasion to the flesh, but by love serve one another".

- **Chapter 5** concludes by emphasising what love **does not do:** it is not "desirous of vain glory, provoking one another, envying one another" (5: 26). The word "provoke" (*prokaleo*) means 'to call forth, as to a contest, hence to stir up what is evil in another' (W.E.Vine) The attitude reeks of jealousy ('I'm better than you, and I'll prove it') and envy (you're better than me, and I resent it').

- **Chapter 6** commences by emphasising what love **does do:** "Brethren, if a man be overtaken in a fault, ye which are spiritual, restore such an one in the spirit of meekness" (6: 1). Love seeks the interests of others. The contrast between the two attitudes is stressed by the inclusion of 'even' in the revised text: "Brethren, **even** if a man be overtaken in any trespass ... restore such an one" (RV); "Brethren, if **even** a man be taken in some fault ... restore such an one" (JND).

The chapter may be divided as follows: *(1) The law of Christ (vv.1-5)*: "Bear ye one another's burdens, and so fulfil the law of Christ" (v.2); *(2) The law of harvest (vv.6-10)*; "whatsoever a man soweth, that shall he also reap" (v.7); *(3) The law of the new creation (vv.11-18):* "For in Christ Jesus neither circumcision availeth any thing, nor uncircumcision, but a new creature (creation)" (v.15).

Each of these sections reflects the conflict between "the flesh" and "the Spirit". In Paul's words, "For the flesh lusteth against the Spirit, and the Spirit against the flesh: and these are contrary the one to the other" (5: 17). So:

- **Verses 1-5.** *"The flesh":* "if a man be overtaken in a fault"; *"the Spirit":* "ye which are spiritual restore such an one". See also verses 3-4: "For if a man thinketh himself to be something, when he is nothing, he deceiveth himself ('the flesh'). But let every man prove his own work ('the Spirit')..."

- **Verses 7-10.** *"The flesh":* "he that soweth to the flesh": *"the Spirit":* "he that soweth to the Spirit".

- **Verses 11-18.** *"The flesh:* "a fair show in the flesh"; *"the Spirit":* "glory ... in the cross of our Lord Jesus Christ".

1) THE LAW OF CHRIST, vv.1-5

"Bear ye one another's burdens, and so fulfil the law of Christ." The apostle refers to three ways in which God's people are to bear burdens: *(a)* in connection with an erring believer (v.1); *(b)* in connection with believers generally (v.2); *(c)* in connection with ourselves (vv.3-5). (Incidentally, Galatians 6 has been called 'the chapter of the three bears': see vv.2, 5, 17.)

a) In connection with an erring believer, v.1

We must notice the following: *(i)* the need for restoration; *(ii)* the means of restoration.

i) The need for restoration

"Brethren, if a man be overtaken in a fault (*paraptoma*, a false step, a trespass)" or, as noted, "Brethren, **even** if a man be overtaken in any trespass ... restore such an one" (RV). We should notice the word "**brethren**". It denotes a relationship which should provoke kindly dealings. Hence, "Let brotherly love continue" (Heb. 13: 1); "love as brethren" (1 Pet. 3: 8). The assembly at Thessalonica excelled in this: "But as touching brotherly love ye need not that I write unto you ... but we beseech you, brethren, that ye increase more and more" (1 Thess. 4: 9-10).

The word "***overtaken***" must be emphasised: it means, not 'caught in the act', but rather 'caught by a trespass through being off guard'. See, for example, Noah (Gen. 9: 20-21). Paul envisages something unpremeditated here. As W.E.Vine points out, this contrasts vividly with the deliberate, premeditated and impenitent practice of evil described earlier: "they which **do** (practice) such things shall not inherit the kingdom of God" (5: 21). The difference may be illustrated by contrasting the pig returning to wallowing in the mire, its natural environment (2 Pet. 2: 22) - the pig is perfectly happy there! Not so a sheep which will endeavour to extricate itself.

ii) The means of restoration

"Ye which are spiritual restore such an one ..." It has been observed that Judaism would condemn the guilty party out of hand. It has also been said that in this epistle Paul exemplifies his own ministry. While it is not an exact parallel, he is in the process of restoring fellow-believers. Attention is drawn to the following:

- ***Who is to do it?*** "Ye which are spiritual." That is, the believer in Chapter 5 verses 16, 18 and 25. The believer in whom is formed "the fruit of the Spirit" (5: 22-23). The believer who has attained spiritual maturity, unlike the Corinthians: "And I, brethren, could not speak unto you as unto spiritual, but as unto carnal, even as unto babes in Christ" (1 Cor. 3: 1). When Paul became aware of personal problems at Philippi ("I beseech Euodias and beseech Syntyche, that they be of the same mind in the Lord") he sought the help of a spiritually minded brother: "I intreat thee also, **true yokefellow**, help those women which laboured with me in the gospel ..." (Phil. 4: 2-3).

- ***What is to be done?*** "*Restore* such an one." The word (*katartizo*) means 'to mend'. It is used of the disciples "mending their nets" (Matt. 4: 21). So "restore" to their former position. As Wm.True so rightly observes, "Torn nets are not much good for catching fish, nor are rent assemblies". The same word (*katartizo*) is also used in 1 Corinthians 1 verse 10, "That ye may be perfectly **joined together** in the same mind and in the same judgment". According to Kenneth Wuest, the Greeks often used this word when they were speaking of 'setting broken limbs'. As Wm.Trew observes, "This is an operation that needs both skill and tenderness, and it is the spiritual man who possesses these qualifications. The spirit in which he sets about his loving ministry is the evidence of his deep spirituality". This is an important, mandatory work. It is so necessary for the Lord's people to be maintained in good health. William Trew is so right in saying "How many, compassed by infirmities who have now fallen, would have been helped to stand, or would have been recovered for God and restored to spiritual health again, had there been spiritual men to carry their burden before God, fulfilling thus the law of Christ, the royal law of love".

It has been nicely said that this ministry of restoration may be illustrated from Genesis 14 where Abraham recovered and restored Lot after his capture by Chedorlaomer and his fellow-kings. But, at the same time, we should also notice that Melchizedek, a king/priest, strengthened Abraham for his encounter with the king of Sodom, reminding us of the high-priestly ministry of the Lord Jesus.

- *How is it to be done?* "In the spirit of meekeness": that is, not in a self-assertive manner. "Considering thyself, lest thou also be tempted": that is, in humility, conscious of personal frailty. Acting in the spirit of self-judgment, rather than acting with a judgmental spirit towards others.

b) In connection with believers generally, v.2

It does seem possible that Paul now takes the opportunity to move from specific cases, where "a man be overtaken in a fault" (v.1), to the general circumstances of life, which can certainly bring anxiety and disquiet to God's people. Thus: "Bear ye **one another's burdens**, and so fulfil the law of Christ". According to the linguists, the words "Bear ye" are in the continuous tense. On the other hand, in keeping with the immediate context, Paul may well be stressing that *all* spiritually-minded believers ("ye which are spiritual") should be ready "to put a shoulder under the burden another is carrying" perhaps with the idea of "helping our brother (or sister) to overcome the result of spiritual weakness (v.1)" (J.Hunter - *What the Bible Teaches – Galatians*).

The spiritual health of the Lord's people should be a matter of personal and mutual concern to every believer. The word "burdens" *(baros)*, denotes a weight, and W.E.Vine notes that it "always suggests what is heavy or burdensome". See, for example, Matthew 20 verse 12, "thou hast made them equal unto us, which have borne the **burden** (*baros*) and heat of the day". It is a **crushing** burden whereas, in verse 5 ("every man shall bear his own burden"), it is a burden (*phortion*) that can be **carried.**

But this is not all: "Bear ye one another's burdens, and so fulfil ('thus have it fulfilled', JND margin) the **law of Christ**". We may well ask, 'What law?' It would certainly not be unreasonable to cite the words of the Lord Jesus, "A new commandment I give unto you, That ye love one another ... By this shall all men know that ye are my disciples, if ye have love one to another" (John 13: 34-35). See also Galatians 5 verse 13, "By love serve one another". Or, alternatively, Paul may well be referring here to the law by which Christ Himself lived: "Surely he hath borne our griefs and carried our sorrows" (Isa. 53: 4: cited in Matthew 8: 17). In the Saviour's own words, "the Son of man came not to be ministered unto, but **to minister**, and to give his life a ransom for many" (Mark 10: 45).

> *Others, Lord: yes, others:*
> *Let this my motto be:*
> *Help me to live for others,*
> *That I might live like Thee.*

It has been pointed out that "to do this is to fulfil the law of Christ, not the Law of Moses" (J.Hunter). Jack Hunter continues: "The Law of Moses imposed burdens that they were not able to bear (see Acts 15: 10): the law of Christ taught them to share burdens".

c) *In connection with ourselves, vv.3-5*

After what might appear to be a slight digression, in which he possibly refers to burden-bearing amongst the Lord's people generally, Paul returns to his main theme which may be highlighted as follows: "ye which are spiritual, restore such an one in the spirit of meekness, considering thyself, lest thou also be tempted ... For if a man thinketh himself to be something, when he is nothing, he deceiveth himself ..." The man who regards "himself to be something" is devoid of the necessary "meekness", and is therefore the wrong man for the job. Moreover, anyone who regards himself as being "something" proves, by that very fact – his high opinion of himself – that he is in fact "nothing". There is no spiritual strength in self-promotion.

In these verses Paul dwells upon the folly of self-approval (v.3) and the necessity for divine approval (vv.4-5).

i) **Self-approval, v.3.** The self-opinionated man: "For if a man thinketh himself to be something, when he is nothing, he deceiveth himself". Solomon said, "Seest thou a man wise in his own conceit? There is more hope of a fool than of him" (Prov. 26: 12). The word "for" links verse 3 with the preceding verses. It indicates that if a believer enters on such ministry with a sense of spiritual superiority, he is self-deceived. We should now listen to Paul in Romans 12 verse 3, "For I say, through the grace given unto me, to every man that is among you, not to think of himself more highly than he ought to think ..." The word "deceiveth" here (*phrenapatao*) means 'to deceive by fancies' (quoted by W.E.Vine): 'to be deceived in one's mind'. (A different word, *planao*, to go astray, to wander, is used in v.7). Self-conceit is self-deceit. The attitude of the proud Pharisee (Luke 18: 11-12) illustrates the point perfectly.

ii) Divine approval, vv.4-5. We are now asked to contemplate, not the self-opinionated man, but the spiritual man. He tests his conduct and service by the Word of God, the divine standard by which everything must be measured: "But let every man prove his own work" (v.4). The word "prove" (*dokimazo*) means 'to put to the test with the expectation of approving', as in 1 Peter 1 verse 7 and 2 Corinthians 13 verse 5. This man scrutinises his conduct and service in the presence of God, and is conscious of divine approval. He can "have rejoicing in himself alone". He does not rejoice "in another", that is, by measuring himself against those who have stumbled, like the man "overtaken in a fault". He measures himself against the Word of God. He does not rejoice out of personal conceit, but in the sense of divine approval on his work. He does not "think himself to be something". He brings the whole matter of life and conduct to God, the only arbiter. Here is the man who lives in the spirit of Galatians 5 verse 26: "Let us not be desirous of vain glory, provoking one another, envying one another".

The necessity for this is stressed in the words, "For every man shall bear his own burden" (v.5). The word translated "burden" here *(phortion)* means something carried, but without reference to its weight, as in *baros* (v.2). The word was commonly used for a man's pack. Here, therefore, it refers to a personal burden of responsibility for our own conduct and service. (Note the expressions: "own work" (v.4) and "own burden" (v.5)). The man who is deeply conscious of his personal responsibility is not likely to "think himself to be something, when he is nothing".

The words, "and then shall he have rejoicing", look ahead to the 'judgment seat of Christ'. Compare 1 Thessalonians 2 verse 19, "For what is our hope or joy, or crown of ***rejoicing*** ..."; Philippians 2 verse 16, "That I may ***rejoice*** in the day of Christ"; 2 Corinthians 1 verse 14, "as also ye have acknowledged us in part, that we are your ***rejoicing,*** even as ye also are ours in the day of the Lord Jesus". This brings us to:

2) THE LAW OF HARVEST, vv.6-10

The connection between the two sections is clear. While it is true that "every man shall bear his own burden", part of that burden of responsibility is to support servants of the Lord. While verse 6 might appear, at first glance, to be a random injunction, this cannot be the case. It would not be good exposition. Contextual interpretation is vital! "Let him that is taught in the word communicate unto him that teacheth in all good things." That is, in view of what has been taught in verse 5 - "for every man shall bear his own burden" - there is to be a sense of responsibility in connection with displaying practical fellowship with those who teach the Word of God. It is, in fact, a case of 'sowing and reaping': *(a)* the **teacher** sows and reaps and *(b)* those who **support** them also sow and reap.

a) Those who teach sow and reap, v.6

"Let him that is taught in the word communicate unto him that teacheth in all good things." This exhortation could have been generated by the fact that because of Judaistic teachers, the true servant of God had been unsupported. However, see, for example, 1 Corinthians 9 verse 11: "If we have sown unto you spiritual things, is it a great thing if we shall reap your carnal things?"

We must carefully notice the wording: "Let him that is taught in the **word**". The word "taught" here *(katecheo)* means to be taught orally, literally 'to sound down the ears'. Notice that it is "taught in the **word** *(logos)*". Here our individual support is emphasised. We should observe that this embraces more than financial support. See, for example, the way in which John commends Gaius (3 John 5-8). Assembly support is emphasised in Philippians 4 verses 15-16.

The word "**communicate**" *(koinoneo)* means 'to share'. See Philippians 4 verses 14-15, "Ye have well done, that ye did **communicate** (have fellowship) with my affliction ... Now ye Philippians know also, that in the beginning of the gospel, when I departed from Macedonia, no church **communicated** with me as concerning giving and receiving, but ye only". See also Hebrews 13 verse 16, "But to do good and to **communicate** forget not: for with such sacrifices, God is well pleased".

Here, then, is a sphere in which we bear other people's burdens! Verse 6 is a 'link' verse: it completes the section dealing with bearing burdens and, at the same time, introduces the idea of sowing and reaping.

b) Those who are taught sow and reap, vv.7-10

This is now developed: "Be not deceived; God is not mocked: for whatsoever a man soweth, that shall he also reap. For he that soweth to his flesh shall of the flesh reap corruption; but he that soweth to the Spirit shall of the Spirit reap life everlasting". While these well-known words state a general principle, applicable to every aspect of life, the context must be born in mind. Paul is continuing to think of material support for the servants of God, and warns against self-indulgence on the part of believers. Our use of material things entrusted to us by God is elsewhere compared to a 'sowing' that will certainly result in a 'reaping'. See 2 Corinthians 9 verses 6-7, "But this I say, He which soweth sparingly shall reap also sparingly; and he which soweth bountifully shall reap also bountifully. Every man according as he purposeth in his heart, so let him give; not grudgingly, or of necessity: for God loveth a cheerful giver". Compare Philippians 4 verse 17: "Not that I desire a gift: but I desire fruit that may abound to your account".

> *We lose what on ourselves we spend,*
> *We have as treasure without end*
> *Whatever, Lord, to Thee we lend,*
> *Who givest all.*

We should note the following:

i) What we are to do, vv.7-8. We must sow "to the Spirit", as opposed to "the flesh". That is, we must pursue the interests of the Spirit of God. We must seek to do what the Spirit desires. This is not the means of **possessing** eternal life, but of **enjoying** eternal life. As always, every word counts:

- **"Be not deceived."** As already noticed, the underlying word (*planao*) is reflected in our English 'planet'. It means 'to wander' or 'to go astray'.

- **"God is not mocked."** The word "mocked" (*mukterizo*) comes from *mukter*, the nose. In other words, 'you cannot turn up your nose at God without incurring the direst consequences'. Men may fool themselves, but they cannot fool God. God is not to be sneered at - neither is He outwitted: He is the Lord of the harvest. So

- **"For whatsoever a man soweth that shall he also reap."** This emphasises a general principle. We should notice that "flesh" and "Spirit" are used again here, but not in quite the same way as in Chapter 5, where the "works of the flesh" are described in all their ugliness. In passing, while Romans 8 verse 13 appears, at first glance, to be a parallel passage, its context demands a different interpretation. Paul is referring there to the unregenerate and regenerate man respectively.

- **"For he that soweth to his flesh shall of the flesh reap corruption."** The margin reading 'own flesh', (JND/RV) suggests, bearing in mind the context of verse 6, that it is personal comfort and satisfaction that is in view. If, instead of 'communicating' with the servants of the Lord, we live for ourselves in utter selfishness, the ultimate result will be "corruption". It is selfishness ending in nothing. W.E.Vine puts it very clearly: "To sow to the flesh does not necessarily mean to do gross, immoral things. There is nothing in this passage to show that these kinds of things are at present in the mind of the apostle. If the believer considers only his own material comforts and the needs of his body, devoting his substance solely to supply these in selfish pleasure and in self-indulgence or in worldly luxury, then, since these are only temporary, and the body in its present constitution must pass away into corruption, our harvest will end with this world. But if taught by the Spirit, we take the larger and true view of life, and we use our substance to encourage that ministry of the Word by which is maintained and developed the life of our spirit, then, since that life is eternal, our harvest will be fully reaped in the region of life which is life indeed, not only in time, but in scenes of heavenly glory". The word "corruption" suggests, among other things, transience, whereas "life everlasting" suggests permanence.

Bearing in mind the context, support for those who teach the word of God, we should notice that in 1 Corinthians 16, Galatia is mentioned and, of course, Corinth itself (v.1). So is Macedonia (v.5). But Romans 15 verse 26, while mentioning Corinth and Macedonia, omits Galatia. Is this why we have this particular injunction here?

- **"But he that soweth to the Spirit shall of the Spirit reap life everlasting."** The expression, "soweth to the Spirit" is defined in verses 9-10: "Let us not be weary in well-doing ... let us do good to all men ... ." We should remember that "life everlasting" is not just living for ever: it is a quality of life. See John 17 verse 3, "And this is life eternal, that they might

Chapter 6:1-18

know thee the only true God, and Jesus Christ, whom thou hast sent". "Life everlasting" is life in fellowship with God. We could say that if "corruption" follows 'sowing to the flesh', then holiness follows 'sowing to the Spirit'. See Job 4 verse 8, "They that plough iniquity and sow mischief, (JND) reap the same"; Hosea 8 verse 7, "For they have sown the wind, and they shall reap the whirlwind" ..."

ii) How we are to sow, v.9. "And let us not be weary in well doing." We must not lose heart: "For in due season we shall reap, if we faint not". The words "in due season" indicate the time of divine appointment. Compare "in its own times" (1 Tim. 2: 6). The words "in due season we shall reap" evidently refer to the present time (we are to be unwearied farmers), but we are not amiss, surely, in adding that they look on to the judgment seat of Christ.

iii) When we are to sow, v.10. "As we have therefore **opportunity**, let us do good unto all men, especially unto them who are of the household of faith." Notice that there is a 'season' for reaping (v.9), and a 'season' for sowing (v.10): the word translated "opportunity" is the same as the word translated "season" (*kairos*). It carries the idea of 'making opportunity'. This highlights the danger of giving indiscriminately, rather than giving as the result of spiritual exercise.

iv) Where we are to sow, v.10. "Let us do good unto *all* men, **especially** unto them who are of the household of faith." No comment needed!

3) THE LAW OF THE NEW CREATION, vv.11-18

In the closing verses of the epistle, we should notice the following: *(a)* the concern of Paul (v.11); *(b)* the value of circumcision (vv.12-15); *(c)* the concluding remarks (vv.16-18).

a) The concern of Paul, v.11

"Ye see how large a letter (perhaps, 'in what large letters', JND margin) I have written unto you with mine own hand." The epistle must have been written slowly and painfully, possibly, as some say, because of his chronic ophthalmia (Gal. 4: 15). Such was his burden for the saints in Galatia. Does our ministry flow out of a burden for the saints, or is it purely an academic exercise?

Galatians

b) The value of circumcision, vv.12-15

This section takes us back to the ***immediate circumstances of writing.*** "And certain men which came down from Judaea taught the brethren, and said, Except ye be circumcised after the manner of Moses, ye cannot be saved … But there rose up certain of the sect of the Pharisees which believed, saying, That it was needful to circumcise them, and to command them to keep the law of Moses" (Acts 15: 1, 5). In this connection, Paul is careful to note that he was accompanied to Jerusalem by Titus, an uncircumcised Gentile, but "neither Titus, who was with me, being a Greek, was compelled to be circumcised" (Gal. 2: 3). In fact, in Paul's own words, they "added nothing to me" (Gal 2: 6): Paul's fellow apostles at Jerusalem recognised that salvation was by faith alone, without the necessity for circumcision.

We should notice three things about circumcision here. In the first two cases, it was valuable to the false teachers: in the last case it had no value at all.

i) It avoided persecution, v.12. "As many as desire to make a fair show, in the flesh, they constrain you to be circumcised; only lest they should suffer persecution for the cross of Christ." As J.Hunter points out, "To insist on circumcision removed the offence of the cross, and saved them from being the target of the hatred of their fellow-Jews". He continues: "This same mistake has been perpetuated down the ages. Christianity without the cross appeals to the natural man, while doing something for his salvation ministers to his pride".

ii) It advanced their position, vv.13-14. "For neither they themselves who are circumcised keep the law; but desire to have you circumcised, that they may glory in your flesh." Paul now stresses the impure motives of the Judaisers. They were not really concerned about the Galatians: they did not keep the law themselves, but sought only the aggrandisement of their own position: "that they may glory in your flesh".

These two verses are in sharp contrast. To 'glory in the flesh' is to honour what God finished at the cross. Christ bearing sin ***fits me for heaven.*** Christ on the cross ***finishes me for the world.*** The idea here is that the believer and the world, particularly the religious world, have passed sentence on each other. There is mutual disassociation.

In what sense did Paul write: "But God forbid that I should glory, save in the cross of our Lord Jesus Christ, by whom the **world is crucified unto me, and *I unto the world?*"**

- Paul looked at the world *(kosmos)*, and said, 'so far as I am concerned, the world is crucified'. He regarded it as obnoxious and accursed.

- The world looked at Paul, and said, 'so far as we are concerned, Paul is crucified'. He is obnoxious and accursed.

Paul 'gloried' ('boasted') in the cross "for through it he had been saved from the penalty due to him as a sinner. He had been delivered from the deadness of Judaism and from this present evil age. It may be a stumbingblock to the Jew and foolishness to the Greek (1 Cor. 1: 23), but to Paul it was the revelation of God's love and grace and wisdom, and through it he had been brought into contact with the Man who died there" (J.Hunter).

We should notice that this is the last of four references in the epistle to crucifixion. The crucifixion of the Lord Jesus is presented *legally* (2: 20), *historically* (3: 1), *morally* (5: 24) and *socially* (6: 15). Crucifixion is not natural or accidental: it is ***judicial.***

iii) It availed nothing, v.15. "For in Christ Jesus neither circumcision availeth any thing, nor uncircumcision, but a new creature" or "new creation" (JND).

Men and women are not saved either because they are circumcised, or because they are not circumcised. In Christ, they are brought into an entirely new realm in which all such distinctions have no place. Compare 2 Corinthians 5 verses 14-17, "For the love of Christ constraineth us; because we thus judge, that if one died for all, then were all dead: and that he died for all, that they which live should not henceforth live unto themselves, but unto him which died for them, and rose again. Wherefore henceforth know we no man after the flesh: yea, though we have known Christ after the flesh, yet now henceforth know we him no more. Therefore if any man be in Christ, he is a new creature ('there is a new creation', JND): old things are passed away; behold, all things are become new".

c) The concluding remarks, vv.16-18

We should notice the following: *(i)* walking 'in line' (v.16); *(ii)* bearing 'brand marks' (v.17); *(iii)* praying for blessing (v.18).

i) **Walking 'in line', v.16.** "And as many as walk (*stoicheo,* as in 5:25, meaning 'to keep in rank') according to this rule (*kanon*: the 'rule' spelt out in verses 14-15), peace be on them, and mercy, and upon the Israel of God." Paul refers here, as noted, to 'walking in line': that is, an ordered walk by the standard of verses 14-15. W.Trew: "Every member of the assembly is called upon to guide his steps according to the standard of the new creation" (W.Trew). It has been suggested that "mercy" is used with particular reference to the Gentiles.

The expression "Israel of God" (v.16) is not an allusion to the church, which has been mistakenly called 'the spiritual Israel', or 'an extension of Israel'. Romans 2 verse 29 defines "the Israel of God": "But he is a Jew, which is one inwardly; and circumcision is that of the heart, in the spirit, and not in the letter; whose praise is not of men, but of God". See also Romans 9 verse 6, "For they are not all Israel (spiritually), which are of Israel (naturally)". The "Israel of God" are converted Jews: "the remnant according to the election of grace" (Rom. 11: 5). The only Israel that God recognises in the present dispensation.

ii) **Bearing 'brand marks', v.17**. "From henceforth let no man trouble me: for I bear in my body the marks of the Lord Jesus" (v.17). Although "circumcised the eighth day", the only marks in his body that meant any thing to him were the *stigmata* (brand marks) of the Lord Jesus. Perhaps Paul refers here to the beatings mentioned in 2 Corinthians 11 verse 24, or to the physical sufferings he had endured, for example, at Lystra (Acts 14: 19). "It is probable, too, that this reference to his scars was intended to set off the insistence of the Judaisers upon a body mark which cost them nothing. Over against the circumcision they demanded as a proof of obedience to the law, he set the indelible tokens, sustained in his own body, of his loyalty to the Lord Jesus" (W.E.Vine).

iii) **Praying for blessing, v.18.** "Brethren, the **grace** of our Lord Jesus Christ (not the 'law of Moses') be with your spirit" (v.18). Paul commenced the epistle, writing as **an apostle**, with "Grace be unto you and peace ..." (1: 3). He concludes the epistle, writing now as **a brother**, "the **grace** of our Lord Jesus Christ be with your spirit". Since the word "spirit" is in the singular, this may well express Paul's desire that the assembly should be completely united in love and fellowship.

EPHESIANS

by
John M Riddle

THE EPISTLE TO THE EPHESIANS

Introduction

Read the whole epistle

While we are not in the habit of long detailed introductions, we ought at least to say something about *(1)* the city of Ephesus, *(2)* the preaching at Ephesus, and *(3)* the church at Ephesus, followed, of course, by *(4)* the letter to Ephesus.

1) The city of Ephesus

The New Testament first refers to Ephesus in Acts 18 which notes Paul's brief visit to the city during the homeward leg of his second 'missionary journey'. Having left Corinth and embarked at Cenchrea, the eastern sea-port of Corinth, from which it was separated by about nine miles, Paul "sailed thence into Syria". The journey eastwards took him to Ephesus, where he left Aquila and Priscilla, his fellow-travellers, having made a brief visit to the synagogue, and promised the Jews there that he would return "if God will" (Acts 18: 18-21). He was as good as his word, and did so in the early stages of his third 'missionary journey' (Acts 19: 1 - 20: 1). In the meantime, Apollos arrived in Ephesus and before he left for Corinth, Aquila and Priscilla did some excellent 'running repairs' to his theology (Acts 18: 24-28). It was obviously God's will for them to remain at Ephesus when Paul sailed off into 'the wide blue yonder' (Acts 18: 21). We should mention:

a) The commercial history of the city

We are told that the city had been established for something like a thousand years before Paul arrived. At one time, Ephesus was a flourishing port with a busy harbour at the mouth of the Cayster River, which emptied into the Aegean Sea. The river was evidently partly silted up by the time of Paul's visit. According to Morrish's *New and Concise Bible Dictionary* "the ruins are extensive: the sea has retired, leaving a pestilential morass of mud and rushes" or, as it has been said, "It is now stinking malarial swamp". Perhaps, hopefully, the environment has improved since all this was written!

In the words of J.Allen (*Revelation Revisited*), "Ephesus was the trading port through which the trade of the Asian continent passed to and from Europe". Lying at an intersection of major trade routes, the city boasted "huge warehouses", which indicated the size of its trade, and "magnificent villas which reflected the wealth of the city". Ephesus also hosted the world-famous Asian Games.

Excavations have revealed a great deal of ancient Ephesus, including a large paved road and numerous foundations of the many silversmiths' shops in the city. As we shall see, the silversmiths did not like the Gospel one little bit. Acts 19 verses 23-41 describes their disquiet, culminating in a noisy meeting of the "Metal Workers Union" in the theatre. In fact, Paul met opposition from religion (Acts 19: 8-9), from spiritism (Acts 19: 13- 20), and, as noted above, from big business (Acts 19: 23-41).

b) *The religious life of the city*

As we shall see, the commercial and religious lives of the city were intertwined. When the Greeks colonized the area, they found a religious cult very similar to their own pagan ideas. The Greeks, like the Romans later, had the habit of absorbing other beliefs. They saw no difference between the gods of Ephesus and their own.

Ephesus was famed for its religious life, and the temple of Diana (the Latin name for Artemis) there was considered one of the seven wonders of the world, along with, for example, the pyramids and the hanging gardens of Babylon.

The temple of Diana was a great tourist attraction – it was the main 'industry' at Ephesus - and the local silversmiths made a good living out of the visitors: they "made silver shrines ('silver niches, containing an image of the goddess', F.F.Bruce) for Diana", which "brought no small gain to the craftsmen" (Acts 19: 24).

The temple that Paul saw replaced an earlier one which was burnt down, it is said, on the night that Alexander the Great was born (in July, 356 B.C.).

By 350 B.C. its replacement was under construction and took 120 years to build. It covered a very large area (the chief building was four times larger than Athen's most famous building, the Parthenon) and was supported by 127 pillars, each of them sixty feet high. "All knowledge of its whereabouts (it stood about a mile and half northeast of the city which Paul knew) had been forgotten for centuries, when its foundations were discovered (by J.T.Wood) on the last day of 1869. The great altar, west of the main building, was discovered in 1965" (F.F.Bruce).

Significantly, it is in the Epistle to the Ephesians that Paul describes the church as a "building fitly framed together" that "groweth unto an **holy temple** in the Lord" (Eph. 2: 21). The temple of Diana was anything but holy.

But in A.D.56 (according to the Scofield Bible) the tradesmen were getting worried. If people were becoming Christians, they wouldn't be interested in buying "silver shrines" anymore! Paul tells us that the believers at Thessalonica had "turned to God from idols to serve the living and true God" (1 Thess. 1: 9). It was now happening at Ephesus. Trouble began to brew. The Metal Workers Union shouted "Great is Diana of the Ephesians" for two hours, and the "town clerk", not a 'happy-chappy', had to "appease the people" (Acts 19: 34-35).

2) The preaching at Ephesus

It was into this corrupt, commercial paganism, that Paul came with the Gospel of Jesus Christ. His brief visit in Acts 18 verses 19-21 was followed by a three-year stay (Acts 20: 31) of which the details are recorded in Acts 19.

On arriving at Ephesus for what proved to be an extended visit, Paul evidently made it his business to contact "certain disciples", twelve or so in number (Acts 19: 1, 7), who had evidently listened to the preaching of Apollos (compare Acts 18: 26 with Acts 19: 2-3). The discussion had a happy outcome (Acts 19: 5-6), and Paul evidently alludes to this in saying, "that we should be to the praise of his glory (God's glory), who first trusted in Christ. In whom ye also trusted, after that ye heard the word of truth, the gospel of your salvation: *in whom also after that ye believed ('having believed', JND), ye were sealed with that Holy Spirit of promise"* (Eph. 1: 12-13).

The Gospel spread. Paul "went into the synagogue, and spake boldly for the space of three months", then "disputing daily in the school of one Tyrannus (probably a lecture hall). And this continued by the space of two years; so that all they which dwelt in Asia heard the word of the Lord, both Jews and Greeks" (Acts 19: 8-10). According to some authorities Paul had the use of the "school" from 11 a.m. to 4 p.m. (F.F.Bruce). It has been calculated (Justin Waldron) that over a period of two years this would mean, omitting the sabbaths, 3,130 hours of teaching!

At this time, Ephesus was the capital of the area known in the New Testament as "Asia". This was a Roman province in what we now call Turkey. It seems likely that all "seven churches which are in Asia" (Rev. 1: 4) were founded about this time. This reminds us that every Christian has the same mission - to spread the gospel.

We should add that Paul was exposed to terrible risk at Ephesus. "If after the manner of men (i.e. to speak after the manner of men) I have fought with (wild) beasts at Ephesus, what advantageth it me, if the dead rise not? Let us eat and drink; for tomorrow we die" (1 Cor. 15: 32). W.E.Vine points out that as a Roman citizen Paul "could not be compelled to fight with actual beasts in an arena; nor could he be flung to the lions", and concludes by explaining that the words, "I have fought with wild beasts at Ephesus", refer "to his experiences at the hands of an infuriated mob". He continues, "His stay there was long, and what he here mentions was no doubt previous to the occurrence recorded in Acts 19". There is certainly no reference to this in Acts 19.

3) *The church at Ephesus*

The assembly at Ephesus was well founded. In Paul's own words at Miletus, "I kept back nothing that was profitable unto you, but have shown you, and have taught you publicly, and from house to house, testifying both to the Jews, and also to the Greeks, repentance toward God, and faith toward our Lord Jesus Christ" (Acts 20: 20-21). He reminded the elders of their God-given responsibilities, and warned them of dangers ahead: "Take heed therefore unto yourselves, and to all the flock, over the which ('in the which', RV) the Holy Ghost hath made you overseers, to feed the church of God, which he hath purchased with his own blood. For I know this, that after my departing shall grievous wolves enter in among you, not sparing the flock. Also of your own selves shall men arise, speaking perverse things, to draw away disciples after them. Therefore watch, and remember, that by the space of three years

I ceased not to warn every one night and day with tears" (Acts 20: 28-31). Ephesus was an assembly with excellent foundations. As noted, Paul preached there (Acts 18 & 19). Aquila and Priscilla were there (Acts 18: 18-19, 26). As also noted, the assembly elders had a personal meeting with Paul (Acts 20: 17-38). Timothy ministered there (1 Tim. 1: 3), and we have an epistle addressed to the assembly in which Paul prays "that Christ may dwell in your hearts by faith; that ye, being rooted and grounded in love, may be able to comprehend with all saints, what is the breadth, and length, and depth, and height; and to know the love of Christ, which passeth knowledge, that ye might be filled with all the fulness of God" (Eph. 3: 17-19).

But it is to **this very assembly** that the Lord Jesus says, "Remember therefore from whence thou art fallen, and repent, and do the first works; or else I will come unto thee quickly, and will remove thy candlestick out of his place, except thou repent" (Rev. 2: 5). Why? Not because they had become lazy; not because they had compromised; not because of erroneous doctrine; but because "thou hast left thy first love". An assembly can have all the marks of a New Testament church, but lack the one thing vital to its life, without which it ceases to have the very reason for its existence.

4) The letter to Ephesus

As F.F.Bruce observes "A comparison with Ephesians 6: 21f. with Colossians 4: 7f. makes it evident that Ephesians was sent to its destination by the hand of Tychicus at the same time as Colossians. We may therefore look for the destination of both letters in the same area. Colossians was manifestly sent to the church at Colosse, in the Phrygian region of the province of Asia. The words "at Ephesus" in Ephesians 1: 1 might seem to put the matter beyond question were it not that some of our earliest authorities for the text omit these two words. The most acceptable view is that the letter was intended to be read not only by the Christians at Ephesus but by those in other cities of the province of Asia as well. There are no personal references in this letter which would limit its full application to any one local church. We are quite justified in calling it 'The Epistle to the Ephesians' if we bear in mind that it was sent also to other churches in the province of which Ephesus was the capital".

The suggestion that the epistle was in fact a circular letter could be supported by the fact that the believers at Colosse were told, "And when this epistle is read among you, cause that it be read also in the church of the Laodiceans; and that ye likewise read the epistle *from* Laodicea" (Col. 4:16), where "the epistle *from* Laodicea was" was actually the 'The Epistle to the Ephesians'.

While it has been nicely said that the epistle describes the wealth, wisdom, walk, and warfare of God's people, it might be better to say, spoiling the alliteration, that their wealth, walk, relationships and warfare might be more appropriate. Very clearly the Epistle falls into two major sections which F.F.Bruce calls *(1) The New Community in the purpose of God (Chs. 1-3)* and *(2) The New Community in the life of believers (Chs. 4-6)*. He explains that "Part 1 and Part 2 are logically bound together by the 'therefore' of 4: 1. Part 2 is the practical outworking of the truth revealed in Part 1".

In using the expression 'The Divine Community', F.F.Bruce refers to Paul's teaching in connection with the church, where Christ has reconciled Jew and Gentile "unto God in one body by the cross, having slain the enmity thereby: and came and preached peace to you which were afar off (the Gentiles), and to them that were nigh (the Jews). For through him we both have access by one Spirit unto the Father. Now therefore ye are no more strangers and foreigners, but fellowcitizens with the saints, and of the household of God" (Eph. 2: 16-19).

This was something, not only amazingly wonderful to Paul, but to unseen observers as well! Just listen to this: "by revelation he (God) made known unto me the mystery ... which in other ages was not made known unto the sons of men, as it is now revealed unto his holy apostles and prophets by the Spirit; that the Gentiles should be fellow-heirs, and of the same body, and partakers of his promise in Christ by the gospel ... Unto me, who am less than the least of all saints, is this grace given, that I should preach among the Gentiles the unsearchable riches of Christ; and to make all men see what is the fellowship of the mystery, which from the *beginning of the world* hath been hid in God, who created all things by Jesus Christ: to the intent that *now* unto the principalities and powers in heavenly places might be known by the church the manifold wisdom of God, according to the eternal purpose which he purposed in Christ Jesus our Lord" (Eph. 3: 3-11).

In an excellent summary of the epistle supplied by our contributor Justin Waldron, the same two major sections are called: *(1) Doctrine – our riches in Christ (1: 3 - 3: 21)* and *(2) Duty – our responsibilities in Christ (4:*

Introduction

1 – 6: 24). In the first case, amongst other things, attention is drawn to our spiritual possessions in Christ (1: 3-14) and our spiritual position in Christ (2: 1-22). In the second case, attention is drawn, amongst other things, to walking in unity (4: 1-16), walking in purity (4: 17 - 5: 21), walking in harmony (5: 22 – 6: 9) and walking in victory (6: 10-20).

Here is F.F.Bruce on the subject: "As Paul considered the answer to the Colossian heresy, he was led to develop the theme of Christ's person and work in relation to the whole universe, including the hierarchies of principalities and powers of which that heresy made so much. As members of the body of Christ, he assured the Colossian Christians that they shared in His victory over these hostile forces and had no need to pay them homage.

But he continued to pursue this line of thought after he had dealt with the Colossian heresy. What is the relation of the Church, as the body of the exalted Christ, to the universe over which He is Lord, and to God's eternal purpose? *He takes up this sublime question in the epistle now before us, not in the swift, argumentative style with which we are so familiar from other letters of his, but in a mood of meditative adoration and prayer.* Then he draws out for his readers the implications of the truth thus unfolded for their everyday life in this world". It sounds, doesn't it, as though F.F.Bruce enjoyed his studies immensely, and, undoubtedly, we will do the same!

We will not attempt now a detailed summary of each chapter, but simply repeat some headings quoted by the late John Parker of Kilbarchan. In each chapter, Paul refers to the church as follows:

Chapter 1

A body that cannot be dissected. "And hath put all things under his feet, and gave him to be the head over all things to the church, which is his body, the fulness of him that filleth all in all" (vv.22-23).

Chapter 2

A building that cannot be destroyed. "Now therefore ye … are built upon the foundation of the apostles and prophets, Jesus Christ himself being the chief corner stone; in whom all the building fitly framed together groweth unto an holy temple in the Lord: in whom ye also are built together for

an habitation of God through the Spirit" (vv19-22).
Chapter 3

A bank that cannot default. "For this cause I bow my knees unto the Father of our Lord Jesus Christ, of whom every family in heaven and earth is named, that he would grant you, according *to the riches of his glory*, to be strengthened with might by his Spirit in the inner man" (vv.14-16).

Chapter 4

A brotherhood that cannot be dissolved. "Endeavouring to keep the unity of the Spirit in the bond of peace. There is one body, and one Spirit, even as ye are called in one hope of your calling ..." (vv.3-4).

Chapter 5

A bride that cannot be divorced. "Christ also loved the church, and gave himself for it; that he might sanctify and cleanse it with the washing of water by the word, that he might present it to himself a glorious church, not having spot, or wrinkle, or any such thing; but that it should be holy and without blemish" (vv.25-27).

Chapter 6

A battalion that cannot be defeated. "Put on the whole armour of God, that ye may be able to stand against the wiles of the devil ... Wherefore take unto you the whole armour of God, that ye may be able to withstand in the evil day, and, having done all, to stand" (vv.11-18).

We must now heed the good advice of Joshua, and "go to possess the land, which the LORD God ... hath given you" (Josh. 18: 3). We shall find that the Epistle to the Ephesians is indeed "a land that floweth with milk and honey" (Josh. 5: 6).

THE EPISTLE TO THE EPHESIANS

"Blessed be the God and Father of our Lord Jesus Christ"

Read Chapter 1: vv.1-3

In introducing the epistle we noted that it comprises two major sections. The first is represented by chapters 1-3, and may be entitled **'Doctrine - our riches in Christ'.** The second is represented by Chapters 4-6, and may entitled **'Duty - our responsibilities in Christ'.** It has been nicely said that over Chapters 1-3 we could write: "this is the way", and over Chapters 4-6, "walk ye in it" (Isa. 30: 21).

Both titles ('Doctrine - our riches in Christ' and 'Duty - our responsibilities in Christ') supplied by Justin Waldron, are well-chosen, and the first is quickly confirmed. In Paul's own words, "In whom (the Lord Jesus) we have redemption through his blood, the forgiveness of sins, according to the **riches** of his grace …" (1: 7). Read a little further: "that ye may know what is the hope of his calling, and what the **riches** of the glory of his inheritance in the saints …" (1: 18). Keep reading: "God, who is **rich** in mercy, for his great love wherewith he loved us" (2: 4). Don't stop reading: "Unto me, who am less than the least of all saints, is this grace given, that I should preach among the Gentiles the unsearchable **riches** of Christ" (3: 8). A little further still: "I bow my knees unto the Father of our Lord Jesus Christ … that he would grant you, according to the **riches** of his glory, to be strengthened with might by his Spirit in the inner man …" (3: 14-16).

Ephesians 1 may be divided as follows: *(A)* the greetings to the Ephesians (vv.1-2); *(B)* the blessings of the Ephesians (vv.3-14); *(C)* the prayer for the Ephesians (vv.15-23).

A) THE GREETINGS TO THE EPHESIANS, vv.1-2

"Paul, an apostle of Jesus Christ by the will of God, to the saints which are at Ephesus, and to the faithful in Christ Jesus: Grace be to you, and peace, from God our Father, and from the Lord Jesus Christ".

We should briefly notice the reference here to *(1)* the writer; *(2)* the readers; *(3)* the place; *(4)* the greeting.

1) The writer, v.1

Paul describes himself as "an apostle of Jesus Christ by the will of God". He gives a more detailed account of his apostleship, and for good reasons, in writing to the Galatians. See Galatians 1 verse 1. In saying here that he was "an apostle of Jesus Christ by the will of God", Paul is making the point (as in Galatians), that no human agency was involved in his appointment. But more than that, he reminds us the apostles spoke with divine authority, and that to reject their teaching was to reject the Word of God, therefore rejecting God Himself. Paul himself makes this clear: "I marvel that ye are so soon removed" – not from the truth of the Gospel only – but "from **him that called you** into the grace of Christ" (Gal. 1: 6). See also 1 Corinthians 14 verse 37, "If any man think himself to be a prophet, or spiritual, let him acknowledge that the things that I write unto you are the commandments of the Lord". Compare 2 Peter 3 verse 2.

It has been said that Paul often refers to himself as an 'apostle of Christ Jesus' (see RV here) because the Lord Jesus first spoke to Paul from heaven as the exalted Christ, whereas Peter refers to himself as 'an apostle of Jesus Christ' (1 & 2 Pet. 1: 1) because his association with Him began on earth.

2) The readers, v 1

"To the saints which are at Ephesus, and to the faithful in Christ Jesus ('to the saints and faithful in Christ Jesus who are at Ephesus', JND)". We should notice how Paul describes them:

- **"The saints which are at Ephesus."** The word "saints" describes what we are, not what we will become! We became "saints" (*hagios* meaning 'holy ones'; 'sanctified' or 'set apart') on faith in Christ. The believers at Corinth were not altogether 'saintly' at times in their behaviour, but Paul addresses them as "them that are sanctified in Christ Jesus, called (*to be*) saints, with all that in every place call upon the name of Jesus Christ our Lord ('our Lord Jesus Christ', JND), both theirs and ours" (1 Cor. 1: 2). This is something that God accomplishes. In the religious world, a person becomes a saint by a process called 'canonization'. The person concerned is dead, their life was beyond reproach, and they had performed at least two miracles. The "saints" at Ephesus were *alive!* They had been set apart by God, and whilst they had never performed any miracles, they had experienced a miracle!

- **"The faithful in Christ Jesus."** The description, "the faithful", refers, "not so much to their fidelity, but to their exercise of faith (see 1 Tim. 6: 2)". The words, "In Christ Jesus" describe "the position into which their faith had placed them" (A.Leckie, *What the Bible Teaches – Ephesians*). The expression is said to occur twenty-seven times in this epistle. We were once "in Adam", but now "in Christ." See 1 Corinthians 15 verse 22, "For as in Adam all die, even so in Christ shall all be made alive." The teaching of this epistle is not that Christ is in us, but that we are "in Christ".

3) The place, v.1

As noted in our Introduction, we are told that the words "at Ephesus" are absent in some of the earliest texts, giving rise to the suggestion that this epistle was in fact a circular epistle, some suggesting that it was sent, they say, to the 'Ephesian area' or 'Greater Ephesus'. While F.F.Bruce, on reasonable grounds, sees no problem if this were the case, J.N.Darby (in his footnote) is somewhat doubtful, saying "Some, without sufficient ground, have considered it as a kind of circular".

4) The greeting, v.2

"Grace be to you, and peace, from God our Father, and from the Lord Jesus Christ." Preachers and commentators always remind us that "grace" (*charis*) is the characteristic Greek greeting, and "peace" (*shalom*) is the characteristic Hebrew greeting, something of particular significance in this epistle (2: 11-22). The letter concludes with "peace" and "grace" (6: 23-24).

We should notice that "grace ... and peace" come conjointly from the Father and the Son, indicating their equality. They come from "God our Father", as the divine source, and from "the Lord Jesus Christ", as the divine channel. The order is important. Grace is the source of divine blessing, and peace is the nature and result of divine blessing. Grace and peace rest on a historical event which exhibited grace, and from which peace is derived. That event is wholly divine: the death of the Lord Jesus Christ.

Ephesians

It reminds us that all we possess, grace and peace, flows from the work of the Lord Jesus. Grace is what Christ brought (Titus 2: 11), and peace is what He left (John 14: 27).

This brings us to:

B) THE BLESSINGS OF THE EPHESIANS, vv.3-14

Praise (vv.3-14) is followed by prayer (vv.15-23). "Blessed be the God and Father of our Lord Jesus Christ, who hath blessed us with all spiritual blessings in heavenly places in Christ … Wherefore I also, after I heard of your faith in the Lord Jesus, and love unto all the saints, cease not to give thanks for you, making mention of you in my prayers …" (vv. 3, 15-16). Later instruction in the epistle flows from Paul's heart, permeated by praise and prayer. His heart is full!

This immense passage describes three wonderful aspects of our blessings: **(1) we are chosen by God** (vv.3-6): **(2) we are redeemed by the Son** (vv.7-12); **(3) we are sealed by the Spirit** (vv.13-14). Put succinctly, Paul refers to the will of God (vv.3-6), to the work of Christ (vv.7-12), and to the witness of the Spirit (vv.13-14). These blessings are bestowed upon us by the Godhead. What privileged people we are!

1) WE ARE CHOSEN BY GOD, V3-6

Before Paul describes the will of God for us (vv.4-6), he lifts his heart to Him in thanksgiving (v.3). We will therefore ponder these verses (vv.3-6) by noticing **(a)** how Paul blessed God (v.3); **(b)** how God has blessed us (vv.4-6). It is a case of:

"Praise God from whom all blessings flow!"

a) How Paul blesses God, v.3

"Blessed be the God and Father of *our* Lord Jesus Christ, who hath blessed us with all spiritual blessings in heavenly places in Christ". Every word counts!

i) "***Blessed*** be the God and Father of our Lord Jesus Christ." When used of God, the word "blessed" (*eulogeos*) means 'to speak well of', to praise: to eulogise. It does not mean "blessed" in the sense of adding anything. See Psalm 103 verses 20-22, 2 Corinthians 1 verse 3 and 1 Peter 1 verse 3.

ii) "Blessed be **the God and Father of our Lord Jesus Christ.**" Compare John 20 verse 17, "I ascend unto my Father, and your Father; and to my God, and your God," *not* 'I ascend to our Father and to our God'. The words, "the God and Father of our Lord Jesus Christ", indicate a unique relationship. It has been said that God is the "God of our Lord Jesus Christ" in relation to Christ's manhood, and the "Father of our Lord Jesus Christ" in relation to Christ's deity. He is "the God of our Lord Jesus Christ" - Whom He served, and the "Father of our Lord Jesus Christ"- Whom He loved.

We cannot leave this without noticing that although there is a distinction between "God *our* Father" (v.2) and "the God and Father of *our Lord Jesus Christ* (v.3) - as pointed out above (John 20: 17) - there is also a marvellous connection. What God is to Christ in a unique sense, He is also to us. This wonder of wonders is all part of being "accepted in the Beloved" (v.6). What Christ enjoys, we enjoy too!

Note, in passing, that Paul addresses his first prayer to "the God of our Lord Jesus Christ" (1: 17), and the second to the "Father of our Lord Jesus Christ" (3: 14).

iii) "Who hath blessed us with all **spiritual blessings in heavenly places in Christ.**" There is so much here. We should notice:

- **The source of our blessings.** As the "God and Father of our Lord Jesus Christ" He is the Source of all. "**He** hath chosen us ... having predestinated us ... **He** hath made us accepted" (vv.4-6). There is no chance or uncertainty, nothing casual, about this: it is in accordance with the "good pleasure of **His** will (v.5) ... the mystery of **His** will (v.9) ... the counsel of **His** own will (v.11). All has been done by "**His** grace" (vv.6-7). Our personal enjoyment of His blessings upon us began at conversion, but they were conceived in eternity!

- **The scope, or sum, of our blessings.** He has "blessed us with all spiritual blessings" or "every spiritual blessing" (JND). His blessings are immense. He is not a cheese-paring God! He has "**abounded** toward us" (v.8). There are no 'second blessings' here! We have it all in Christ now. They are "spiritual blessings", not temporal blessings, which brings us to:

- **The sphere of our blessings.** They are located "in heavenly places" or "in the heavenlies" (JND). Not 'in Canaan', or 'Immanuel's land!' (Isa. 8: 8).

The epistle begins with the saints "in the heavenlies". This is a characteristic phrase. It is where Christ sits, Chapter 1 verse 20. It is where we sit with Him, Chapter 2 verse 6. It is where the principalities and powers see the wonder of the church, Chapter 3 verse 10. It is where the emissaries of Satan are active, Chapter 6 verse 12. "The heavenlies" is a general term, not referring directly to heaven itself, but to what is heavenly in nature as opposed to what is earthly in nature. The believer's blessings are not therefore connected with the land or the throne of Israel. "In the heavenlies" indicates the character of our blessings.

The word translated 'heavenlies' (*epouranios*) is used in John 3 verse 12: "If I have told you earthly things, and ye believe not, how shall ye believe if I tell you of heavenly things". See also Matthew 18 verse 35, "My heavenly Father...."

- **The security of our blessings.** "Who hath blessed us with all spiritual blessings in heavenly places *in Christ*" (v.3). Everything is secure in Him. God has "chosen us *in Him* (v.4) ... predestinated us unto the adoption of children *by Jesus Christ* to himself" (v.5). We are "accepted *in the Beloved*" (v.6); "*in whom* we have redemption through his blood" (v.7); "*in whom,* also we have obtained an inheritance, being predestinated ..." v.11). Paul refers to the past ("chosen ... predestinated"), to the present ("accepted"), and to the future ("obtained an inheritance"). That is, if we accept that the verb *kleroo* is understood in the middle voice as opposed to the passive voice. If the latter, then it must be rendered, 'in whom also we were made a heritage', RV.

All God's purposes are secured in Christ: not only His purpose for ourselves, but for "all things": "that in the dispensation of the fulness of times he might gather together in one *all things* in Christ, both which are in heaven, and which are on earth" (v.10).

This brings us to:

b) How God has blessed us, vv.4-6

"According as ('even as', RV) he hath **chosen us** in him ... having **predestinated us** unto the adoption of children by Jesus Christ to himself ...to the praise of the glory of his grace, wherein he hath made us **accepted in the beloved.**" The words "according as" refer to the general statement in verse 3.

THE EPISTLE TO THE EPHESIANS

"Chosen in him ... redemption through his blood"

Read Chapter 1: 4-8

As we have already noted, Ephesians 1 may be divided as follows: **(A)** the greetings to the Ephesians (vv.1-2); **(B)** the blessings of the Ephesians (vv.3-14); **(C)** the prayer for the Ephesians (vv.15-23).

A) THE GREETINGS TO THE EPHESIANS, vv.1-2

We noticed references here to **(1)** the writer; **(2)** the readers; **(3)** the place; **(4)** the greeting.

B) THE BLESSINGS OF THE EPHESIANS, vv.3-14

This immense passage describes three wonderful aspects of our blessings: **(1) we are chosen by God** (vv.3-6): **(2) we are redeemed by the Son** (vv.7-12); **(3) we are sealed by the Spirit** (vv.13-14). Put succinctly, Paul refers to the will of God (vv.3-6), to the work of Christ (vv.7-12), and to the witness of the Spirit (vv.13-14).

1) THE WILL OF GOD, vv.3-6

We noticed in these verses **(a)** how Paul blessed God (v.3); **(b)** how God has blessed us (vv.4-6).

a) How Paul blessed God, v.3

"Blessed be the God and Father of *our* Lord Jesus Christ, who hath blessed us with all spiritual blessings in heavenly places in Christ." We dealt with this in our previous study.

b) How God has blessed us, vv.4-6

Paul now outlines three marvellous aspects of the will of God for us: *(i)* He has chosen us in Christ (v.4); *(ii)* He has predestinated us in Christ (v.5); *(iii)* He has accepted us in Christ (v.6).

i) He has chosen us in Christ, v.4

Why raise the subject here? We must remember that the preaching in the area of Ephesus involved Jews and Gentiles: "all they which dwelt in Asia heard the word of the Lord Jesus, both Jews and Greeks" (Acts 19:10). Israel was, of course, the 'elect nation', but now God has, according to His eternal purpose, **another elect people** - "According as he hath chosen us (*eklego*, to 'pick out', 'select', W.E.Vine) in him before the foundation of the world, that we should be holy and without blame before him in love". It was an eternal choice. It was made before the earth and the human race existed. "We dare not diminish what Paul writes here. God chooses believers, and they are chosen before they *have done* anything or *have been* any thing for God. 'It is the infinite Free-Will of God (even more sacred than the free-will of man), a purpose and a plan older than the oceans and the skies' (Moule)" (supplied by Justin Waldron). In the words of F.F.Bruce, "So far as the personal experience of believers is concerned, their entry into the relationship described by the words "in Christ" took place when they were born from above, and was symbolized in baptism; but from God's point of view it has no such temporal limitation. They have been the objects of His eternal choice, and that eternal choice is so bound up with the person of Christ that in the light of divine purpose they are described as being 'in Christ' before the world's foundation".

We should now read the following: "God hath from the beginning chosen you to salvation" (2 Thess. 2: 13); "Who hath saved us, and called us with an holy calling, not according to our works, but according to his own purpose and grace, which was given us in Christ Jesus, before the world began" (2 Tim. 1: 9); "Elect according to the foreknowledge of God the Father ..." (1 Pet. 1: 2); "For whom he did foreknow, he also did predestinate to be conformed to the image of his Son" (Rom. 8: 29). Compare Romans 9 verse 11: "For the children being not yet born, neither having done any good or evil, that the purpose of God according to election might stand, not of works, but of him that calleth" and Romans 11 verses 5-6: "Even so then at this present time also there is a remnant according to the election of grace, And if by grace, then is it no more of works: otherwise grace is no more grace."

As Wm.Hoste (*Bible Problems and Answers,* pp. 29/30) observes. "Generally when man's responsibility and God's electing grace are mentioned on the same page of Scripture, it is the former that comes first. Thus in John 5: 40, the Lord said to the Jews, 'Ye will not come to me that ye might have life' (not, 'ye cannot'), and in the following chapter (v.44) we hear His words, 'No man can come to me, except the Father, which hath sent me, draw him'. See also Acts 13: 46, 'Seeing ye put it (the word of God) from you, and judge yourselves unworthy of everlasting life, lo, we turn to the Gentiles'; and then two verses on, 'As many as were ordained to eternal life believed'. In Acts 18: 8, 'Many of the Corinthians, hearing, believed, and were baptized', and in v.10, referring to people not believers at the time, 'I have much people in this city'".

We should notice:

- **The sphere in which we were chosen**. "According as he hath chosen us in him". Not 'to be in him', but "in him." It has been said that all that Christ is, we are. So, for example, He is the chosen One, and we are chosen in Him. He is the accepted One, and we are accepted in Him (v.6). Hendriksen puts it a little differently in saying, "the basic answer must be that from before the foundation of the world Christ was the Representative and Surety of all those who in time would be gathered into the fold".

- **The time in which we were chosen**. "Before the foundation of the world". Compare John 17 verse 24, "Thou lovest me before the foundation of the world"; 1 Peter 1 verse 20, "Who verily was foreordained before the foundation of the world". Compare (just compare) Revelation 13 verse 8: "And all that dwell on the earth shall do it homage, [every one] whose name had not been written from [the] founding of [the] world in the book of life of the slain Lamb" (JND).

- **The purpose for which we were chosen**. "That we should be holy and without blame before him in love." (Compare Zephaniah 3: 17.) God desired to have people suited for His holy presence and suited to His holy nature. Compare, for example, Ephesians 2 verse 10 and 2 Peter 1 verse 10. The words at the end of verse 4 and the beginning of verse 5 are sometimes rendered: "that we should be holy and without blame before him. In love having predestinated us ..." Election has in view sanctification. Compare, again, Ephesians 2 verse 10, "For we are his workmanship, created in Christ Jesus unto good works, which God hath before ordained that we should walk in them". The doctrine of election is never taught in a vacuum. In the words of F.F.Bruce, "In the presence of such a mystery we do well to be humble, acknowledging the limits of our understanding and paying heed to the solemn practical purpose of God's electing grace".

It should be said that men and women are not elected because God saw that they would be holy. Election is not conditional on man's foreseen merits, or even on his foreseen faith.

ii) He has predestinated us in Christ, v.5

"(In love) having predestinated us unto the adoption of children by Jesus Christ to himself, according to the good pleasure of his will." This brings before us the subject of **predestination.**

Election concerns individual people, and concerns the past counsels of God. **Predestination** concerns the status and place of those people: it points to the status of those chosen, the elect. Hence 'unto sonship'. See also verse 11. The word is used only of saved people: unsaved are not said to be predestinated to judgment. It is connected, not with the past, as election, but with the future, and concerns the position marked out for believers. It determines the special character of that eternal blessing belonging to the elect. That is, **sonship.** Compare Romans 8 verses 29-30, "For whom he did foreknow, he also did **predestinate to be conformed to the image of his Son**, that he might be the firstborn among many brethren". See 1 Corinthians 2 verse 7, "But we speak the wisdom of God in a mystery, even the hidden wisdom, which God ordained (predestinated - predetermined) before the world unto our glory".

The words, "unto the adoption of children by Jesus Christ to himself", refer to our placement as sons. See Romans 8 verse 15, "For ye have not received the spirit of bondage again to fear; but ye have received the Spirit of adoption". See also Romans 8 verse 23, "Waiting for the adoption, to wit, the redemption of the body". See also Galatians 4 verse 5.

W.W.Wiersbe *(Ephesians - Be Rich)* explains 'adoption' lucidly: "'Adoption' has a dual meaning, both present and future. You do not get into God's family by adoption. You get into His family by regeneration, the new birth (John 3: 1-18; 1 Peter 1: 22-25). Adoption is the act of God by which He gives His 'born ones' an adult standing in the family".

Adoption is therefore connected with sonship, and therefore with privilege, standing, character and destiny. Mephibosheth was given a position "as one of the king's sons" (2 Sam. 9: 11). Sonship is more than a relationship. It carries the idea of the privilege and responsibility of full-grown sons. It involves dignity and deportment.

In the Old Testament, Israel was "My son" corporately. See Romans 9 verse 4, "Who are Israelites, to whom pertaineth the adoption".

All this is "according to the good pleasure of his will". Compare verse 9, "according to his good pleasure". We have to leave it there: human reasoning must give place to "the good pleasure of his will". Compare Luke 2 verse 14, "Glory to God in the highest, and on earth peace, good will toward men" or "good pleasure in men". But God did not find 'pleasure' in men. He found it in His Son! "My beloved Son, in whom I am well pleased". And, wonder of wonders, in us as well. Fully so, in time to come.

iii) He has accepted us in Christ, v.6

If in verse 5, we have "his will", now, in verse 6, we have "his grace". All that we have considered in verses 4-5 is "To the praise of the glory of his grace, wherein he hath made us accepted in the Beloved". The word "accepted" *(charitoo)* means 'taken into favour' and occurs as "highly favoured" in Luke 1 verse 28. "Grace" is the basis of verses 4-5. In "grace" we have been 'highly favoured' ("accepted", AV). We have been 'begraced', not because of anything in us, not because He found us acceptable, not even because He foresaw that we would believe the gospel. This grace must be found exclusively in His gracious character. Note the beautiful term to describe the Lord Jesus: "in the **Beloved**". See, for example, "This is my beloved Son, in whom I am well pleased" (Matt. 3: 17). "Beloved" here (v.6) is a noun. The Lord Jesus is "the Son of his love" (Col. 1: 13, JND). The Lord Jesus said, "Thou lovest me before the foundation of the world" (John 17: 24).

> *So near, so very near to God,*
> *Nearer I cannot be,*
> *For in the Person of His Son*
> *I am as near as He.*

> *So dear, so very dear to God,*
> *Dearer I cannot be,*
> *The love wherewith He loves the Son,*
> *Such is His love for me.*

The section ends with praise: "To the praise of the glory of his grace". Justin Waldron calls this "a holy gasp from the apostle at the wonders of such grace". The next two sections (vv.7-12) also end with praise (vv.13-14).

2) THE WORK OF CHRIST, vv.7-12

God has "predestinated us unto the adoption of children by Jesus Christ to himself, according to the good pleasure of his will, to the praise of the glory of his grace, wherein he hath made us accepted in the beloved ('Beloved', JND): **in whom we have redemption through his blood** ..." (vv.5-7). As W.W.Wiersbe observes, "We should not think that each Person of the Godhead works independently, because they all worked together to make possible our salvation".

This section explains how the calling described in verses 4-6 has already become effective and will be perfectly completed in the future. The will of God for us could not be realised apart from the work of Christ. We could not be 'highly favoured' ("accepted", AV) unless Christ had first dealt with our sin.

In these verses, our attention moves from heaven to earth and from eternity to time. We should note the following: *(a)* the Person (v.7); *(b)* the people (v.7); *(c)* the price (v.7); *(d)* the pardon (v.7) *(e)* the provision (vv.7-8); *(f)* the prospect (vv.9-10); *(g)* the present position (vv.11-12).

a) The Person, v.7

"**In whom** we have redemption through his blood, the forgiveness of sins, according to the riches of his grace." The expression, "In whom", is repeated in verses 11 and 13, reminding us that "all the promises of God in him are yea, and in him, Amen" (2 Cor. 1: 20) or "For whatever promises of God [there are], in him is the yea, and in him the amen ..." (JND). Everything prefaced by "In whom", must be perfectly and eternally secure.

b) The people, v.7

"In whom **we** have redemption through his blood, the forgiveness of sins, according to the riches of his grace." We were slaves: now we are sons. What an amazing combination: "In whom" and "we have ..."

c) The price, v.7

"In whom we have **redemption** (*apolutrosis*: paying the ransom price) through his blood, the forgiveness of sins ..." In the words of F.F.Bruce, "This redemption is something that He has procured on our behalf; the word implies that our former existence was one of slavery from which we needed to be ransomed. The ransom-price is expressly mentioned ... it was a price of immeasurable costliness, nothing less than the blood of Christ (cf. Rom. 3: 24 f. ; 1 Pet. 1: 18 f.)". W.W. Wiersbe reminds us that "To redeem means 'to purchase and to set free by paying a price'". He continues, "There were six million slaves in the Roman Empire, and often they were bought and sold like pieces of furniture. But a man could purchase a slave, and set him free, and this is what the Lord Jesus did for us".

d) The pardon, v.7

"In whom **we** have redemption through his blood, **the forgiveness of sins**, according to the riches of his grace." This has been called 'the accompaniment of redemption'.

The word rendered "forgiveness" (*aphesis*) "denotes a dismissal, release" (W.E.Vine). The word reminds us of procedure on the Day of Atonement, when "the high priest sent the scapegoat into the wilderness ... Christ died to carry away our sins so that they might never again be seen (John 1: 29; Psalm 103:12). No written accusation stands against us because our sins have been taken away!" (W.W. Wiersbe).

The word rendered "sins" (*paraptoma*), meaning 'trespasses', denoting, literally, 'a fall beside', and refers to "a deviation from uprightness and truth" (W.E.Vine).

e) The provision, vv.7-8

"In whom we have redemption through his blood, the forgiveness of sins, according to the ***riches of his grace; wherein he hath abounded toward us in all wisdom and prudence.***" The abundance of God's provision for us in this way is stressed: it is

- **Not** "according to his grace"

- **But** "according to the ***riches*** of his grace" (v.7). Such abundance! For "riches", see also Chapter 1 verse 18; Chapter 2 verses 4 and 7 and Chapter 3 verses 8 and 16. This is a very 'rich' epistle! Notice too that it is not '***out*** of the riches of his grace', but "***according*** to the riches of his grace". Compare Philippians 4 verse 19. The grace of God certainly provides the forgiveness of sins, but, let it be said, it provides so much more as well!

Paul therefore draws our attention to the ***dimensions*** of divine grace: "Wherein he hath ***abounded*** toward us in ***all wisdom and prudence***" (v.8). M.R.Vincent calls this "the wisdom and prudence with which He abundantly endows His followers". His grace - 'abounding' grace – not only bestows "redemption" and the "forgiveness of sins", but "spiritual wisdom (*sophia*) and discernment (*phronesis*) are imparted as well, so that we may grasp something of the divine purpose of the ages and of the place which we occupy therein " (F.F.Bruce). Hence, having said "wherein (in the riches of his grace) he hath abounded to toward us in all wisdom and prudence" (v.8), Paul continues: "having made known unto us (or 'in that he made known to us') the mystery of his will (defined in v.10), according to his good pleasure which he purposed in himself" (v.9).

For "wisdom and prudence" see Proverbs 8 verse 12. The Lord gave Bezaleel and Aholiab "wisdom and understanding" (Exod. 36: 1). Compare Colossians 1 verse 9.

So, in grace we have ***redemption,*** but in that same grace God gives us enlightenment in connection with His plan and purpose which will be consummated "in the dispensation of the fullness of times" (v.10). So in grace, we have both ***redemption*** and ***revelation.*** This leads to:

f) The prospect, vv.9-10

"Having made known unto us the mystery of his will, according to his good pleasure which he hath purposed in himself: that in the dispensation of the fulness of times he might gather together in one all things in Christ, both which are in heaven, and which are in earth; even in him."

THE EPISTLE TO THE EPHESIANS

"In whom we have received an inheritance"

Read Chapter 1: vv.9-14

As we have already noted in previous studies, Ephesians 1 may be divided as follows: *(A)* the greetings to the Ephesians (vv.1-2); *(B)* the blessings of the Ephesians (vv.3-14); *(C)* the prayer for the Ephesians (vv.15-23).

A) THE GREETINGS TO THE EPHESIANS, vv.1-2

In this connection, we noticed *(1)* the writer; *(2)* the readers; *(3)* the place; *(4)* the greeting.

B) THE BLESSINGS OF THE EPHESIANS, vv.3-14

This immense passage describes three wonderful aspects of our blessings: *(1) we are chosen by God* (vv.3-6): *(2) we are redeemed by the Son* (vv.7-12); *(3) we are sealed by the Spirit* (vv.13-14). Put succinctly, Paul refers to the will of God (vv.3-6), to the work of Christ (vv.7-12), and to the witness of the Spirit (vv.13-14).

1) THE WILL OF GOD, vv.3-6

Having observed how Paul blessed God (v.3), we continued by noticing how God has so wonderfully blessed us (vv.4-6): *(a)* He has chosen us in Christ (v.4); *(b)* He has predestinated us in Christ (v.5); *(c)* He has accepted us in Christ (v.6).

a) He has chosen us in Christ, v.4

"According as he hath chosen us (*eklego,* to 'pick out', 'select', W.E.Vine) in him before the foundation of the world, that we should be holy and without blame before him in love." Election has in view sanctification. The doctrine of election is never taught in a vacuum. In the words of F.F.Bruce, "In the presence of such a mystery we do well to be humble, acknowledging the limits of our understanding and paying heed to the solemn practical purpose of God's electing grace".

b) *He has predestinated us in Christ, v.5*

"(In love) having predestinated us unto the adoption of children by Jesus Christ **to himself** (we are "children of **God**", Rom. 8: 16-17), according to the good pleasure of his will." **Election** concerns individual people, and involves the past counsels of God. **Predestination** concerns the status and place of those people: hence 'unto sonship' ("the adoption of children", AV). God's purpose ("having predestinated us ...") is His pleasure ("according the good pleasure of his will").

c) *He has accepted us in Christ, v.6*

All that we considered in verses 4-5 is "To the praise of the glory of his grace, wherein he hath made us accepted in the Beloved". The word "accepted" *(charitoo)* means 'taken into favour' and occurs as "highly favoured" in Luke 1 verse 28. We noted the beautiful term to describe the Lord Jesus: "in the **Beloved**". The Lord Jesus is "the Son of his love" (Col. 1: 13, JND).

2) *THE WORK OF CHRIST, vv.7-12*

This section describes how the calling described in verses 4-6 has already become effective and will be perfectly completed in the future. The will of God for us could not be realised apart from the work of Christ. We could not be 'highly favoured' ("accepted", AV) unless Christ had first dealt with our sin.

We noted that in these verses, our attention moves from heaven to earth and from eternity to time, and suggested the following: *(a)* the Person (v.7); *(b)* the people (v.7); *(c)* the price (v.7); *(d)* the pardon (v.7) *(e)* the provision (vv.7-8); *(f)* the prospect (vv.9-10); *(g)* the present position (vv.11-12).

a) The Person, v.7

"***In whom*** we have redemption through his blood, the forgiveness of sins, according to the riches of his grace."

b) The people, v.7

"In whom ***we*** have redemption through his blood, the forgiveness of sins, according to the riches of his grace." It has been nicely said that the words, "the glory of his grace" (v.6) have our sonship in view, whereas "the riches of his grace" have our sinnership in view.

c) The price, v.7

"In whom we have ***redemption*** (*apolutrosis*: paying the ransom price) through his blood, the forgiveness of sins..." See Addenda (1)

d) The pardon, v.7

"In whom we have redemption through his blood, ***the forgiveness of sins***, according to the riches of his grace."

e) The provision, vv.7-8

"In whom we have redemption through his blood, the forgiveness of sins, according to the ***riches of his grace; wherein he hath abounded toward us in all wisdom and prudence.***" God has not only forgiven our trespasses ("sins", AV), He has made us His confidantes. Compare Genesis 18 verse 17, "Shall I hide from Abraham that thing which I do ..." This leads to:

f) The prospect, vv.9-10

"Having made known unto us the mystery of his will, according to his good pleasure which he hath purposed in himself: that in ***the dispensation of the fulness of times he might gather together in one all things in Christ,*** both which are in heaven, and which are in earth; even in him."

God purposes that everything, in heaven and in earth, will then be subject to Christ as absolute Head of all creation, whether heaven or earth. F.F.Bruce puts it as follows: "Everything in heaven and earth will then be summed up in Christ; the verb used is *anakephalaioo* (to 'head up', 'sum up' or 'recapitulate'), which here implies 'the entire harmony of the universe, which shall no long contain alien and discordant elements, but of which all the parts shall find their centre and bond of union in Christ'" (J.B.Lightfoot). See Colossians 1 verse 20.

The meaning of the word "mystery" (v.9) is clearly apparent from its next occurrence (where it is used in a different connection – the church): "by revelation he made known to me the mystery ... which in other ages **was not made known** unto the sons of men, **as it is now revealed** unto his holy apostles and prophets by the Spirit; that the Gentiles should be fellow-heirs, and of the same body, and partakers of his promise in Christ by the gospel" (Eph. 3: 3-6). The "mystery" here (Eph.1: 9) is that "all things" will 'headed up' in Christ – not only "all things" on earth (that had been revealed in the Old Testament) but "all things" *in the heavenly realm as well.*

The words, "the dispensation of the fulness of times" do not have the same meaning as Galatians 4 verse 4. They refer, rather, to the future administration ('dispensation', AV) of the last phase in human history. That is, the Millennium. It will be the fulness (the complement: the full extent/number) of the ages. In the words of Albert Leckie *(What the Bible Teaches - Ephesians),* "The primary thought in 'dispensation' (the idea of 'dispensing') is not a period of time, but rather administration, or how matters are dispensed ... Paul is therefore writing of the coming millennial age, and we learn that God's purpose then is to gather together in one all things in Christ ... All things therefore in heaven and earth will converge on Christ, become subject to Him, and take character from Him". It has been said that all other 'stewardships' (Adam, Noah, Zedekiah, etc) have ended in failure. But *not* this stewardship!

But why mention this here? This brings us to:

g) The present position, vv.11-12

These verses may be summarised as follows: *(i)* the purpose of our predestination (v.11); *(ii)* the power in our predestination (v.11); *(iii)* the praise arising from our predestination (v.12).

i) The purpose of our predestination, v.11

"In him, in whom also we **have obtained an inheritance** (JND concurs) being predestinated according to the purpose of him who worketh all things after the counsel of his own will" (v.11). See Psalm 33 verse 11, "The counsel of the LORD standeth for ever: the thoughts of his heart to all generations". This refers to the fact that having been predestinated to sonship, as sons, we have an inheritance: **we are made heirs**. We will receive the inheritance when all things are brought together in Christ. **When He receives His inheritance** (Heb. 1: 2) as "heir of all things", **we will receive ours** as "heirs of God and joint heirs with Christ". We will not receive it apart from Him! He will not receive it apart from us! Hence, "**In whom** we have obtained an inheritance". Once we were slaves, but **now** we are sons! Once we were poor, but **now** we are rich!

It has been said that since an inheritance is to be enjoyed, how then can this be accomplished in our case now? The suggested answer lies in Acts 20 verse 32: "And now, brethren, I commend you to God, and to the word of his grace, which is able to build you up, and to give you an inheritance among all them that are sanctified". The Word of God (called here "the word of his grace") both builds us up (*oikodomeo*, to build a house) and enables us to enjoy all the blessings that belong to the children of God *now*, as well as in the future.

It should be said at this juncture, that some scholarly and conservative expositors, including F.F.Bruce and W.E.Vine, lean towards the rendering, "In whom also we have obtained an inheritance (or 'made a heritage')" (RV). See Addenda (2)

ii) The power in our predestination, v.11

"Being predestinated according to the purpose of him who **worketh all things** after the counsel of his own will." In the words of F.F.Bruce, "Whatever God has purposed is sure of fulfillment; He is described here as the One 'who worketh all things after the counsel of his will'. That is to say, when once His will has decreed that something shall be so, His wisdom, power and love combine to overrule the course of events so that all things are made to work together for the accomplishment of what He has planned". We should note the present tense here: "who **worketh** all things after the counsel of his will".

iii) The praise arising from our predestination, v.12

"That we (Jewish believers) should be to the praise of his glory, who first trusted (*proelpizo'*, meaning 'hoped before', RV) in Christ ..." (v.12). Albert Leckie,

Ephesians

helpfully, understands this to mean that "Whereas restored Israel in a coming age will be blessed as they become subject to the reign of Christ in His manifested glory, believing Jews of this day of grace will share with Christ in that glory (Col. 3: 4), and will become the theme of praise by adoring hosts". Paul goes on to say the believing Gentiles also have the same glorious prospect (vv.13-14).

F.F.Bruce writes clearly and helpfully on the subject: "the words 'ye also' in verse 13, with their evident allusion to Gentile Christians, indicate clearly enough that 'we' in verses 11 and 12 are Jewish Christians. They represent the people of God, the believing remnant of Israel, **whose hope was fixed on the Messiah before He came**, and who accepted Him when He appeared, either immediately (like the original disciples) or after an interval (like Paul himself). The gospel order, 'to the Jew first, and also to the Greek' (Rom. 1: 16; cf. 2: 9 f.) is illustrated historically by the fact that for the first few years after the death and resurrection of Christ, the message of life through faith in Him was proclaimed 'to none save unto the Jews' (Acts 11:19); its direct presentation to Gentiles marks the second stage in its progress".

So the second section (vv.7-12) in this part of the chapter (vv.4-14) concludes with praise.

This brings us to:

3) THE WITNESS OF THE SPIRIT, vv.13-14

Before we address the teaching in these verses, we should notice the changing pronouns: "In whom **we** also have obtained an inheritance ... that **we** should be to the praise of his glory, who first trusted in Christ. In whom **ye** also trusted, after that **ye** heard the word of truth, the gospel of **your** salvation: in whom also after that **ye** believed (*pistuo*, meaning 'reliance upon') **ye** were sealed with that Holy Spirit of promise, which is the earnest of **our** inheritance until the redemption of the purchased possession, unto the praise of his glory" (vv.11-14). Paul is evidently referring to **"we"** Jews in verses 11 and 12 and **"ye"** Gentiles in verse 13. In verse 14, it is "**our** inheritance", that is, Jew and Gentile together. This is developed in Chapter 2.

Having said, of Jewish believers, "In whom also **we** have obtained an inheritance" (v.11), Paul completes the picture in saying "In whom ye also (omit *trusted*, and insert - to give the sense - *were made a heritage*), after that ye heard the word of truth, the gospel of your salvation...." (v.13).

As F.F.Bruce points out, "Paul points out the distinction between Jewish believers ('we') and Gentiles believers ('ye also') in order to bring out more fully the central emphasis of this epistle – that Gentile believers have been incorporated along with Jewish believers as members of the body of Christ and sharers of the heritage of God".

We must emphasise the important *order* here: "In whom (again, it is in Christ) ye also trusted, after that ye heard the word of truth, the gospel of your salvation: in whom also after that ye believed, ye were sealed with that Holy Spirit of promise" (v.13). So it was "after that ye heard" ('having heard', JND) and "after that ye believed" ('having believed', JND), that "ye were sealed with that Holy Spirit of promise" (v.13).

These verses therefore emphasise three things: *(a)* what they heard: "***ye heard***" (v.13); *(b)* what they did: "***ye believed***" (v.13); *(c)* what they became: "***ye were sealed***" (v.13-14).

a) What they heard, v.13

"Ye heard the word of truth, the gospel of your salvation." Each word will bear close examination; each word counts:

- "Ye heard the **word** of truth." Paul uses the word *logos* here. Compare "the **word** (*logos*) of reconciliation" (2 Cor. 5: 19); "the **word** (*logos*) which God sent unto the children of Israel. Preaching peace by Jesus Christ (he is Lord of all): that word (*rhema*), I say, ye know, which was published throughout all Judaea ..." (Acts 10: 36-37).

The Greek word *logos* indicates what is true and trustworthy, as opposed to *mythos* which indicates what is fictional and spurious. The word *logos* therefore indicates the quality of truth, whereas *rhema* refers to the spoken word. The word *logos* therefore emphasises that the gospel involves preaching truth, not playing on people's feelings or emotions. We have a marvellous example of *mythos* in Acts 19 verse 35. Just listen to the "townclerk": "Ye men of Ephesus, what man is there that knoweth not how that the city of the Ephesians is a worshipper of the great goddess Diana, and of the image which fell down from Jupiter?"

- "The **gospel** of your salvation." The "word of truth" is good news: it conveys the message of salvation. The word "gospel" (*euangelion*) itself signifies good news. There cannot be better news than that of salvation!

b) What they did, v.13

"In whom also after that ye **believed**." While, as F.F.Bruce points out, "The phrase 'in whom' does not so much imply that Christ was the one in whom they believed (that was true, of course), as that He was the One in whom they were sealed with the Spirit", nevertheless the gospel became 'the gospel of their salvation' through their faith in the Lord Jesus. We must remember that: "Faith cometh by hearing, and hearing by the word (*rhema*) of God" (Rom. 10: 17).

c) What they became, vv.13-14

They became God's possession. "Ye were sealed with that Holy Spirit of promise, which is the earnest of our inheritance until the redemption of the purchased possession, unto the praise of his glory." There is so much to consider here.

- "Ye were **sealed** with that Holy Spirit of promise." The word "sealed" indicates ownership. See, for example, 2 Timothy 2 verse 19: "the foundation of God standeth sure, having this **seal,** The Lord knoweth them that are his ..."; 2 Corinthians 1 verses 21-22: "Now he which stablisheth us with you in Christ, and hath anointed us, is God; who hath also **sealed** us, and given the earnest of the Spirit in our hearts"; Ephesians 4 verse 30: "And grieve not the holy Spirit of God, whereby ye are **sealed** unto the day of redemption". F.F.Bruce explains that "An owner seals his property with his signet to mark it as his; if at a later date he comes to claim it and his right to it is questioned, his seal is sufficient evidence, and puts an end to such questioning".

In an address many years ago at Cheshunt, Mr. Ray Dawes pointed out that the Customs and Excise authorities at London Airport, having retrieved and packaged contraband, seal it to indicate that it was now the property of the Crown.

- "Ye were sealed with that **Holy Spirit of promise.**" The context suggests, not so much 'the promised Holy Spirit', but the Holy Spirit whose presence guarantees the fulfilment of the promise. He is the Guarantee of these blessings.

- "Ye were sealed with that Holy Spirit of promise, which is **the earnest of our inheritance** ..." It has been pointed out that the Greek word here (*arrhabon*) "is derived from a Semitic root represented in the Hebrew Bible by the term rendered 'pledge' three times in Genesis 38: 17-20. There Judah gave his daughter-in-law Tamar certain articles of his personal property as a pledge until he could redeem his promise to present her with 'a kid of the goats'. The word is used in modern Greek for an engagement ring, a fact that speaks for itself" (F.F.Bruce). Compare "*our* inheritance" (all believers) with the words "in whom also *we* (we Jews) have obtained an inheritance … In whom *ye* (ye Gentiles) also … (vv.11,13).

- "Ye were sealed with that Holy Spirit of promise, which is the earnest of our inheritance **until (unto) the redemption of the purchased possession**, unto the praise of his glory." "Believers are God's redeemed possession already, but the consummation of His redeeming work remains to be experienced by us. We 'have the firstfruits of the Spirit', but the harvest still lies in the future; meanwhile we are 'waiting for the adoption, to wit, the redemption of our body' (Rom. 8: 23)" (F.F.Bruce).

In view of the Lord's words in Matthew 13 verse 44 ("Again the kingdom of heaven is like unto treasure hid in a field; the which when a man hath found, he hideth, and for joy thereof goeth and selleth all that he hath, and buyeth that field"), it is often said said that "the redemption of the purchased possession" refers "to what Christ has acquired for himself, meaning the world ('the field is the world', Matt.13: 38)", but while, of course, the Lord Jesus has every right to acquire the world for Himself – and will do so – this hardly fits the context of our current passage.

The third section ends with praise: all this will be "Unto the praise of his glory" (v.14). As W.W.Wiersbe observes, "Did you notice that after each of the main sections in verses 4-14, Paul has added the purpose behind these gifts? Why has God the Father chosen us, adopted us, and accepted us? It is "to the praise of the glory of his grace" (v.6). Why has the Son redeemed us, forgiven us, revealed God's will to us, and made us part of God's inheritance? It is "that we should be to the praise of his glory" (v.12). Why has God the Spirit sealed us and become the Guarantee of our future blessing? It is "unto the praise of his glory" (v.14)".

ADDENDA

1) *"In whom we have redemption though his blood", v.7*

The Jewish background is evident here. See 1 Peter 1 verses 18-19: "Forasmuch as ye know that ye were not redeemed with corruptible things, as silver and gold, from *your vain conversation received by tradition from your fathers*, but with the precious blood of Christ ..." But *now* "we" (we Christians – both Jews and Gentiles) have *redemption through his blood* ..."

It has been nicely said that the man who would not redeem would have his shoe loosed (Deut. 25: 7-9 c/f Ruth 4: 7-8), but John the Baptist would not unloose the Saviour's shoe (Luke 3:16) because He had come to redeem! (Yes, there *is* another reason!).

2) "In whom also we have obtained an inheritance", v.11

The differing renderings of verse 11 arise from the fact that the AV translators understood the wording to be in the Middle Voice ("In whom also we have obtained an inheritance") whereas the RV translators understood the wording to be in the Passive Voice ("In whom also we were made a heritage"). In this connection F.F.Bruce observes, "Both statements are true, but the apostle is thinking here of 'God's own possession' (v.14, RV), 'his inheritance in the saints' (v.18). So, in Old Testament days, it was revealed that 'the Lord's portion is his people; Jacob is the lot of his inheritance' (Deut. 32: 9)".

Others, including Albert Leckie, following the AV rendering, suggest that the saints are predestinated to the position of sons (v.5), and predestinated to receive and enjoy an inheritance (v.11). "Sonship and heirship are linked together: we are heirs because we are sons ... Furthermore, believers have the seal of the Holy Spirit of promise and this is the earnest of their inheritance (vv.13-14)".

However, it must be said that F.F.Bruce's understanding of the words that "we should be to the praise of his glory who first trusted in Christ" (v.12) is particularly attractive. While agreeing that Paul has in mind believers of Jewish origin, he remarks that "if in verse 6, the foreordination of believers to adoption as sons tends 'to the praise of the glory of his grace'; so here their foreordination to be His special heritage means that the 'praise of his glory' will shine forth in them: that is to say, the glory of God unveiled in His people is to draw forth the admiring praise of the universe (cf. Eph. 3: 10)".

THE EPISTLE TO THE EPHESIANS

"Making mention of you in my prayers"

Read Chapter 1: 15-23

As we have noted in all our previous studies, this chapter may be divided into three sections: *(A)* the greetings to the Ephesians (vv.1-2); *(B)* the blessings of the Ephesians (vv.3-14); *(C)* the prayer for the Ephesians (vv.15-23).

A) THE GREETINGS TO THE EPHESIANS, vv.1-2

We noticed the references here to *(1) the writer*: "Paul, an apostle of Jesus Christ"; *(2) the readers*: "the saints ... and ... the faithful in Christ Jesus; *(3) the place*: "to the saints ... at Ephesus"; *(4) the greeting*: "Grace be to you, and peace ..."

B) THE BLESSINGS OF THE EPHESIANS, vv.3-14

This immense passage describes three wonderful aspects of our blessings: *(1) we are chosen by God* (vv.3-6): *(2) we are redeemed by the Son* (vv.7-12); *(3) we are sealed by the Spirit* (vv.13-14). As we have said, put succinctly, Paul refers to the will of God (vv.3-6), to the work of Christ (vv.7-12), and to the witness of the Spirit (vv.13-14). This brings us to:

C) THE PRAYER FOR THE EPHESIANS, vv.15-23

This is the first of Paul's two recorded prayers for the believers at Ephesus. He prays for the enlightenment of their understanding of God's provision for them: "the eyes of your understanding being enlightened (v.18). In his second prayer (3: 13-21), he prays for the enrichment of their appreciation of Christ's love for them: "to know the love of Christ which passeth knowledge" (3: 19).

The current passage may be divided as follows: *(1)* the background to his prayer (v.15); *(2)* the regularity in his prayer (v.16); *(3)* the titles in his prayer (v.17a); *(4)* the content of his prayer (vv.17b-23).

1) THE BACKGROUND TO HIS PRAYER, v.15

"Wherefore I also, after I heard of your faith in the Lord Jesus, and love unto all the saints, cease not to give thanks for you, making mention of you in my prayers." "Paul shows us here that preachers must do more than preach to their audience – they must also **pray** for them" (supplied by Justin Waldron). It is thought that this epistle was written some four years after Paul's ministry at Ephesus. He acted on information received. "Their faith told Paul that they were honouring the Head, and their love told him that they were functioning in the Body" (A.G.Muir, *The Believer's Magazine, 1972*). We are told that the words "faith" and "love" are used here, not in the aorist voice (something accomplished in the past and complete), but in the continuous tense. Our "faith in the Lord Jesus" ought to be demonstrated, amongst other things, in "love unto all the saints". See 2 Thessalonians 1 verse 3. Compare Hebrews 6 verse 9-10. Compare Colossians 1 verse 4. Note the connection between "faith" and "love" in Galatians 5 verse 6.

- *"Your faith in Christ Jesus."* This is where faith rests. Paul calls this "the obedience of faith" (Rom. 1: 5, AV margin; 16: 26). See also Romans 6 verse 17.

- *"Your…love unto all the saints."* So it is "faith in the **Lord Jesus**, and love *(phileo)* unto all **the saints**". Paul uses the word *phileo* here because he is speaking about brotherly relationships – mutual relationships. He uses the word *agape* when speaking of love in its intrinsic character. It has been said that 'the magnet that draws sinners to God, also draws them together'.

These excellent qualities in the believers at Ephesus engendered prayer for further spiritual growth. The reverse happened at Corinth. Conditions there made correction necessary. Progress is only possible when conditions are right. Paul's prayers convey the need for progress, however excellent the existing conditions. See, for example, Philippians 1 verses 3-11 ("I thank my God upon every remembrance of you … And this I pray, that your love may abound yet more and more in knowledge and in all judgment"); Colossians 1 verses 3-4 ("We give thanks to God … since we heard of your faith in Christ Jesus, and of the love which ye have to all the saints … we do not cease to pray for you, and to desire that ye might be filled with the knowledge of his will"). Similarly in our current passage. A stationary believer is not contemplated! Now read 1 Thessalonians 4 verses 9-10.

As we shall have already noted and will see further, Paul not only taught the saints (as in 1: 3-14), but prayed that his teaching might be understood and effective in their lives (1: 17-23). How often do **we** (we preachers) pray in such terms for God's people?

2) THE REGULARITY OF HIS PRAYER, v.16

"*I ... cease not to give thanks for you, making mention of you in my prayers*". Compare Chapter 5 verses 4 and 20. The words, "cease not ... making mention" convey Paul's prayerful remembrance of them. See Romans 1 verse 9 ("God is my witness ... that without ceasing I make mention of you always in my prayers"); 1 Thessalonians 1 verse 2 ("We give thanks to God always for you all, making mention of you in our prayers; remembering without ceasing your work of faith ..."); Philemon verse 4 ("I thank my God, making mention of you always in my prayers"). As F.F.Bruce observes, "What an intercessor he must have been!"

Information should lead to intercession. See, for example, Nehemiah 1 verses 1-4. The regularity of Paul's prayers ("cease not") is all the more remarkable bearing in mind his imprisonment. He might well have concentrated on himself! The late Mr. G.B.Fyfe, of happy memory, was heard to say that although, because of his blindness, he was unable to continue reading and preaching, he now had more time to pray.

Paul's prayer here, and elsewhere, includes praise in prayer and petition in prayer.

- **Praise**. "I ... cease not to **give thanks** for you." Paul evidently practised his own ministry: "Continue in prayer, and watch in the same with **thanksgiving**" (Col. 4: 2). We should notice that he begins with thanksgiving: we are often all too quick to begin with our petitions! This recalls the familiar words of advice which Paul gave to the believers at Philippi: "In nothing be anxious, but in everything by prayer and supplication with **thanksgiving** let your requests be made known unto God" (Phil. 4: 6 RV).

- **Petition**: "making mention of you in my **prayers**". See, again, Colossians 4 verse 2; Philippians 4 verse 6. As we shall see, Paul prayed, not so much for progress in knowing and understanding "things or "facts", but rather for progress in "the personal knowledge of God" (F.F.Bruce). Hence he prays that "the God of our Lord Jesus Christ, the Father of glory, may give unto you the spirit of wisdom and revelation *in the knowledge of him"* (v.17).

Are *we* consistent and regular in our thanksgiving and prayers, even in adverse circumstances? This brings us to:

3) THE TITLES IN HIS PRAYER, v.17a

"That the God of our Lord Jesus Christ, the Father of glory, may give unto you the spirit of wisdom and revelation in the knowledge of him: the eyes of your understanding being enlightened…" It has been nicely said that as God, He undertakes, and that as Father, He understands.

In the Old Testament, prayer was addressed to the 'God of Abraham' (see, for example, Gen. 24: 12, 42; 1 Kings 18: 36) and the 'God of Israel' (see, for example, Psalm 59: 5; 69: 6). God was addressed in national terms. While He is still the "God of Israel", *we* pray to Him as "the *God* of *our* Lord Jesus Christ" and as "the *Father* of *our* Lord Jesus Christ" (3: 14). The reason for the change is given in Ephesians 2 verses 11-22.

- He is *"the God of our Lord Jesus Christ".* "The expression, 'the God of our Lord Jesus Christ', refers to our Lord in His humanity, as worshipping and being obedient to God the Father" (Kenneth S. Wuest, *Word Studies in Ephesians and Colossians*). Albert Leckie (*What the Bible Teaches – Ephesians*) concurs: "The 'God of our Lord Jesus Christ' is God in relation to Christ as a man: Psalm 22 verse 10, from His birth ('thou art my God from my mother's belly'); Psalm 22 verse 1, in the darkness of Golgotha ('My God, my God, why hast thou forsaken me'); John 20 verse 17, as a man risen from the dead ('I ascend unto my Father, and your Father; and to my God, and your God'); Hebrews 1 verse 9, as an exalted man in heaven ('Thou hast loved righteousness, and hated iniquity; therefore God, even thy God, anointed thee with the oil of gladness above thy fellows')".

But why does Paul state that He is "the God of our Lord Jesus Christ" here? He does so to emphasise that the same God whose mighty power raised Christ from the dead and elevated Him, as man, to heaven (vv.19-20) is wonderfully able to bless His people. See verses 19-23.

- He is "the Father of glory". Kenneth Wuest suggests that "He is 'the Father of (the) glory' in the sense that He is the Father to whom glory belongs", and that is certainly true in Chapter 1 verse 6 ("having predestinated us ... the praise of the glory of his grace"); Chapter 1 verse 12 ("that we should be to the praise of his glory"); Chapter 1 verse 14 ("unto the praise of his glory"); Chapter 1 verse 10 ("the riches of the glory of his inheritance in the saints"). It is equally true to say (as preachers normally do) that He is 'the source of all glory'. See, for example, Romans 6 verse 4; Colossians 1 verse 11. As the "Father of glory", He "glorified his Son, Jesus ..." (Acts 3: 13), whom He "raised ... up from the dead, and gave him glory" (1 Pet. 1: 21). He has planned glory for us: see, for example, Romans 8 verse 30; Hebrews 2 verse 10. W.K.Morrison puts it nicely in saying, as the "Father of glory He is not only the Creator and Originator of glory, but that glory is His essential attribute".

Preachers love to say (and why not?!) that God is "the Father of glory", that the Lord Jesus is "the Lord of glory" (1 Cor. 2: 8), and that the Holy Spirit is "the Spirit of glory" (1 Pet. 4: 14).

4) THE CONTENT OF HIS PRAYER, v.17b-23

We should notice here that Paul prays *(A)* for their general spiritual development (vv.17b-18), and *(B)* for their grasp of specific truth (vv.18b-23).

A) His prayer for them generally, v.17b-18a

Paul prays that God "may give unto you the spirit of wisdom and revelation in the knowledge of him; the eyes of your understanding being enlightened ..." In the first place, he refers to God who *imparts* "wisdom and revelation" and, in the second, to the Lord's people (in the case, at Ephesus) who *receive* "wisdom and revelation".

a) God who reveals, v.17b

Paul prays that God would give them "the spirit of wisdom and revelation in the knowledge of him" or "a spirit of wisdom and revelation in the knowledge of him" (RV). It is worth noting that the Holy Spirit is elsewhere called "the Spirit of truth" (John 15: 26) and "the Spirit of adoption" (Rom. 8: 15)

The words here, "give unto you [the] spirit of wisdom and revelation" (JND), indicate that this is not a direct reference to the Holy Spirit. Compare Chapter

1 verse 13 and Chapter 3 verse 16. We have already received the Holy Spirit! It refers, rather, to the enabling that the Holy Spirit imparts. As F.F.Bruce points out, "While the reference is not actually to the personal Spirit of God here, yet such a spirit of wisdom and revelation cannot be possessed apart from Him who is 'the Spirit of wisdom and understanding, the Spirit of counsel and might, the Spirit of knowledge and of the fear of the Lord' (Isa. 11: 2)". See 1 Corinthians 2 verses 10-13.

F.F.Bruce continues: "Knowledge without wisdom can be a menace; wisdom is that insight into the nature of things, that sense of what is fitting, which enables one to co-ordinate and use one's knowledge aright ... But the knowledge of which the apostle speaks is not primarily a knowledge of things or facts; it is the personal knowledge of God. And this knowledge is impossible unless God is pleased to make Himself known. Hence the spirit which the apostle desires for his readers is a spirit of *revelation* as well as one of wisdom". See 1 Corinthians 2 verses 6-11.

At this juncture, we should add the following:

- **"The spirit of wisdom."** For its practical implications, see James 3 verse 17; "The wisdom that is from above is first pure, then peaceable, gentle, easy to be intreated, full of mercy and good fruits, without partiality, and without hypocrisy". This must include, "a word in season to him that is weary" (Isa. 50: 4).

- **"The spirit of...revelation (apokalupsis)."** W.E.Vine defines this as "the communication of the knowledge of God to the soul". See 1 Corinthians 2 verses 9-12. Since "wisdom" is divinely-given ability, and "revelation" is divinely-given truth, Paul therefore prays, not only that the Lord's people might be depositaries of divine information, but that they might have the ability to use it effectively.

We have every reason to thank God for "the spirit of ... revelation". Zophar the Naamathite speaks for us all in saying, "Canst thou by searching find out God? Canst thou find out the Almighty unto perfection?" (Job 11: 7). God is self-revealing. He reveals Himself by the Holy Spirit. See 1 Corinthians 2 verses 9-12, "Eye hath not seen ... but God hath revealed them unto us by his Spirit: for the Spirit searcheth all things, yea, the deep things of God ... the things of God knoweth no man, but the Spirit of God. Now we have received not the spirit of the world, but the Spirit which is of God; that we might know the things that are freely given us of God".

As already noted. such "wisdom" and "revelation" is "in the knowledge of *him"*, where *epignosis* (AV 'knowledge) refers to the experimental knowledge of God. Compare Psalm 103 verse 7, "He made known his **ways** unto Moses, his **acts** unto the children of Israel". This of necessity involves our devotional life, as demonstrated in Acts 13 verse 2, "As they ministered **unto the Lord** and fasted the Holy Ghost said ..." We must remember that "wisdom" and "revelation" are not isolated spiritual assets. They are the product of communion and fellowship with God.

b) God's people who receive, v.18a

"The eyes of your understanding being enlightened" or "being enlightened in the eyes of your heart" (JND). "The weight of authority favours 'heart' (*kardia*) and not understanding (*dianoia*)" (A Leckie). In the Old Testament, a prophet was called a 'seer', which implied that he had an eye for the things of God. Here we have inward vision. The heart is used in Scripture to convey the inner life, whether regenerate or unregenerate. See Proverbs 4 verse 23, "Keep thy heart with all diligence; for out of it are the issues of life"; Proverbs 23 verse 7, "For as he thinketh in his heart, so is he".

The enlightenment here stands in direct contrast to "having the understanding darkened" (Eph. 4: 18). The two verses describe saved and unsaved people respectively. So wisdom and understanding are not spiritual sensations, feelings of elation, or unexplainable and unintelligible emotions. To the contrary, they derive from intelligence in the ways of God. Compare 1 Corinthians 14 verse 15. This brings us to:

B) His prayer for them particularly, vv.18b-23

That "ye may know" three things: *(a)* "*what* is the hope of his calling, and *(b) what* the riches of the glory of his inheritance in the saints, and *(c) what* is the exceeding greatness of his power to us-ward who believe". Whilst we must use our academic apparatus, it remains that understanding comes through "the spirit of wisdom and understanding in the knowledge of him".

a) "What is the hope of his calling", v.18

There is encouragement for God's people. They "rejoice in hope of the glory of God ... and hope maketh not ashamed; because the love of God is shed abroad in our hearts by the Holy Ghost, which is given unto us" (Rom.

5: 2, 5). The "calling" is defined in Chapter 1 verse 4, "According as he hath chosen us in him before the foundation of the world". See also Chapter 4 verse 4: "There is one body, and one Spirit, even as ye are called in one hope of your calling." It is an eternal calling: "God ... who hath saved us, and called us with an holy calling, not according to our works, but according to his own purpose and grace, which was given us in Christ Jesus before the world began" (2 Tim. 1: 9); "Moreover whom he did predestinate, them he also called" (Rom. 8: 30). The latter passage stresses the consummation of the divine call: we are predestinated "to be conformed to the image of his Son ... them he also glorified". We are "the called according to his purpose" (Rom. 8: 28). In J.N.Darby's beautiful words –

> *And is it so? I shall be like Thy Son!*
> *Is this the grace which He for me hath won?*
> *Father of glory, thought beyond all thought*
> *In glory, to His own blest likeness brought.*

For other references to our 'calling', see 1 Thessalonians 2 verse 12, "Walk worthy of God, who also hath called you unto his kingdom and glory". There are practical implications: "As he which hath called you is holy, so be ye holy" (1 Pet. 1: 15); "Walk worthy of the vocation wherewith ye are called" (Eph. 4: 1); "And every man that hath this hope in him, purifieth himself, even as he is pure" (1 John 3: 3).

b) "What the riches of the glory of his inheritance in the saints", v.18

There is enrichment for God's people. This chapter deals with the subject of inheritance in two ways:

- Firstly, as believers, **we** have an inheritance in **Christ**: Paul refers to "that Holy Spirit of promise, which is the earnest of our inheritance" (vv.13-14). This reminds us of the Levites who "shall have no part nor inheritance with Israel ... the LORD is their inheritance, as he said unto them" (Deut. 18: 1-2).

- Secondly, and this is the emphasis here, God has an inheritance in **us.** Note, then, that it is "his inheritance". Not '*our* inheritance', but "*his* inheritance", as in verse 11 (if you follow the RV): "in whom also we were made a heritage". Compare the following: "But the LORD hath taken you ... to be unto him a people of inheritance, as ye are this day" (Deut. 4: 20); "For the Lord's portion is his people; Jacob is the lot of his inheritance" (Deut. 32:

9); "Blessed is the nation whose God is the LORD; and the people whom he hath chosen for his own inheritance" (Psalm 33: 12). The Lord Jesus referred to His disciples as "them whom thou hast given me ... all mine are thine, and thine are mine"(John 17: 9-10). The words, "the riches of the glory of his inheritance in the saints", are perhaps an allusion to Exodus 19 verse 5, "Ye shall be a peculiar treasure unto me above all people". If there, in the Old Testament, the value and preciousness of Israel to God is emphasised, how much more the church here (v.18). In the delightful words of W.K.Morrison, "It is a stupendous and humbling thought that God regards the saints as a rich possession laid up in store for His own delight, and yet that is what the expression means". The high priest bore the names of the children of Israel, engraved on precious stones, upon the shoulders and breastplate of his garment. This was how God saw them – and how He sees us!

One aspect of the "riches of the glory of his inheritance in the saints" is stressed by the way in which unseen "principalities and powers" see in the church "the manifold wisdom of God", particularly in the dissolution of the barriers between Jew and Gentile (Eph. 3: 10).

iii) "What is the exceeding greatness of his power to us-ward who believe", vv.19-23

There is enabling for God's people. It has been observed that Paul summons the whole resources of his vocabulary to describe the power available to the believer, and does so in view of the supreme demonstration of that power in the resurrection of the Lord Jesus. It has been nicely said that Paul's prayer for their spiritual enlightenment challenges his readers to action. Prayer "is not a sedative, but a stimulant" (W.K.Morrison, *Believer's Magazine, August 1962*). As C.H.Spurgeon points out, this is the power that "raises the drunkard from his drunkenness, the thief from his dishonesty, the Pharisee from his self-righteousness, the Sadducee from his unbelief" (supplied by Justin Waldron).

F.F.Bruce is well worth quoting *in extenso* here: "When Paul thinks of the power of God, he presses all the terms for power in his vocabulary into service in order to convey something of its all-surpassing character. Paul is the only New Testament writer to use the participle rendered "exceeding" *(hyperballon),* and does so in four other passages: 2 Corinthians 3 verse 10; 2 Corinthians 9 verse 14; Ephesians 2 verse 7; Ephesians 3 verse 19. But not content with this superlative word, he piles synonym on synonym as he describes how God's 'power' *(dynamis:* unquestioned ability*)* operates according to the inworking *(energeia:* efficient operation) of the strength *(kratos:* force superior to all opposition) of His might *(ischys:* inherent vital power). Why this attempt to exhaust the resources of language to convey something of the greatness of God's power? Because he is thinking of one supreme occasion when that power was exerted. This follows:

- **His resurrection.** When referring to divine power, Paul cites the resurrection rather than creation. The power present in the resurrection of the Lord Jesus is the power that enables men and women to live for God: "Therefore we are buried with him by baptism into death: that like as Christ was raised up from the dead by the glory of the Father, even so we also should walk in newness of life" (Rom. 6: 4); "I am crucified with Christ: nevertheless I live; yet not I, but Christ liveth in me" (Gal. 2: 20); "Now unto him that is able to do exceeding abundantly above all that we ask or think, according to the power that worketh in us" (Eph. 3: 20); "That I might know him, and the power of his resurrection" (Phil. 3: 10).

We are to be "strong in the Lord, and in the power of his might" (Eph. 6: 10) The power which exalted the Lord Jesus to utter supremacy is available to us in our combat with the dark powers which we engage in spiritual conflict. His resurrection and ascension are the pattern of our blessings: "And hath raised us up together, and made us sit together in heavenly places in Christ Jesus" (Eph. 2: 6). We, by grace alone, share with Christ in the glory of the heavenlies. We too are above the very enemies we encounter! "There never needs to be a 'power shortage' in the Christian life" (Justin Waldron).

- **His ascension.** The power that operated in His resurrection continued to operate in His exaltation: "the working of his mighty power, which he wrought in Christ, when he raised him from the dead, and set him at ***his (own) right hand in the heavenly places***" (v.20). See Psalm 110 verse 1. No angel can sit there (Heb. 1: 13). The Lord Jesus "ascended up far above all heavens" (Eph. 4: 10) or, in the words now before us, he ascended "far above all principality, and power, and might, and dominion, and every name that is named, not only in this world, but also in that which is to come" (v.21). That is, "far above" all "principalities ... powers ... the rulers of the darkness of this world ... spiritual wickedness in high places" (Eph. 6: 12)

The Lord Jesus is not only above them (v.21) – He has dominion over them: God "hath put all things under his feet" (v.22), alluding here to Psalm 8 verse

6, "Thou hast put all things under his feet". All things were placed beneath Adam's feet on **earth**, and beneath Christ's feet in **heaven.** As Paul points out elsewhere (Col. 2: 9, 18), since Christ is "the head of all principality and power" there is no question of 'worshipping angels'. This 'Gnostic' practice may have been in Paul's mind here.

While all the 'principalities and powers' in verse 22 are beneath the **feet** of the Lord Jesus: the church is identified with Christ as its glorified **Head.** If "all things" are put under "his feet" (v.22) then this must exclude the church since it is described as "his body". As "head over all things to the church (the first mention of *ekklesia* in the epistle)" (v.22), He would be incomplete without His body. But God has given Him "to be the head over all things to the church (see Addendum), which is his body, the fulness of him that filleth all in all" (vv.22-23).

The word translated "fulness" (*pleroma*) means 'the complement'. Adam was incomplete without Eve. "The church is described as the fulness or complement of Christ, just as the body is the necessary complement of the head in order to make up a complete man" (F.F.Bruce). "Principalities and powers" are **subject** to Him, but "believing men are **joined** to Him" (Moule). Compare 1 Corinthians 12 verse 12.

The words "that filleth all in all" refer to the fact that Christ fills the entire universe, and anticipates the day when God gathers "together in one all in Christ, both which are in heaven, and which are on earth; even in him" (v.10). In that day, Christ will be "glorified in his saints and to be admired in all them that believe" (2 Thess. 1: 10). As the body is the vehicle through which the will and desires of the head are accomplished, so in like manner, will the church be identified with Christ - united with Him - in His glory. The church will be complete in Him, and, wonder of wonders, He will be complete in the church for, "as an exalted head, Christ would be incomplete without the church His body" (A.Leckie). Staggering, isn't it!

ADDENDUM

Some commentators read the words "and gave him *to be* (italicised, AV) the head over all things to the church" (v.22) as 'and gave him, the head of all things (referring to v.10), to the church'.

THE EPISTLE TO THE EPHESIANS

"God ... hath quickened us together with Christ"

Read Chapter 2: 1-10

Having, in Chapter 1, described the immense blessings bestowed upon his readers - **chosen by God** (vv.3-6), **redeemed by the Son** (vv.7-12) and **sealed by the Spirit** (vv.13-14) - Paul then records his prayer for them: "that ye may know **what** is the hope of his calling, and **what** the riches of the glory of his inheritance in the saints, and **what** is the exceeding greatness of his power to us-ward who believe, according to the working of his mighty power, which he wrought in Christ, when he raised him from the dead ..." (vv.18-20).

Coming now to Chapter 2, we learn that "God did not only raise Christ from the dead by His mighty power: He has raised the people of Christ from the dead as well" (F.F.Bruce). Bruce continues, "in the present passage, the death from which God has 'quickened us together with Christ' (v.5) is not our death-with-Christ (as, for example, in Romans 6: 3-5), but our moral and spiritual death brought about through our 'trespasses and sins' (v.1)". Compare Ephesians 1 verse 7.

Albert Leckie (*What the Bible Teaches – Ephesians*) points out the connection between the two chapters as follows: "From an introduction in Chapter 1 to divine counsel and purpose concerning the church in the matter of election, predestination and inheritance, we now have the **dreadful material** upon which God had to work. None save God could have done anything with such apparently hopeless material". How thankful we are for those two words – "**But God ...**" (v.4). Hence the emphasis in the passage on God's mercy (v.4), love (v.4), grace (vv.5, 7, 8), and kindness (v.7). We are "**his workmanship,** created in Christ Jesus unto good works" (v.10).

With this in mind, Ephesians 2 may be divided as follows: in verses 1-10,

Chapter 2:1-10

Paul deals with Jew and Gentile morally, and in verses 11-20, he deals with Jew and Gentile dispensationally.

- **Jew and Gentile morally, vv.1-10.** Both are alike dead. They occupy the common ground of sinners. They are both "dead in trespasses and sins". But, in the case of believers, God has dealt with their sinnership. Hence the expressions, "in time past" (v.2) and "in times past" (v.3). The section commences with "wherein in time past ('once', JND) ye **walked** according to the course of this world ..." (v.2), and concludes with "we are his workmanship, created in Christ Jesus unto good works, which God hath before ordained that we should **walk** in them" (v.10).

Both Jew and Gentile are certainly comprehended in verses 1-10: "And **you** (you Gentiles) hath he quickened who were dead in trespasses and sins; wherein in time past **ye** (you Gentiles) walked according to the course of this world ... among whom also **we all** (Jews and Gentiles) had our conversation in times past ... But God, who is rich in mercy, for his great love wherewith he loved **us** (Jews and Gentiles) even when **we** (Jews and Gentiles) were dead in sins, hath quickened **us** (Jews and Gentiles) together with Christ ..."

- **Jew and Gentile dispensationally, vv.11-20.** We should notice the repetition of "**both**" (vv.14, 16, 18, 22). Gentiles, "sometimes afar off", are "made nigh by the blood of Christ. For he is our peace, who hath made **both** one, and hath broken down the middle wall of partition between us" (v.14).

This extends and amplifies Ephesians 1 verses 12-14, "That **we** (that is, 'we Jews') should be to the praise of his glory, who first trusted in Christ. In whom **ye** (that is, 'ye Gentiles') also trusted ... in whom **ye** ('ye Gentiles') also, after that ye believed, **ye** were sealed with that Holy Spirit of promise, which is the earnest of **our** inheritance (that is, the inheritance belonging to Christians, both Jews and Greeks) until the redemption of the purchased possession ..."

In summary, Gentiles, like Jews, were sinners, "dead in trespasses and sins", but the "dead" have new life (vv.1-10); Gentiles were strangers, but, no longer "afar off", they have been "made nigh" (vv.11-20).

Purely for the record, Ephesians 2 verse 1 to Chapter 3 verse 13 may be divided as follows: *(i)* the human material (2: 1-10); *(ii)* the divine masterpiece (2: 11-22); *(iii)* the hidden mystery (3: 1-13). This brings us to:

1) JEW AND GENTILE MORALLY, vv.1-10

The epistle to the Ephesians discloses the highest aspects of Christian calling, and here (2: 1-10) Paul traces the history, in time, of the believer from the past to the future. It begins, as already noted, "in time past" or in "times past" (vv.2, 3), and concludes with "the ages to come" (v.7), stressing, at the same time, the current relevance of our calling: "we are his workmanship, created in Christ Jesus unto good works, which God hath before ordained that we should walk in them" (v.10).

In this connection, we should notice reference to **the past** (vv.1-3), to **the present** (vv.4-6), and to **the future** (v.7).

a) The past, vv.1-3

"And you (in the good of all the blessings described in Chapter1) hath he quickened, who were dead in trespasses and sins; wherein in time past ye walked according to the course of this world, according to the prince of the power of the air, the spirit that now worketh in the children of disobedience: among whom also we all had our conversation in times past in the lusts of our flesh, fulfilling the desires of the flesh and of the mind; and were by nature the children of wrath, even as others." We should notice the following: we were *(i)* dead, *(ii)* dominated, *(iii)* disobedient, and *(iv)* doomed. Only God can do something with material like that!

i) We were dead, v.1

We were "dead in ('through', RV) trespasses and sins". The word "trespasses" (*paraptoma*) denotes "a trespass, a deviation, from uprightness and truth" (W.E.Vine); "to deviate from the right path, to turn aside, to wander" (Kenneth S. Wuest). The word "sins" (*hamartia* from *hamartano*, 'to miss the mark') "speaks of sin as the act of a person failing to obey the Word of God, failing to measure up in his life to the will of God. Its use is excellently illustrated in Romans 3 verse 23, 'all have sinned (missed the mark), and at present come short of the glory of God'" (K.S.Wuest).

The figure of death ("dead in trespasses and sins") is explained by Isaiah 59 verse 2, "Your iniquities have separated between you and your God, and your sins have hid his face from you"; Ephesians 4 verse 18, "Having the understanding darkened, being alienated from the life of God through the ignorance that is in them, because of the blindness of their heart". Death is not cessation of existence, but separation from God.

ii) We were dominated, vv.2-3

Mankind has become subject to a trinity of evil. Paul refers to our environment (v.2), our enemy (v.2) and our evil nature (v.3). Put another way, 'the world the flesh and the devil'.

- **Our environment, v.2.** "Wherein (in 'trespasses and sins') in time past ye walked according to the course (*aion*) of this world", meaning here 'the spirit of the age' (quoted by K.S.Wuest), that is, the sinful atmosphere of the world. Or, connecting it with what follows, the world system organised by Satan. Now, of course, we 'walk' differently. See Ephesians 2 verse 10; Chapter 4 verses 1 and 17, Chapter 5 verses 2, 8 and 15.

The "course of this world" can be determined from the following: "the **world** (*kosmos*) by wisdom knew not God" (1 Cor. 1: 21); "If the **world** (*kosmos*) hate you, ye know that it hated me before it hated you" (John 15: 18); "the corruption that is in the **world** (*kosmos*) through lust" (2 Pet. 1: 4); "all that is in the **world** (*kosmos*), the lust of the flesh, and the lust of the eyes, and the pride of life ..." (1 John 2: 16); "the whole **world** (*kosmos*) lieth in wickedness" (1 John 5: 19); "the god of this **world** (*aion*)" (2 Cor. 4: 4). We should note that *kosmos* denotes the world in the sense of its order and arrangement, whereas *aion* denotes a period of time. (W.E.Vine's *Expository Dictionary of New Testament Words* is essential reading here.)

- **Our enemy, v.2.** "According to the prince of the power of the air, the spirit that now worketh in the children ('sons', suggesting responsibility) of disobedience."

He is called "the **prince** (*archon*, meaning 'chief'or 'ruler') of the power of the air". Compare "the **prince** of the devils" (Mark 3: 22); "the **prince** of this world" (John 12: 31; Chapter 14: 30; Chapter 16: 11). Hence his statement, "All this power (*exousia*, meaning 'freedom of action') will I give thee, and the glory of them: for that is delivered unto me" (not by God, but by men) (Luke 4: 6). He is called "the god of this world" (2 Cor. 4: 4). But he is not omnipresent. He walks "to and fro in the earth ..." (Job 1: 7; 2: 2)

Here, he is called "the prince of the power of the air". That is, his sphere of operation. His influence, and that of his associates, is as pervasive as the air man breathes. He implants evil thoughts in men's hearts: see, for example, Judas Iscariot and Ananias and Sapphira. There is only One who was never subject to him: the Lord Jesus said, "the prince of this world cometh, and hath nothing in me" (John 14: 30).

- *Our evil nature, v.3.* "Among whom also we all had our conversation in times past in the lusts of our flesh, fulfilling the desires of the flesh and of the mind" or "doing what the flesh and thoughts willed to do" (JND). The "desires ... of the mind" does not necessarily mean only base things: it includes such things as arrogance and intolerance. We were subject to our sinful fallen nature, condemned for what we were in ourselves. See Romans 8 verses 7-8, "the carnal mind is enmity against God; for it is not subject to the law of God, neither indeed can be. So then they that are in the flesh cannot please God"; Galatians 5 verses 19-21, "Now the works of the flesh are manifest, which are these; Adultery, fornication, uncleanness, lasciviousness, idolatry, witchcraft, hatred, variance, emulations, wrath, strife, seditions, heresies, envyings, murders, drunkenness, revellings, and such like".

iii) We were disobedient, v.2

We were once "children of disobedience", as we were once "the servants of sin", but like the believers at Rome, it can be said of us, "God be thanked, that ye were the servants of sin, but ye have obeyed from the heart that form of doctrine which was delivered you" (Rom. 6: 17).

At one time, we were "foolish, **disobedient**, deceived ..." (Titus 3. 3), but we believed the gospel which has been "made known to all nations for the **obedience** of faith" (Rom. 16: 26).

Satan is called "the spirit that now worketh in the children of disobedience". We observe him working "in the children of disobedience" when the Lord Jesus was here: "But now ye seek to kill me, a man that hath told you the truth, which I have heard of God: this did not Abraham (whom they claimed to be their father). Ye do the deeds of your father ... Ye are of your father the devil, and the lusts of your father ye will do. He was a murderer from the beginning, and abode not in the truth, because there is no truth in him. When he speaketh a lie, he speaketh of his own: for he is a liar, and the father of it" (John 8: 40, 41, 44).

Chapter 2:1-10

We observe him working in another 'child of disobedience'. Bar-Jesus, in Cyprus, "withstood them (Barnabas and Saul), seeking to turn away the deputy from the faith", for which he was called "thou child of the devil, thou enemy of all righteousness" (Acts 13: 8-10).

iv) We were doomed, v.3

We (Jew and Gentile are on the same ground) were " by nature the children of wrath (*orge*), even as others". We were "children of wrath" because "children of disobedience". Paul makes it clear that the wrath of God is already operative in the world: "the **wrath of God** (*orge*) is revealed from heaven against all ungodliness and unrighteousness of men, who hold the truth in unrighteousness; because that which may be known of God is manifest in them, for God hath shewed it unto them. For the invisible things of him from the creation of the world are clearly seen ... so that they are without excuse" (Rom. 1: 18-20).

One day, men and women on earth will experience the wrath of God as never before: "The Lord Jesus shall be revealed from heaven with his mighty angels, in flaming fire taking vengeance on them that know not God, and that obey not the gospel of our Lord Jesus Christ: who shall be punished with everlasting destruction from the presence of the Lord, and from the glory of his power" (2 Thess. 1: 7-9). In that day men and women will say "to the mountains and rocks, Fall on us, and hide us from the face of him that sitteth on the throne, and from the **wrath** (*orge*) of the Lamb" (Rev. 6: 16). This brings us to:

b) The present, vv.4-6

"But God, who is rich in mercy, for his great love wherewith he loved us, even when we were dead in sins, hath quickened us together with Christ (by grace ye are saved); and hath raised us up together, and made us sit together in heavenly places in Christ Jesus ..." There has been divine intervention. There was no alternative. God alone could deal with the situation. Although dead, dominated, disobedient and doomed, God has wonderfully acted toward us in mercy (v.4), love (v.4) and grace (v.5). We should notice *(i)* why He has so blessed us and *(ii)* how He has so blessed us.

i) Why He has blessed us

"But God, who is rich in **mercy**, for his great **love** wherewith he loved us, even when we were dead in sins, hath quickened us together with Christ (by **grace** ye are saved) …" (vv.4-5).

- *His mercy.* God is "**rich** in mercy". David puts it like this: "The LORD is merciful and gracious, slow to anger and plenteous in mercy … He hath not dealt with us after our sins, nor rewarded us according to our iniquities. For as the heaven is high above the earth, so great is his mercy toward them that fear him" (Psalm 103: 8-11). He is not only merciful, He is "rich in mercy". In the words of Albert Leckie, "If Jew and Gentile deserved wrath, God would exercise rich mercy". Compare Chapter 1 verse 7, "the riches of his grace"; Chapter 2 verse 7, "the exceeding riches of his grace"; Chapter 3 verse 16, "the riches of his glory".

- *His love.* He has shown us, not just love (that, in itself, is wonderful, but "great love". Compare Chapter 1 verse 4 (that is, if you accept the amended punctuation): "In love having predestinated us"; Chapter 3 verse 19, "the love of Christ which passeth knowledge"; Chapter 5 verse 25, "Christ also loved the church, and gave himself for it". John refers to His "great love" in saying, "Hereby perceive we the love of God, because he laid down his life for us" (1 John 3: 16); "In this was manifested the love of God toward us, because that God sent his only begotten Son into the world, that we might live through him. Herein is love, not that we loved God, but that he loved us, and sent his Son to be the propitiation for our sins" (1 John 4: 9-10).

- *His grace.* "By grace ye are saved." Paul has something more to say about this in verses 8-9. His words elsewhere are relevant: "But where sin abounded, grace did much more abound: that as sin hath reigned unto death, even so might grace reign, through righteousness, unto eternal life, by Jesus Christ our Lord" (Rom. 5: 20-21).

ii) How He has blessed us

"Even when we were dead in sins, hath quickened us **together** with Christ (by grace ye are saved) and hath raised us up **together**, and made us sit **together** in heavenly places in Christ Jesus." Here is new life! No longer "dead in trespasses and sins", we are, to quote out of context (oh dear!), "as those that are alive from the dead" (Rom. 6: 13).

Looking at our passage overall, some comparisons emerge. They look something like this:

- *In Christ, we have new life.* Before conversion we were "dead in trespasses and sins" (v.1). Now, God has "quickened us together with Christ" (v.5).

- *In Christ, we enjoy a new environment.* Before conversion we "walked according to the course of *this world*" (v.2). Now, God "hath raised us up together, and made us sit together in *heavenly places* in Christ Jesus" (v.6). This is not where the world sees us – in the visible and material world: it is, rather, the place were God sees us – in the unseen spiritual realm. It has been said that He does not see us in a garden with Adam, or in a tent with Abraham, or on a throne with David, but with Christ 'in the heavenlies'. We must, therefore, "seek those things which are above" and set our "affection on things above, not on things on the earth" (Col, 3: 1-2). (See also 1 John 2: 15.)

- *In Christ, we are subject to a new authority.* Before conversion we were subject to the "prince of the power of the air, the spirit that now worketh in the children of disobedience" (v.2). Now, being "in Christ Jesus" (v.7 JND), we are "*his* workmanship" (v.10). Therefore, we must not "give place to the devil" (4: 27).

- *In Christ, we have a new character.* Before conversion, we obeyed "the lusts of our flesh, fulfilling the desires of the flesh and of the mind" (v.3). Now, we have been "created in Christ Jesus unto good works" (v.10). Therefore we are to "put off concerning the former conversation the old man, which is corrupt according to the deceitful lusts ... and put on the new man which after God is created in righteousness and true holiness" (4: 22-24).

- *In Christ, we have a new future*. Before conversion, we were "the children of wrath, even as others" (v.3). Now, we look forward to "the ages to come" when we will enjoy "the exceeding riches of his grace in his kindness towards us through Christ Jesus" (v.7). This brings us to

c) The future, vv.7-10

"That in the ages to come he might shew the exceeding riches of his grace in his kindness (*chrestotes*, meaning 'goodness', as opposed to 'severity: Rom 11: 22), toward us through Christ Jesus ('in Christ Jesus', JND). For by grace are ye saved through faith; and that not of yourselves; it is the gift of God; not of works, lest any man should boast. For we are his workmanship,

Ephesians

created in Christ Jesus unto good works, which God hath before ordained that we should walk in them."

The "***exceeding*** (*huperballo*: to throw over or beyond) riches of his grace" (v.7) remind us of the "***exceeding*** (*huperballo*) greatness of his power" (1: 19), and that He is able to do "***exceeding abundantly*** *(huperekperissou)* above all that we ask or think" (3: 20).

"The ages to come" are distinct from the "age to come" (1: 21) and suggest that the display of "the exceeding riches of his grace" will "remain undiminished as long as time shall last" (A.Leckie).

The oft-quoted (and rightly so) words, "For by grace are ye saved through faith; and that not of yourselves; it is the gift of God, not of works, lest any man should boast" emphasise that the salvation which brings such a glorious prospect is solely divine. This is emphasised in earlier verses by the expressions, "with Christ" (v.5); "in Christ Jesus" (v.6); "through Christ Jesus" (v.7). The salvation which we now enjoy, and which provides such a glorious future is:

- **Available through grace**. "By **grace** are ye saved (that is, saved from the things described in vv.1-3) through faith ..." See also verse 8.

- **Appropriated by faith.** "By grace are ye saved through ***faith.***" Compare, for example, John 1 verse 12; Romans 5 verse 1. Remember Abraham!

- **Accepted as a gift.** "For by grace are ye saved through faith; and that not of yourselves; it is the ***gift of God*** ..." There are good grammatical arguments for saying that faith is the "gift of God" here, and 2 Peter 1 verse 1 is usually cited in this connection. See also Romans 10 verse 17. However, not a few commentators (including F.F.Bruce) tell us that other grammatical considerations could suggest that it is "the whole concept of salvation by grace through faith, that is described as "the gift of God". F.F.Bruce adds that "this, incidentally, was Calvin's interpretation, although many of his followers have preferred to take faith itself as the gift of God here".

- **Apart from works**. Whatever view we take in connection with the above, there is no doubt that salvation is "not of works, lest any man should boast". In fact, God does the work, "We are his workmanship, created in Christ

Jesus unto good works" (v.10). This emphasises the place of "works": not in salvation, but as the fruit of salvation. The word translated "workmanship" (*poiema*), whence the English word 'poem', conveys the ideas of beauty and symmetry. "It is workmanship with an end in view, to produce a beautiful design" (A.Leckie). We must give evidence of this. "Faith without works is dead" (Jas. 2: 20).

We cannot leave this without noting the practical application of God's sovereignty. In considering Ephesians 1 verse 4 ("he hath chosen us in him before the foundation of the world, that we should be holy and without blame before him ..."), we noted that the doctrine of election is never taught in a vacuum. F.F.Bruce's comment at this point is well worth repeating: "In the presence of such a mystery we do well to be humble, acknowledging the limits of our understanding and paying heed **to the solemn practical purpose of God's electing grace".**

Having considered the position of the Jew and Gentile morally (vv.1-10), in our next study we will consider the Jew and Gentile dispensationally (vv.11-22).

THE EPISTLE TO THE EPHESIANS

"He is our peace, who hath made both one"

Read Chapter 2: 11-22

In our previous study, we noted that Ephesians 2 may be divided as follows: **(1)** Jew and Gentile morally (vv.1-10); **(2)** Jew and Gentile dispensationally (vv.11-22).

1) JEW AND GENTILE MORALLY, vv.1-10

Both Jew and Gentile occupy common ground. They are both "dead in trespasses and sins". While Paul is seemingly referring to Gentile believers in saying, "and **you** being dead in your offences and sins ..." (v.1, JND), he goes on to say, "among whom **we** (Jews) also all once walked according to the age of this world ..." (v.2, v.3, JND). But Paul does say that all this belonged to the past. Hence the expressions, "in time past" (v.2) and "in times past" (v.3. A marvellous change has taken place! It all begins with two words, "**But now** ..."

These verses (vv.1-10) commence with the words, "wherein in time past ('once', JND) ye **walked** according to the course of this world ..." (v.2), and conclude with, "we are his workmanship, created in Christ Jesus unto good works, which God hath before ordained that we should **walk** in them" (v.10). This brings us to:

2) JEW AND GENTILE DISPENSATIONALLY, vv.11-22

Whereas "in times past" (v.3) Jew and Gentile shared the same ground in that "all have sinned, and come short of the glory of God" (Rom. 3: 23), there was, at the same time ("at that time", v.12), a deep division between Jew and Gentile. The division was in fact so deep that it has been described as the *deepest* of all human divisions. The division in question concerned proximity to God. To summarise, the Gentiles were "far off" from God, and the Jews were "nigh" to God (v.17). This was the position in Old Testament days. But there has been a radical change. Gentiles (that is, believing Gentiles), who "sometimes were far off, are made nigh by the blood of Christ" (v.13). As a result of the death of the Lord Jesus, "the middle wall of partition", referring to "the law of commandments contained in ordinances", Paul's way of describing the division between Jew and Gentile, has been "broken down", and while the two parties (Jew and Gentile) remain, in the case of believing Jews and Gentiles, there is now "one new man" (v.15), also described as "one body" (v.16). Hence we read such expressions as "***both*** one" (v.14); "reconcile ***both*** unto God" (v.16); "through him we ***both*** have access by one Spirit unto the Father" (v.18).

This would have been of particular interest to the believers at Ephesus since Paul had "disputed ('reasoned', JND) daily in the school of one Tyrannus. And this continued by the space of two years; so that all they which dwelt in Asia heard the word of the Lord, ***both Jews and Greeks***" (Acts 19: 9-10).

In summary:

- We learn from verses 1-10 that Gentile believers, like Jewish believers, ***were once sinners***, "dead in trespasses and sins", but that they have now been "quickened ... together (*sunzoopoieo,* 'to make alive with') with Christ" (v.5).

- We learn from verses 11-22 that Gentile believers who, like all Gentiles, ***were once strangers*** ("sometimes ... far off"), have now been "made nigh".

In fact, the chapter has been divided like this: from death to life (vv.1-10); from distance to nearness (vv.11-22).

Our current passage (vv.11-22), may be divided as follows: *(A) "In time past"* (vv.11-12): "Wherefore remember, that ye being in *time past* Gentiles in the flesh ..." (v.11); *(B) "But now"* (vv.13-22): "But ***now*** in Christ Jesus ... ***Now*** therefore ye are no more strangers and foreigners" (vv.13, 19).

A) *"In time past", vv.11-12*

"Wherefore remember, that ye being in time past Gentiles in the flesh, who are called Uncircumcision by that which is called the Circumcision in the flesh made by hands: that at that time ye were without Christ, being aliens from the commonwealth of Israel, and strangers from the covenants of promise, having no hope, and without God in the world." Paul outlines the position of "Gentiles in the flesh", a term which evidently refers to natural descent:

a) They were without faith, v.11

They were "called Uncircumcision by that which is called the Circumcision in the flesh made by hands". This is certainly borne out by such passages as, "Is there never a woman among the daughters of thy brethren, or among all my people, that thou goest to take a wife of the **uncircumcised** Philistines" (Judges 14: 3); "Come, and let us go over unto the garrison of these **uncircumcised**" (1 Sam. 14: 6).

Circumcision was instituted with Abraham. It was "a seal of the righteousness of the faith which he had yet being uncircumcised" (Rom. 4: 11). The 'rolling away' of the flesh signified no faith in self, and faith in God. Hence, "**we** (that is, 'we' Christians) are the circumcision, which worship God in the spirit, and rejoice in Christ Jesus, and have **no confidence** in the flesh" (Phil. 3: 3).

We should notice Paul's exact words: not just 'circumcision', but "Circumcision ... **made by hands**". Paul explains this in Romans 2 verses 28-29, "For he is not a Jew, which is one outwardly; neither is that circumcision, which is outward in the flesh: but he is a Jew, which is one inwardly; and circumcision is that of the heart, in the spirit, and not in the letter; whose praise is not of men, but of God".

Ideally, circumcision was the mark in the flesh of the people who trusted in God. But although they possessed the sign, and gloried in it, they did not possess the faith it signified. They were "uncircumcised in heart and ears" (Acts 7: 51).

b) They were without Christ, v.12

"At that time ye (Gentiles) were without Christ." This emphasises that the Messiah, "according to the flesh" (Rom. 1: 3), was Jewish. He was not of Gentile origin, and Gentiles had no claim on Him:

- **He was born of a Jewish tribe:** "It is evident that our Lord sprang out of Juda" (Heb. 7: 14).

- *He was born in a Jewish city*: "And thou Bethlehem ... out of thee shall come a Governor, that shall rule my people Israel" (Matt. 2: 6).

- *He was born to a Jewish throne:* "The Lord God shall give unto him the throne of his father David" (Luke 1: 32).

Paul deals with this in referring to his "brethren, my kinsmen according to the flesh: who are Israelites; to whom pertaineth the adoption, and the glory, and the covenants, and the giving of the law, and the service of God, and the promises; whose are the fathers, and of whom as concerning the flesh Christ came, who is over all, God blessed for ever. Amen." (Rom. 9: 4-5).

But the people to whom Paul is writing were no longer "without Christ"!

c) They were without claim, v.12

They were "aliens from (literally, 'strangers from') the commonwealth of Israel". The word translated "commonwealth" (*politeia*) belongs to the same family as the word translated "fellowcitizens" (*sumpolites*) in verse 19.

The Gentiles had no national claim on God. See Amos 3 verse 2: "You only (Israel) have I known of all the families of the earth"; Numbers 23 verse 9, "Lo, the people (Israel) shall dwell alone, and shall not be reckoned among the nations"; Exodus 19 verses 5-6, "Ye shall be a peculiar treasure unto me above all people ... ye shall be unto me a kingdom of priests, and an holy nation". As a nation, Israel had special privileges. See, again, Romans 9 verses 4-5.

In the Old Testament, the community of God's people was confined to the national frontiers of Israel.

d) They were without hope, v.12

They were "strangers from the covenants of promise, having no hope". No covenants were made with the Gentile nations. Gentiles were excluded from the blessings pertaining to the Jewish theocracy. The Noahic covenant (Gen. 9: 9-17) was made with the human race in general. There were no Jews or Gentiles at the time!

The words, "strangers from the covenants of promise" are, literally, 'strangers from the covenants of ***the*** promise' (RV). The covenants made with Israel, including those concerning the land and the throne, formed the basis of its national life, and of future glory. Hence, of the Gentiles we read, "having no hope". The covenants were the foundations on which the nation rested.

e) *They were without God, v.12*

They were "without God in the world". The presence of God was peculiar to Israel. He did not dwell amongst the Gentile nations. The nation of Israel was unique. Moses put it like this: "For what nation is there so great, who hath God so nigh unto them, as the LORD our God is in all things that we call upon him for?" (Deut. 4: 7). The tabernacle bore witness to His desire to dwell among them: "Let them make me a sanctuary; that I may **dwell** among them" (Exod. 25: 8). So did the temple: at its dedication, "The glory of the LORD had filled the house of the LORD" (1 Kings 8: 11).

Israel had the 'Shekinah', God dwelling in their midst. The "pillar of the cloud by day" and the "pillar of fire by night" (Exod. 13: 22) were 'the badge' of His presence during Israel's wilderness journey.

B) "But now", vv.13-22

The Gentiles had nothing. "But now!" When dealing with Jew and Gentile morally, Paul says, "***But God** ...*" (v.4). Now, in dealing with Jew and Gentile dispensationally, he says, "***But now** ...* " (v.13). Having described the Gentile position "in time past" (vv.11-12), Paul now describes the amazing change that has taken place. "But now", behold "one new man" (v.15); "one body" (v.16); "fellow-citizens" (v.19); "of the household of God" (v.19); "an holy temple in the Lord" (v.21); "an habitation of God through the Spirit" (v.22). There is no hint of friction. "One" and "both" are 'key words in the passage: Christ "is our peace, who hath made ***both one***" (v.14). He has made "in himself ***one new man***, so making peace" (v.15). He has reconciled "***both*** unto God in ***one body*** by the cross" (v.16). "Through him we ***both*** have access by one Spirit unto the Father" (v.18).

The word "now" occurs twice in this section. In verses 13-18 emphasis is placed on "one body", and in verses 19-22 emphasis is placed on one building. There is now:

a) One body, vv.13-18

In this "one body", distance (v.13), disunion (v.14), division (v.14), dissension (v.15) and distinction (vv.15-18) are all done away.

i)   Distance is done away, v.13. "But now in Christ Jesus (the incarnate Messiah) ye (you Gentiles who are now in Christ) who sometimes were far off are made nigh by the blood of Christ (the death of the incarnate Messiah)." The reference to "the blood of Christ" means that guilt was involved, and must be dealt with.

Gentiles have not been brought on to Jewish ground. This was where the Judaisers erred. Neither, as far as the "one body" is concerned, have the Jews been left on Jewish ground!

ii)   Disunion is done away, v.14. "For he is our peace, who hath made both one." The words, "he is our peace", refer, in context, not to peace with God, but to peace between Jew and Gentile. Someone has observed in this connection that a Jew was able to say to a Gentile, "Believe on the Lord Jesus Christ, and thou shalt be saved ..." (Acts 16: 31). Peter was able to do the same in the house of Cornelius (Acts 10: 36-48).

iii)   Division is done away, v.14. He has "broken down the middle wall of partition between us." The 'woman of Samaria' certainly knew about the "middle wall of partition" (John 4: 9), and the Lord Jesus showed her how it would be "broken down" (John 4: 19-24), reminding us that "Joseph (a lovely picture of the Lord Jesus) is a fruitful bough, even a fruitful bough by a well; whose branches run over the wall".

While there might be an allusion to the wall between the court of the Gentiles and the inner courts, into which only Jewish worshippers might enter (see Addenda), it is much more likely that this refers to the dismantling of the national fence which divided Jew and Gentile. **There is now no dividing barrier.** No longer can it be said, amongst believers, "the Jews have no dealings with the Samaritans". But the "middle wall of partition" is, surely, defined by what follows, that is, "the law of commandments contained in ordinances". So:

iv)   Dissension is done away, v.15. Christ has "abolished in his flesh the enmity, even the law of commandments contained in ordinances". In saying that He has "abolished in his **flesh** the enmity ...", Paul is emphasing that it was "as a true man, by giving His body in sacrifice on the cross, that Christ annulled the state of war between those two divisions of mankind" (F.F.Bruce). The word "enmity" certainly describes the relationship between Jew and Gentile. We have only to think of the animosity of Jews towards Gentiles, whom the Jews regarded as the 'dogs of the Gentiles'. After all, they, the Jews, had "the covenants, and the giving of the law, and the service of God, and the promises" (Rom. 9: 4). It was therefore quite unthinkable that they should have any 'truck' with such 'lower forms of life' like Gentiles, who did not keep the law.

The death of Christ brought to an end those things that divided Jew and Gentile. Salvation does not rest in the observance of "commandments contained in ordinances", but in the work of Christ, enabling all believers to say, as already noted, "we are the circumcision, which worship God in the spirit, and rejoice in Christ Jesus, and have no confidence in the flesh". **There is now no dividing ritual. The suffering and death of the Lord Jesus put an end to "the law of commandments contained in ordinances", which had served their purpose.**

v) Distinction is done away, vv.15-18. Christ has "abolished in his flesh the enmity, even the law of commandments contained in ordinances; **for to make in himself of twain one new man,** so making peace (that is, peace between Jew and Gentile); and that he might reconcile both unto God in one body by the cross, having slain the enmity thereby: and came and preached peace to you which were afar off, and to them that were nigh". Through the death of Christ, believing Jews and Gentiles have been made one new man (that "one new man" is the church). In praying for those who would believe through the preaching of His disciples, the Lord Jesus said, "that they all may be **one** ..." (John 17: 21). He also said, "And other sheep I have, which are not of this fold: them also I must bring, and they shall hear my voice; and there shall be one fold ('flock', JND), and one shepherd" (John 10: 16). As such, they enjoy:

- **Joint reconciliation.** He has reconciled "both unto God in one body by the cross, having slain the enmity thereby". Jew and Gentile have not only been reconciled **amongst themselves** in this way, they have both, as "one man", been reconciled to **God.** The cross is the instrument. Only when sinners have been reconciled to God through the cross will they truly be reconciled to each other.

- **_Joint peace._** The death of the Lord Jesus enabled Him to come and preach "peace to you which were afar off, and to them that were nigh". Compare Isaiah 52 verse 7, "How beautiful upon the mountains are the feet of him that bringeth good tidings, that publisheth peace"; Isaiah 57 verse 19, "I create the fruit of the lips; Peace, peace to him that is far off, and to him that is near, saith the Lord". We should notice the expressions, "He is our peace" (v.14); "making peace" (v.15); "preached peace" (v.17). (There are seven references to " peace" in this Epistle.)

- **_Joint access._** "For through him we both have access by one Spirit unto the Father." **_There is now no limited access._** Here is the evidence that the Lord Jesus has "abolished in his flesh the enmity, even the law of commandments contained in ordinances", reminding us, again, of the Lord's words, "Other sheep I have which are not of this fold: them also I must bring, and they shall hear my voice; and there shall be one fold, and one shepherd" (John 10: 16).

We must notice the involvement of the Godhead in our approach to God: "For through **_him_** (the Lord Jesus) we both (Jew and Gentile) have access by one **_Spirit_** unto the **_Father_**".

As already noted, the word "now" occurs twice in this section. As we have noticed, in verses 13-18 emphasis is placed on "one body". Now we must notice that in verses 19-22 emphasis is placed on one building. So:

b) **_One building, vv.19-22_**

We should notice **_(i)_** the household (v.19): "the household of God"; **_(ii)_** the house (vv.20-22): "an holy temple in the Lord".

i) The household, v.19. "**_Now_** therefore ye are **_no more_** strangers (as they were in v.12) and foreigners (literally, 'sojourners'), but fellow-citizens with the saints, and of the household of God." **_There is now no national barrier._** There is now a new community. The word translated "foreigners" (_paroikos,_ meaning 'dwelling near', but not a citizen) refers to Gentiles residing in Israel, but that is all.

The word 'citizenship' carries the idea of partaking in a common privilege. "Fellow-citizens with the **_saints_**", reminds us that while, in the Old Testament, the word "saints" is associated with the Jewish nation, now it has a wider and more comprehensive connotation. The common relationship is expressed by the phrase, "household of God". In the words of W.E.Vine, "'the household of God' denotes the company of the redeemed; in Galatians 6 verse 10, it is called 'the household of the faith', RV". Albert Leckie explains the passage with clarity: "If in God's dealings with men anterior to Calvary, the Gentile was considered a stranger, outside of the family and a foreigner without any personal rights, now by divine grace they were fellow-citizens with all the saints of this era, having equal rights and privileges as those who belong to the same city (Luke 15: 15), or country (Acts 21: 39.) They were of the same household of God, and of the same spiritual family". Paul now speaks about the house itself.

ii) The house, vv.20-22. We should notice its foundation (v.20); its corner stone (v.20); its growth (v.21); its purpose (v.21). It has been nicely said that: "This tells us that the Church is a building, perfectly designed by the Great Architect. It is not a haphazard pile of stones, randomly dumped in a field. God *arranges* the Church for His own glory and purpose" (supplied by Justin Waldron).

- *Its foundation*. "And are built upon the foundation of the apostles and prophets, Jesus Christ himself being the chief corner stone." "Built" *not* 'upon the patriarchs', but upon "the foundation of the apostles and prophets". 1 Peter 2 verses 1-6 is now compulsory reading!

The word "of" ("built upon the foundation *of* the apostles and prophets") is not subjective, but objective. That is, the apostles and prophets are not themselves the foundation: they laid the foundation. In laying the foundation, they emphasised the most important point of all, viz. that the Lord Jesus is the "chief corner stone".

- *Its corner stone*. "Jesus Christ himself being the chief corner stone." This conveys stability. The cornerstone was laid to give strength to the two walls which it connected. Thus Christ unites Jew and Gentile. All other stones are laid in relation to the corner stone. Hence our lives must be regulated with reference to Christ.

- *Its growth*. "In whom all the building fitly framed together groweth unto an holy temple in the Lord; in whom ye also (the Ephesians were part of that 'holy temple') are builded together for an habitation of God through the Spirit." We should notice that Paul does not say '*on* whom', but "*in* whom":

the building grows in vital union with Christ. He is the builder. He said, "I will build my church" (Matt. 16: 18).

The expression "fitly framed" occurs again in Ephesians 4 verse 16 ("fitly joined") in connection with the body. The question is, what is "fitly framed together"? It is certainly not each local church! These are not "fitly framed together" to form the church! It must therefore be the individual believer. This is most certainly the case in Chapter 4 verse 16: "From whom (Christ) the whole body **fitly joined** together and compacted by that which **every joint** supplieth, according to the effectual working in the measure of **every part**, maketh increase of the body unto the edifying of itself in love". The translation 'every or each several building' does not fit the context at all, and A.Leckie is surely correct in saying, 'the apostle is speaking of believing Jews and believing Gentiles being joined together in this building that is growing "unto an holy temple in the Lord"'.

- ***Its purpose.*** It "groweth unto an holy temple in the Lord: in whom ye also are builded together for an habitation of God through the Spirit".

The words, "groweth unto a holy temple in the Lord", could well look on to the future and permanent glory of the church: "A glorious church, not having spot, or wrinkle, or any such thing; but that it should be holy and without blemish" (Eph. 5: 27). The Old Testament temple was a sacred building, an epithet which it shares with the coming millennial temple.

This wonderful spiritual building is, equally, a "holy temple", in contrast to the idolatrous, unholy temple of Diana. This spiritual temple is not only owned but occupied. God fills it. It is "an habitation of God through the Spirit". The same life permeates the whole structure and is in each individual member (A.Swanson, *From my Notebook, Galatians & Ephesians*). Never was there another temple like this. Under the old dispensation, God localised His presence in the tabernacle and in the temple (John 4: 20-21). The Jew had to journey to these buildings in order to worship God. God had a tabernacle for His people, but now, under grace, His people are His tabernacle or dwelling place. The church is the "habitation of God through the Spirit". The word translated "habitation" *(katoiketerion)* implies a permanent dwelling place.

So Gentiles now belong to the same country, the same city, the same family, the same foundation, the same temple. Angus Swanson (see above) sums it up like this:

Its social nature	-	fellow-citizens
Its spiritual nature	-	household of God
Its stable nature	-	upon the foundation
Its symmetrical nature	-	fitly framed together
Its sanctified nature	-	holy temple
Its sublime nature	-	habitation of God

"And so this chapter, which began with a description of these Gentiles as dead, depraved, diabolical and disobedient, now ends with these same Gentiles as cleansed from all guilt and defilement, and established (with all believers, Jew or Gentile) as a holy spiritual temple in Christ ... " (supplied by Justin Waldron). We should add that, strictly speaking, in Christ "there is neither Greek, nor Jew ... but Christ is all, and in all" (Col. 3: 11).

If in verses 1-10, we have the **human material**, and in verses 11-22, the **divine masterpiece**, then in Chapter 3 verses 1-13, we have the **hidden mystery**. In our next study, we will consider Paul's teaching in connection with the last of these.

Addenda

1) "He ... hath broken down the middle wall of partition between us" (v.14).

We are told that on the wall between the court of the Gentiles and the inner courts, there was an inscription written in Greek and Latin: "No foreigner may enter within the barricade which surrounds the sanctuary and enclosure. Anyone who is caught doing so will have himself to blame for his ensuing death". It nearly happened to Paul. See Acts 21 verses 27-32.

2) "In whom all the building ... groweth unto an holy temple in the Lord" (v.21).

The Revised Version rendering, "in whom each several building, fitly framed together, groweth into a holy temple in the Lord", suggests that "the completed temple will consist of the aggregate of a large number of smaller buildings" (F.F.Bruce). However, having quoted the Revised Version, F.F.Bruce goes on to say that he does not agree with it!

THE EPISTLE TO THE EPHESIANS

"The mystery ... which in other ages was not made known unto the sons of men"

Read Chapter 3: 1-13

If Ephesians 1 emphasises God's **purpose**, and Chapter 2 emphasises His **power** (in respect of the dead, vv.1-10, and in respect of the distant, vv.11-22), then Chapter 3 emphasises His **programme.**

God's 'programme' centres here on the "mystery" which "in **other ages** was not known unto the sons of men, as it is **now** revealed unto his holy apostles and prophets by the Spirit; that the Gentiles should be fellowheirs, and of the same body, and partakers of his promise in Christ by the gospel" (vv.3-6).

We should say at this juncture that in the New Testament, the word "mystery" refers, not to something totally inexplicable, but to something hitherto hidden "in God" which has now been revealed by Him. Paul puts it like this: "Unto me, who am less than the least of all saints, is this grace given, that I should preach among the Gentiles the unsearchable riches of Christ, and to make all men see what is the fellowship of the mystery, which from the beginning of the world hath been **hid** in God, who created all things by Jesus Christ: to the intent that **now** unto the principalities and powers in heavenly places might be known by the church the manifold wisdom of God, according to the **eternal purpose** which he purposed in Christ Jesus our Lord ..." (vv. 8-11).

In *The Collected Writings of W.E.Vine, Volume 5*, the publishers include a paper entitled 'The Twelve Mysteries of Scripture'. This includes, as we would expect, the "mystery" of believing Jews and Gentiles becoming 'co-members' of the church, the 'body of Christ'. Amongst other 'mysteries' are "the mystery of God" (Col. 2: 2), "the mystery of godliness" (1 Tim. 3: 16), the "mystery" of resurrection (1 Cor. 15: 51), "the mystery of iniquity" (2

Thess. 2: 7), "the mysteries of the kingdom"(Matt. 13: 11). The apostles were "ministers of Christ, and stewards of the mysteries of God" (1 Corinthians 4: 1). We should note that in Ephesians 1 verses 9-10, Paul uses the word "mystery" in connection with God's purpose to "gather together in one all things in Christ, both which are in heaven, and ... on earth".

Albert Leckie points out: "The 'mystery' here (in Ephesians 3: 4, 9) is not simply the gospel in terms of grace reaching out in salvation to the Gentiles ... Nor is the 'mystery' the fact of the church in this day of grace – this was revealed by our Lord in Matthew 16 verse 18. The 'mystery' revealed to Paul was the unique character of the church as the body of Christ in which converted Jew and Gentile are co-members". T.E.Wilson calls the New Testament 'mysteries' – 'sacred secrets'.

With this in mind, Ephesians 3 may be divided into two major sections as follows: *(1)* Paul's stewardship (vv.1-13); *(2)* Paul's supplication (vv.14-21). Both sections are introduced with the words, "For this cause ..." (vv.1, 14).

If, however, we turn the two suggested divisions into three, it looks like this: *(1) the "mystery" revealed to Paul* (vv.2-6): "he made known unto me the mystery" (v.3); *(2) the "mystery" revealed by Paul* (vv.7-12): "to make all men see what is the fellowship of the mystery" (v.9); *(3) the "mystery" understood by the Ephesians* (vv.14-21): that ye "may be able to comprehend with all saints what is the breadth, and length, and depth and height ..." (v.18). That is, the "breadth ... length ... depth and height" of the "mystery".

1) THE "MYSTERY" REVEALED TO PAUL, vv.1-6

In this connection, Paul refers to himself as a steward (see also 1 Cor. 4: 1): "For this cause I Paul, the prisoner of Jesus Christ for you Gentiles, if ye have heard of the **dispensation** of the grace of God which is given me to you-ward ..." According to W.E.Vine, the word rendered "dispensation" (*oikonomia*), which "primarily signifies the management of a household or household affairs (*oikos,* a house, *nonos,* a law), came to include the management or administration of the property of others, and so a stewardship. See Luke 16 verses 2, 3 and 4". W.E.Vine adds, "A dispensation is not a period or epoch (a common, but erroneous, use of the word), but a mode of dealing, an arrangement or administration of affairs". For further occurrences of the word, see 1 Corinthians 9 verse 17 and Colossians 1 verse 25.

It should be said that commentators and preachers generally tell us that Ephesians 3 verses 2-21 is really a parenthesis, or diversion, arising out of Paul's words "for you Gentiles", and that his 'main theme' can be traced by linking his opening words in Chapter 3 with his opening words in Chapter 4: "For this cause I Paul, the prisoner of Jesus Christ for you Gentiles ... I therefore, the prisoner of the Lord, beseech you that ye walk worthy of the vocation wherewith ye are called". Paul was evidently intent on stressing the practical implications for Gentile believers, but before doing so, he first explains his God-given role in detailing the immense privileges bestowed upon Gentile believers, and in praying that they would enjoy them to the full.

Bearing all this in mind, we will divide the passage (vv.1-6) as follows: *(a)* the scope of his stewardship (v.1); *(b)* the source of his stewardship (vv.2-4); *(c)* the uniqueness of his stewardship (v.5); *(d)* the subject of his stewardship (v.6).

a) The scope of his stewardship, v.1

Paul describes himself as "the apostle of the Gentiles" (Rom. 11: 13). In the words of W.E.Vine, "Paul was commissioned directly, by the Lord Himself, after His ascension, to carry the Gospel to the Gentiles". See, for example, Acts 22 verse 21. As we have already noticed, he was able to say, "Unto me, who am less than the least of all saints, is this grace given, that I should preach among **the Gentiles** the unsearchable riches of Christ" (v.8). Compare Galatians 2 verse 9, "And when James, Cephas, and John ... perceived the grace that was given unto me, they gave to me and Barnabas the right hands of fellowship; that **we should go unto the heathen** ('the nations', JND), and they unto the circumcision".

It is in his capacity of "the apostle to the Gentiles" that he now says, "For this cause I Paul, the prisoner of Jesus Christ **for you Gentiles**, if ye have heard of the dispensation of the grace of God which is given me to **you-ward** ..." (vv.1-2). In referring three times to the Gentiles (vv.1, 6, 8), Paul does not in any way suggest that they have been blessed to the detriment of the Jews, but rather that, with believing Jews, believing Gentiles have become "fellowheirs, and of the same body, and partakers of his promise in Christ by the gospel" (v.6).

Having described the wonderful way in which God has made "**both** (Jew and Gentile) **one**" (2: 14), reconciled "**both** unto God in **one body** by the cross" (2:16), and that "through him ... **both** have access by one Spirit unto the Father" (2: 18), Paul says, "for **this cause** ('reason', JND) I Paul, the prisoner of Jesus Christ for you Gentiles ... beseech you that ye walk worthy of the vocation (*klesis,* 'calling') wherewith ye are called" (3: 1 with 4: 1). But before he develops the subject, telling them how their 'calling' should affect **them**, he tells them how it affected **him**.

"For this cause I Paul, **the prisoner of Jesus Christ for you Gentiles** ..." Serving the Lord came with a price-tag. There is nothing glamorous about serving the Lord. Notwithstanding, Paul recognised that his adverse circumstances were in God's hand - an infinitely higher 'hand' than the hand of Rome! He was "the prisoner of Jesus Christ" ('Christ Jesus', margin), or "the prisoner of the Lord" (4: 1). Paul recognised the sovereignty of God in his circumstances. See also Philippians 1 verses 12-13.

We should also notice that Paul was well aware that his imprisonment (or 'house arrest', Acts 28: 16, 30) was not just 'part of the course', or 'a quirk of fate'.

- It was the direct result of his work amongst Gentiles. He was in prison because of Jewish animosity against him for reaching out to the Gentiles. See Acts 22 verses 21-22; Ephesians 3 verse 13 and 1 Thessalonians 2 verses 14-16. We should remember that, from the very beginning, Paul was thoroughly aware that suffering for Christ's sake lay ahead. The Lord told Ananias that He would show Paul "how great things he must suffer for my name's sake" (Acts 9: 16).

- It was part of God's plan for him to address the supreme court of the Roman Empire, and in so doing to bring the Gospel before the highest echelons of Roman society. See 2 Timothy 4 verses 16-17: "The Lord stood with me and strengthened me; that by me the preaching might be fully known, and that all **the Gentiles** might hear ..." Had Paul arrived in Rome as a visitor or traveller, he would never have had opportunity to personally appeal to Caesar (Acts. 25: 11-12; 26: 32).

b) The source of his stewardship, vv.2-4

Having described himself as "I Paul, the prisoner of Jesus Christ for you Gentiles", the apostle begins to explain his position. He commences by saying, "I Paul, the prisoner of Jesus Christ for you Gentiles, if ye have

Chapter 3:1-13

heard of ***the dispensation of the grace of God which is given me to you-ward*** ..."

We should notice that in referring to "the dispensation of the grace of God", Paul evidently has in mind, not so much "the grace that was given him as an unworthy servant of God", but to "the grace of God reaching out to the Gentiles" (A.Leckie). Compare Ephesians 1 verse 7 and Chapter 2 verse 7, where the "riches of his grace" and "the exceeding riches of his grace" relate to salvation. As we shall see, he certainly refers later to the "grace" given him personally (vv.7, 8). However, Paul does stress here that his stewardship in proclaiming "the grace of God" was ***imparted*** to him, reminding us that "the manifestation of the Spirit is given to every man to profit withal ..." (1 Cor. 12: 7-11). All believers are 'gifted' people!

The very word "dispensation", or 'stewardship', intimates that his service for God was assigned to him. Moreover, it was committed to him "by revelation" – "by ***revelation*** he made known unto me the mystery" (v.3). See also verse 5, "the mystery ... which in other ages was not made known unto the sons of men, as it is now ***revealed*** unto his holy apostles and prophets by the Spirit". Quite clearly, this was not something at which he had arrived by deduction or logic. Paul did not make it all up! It was not his invention! (Justin Waldron). As we have already emphasised, the word translated "mystery" (*musterion*) is truth previously hidden from human knowledge or understanding, but now disclosed by divine revelation.

We should notice, in passing, that it was "by revelation" that Paul learnt about the character of the church (v.3), and that it was "by ... revelation" that he learnt about the character of the gospel (Gal. 1: 12). Paul elsewhere refers to other things revealed to him, for example, the Lord's supper (1 Cor. 11: 23); the truths of the Gospel (Gal. 1: 12); the rapture of the saints (1 Thess. 4: 15). 'Revelation' relates to the imparting of God's word, through the Holy Spirit, to the men who were to write it down. 'Inspiration' relates to the transfer of God's word from the minds of the writers to their writings.

Albert Leckie's comments on the parenthetical words, "as I wrote afore in a few words (referring to what he had just written, 2: 11-22), whereby, when ye read, ye may understand my knowledge in the mystery of Christ" (vv. 3-5), are well worth quoting: "The importance of reading is stressed in this verse; this is how understanding is acquired now that divine revelation of our day is complete. 'My knowledge' (*sunesis*), translated 'intelligence' in the JND, is not self-approbation. Here was an intelligence by divine revelation that would be discerned by the reader". Compare Matthew 24 verse 15: "whoso readeth, let him understand".

Do notice that according to the New Translation (JND), Paul refers here, not to "Christ" but to "the Christ". See also 1 Corinthians 12 verse 12 (JND). "***The*** Christ" is Christ ***and*** His body – the church.

c) *The uniqueness of his stewardship, v.5*

"The mystery ... which in other ages (*heteros*, other ages of a different kind) was not made known unto the sons of men, as it is now revealed unto his holy apostles and prophets by the Spirit." It has been said, somewhat humorously, that since foundations do not appear halfway up a building, we do not have apostles and prophets now! We should note at least three things in relation to the "mystery":

i) It was not previously revealed

God's blessing and provision for Gentiles was most certainly anticipated in the Old Testament. See, for example, Genesis 12 verse 3. In the New Testament, Paul refers to passages from the Old Testament writings, law, and prophets which allude six times to the Gentiles (Rom. 15: 9-12).

But, as we have already noticed, the inclusion of Jew and Gentile in "one new man" was ***not*** anticipated in the Old Testament. This was "the mystery ... which in other ages was ***not made known*** unto the sons of men, as it is ***now revealed*** unto his holy apostles and prophets by the Spirit ..."

ii) How it has been revealed

Or, how it was acquired. It had been "revealed unto his holy apostles and prophets ***by the Spirit***". The Lord Jesus said to His disciples, "I have yet many things to say unto you, but ye cannot bear them now. Howbeit when he, the Spirit of truth, is come, he will guide you into all truth" (John 16: 12).

iii) To whom it was revealed

It was "revealed unto ***his holy apostles and prophets*** by the Spirit". That is, to the men who laid the foundation: "ye are ... built upon the foundation of the apostles and prophets, Jesus Christ himself being the chief corner stone" (Eph. 2: 20).

This verse (v.5) provides us with a threefold contrast:

- "Other ages" and "now"

- "Not made known" and "now revealed". This does not mean 'not made known in the same way', but 'not made known *at all*'. Compare Colossians 1 verse 26.

- "Sons of men" and "holy apostles and prophets". Not 'prophets and apostles', but 'apostles and prophets' – pointing, not to Old Testament prophets, but to New Testament prophets. It has been pointed out that even Gamaliel, "a doctor of the law", with a good reputation (Acts 5: 34), knew nothing about it. Paul certainly didn't get it from him! (Acts 22: 3)

d) The subject of his stewardship, v.6

"That the Gentiles should be fellowheirs, and of the same body, and partakers of his promise in Christ by the gospel", or "fellow-heirs, and fellow-members of the body, and fellow-partakers of the promise in Christ Jesus through the gospel" (RV).

Paul says nothing about 'Jewish' blessings and promises. Gentiles have not been brought on to 'Jewish' ground. Rather, both Jew and Gentile have been brought on to totally new ground! Hence the Revised Version's emphasis on 'fellow …' It looks like this:

- Believing Jews and Gentiles have *fellow possessions*: Gentile believers are "fellowheirs".

- Believing Jews and Gentiles have *a fellow position*: Gentile believers are of "the same body".

- Believing Jews and Gentiles are *fellow participants:* Gentile believers are "partakers of his promise in Christ by the gospel".

As Albert Leckie points out, "This situation is unique to this day of grace: not the Gentiles (nations) blessed through the nation of Israel as was the mind of God for a past day and will in fact be realised in an age to come, but Jew and Gentile sharing equally on the same common plane all the blessings of this day of grace". Gentile believers are not 'second class citizens'. They have equal status with their Jewish brethren. Both have been blessed in this way "in Christ ('Christ Jesus', JND) by the gospel". Since Paul says, "partakers of his promise in Christ by the gospel", we have to decide which "promise" he has in mind. Perhaps the answer lies in John 10 verse 16.

Truth revealed is truth to be communicated, which bring us to:

2) THE "MYSTERY" REVEALED BY PAUL, vv.7-12

In these verses, amongst other things, Paul repeats the comparison between past and present (see v.5): he refers to "the mystery, which from **the beginning of the world** hath been **hid** in God, who created all things by Jesus Christ: to the intent that **now** unto the principalities and powers in heavenly places **might be known**, by the church, the manifold wisdom of God" (vv.9-10).

If, in verses 2-3, Paul was given "the **dispensation of the grace of God**", that is, the stewardship of proclaiming "the grace of God", then here (v.7) he was given "the **gift of the grace of God**" in actually preaching "among the Gentiles the unsearchable riches of Christ".

With this in mind, we should notice what has been called 'Paul's dual function': he refers to himself: *(a)* as 'a minister of the gospel' (vv.6-8); *(b)* as a 'preacher of the mystery' (vv.9-12).

a) As 'a minister of the gospel', vv.6-8

"That the Gentiles should be ... partakers of his promise in Christ by the gospel; whereof I was made a minister according to the gift of the grace of God given unto me by the effectual working of his power. Unto me, who am less than the least of all saints, is this grace given, that I should preach among the Gentiles the unsearchable riches of Christ."

It is of interest to note that when Paul says *here*, "I was made a minister", he refers to the gospel, but that when he says "I am made a minister" in **Colossians 1 verse 25**, he refers to the church. Context is so important.

Chapter 3:1-13

We should note the following:

- Paul describes himself as a "minister" (*diakonos,* a servant). He refers to this in Acts 20 verse 19, "***serving*** the Lord with all humility". See also 1 Corinthians 3 verse 5. It is worth noting that he describes himself as a servant (*diakonos*) before describing himself as a preacher (*euangelizo* - to announce glad tidings), vv. 7, 8). Peter does something similar; he describes himself as "a servant and an apostle" (2 Pet. 1: 1). Significant, isn't it! But there is more:

- Paul describes himself as a divinely-equipped servant. He was *not* self-appointed and self-empowered. He was "***made*** a minister", not by an ecclesiastical body or a board of examiners, but because God had appointed him and equipped him: "I was made a minister ***according to the gift of the grace of God given unto me by the effectual working of his power***". The grace of God in selecting Paul to serve Him in this way was accompanied by God-given ability to serve Him. It was "by ('according to', RV/JND) the effectual working (*energeia*) of his power (*dunamis*)". It was ***God's*** power, not ***Paul's*** power. He makes no claims for himself. The Lord Jesus said, "***I will make you*** fishers of men". But there is still more:

- Paul describes himself as quite unworthy of the privilege of serving God: "I was made a minister according to ***the gift of the grace of God given unto me*** ... Unto me, who am ***less than the least of all saints***, is ***this grace given*** ..." But, at the same time, Paul is deeply appreciative of the privilege bestowed upon him. It was bestowed upon him in divine grace (vv.7, 8).

He served with a deep sense of unworthiness: as one who really did believe (Paul is not being rhetorical here) that he was "less than the least of all saints". See 1 Corinthians 15 verses 8-9 and 1 Timothy 1 verse 15. He served, equally, with a deep sense of the honour bestowed upon him. As Albert Leckie points out, 'The undoubted contrast is between Paul, "less than the least", and "the unsearchable riches of Christ"'. This 'sense of honour' permeates his very words: "Unto ***me***, who am less than the least of all saints, is this grace given, that ***I*** should preach among the Gentiles the unsearchable riches of Christ". There is a sense of wonder in Paul's voice here. You can hear it again in 1 Timothy 1 verses 12-14. The once proud Pharisee who would not previously have been in contact with Gentiles, now preached to them!

That sense of wonder comes, not only from the fact that he felt so unworthy to preach, but also from the fact that he was given such a superlative message

– "the unsearchable riches of Christ." The word rendered "unsearchable" (*anexichniastos*) is translated "past finding out" (Rom. 11: 33). It is beyond human understanding. Some one has said that it means 'cannot be probed'.

The "unsearchable riches of Christ" reminds us of "the riches of his grace" (1: 7; 2: 7); "the riches of the glory of his inheritance in the saints" (1. 18); "the riches of his glory" (3: 16).

It is a great honour to preach the Gospel!

This brings us to Paul:

b) As a 'preacher of the mystery', vv.9-12

Having referred to the grace of God in appointing him to "preach among the Gentiles the unsearchable riches of Christ", Paul goes further in adding, "and to make all (men) see, what is the fellowship ('administration', JND: 'stewardship', RV margin) of the mystery, which from the beginning of the world hath been hid in God, who created all things by Jesus Christ ..." (v.9). According to F.F.Bruce, "To make all men see" is, literally, "to enlighten (*photizo*) all men".

We have to decide whether "all men" here means 'all humanity' or 'all who responded to his preaching'. The context strongly suggests the latter. Having preached "among the Gentiles the unsearchable riches of Christ"(v.8), Paul then explained to those who responded, the wonderful way in which God had not only forgiven their sins, but at the same time, incorporated them in one body, the "church".

These verses are an advance on verses 5-6. In these earlier verses Paul refers to the fact that "the mystery" was "**not made known** unto the sons of men, as it is **now revealed unto his holy apostles and prophets** by the Spirit". Now, in verses 9-10, he refers to the fact that "the mystery, which from the beginning of the world ('throughout the ages', JND, or 'from all ages', RV) hath been hid in God" has now been made known, not only to God's "holy apostles and prophets" (vv.5-6), but "**to the principalities and powers in heavenly places**". We should notice the following:

i) That the "mystery" (that is, "That the Gentiles should be fellow-heirs ...", v.6) was not hid in the Old Testament, but "hid in God". So we look in vain for the doctrine of the church in the Old Testament.

ii) That the incorporation of believing Jews and believing Gentiles in one body is an object lesson to unseen observers of the "manifold (*polupoikilos*, 'much varied') wisdom of God". We must not forget that angels have an intense interest in the fulfilment of prophecy (1 Pet. 1: 10-12), in the salvation of sinners (Luke 15: 10), in the suffering of servants (1 Cor. 4: 9), in the conduct of saints (1 Cor. 11: 10) and, here, in the church as the masterpiece of divine wisdom. Wisdom is mentioned three times in this epistle (1: 8; 1: 17; 3: 10). We are told that ten different Hebrew Old Testament words are rendered "wisdom". This just shows how many-sided it really is!

iii) That in creation, God provided a setting in which He would ultimately display His supreme wisdom in this way before the wondering gaze of heavenly observers – both good and evil (see Eph. 6: 12). Very clearly, the reference to creation here is more than a passing observation: it indicates, rather, that there is a link between creation and the amazement of "principalities (those that exercise rule) and powers" (those with the ability exercise power) in heavenly places as they behold the church.

Albert Leckie puts it, rather beautifully, like this: "Little did these angelic beings realise as they witnessed God's power in creation, and in fact sang together (Job 38: 7), that God had a secret hid in His heart - that He was erecting a stage upon which in our day He would introduce the church and display in it to these same angelic beings His very varied wisdom. If Jew and Gentile failed God in everything entrusted to them, and the climax of their guilt was seen in their joint-condemnation to crucifixion of the Son of God, what an object lesson to angelic beings of the multifarious wisdom of God must be seen in Jew and Gentile joint-heirs, a joint-body and joint-partakers of God's promise. Here is the masterpiece of divine wisdom".

It has been nicely said, that "in the big picture, God does not use the angels to reveal His wisdom to the saints, but He does use the saints to reveal His wisdom unto the angelic beings, both faithful and fallen angels. This reminds us that we are called to something far greater than our own individual salvation and sanctification. We are called to be the means by which God teaches the universe a lesson, and a beautiful lesson" (supplied by Justin Waldron).

This was no emergency measure: it is "According to the eternal purpose (literally, 'according to the purpose of the ages') which he purposed in Christ Jesus our Lord" (v.11).

God's "eternal purpose" was not only that Jew and Gentile should be joint-participants in "the same body", but that they should approach Him with confidence, and have unshaken confidence in His will. Thus we read, "In whom we have boldness and access with confidence by the faith of him (or 'through our faith in him", RV: as also in Rom. 3: 22; Gal. 2: 20)", and "Wherefore I desire that ye faint not ('lose heart') at my tribulations for you, which is your glory" (vv.12-13). In view of all that Paul has told them:

*i) **They could confidently pray to God.*** They could pray with "boldness", that is, ability to speak freely; they could pray with "access", that is, ability to come freely; they could pray with 'confidence through faith in him', that is, ability to trust in Him freely. Through faith in Christ we have free, unrestricted, confident access to God.

*ii) **They could confidently trust the purpose of God.*** There was no reason to be disheartened over Paul's tribulations: "Wherefore I desire that ye faint not at my tribulations for you, which is your glory". It is noticeable that Paul was more concerned abut their spiritual welfare than he was for his own. His imprisonment was part of God's eternal purpose. He was suffering on account of, in his own words, "your glory". So there was an end in view, and to this end, Paul was "the prisoner of Jesus Christ for you Gentiles" (v.1). His imprisonment did not mean that he ceased to acquaint Gentiles with the gospel (see Ephesians 6: 19-20; Philippians 1:12-13). The very mention of "your glory" would remind the Ephesians that God's purpose was advancing towards its consummation" (F.F.Bruce).

This brings us to:

3) THE "MYSTERY" UNDERSTOOD BY THE EPHESIANS, vv.13-21

We will consider this in our next study.

THE EPISTLE TO THE EPHESIANS

"The breadth, and length, and depth, and height"

Read Chapter 3: 14-21

In introducing Ephesians 3, we suggested that the passage may be divided as follows: **(1) the "mystery" revealed to Paul** (vv.2-6): "he made known unto me the mystery" (v.3); **(2) the "mystery" revealed by Paul** (vv.7-12): "to make all men see what is the fellowship of the mystery" (v.9); **(3) the "mystery" understood by the Ephesians** (vv.14-21): "that ye may be able to comprehend with all saints what is the breadth, and length, and depth and height ..." (v.18). That is, we suggested, the "breadth ... length ... depth and height" of the "mystery".

1) THE "MYSTERY" REVEALED TO PAUL, vv.1-6

Speaking of himself as a steward (v.2, where the word "dispensation" refers to 'stewardship' or 'administration'), Paul refers to "the mystery ... which in other ages was not made known unto the sons of men, as it is now revealed unto his holy apostles and prophets by the Spirit; that the Gentiles should be fellowheirs, and of the same body, and partakers of his promise in Christ by the gospel" (vv.3, 5, 6).

2) THE "MYSTERY" REVEALED BY PAUL, vv.7-12

Speaking now of himself as a servant ("minister", AV), Paul - with evident amazement on his part - refers to the privilege bestowed upon him in this way: "Unto me, who am less than the least of all saints, is this grace given, that I should preach among the Gentiles the unsearchable riches of Christ; and to make all men see what is the fellowship of the mystery, which from the beginning of the world hath been hid in God ..." (vv.8-9).

This brings us to:

3) THE "MYSTERY" UNDERSTOOD BY THE EPHESIANS, vv.14-21

In these verses, Paul prays: "that ye may be able to comprehend with all saints what is the breadth, and length, and depth and height ..." (v.18). That is, the "breadth ... length ... depth and height" of the "mystery".

These verses contain the second of Paul's two recorded prayers for the believers at Ephesus.

- *In his first prayer* (1: 15-23), he prays for their enlightenment: "I ... cease not to give thanks for you, making mention of you in my prayers; that the God of our Lord Jesus Christ, the Father of glory, may give unto you the spirit of wisdom and revelation in the knowledge of him: the eyes of your understanding being **enlightened**; that ye may know **what** is the hope of his calling, and **what** the riches of the glory of his inheritance in the saints, and **what** is the exceeding greatness of his power to us-ward who believe ..."

- *In his second prayer* (3: 14-21), he prays that they might be enriched in their appreciation of divine love: "that Christ may dwell in your hearts by faith; that ye, being rooted and grounded in love, may be able to comprehend with all saints what is the breadth, and length, and depth, and height; and to know the love of Christ, which passeth knowledge, that ye might be filled with all the fulness of God". As we shall see, Paul is evidently referring, first (v.18), to the dimensions of the "mystery" (see vv.4-6, 9), something which they "may be able to comprehend", and then, secondly (v.19), to something that is incomprehensible, "the love of Christ, which passeth knowledge".

This is, in fact, the second of two requests. The *first* is addressed to *them.* "Wherefore I desire that ye faint not at my tribulations for you, which is your glory", (v.13). The *second* is addressed to *God.* "For this cause I bow my knees unto the Father of our Lord Jesus Christ ... that he would grant you ..." (vv.14, 16).

So Paul not only teaches: he prays that they might understand the teaching - an important lesson for every Bible teacher! We must add that Paul does not only pray that they might understand his teaching, but that they might come to appreciate the divine love which is expressed by that teaching. Hence "that ye may be able to comprehend with all saints what is the breadth, and length, and depth, and height, *and* to know *the love of Christ* which passeth knowledge ..."

We should never forget that Bible doctrine should always lead to a deepening sense of wonder and a deeper appreciation of the love of God. The hymn-writer puts it beautifully:

> *My God, how wonderful Thou art,*
> *Thy majesty how bright!*
> *How beautiful Thy mercy-seat,*
> *In depths of burning light.*
>
> *Oh, how I fear Thee, Living God,*
> *With deepest, tenderest fears,*
> *And worship Thee with trembling hope*
> *And penitential tears!*
>
> *Yet I may love Thee, too, O Lord,*
> *Almighty as Thou art,*
> *For Thou hast stooped to ask of me*
> *The love of my poor heart.*

It would be a profitable study to trace the references to "love" in this epistle, viz: "rooted and grounded in love" (3: 17); "forbearing one another in love" (4: 2); "speaking the truth in love" (4: 15); "the edifying of itself (the body of Christ) in love" (4: 16); "walk in love" (5: 2); "Husbands, love your wives ... Christ loved the church" (5: 25 ff); "love with faith" (6: 23).

We must now ponder the detail in Paul's prayer: *(A)* the address of the prayer (vv.14-15); *(B)* the content of the prayer (vv.16-19); *(C)* the doxology concluding the prayer (vv.20-21).

A) THE ADDRESS OF THE PRAYER, vv.14-15

"For this cause (that they might not be disheartened at his adversity) I bow my knees unto the Father of our Lord Jesus Christ" (v.14). Paul addresses his prayer to the "Father of our Lord Jesus Christ" and does so with reverence. We must notice his "reverent posture" (A.Leckie): "I bow my knees ..." Compare Solomon (1 Kings 8: 54); Daniel (Dan. 6: 10); Stephen (Acts 7: 60); Peter (Acts 9: 40); Paul, again (Acts 20: 36); the Lord Jesus Himself (Luke 22: 41). However, "Abraham stood ... before the LORD" (Gen. 18: 22) and David "sat before the LORD" (2 Sam. 7: 18).

The form of address, "the Father of our Lord Jesus Christ", is appropriate in view of what follows. While "most authorities seem to agree on the omission of the words, 'of our Lord Jesus Christ'" (A.Leckie), JND is not nearly so sure: see his marginal note. As Father, He is the Source of all, and here, of "every family in heaven and earth". The title, "Father", is freighted with divine love.

"Of whom (that is, 'By whom', not 'After whom') every family in heaven and earth is named" (RV). In the Old Testament, the Lord said of Israel, "You only have I known of all the families of the earth" (Amos 3: 2). Here, the words "every family" are used which, in view of previous teaching, may well indicate the inclusion of the Gentiles with Jews as "fellowheirs, and of the same body, and partakers of his promise in Christ by the gospel" (v.6). W.E.Vine suggests that the reference is to "all spiritually related to God the Father, Who is the Author of that spiritual relationship as children, uniting them to one another in family relationship".

The apostle is "not thinking of one family, some of whom are in heaven and some on earth, but rather of different families" (A.Leckie). However, not all agree. Wm.Hendriksen asserts that the AV reads properly, with reference to the context, and that the whole emphasis of the passage is on the unity of the church, rather than a series of families. We suggest, nevertheless, that Paul is intimating that while God is, indeed, the Father of all believers, of whatever period and whether the "innumerable company of angels ... the general assembly and church of the firstborn ... the spirits of just men made perfect" (Heb. 12: 22-23), His 'masterpiece' of family life is the church (Eph. 3: 10-11). He therefore prays "That he would grant *you*, according to the riches of his grace, to be strengthened with all might by his Spirit in the inner man ..." (v.16). The point of saying, "from whom every family in heaven and on earth is named" (RV) is that such a father as this is well able to answer Paul's prayer for the "household of God" (2: 19) This brings us to:

B) *THE CONTENT OF THE PRAYER, vv.16-19*

We should notice *(a)* the resource (v.16): "the riches of his glory", *(b)* the request (vv16-19): this involves strengthening by the Spirit (v.16), the indwelling of Christ (v.17), and the "fulness of God" (v.19): in other words, "the Blessed Trinity".

a) The resource, v.16

Speaking of His Father, the Lord Jesus said, "If ye then, being evil, know how to give good gifts unto your children, how much more shall your Father which is in heaven give good gifts to them that ask him" (Matt. 7:11). We are now to see something of these "good gifts", but first of all, the resources available to us: "That he would grant you, according to the riches of his glory". Divine wealth is liberally scattered in Ephesians 1-3. Note: "the **riches** of his grace" (1: 7), 'the **riches** of his mercy' (2: 4); "the **riches** of his glory" (3: 16).

"The riches of **his glory**" may be explained by the way in which the Lord answered the request of Moses, "I beseech thee, shew me thy glory" (Ex. 33: 18). The answer follows, first of all in words (v.19), and then visibly: "And the Lord passed by before him, and proclaimed, The Lord, the Lord God, merciful and gracious, longsuffering, and abundant in goodness and truth, keeping mercy for thousands, forgiving iniquity and transgression and sin, and that will by no means clear the guilty" (Ex. 34: 6-7). On this occasion, the Lord's glory was the perfect blending of every divine attribute, His absolute ability to meet every circumstance and exigency.

But let's look at it like this: "If I am a billionaire and I give you **ten dollars**, I have given you **out** of my riches. But if I give you a **million dollars**, I have given to you **according** to my riches. The first is a *portion*; the second is a *proportion*" (Warren Wiesbe). In other words, Paul is referring to the limitless resources of God made available to us.

The Ephesians were therefore told that God was completely able to meet Paul's request for them. His resources are infinite. He delights to bless His people out of them: "My God shall supply all your need according to his riches in glory by Christ Jesus" (Phil. 4: 19); "Strengthened with all might according to his glorious power" (Col. 1: 11).

b) The request, vv.16-19

We cannot fail to notice how one part of the prayer merges perfectly with the next in drawing us onwards and upwards to the point when we are "filled with all (unto) the fulness of God" (v.19). With that in mind, Paul uses the conjunction "that" (vv.16, 17, 19) in progressively elevating his petition. W.Hendriksen likens the parts of the prayer to the rungs of a ladder, leading progressively upward. We must notice the following *(i)* the strengthening of the Spirit (v.16); *(ii)* the indwelling of Christ (v.17); *(iii)* the dimensions of the mystery (v.18); *(iv)* the love of Christ (v.19); *(v)* the fulness of God (v.19).

i) The strengthening of the Spirit, v.16

"That he would grant you, according to the riches of his glory, to be strengthened with might by his Spirit in the inner man."

The subject is not so much spiritual power in service in the accepted sense (as, for example, in Acts 1: 8), but inward strengthening. "The Father could strengthen (the Greek word means 'to cause to acquire strength') and that with power *(dunamei)* in the inner man" (A.Leckie). Compare 2 Corinthians 4 verse 16, "though the outward man perish, yet the inward man is renewed day by day". The apostle is not referring here to service in the assembly - the exercise of gifts in the church - a subject developed later. The experience to which Paul refers concerns the daily life of every believer.

Understanding the "mystery" cannot be achieved by natural means. It cannot come by secular education, logical reasoning, or natural genius. It is only "by his Spirit in the inner man".

The Lord Jesus is the perfect example of a man "strengthened with might by God's Spirit in the inner man". "And Jesus being full of the **Holy Ghost** returned from Jordan, and was led by **the Spirit** into the wilderness ... and Jesus returned in the power of **the Spirit** into Galilee ... if I cast out demons by **the Spirit of God**, then the kingdom of God is come unto you ...The former treatise have I made, O Theophilus, of all that Jesus began both to do and teach, until the day in which he was taken up, after that he through **the Holy Ghost** had given commandments unto the apostles whom he had chosen" (Luke 4: 1; Luke 4: 14; Matt. 12: 28; Acts. 1: 1-2). These references disclose a Spirit-controlled life beyond compare. Never to our Lord need it be said, "Do not grieve the Holy Spirit of God" (Eph. 4. 30, JND), or, "Quench not the Spirit" (1 Thess. 5: 19). The experience of the strengthening power of the Holy Spirit in our lives is related to our submission and obedience to the Word of God. "This inward strengthening is in the inner man which delights in the law of God ((Rom. 7: 22), can be renewed (2 Cor. 4: 16), and is by the Spirit of the Father. All that pertains to the flesh and the natural man is excluded: here is a realm beyond their reach" (A.Leckie).

Chapter 3:14-21

The presence and power of the Holy Spirit in the life of the believer leads to a further consideration. It brings us into the enjoyment of:

ii) The indwelling of Christ, v.17

Paul prayed that the believers at Ephesus might "be strengthened with might by his Spirit in the inner man; that Christ may dwell in your hearts by faith (suggesting our dependence on Him) …" Just think of this: Christ, who "in the dispensation of the fulness of times" will be at the centre of the universe (Eph. 1: 10), is even now at the centre of the hearts of His people (T.Miller).

We must now listen carefully to the teaching of the Lord Jesus. "And I will pray the Father, and he shall give you another Comforter, that he may abide with you forever … but ye know him; for **he dwelleth with you and shall be in you.** I will not leave you comfortless, **I will come to you**" (John 14: 16-18). The power of the indwelling Holy Spirit leads to the enjoyment of Christ Himself in our hearts, that is, in our inward lives. We should remember that the Holy Spirit has not come *instead* of Christ, but to make possible the indwelling of Christ in the hearts of His people. This does not refer only to an initial experience, but rather to His constant indwelling. But this is more than His presence (wonderful as that is): the text may be rendered, "may make a home (*katoikeo*, 'to settle down in a dwelling') in your hearts". The purpose of indwelling Spirit is to maintain our appreciation and enjoyment of Christ's presence. Someone who makes a home in our hearts cannot be a stranger. Faith is the key to the experience. In John's Gospel, it is love: "If a man love me, he will keep my words; and my Father will love him, and we will come unto him and make our abode (*mone*) with him" (John 14: 23). *Choice Gleanings* published a touching illustration of this verse. See Addenda (1).

The experience of Christ dwelling in our hearts by faith leads to the constant development and enriching of spiritual life. Having suggested that the usage of "hearts" implies Christ at the centre of our love, we notice what follows: "that ye, being rooted and grounded in love". This carries the figure of a plant healthily rooted, and a building solidly founded. A plant starved of the food essential to its growth and development will become stunted and emaciated: a Christian without Christ at the centre of his affections will be spiritually deficient.

To be rooted in love means: "forbearing one another in love" (Eph. 4: 2) and "speaking the truth in love" (Eph. 4: 15). That is, displaying in our lives that pre-eminent characteristic of Christian conduct required by the Saviour: "As I have loved you, that ye also love one another" (John 13: 34). To be "grounded" in love suggests stability. The Christian whose life is thus founded will not be shaken by the onslaughts of Satan calculated to topple him. We will then be able to "comprehend what is the breadth, and length, and depth, and height, and to know (*ginosko,* the inception and progress in knowledge: to 'get to know') the love of Christ". This brings us to the next part of the prayer. Strengthened by the Spirit in the inner man (v.16), Christ dwelling in the heart by faith and established in divine love (v17) brings strength to "comprehend":

iii) *The dimensions of the mystery, v.18*

The Greek word rendered *"comprehend"* (katalambano) actually means 'apprehend'. That is, "to lay hold of; then, to lay hold of so as to possess as one's own, to appropriate" (W.E.Vine).

We must not overlook the phrase, "with all saints". Progress in understanding any part of God's Word involves fellowship. A believer cannot expect to explore the fulness of any subject, apart from fellowship with fellow-believers. A Christian who habitually absents himself from meetings of the saints cannot be anxious to make progress in the things of God. "With all saints" shows that no one saint in isolation can apprehend "what is the breadth, and length, and depth, and height". The dimensions of the mystery are now given:

- *Its breadth.* This is the subject of the preceding section of the epistle, in which the grand truth of the union of Jew and Gentile in Christ is developed. What breadth of purpose in the words, "hath broken down the middle wall of partition between us"! The Gentile, as well as the Jew, is embraced. "For God so loved the world ..." We have already noted the way in which this is pre-figured in the Old Testament: "Joseph is a fruitful bough, even a fruitful bough by a well: whose branches run over the wall" (Gen. 49: 22). See John 4 verses 4-42.

The "breadth" of the mystery can therefore be understood from this very chapter: "by revelation he made known unto me the mystery ... which in other ages was not made known unto the sons of men, as it is now revealed unto his holy apostles and prophets by the Spirit: that the Gentiles should be fellowheirs, and of the same body, and partakers of his promise in Christ by the gospel ... ***according to the eternal purpose which he purposed*** *in Christ Jesus our Lord*" (Eph. 3: 3-6, 11). The breadth of the "mystery" was purposed from eternity!

As we have already noted, that God would ultimately bless the Gentile nations at large had long been understood by the Hebrew prophets, but when the "mystery" of the church was revealed, something entirely new appeared: that while the Gentile nations would retain their identity under the beneficent reign of Messiah, now, both Jew and Gentiles participate in one body, the church. Of its Head it is written, "to make in himself of twain one new man, so making peace; and that he might reconcile both unto God in one body by the cross" (Eph. 2: 15-16). Thus it is written, "give none offence, neither to the Jews, nor to the Gentiles, nor to the church of God" (1 Cor. 10: 32). The breadth of the "mystery" is seen in the last named, where "there is neither Greek nor Jew, circumcision nor uncircumcision, Barbarian, Scythian, bond nor free: but Christ is all, and in all" (Col. 3: 11).

Paul delighted not only in the sublime truth of the church, but in the fact that to him was extended the privilege of preaching "among the Gentiles the unsearchable riches of Christ; and to make *all men* see what is the fellowship of the mystery". There is its "breadth".

- *Its length*. This dimension recalls earlier teaching in the chapter. The church, incorporating both Jew and Gentile in one body was a "mystery which from the beginning of the world hath been hid in God" (v.9). The church, which displays "the manifold wisdom of God", is "according to the *eternal purpose* which he purposed in Christ Jesus our Lord" (v.11).

In calculating the length of the "mystery", we must therefore begin in eternity! But that is not all: we end in eternity! "That in the ages to come, he might shew the exceeding riches of his grace in his kindness toward us by Christ Jesus" (Eph. 2: 7). Such is its length.

- *Its depth*. "And you hath he quickened who were dead in trespasses and sins ... among whom also we *all* had our conversation in times past ..." (Eph. 2: 1-3).

It is the "all" of Jew and Gentile. "But God who is rich in mercy, for his great love wherewith he loved us (Jew and Gentile) even when we were dead in sins hath quickened us together with Christ" (Eph. 2: 4-5). The great question is, how? On what basis? The answer lies in Ephesians 1 verse 7,

Ephesians

"In whom we have redemption through his blood", and in Ephesians 2 verse 13, "made nigh by the blood of Christ."

- *Its height.* "But God, who is rich in mercy, for his great love wherewith he loved us, even when we were dead in sins, hath quickened us together with Christ (by grace are ye saved) and hath raised us up together, and made us sit together in *heavenly places in Christ Jesus*: that in the ages to come he might shew the exceeding riches of his grace toward us through Christ Jesus" (Eph. 2: 4-7). Once again, it is the "us" of Jew and Gentile.

It is well worth remembering that while "all things", including "all principality and power", are 'under the feet' of the risen and ascended Christ, the church is identified with Him as its "head". God has given "him to be head over all things to the church, which is his body, the fulness of him that filleth all in all" (Eph. 1: 20-23). The "principalities" and "powers" with which we engage in spiritual conflict (Eph. 6: 12) are beneath His feet. Not so the church. The church is not identified with the feet of Christ. The church is one with Him as its glorious Head, and therefore above its enemies! Our foes are beneath our feet! Behold the 'height' of the mystery! This brings us to:

iv) The love of Christ, v.19

The 'dimensions' of the "mystery" reveal, at the same time, the breadth, the length, the depth, and the height of the "love of Christ that passeth knowledge". As Albert Leckie points out, "The love of Christ" in this epistle is *His love to the church.* See Chapter 5 verses 25-27. If the breadth, length, depth and height of verse 18 may be *apprehended,* the love of Christ *surpasses knowledge*; yet it is not unknowable".

But, wonderful as it is, 'knowing the love of Christ which passeth knowledge', is not an end in itself. It will have a transforming effect on our lives. "And to know the love of Christ which passeth knowledge, *that* ye might be filled with all the fulness of God."

v) The fulness of God, v.19

It has been pointed out that the words, "that ye might be filled with all the fulness of God" are better rendered "filled unto (*eis*) all the fulness of God" (RV). That is, "being progressively filled 'up to the measure' of God's fulness" (F.F.Bruce). As A.Leckie points out, "this cannot be 'the fulness of the Godhead' (Colossians

2: 9), for this is incommunicable. Whatever this fulness might be, no-one could contain it. The fulness of God must relate to what of God is communicable to the saints: 'filled with the knowledge of his will (Col. 1: 9); 'fill you with all joy and peace in believing" (Rom. 15: 13); 'partakers of the divine nature' (2 Pet. 1: 4); and 'of his fulness have all we received, and grace for grace' (John 1: 16).

C) THE DOXOLOGY CONCLUDING THE PRAYER, vv.20-21

"Now unto him that is able to do exceeding abundantly above all that we ask or think, according to the power (*dunamis*) that worketh (*energeia*) in us, unto him be glory in the church by Christ Jesus throughout all ages, world without end. Amen". We should notice the words: **(a)** "**unto him** that is able" (v.20); **(b)** "**unto him** be glory" (v.21). See Addenda (2).

a) "Unto him that is able", v.20

Paul does not say 'above all that we **can** ask or think', but "above all that we ask or think". He is thinking of the requests in his prayer! God is able to more than answer these petitions: that the Lord's people should be "strengthened with might by his Spirit in the inner man ... may be able to comprehend with all saints, what is the breadth, and length, and depth, and height; and to know the love of Christ, which passeth knowledge ... filled with (unto) all the fulness of God". The words, "exceeding abundantly" mean 'in over abundance, beyond all measure'. The power to know and enjoy this is resident in every believer: it is "the power that worketh in us".

Warren Wiersbe has a nice piece here: "Some power is dormant; it is available, but not being used, such as the power stored in a battery. But God's energy is effectual power – power at work in our lives. This power works *in* us, in the inner man (v.16). Philippians 2 verses 12-13 are parallel verses, so be sure to read them". Good advice!

b) "Unto him be glory", v.21

The words, "throughout all ages, world without end" are elsewhere rendered, 'unto all generations of the age of ages' (JND). Albert Leckie explains this as follows: "If the age of the ages be the coming millennium, as I judge it to be, then the church in its peculiar and unique relationship to Christ will be seen by generations, to the glory of the Father". Albert Leckie continues by pointing out that if the church now "displays to **angelic beings** in the

Ephesians

heavenlies the multi-varied wisdom of God (v.10)" then in the "age of the ages", from "its place in the heavenlies with Christ Jesus", it will bring glory to the Father on the part of "generations *of men on the earth*".

F.F.Bruce puts it differently: "Paul piles synonym on synonym to emphasise the eternity of God's praise: 'unto all generations of the age of the ages' (as the RV margin renders it literally). Since it is God's will 'in the ages to come' to display the 'exceeding riches of His grace' in those who have been its most signal beneficiaries, so throughout these coming ages, one age supervening upon another into the remotest infinity, it is that excelling grace of His which will redound to His highest glory. Well may the apostle add his 'Amen'; but it is not his 'Amen' alone, but the 'Amen of the whole new creation. On this transcendent note the first part of the epistle ends".

Addenda

1) "That Christ may dwell in your hearts by faith", v17.

"Napoleon was a general who generated tremendous love and loyalty among his troops. The story is told of a soldier badly wounded in battle. The surgeon was cutting deep to remove the bullet. Between groans and cries the soldier muttered, 'probe deeper and you will find the Emperor'. So what is deep in our hearts? What has priority in our lives? Is it money? Is it pleasure? Is it family? Paul's prayer for believers was that Christ might be enshrined in our hearts as our Lord and Saviour. Probe your own heart today".   Donald L.Norbie.

Extracted from *Choice Gleanings* (date unrecorded)

2) "Now unto him that is able to do exceeding abundantly above all that we ask or think", v.20.

Ask
All that we ask
Above all that we ask or think
Abundantly above all that we ask or think
Exceeding abundantly above all that we ask or think
Able to do exceeding abundantly above all that we ask or think.

Extracted from *Choice Gleanings* (date unrecorded)

THE EPISTLE TO THE EPHESIANS

"Walk worthy of the vocation wherewith ye are called"

Read Chapter 4: 1-6

In introducing the Epistle, we drew attention to its two major sections. These were, in the words of Justin Waldron, *(1) Doctrine - our riches in Christ* (1: 3 - 3: 21) and *(2) Duty - our responsibilities in Christ* (4: 1 - 6: 20). In the first case, amongst other things, Paul draws our attention to our spiritual possessions in Christ (1: 3-14) and our spiritual position in Christ (2: 1-22). In the second case, to quote W.W.Wiersbe, attention is drawn, amongst other things, to walking in unity (4: 1-16), walking in purity (4: 17 - 5: 21), walking in harmony (5: 22 – 6: 9) and walking in victory (6: 10-20). The word "walk" occurs five times in this part of the letter.

The same two sections could be summarised in two words – **Belief** (chs. 1-3) and **Behaviour** (chs. 4-6). The first refers to our position "in Christ" (the references should be noted), and the second to our practice "in the Lord" (again, the references should be noted).

We have therefore now reached the second of the two major sections indicated above (Chs.4-6) with its appropriate introduction: "I therefore, the prisoner of the Lord, beseech you that ye walk worthy of the vocation wherewith ye are called" (4: 1). As noted above, Paul stresses, first of all, that to "walk worthy of the vocation (*klesis*, 'a calling', as in v.4) wherewith ye are called", means walking in unity. We should therefore notice *(1) the plea for unity* (vv.1-3): "endeavouring to keep the unity of the Spirit in the bond of peace" (v.3); *(2) the provision for unity* (vv.4-16): with this in mind, Paul discusses *(a)* the unity of the faith (vv.4-6); *(b)* the diversity of the gifts (vv.7-16).

1) THE PLEA FOR UNITY, vv.1-3

Attention is drawn to the following: *(a)* the manner in which Paul appeals to them (v.1); **(b)** the way in which they were to walk (v.2); **(c)** the diligence they were to display (v.3).

a) The manner in which Paul appeals to them, v.1

"I therefore, the prisoner of the Lord, beseech you that ye walk worthy of the vocation wherewith ye are called." We should say, first of all, that bearing in mind the previous teaching in the epistle, Paul is particularly emphasising that **Jew and Gentile have a responsibility to co-exist.** People who had previously been at enmity with one another had now been brought together as "one new man" (2: 15).

This did not mean, however, that strained relationships were unknown, and we have an example in Romans 14 verse 1 to Romans 15 verse 7. Paul concludes the passage by saying, "Now the God of patience and consolation grant you to be like-minded one toward another in Christ Jesus: that ye may with one mind and one mouth glorify God ..." (Rom. 15: 5-6). While our circumstances today differ from those existing in Paul's lifetime, the principles on which he addresses the problem are unchanging. His teaching on the subject is certainly applicable today.

We should now notice the following:

- As already noted, the two words, **"I therefore"**, introduce a new section in the Epistle. Paul introduces a new section in the Epistle to the Romans in the same way: "I beseech you, **therefore**, brethren, by the mercies of God ..." (Rom. 12: 1). But in both cases, it is rather more than a simple division. The use of "therefore" indicates that doctrine is to direct our lives, as well as to inform our minds.

The same lesson is stressed later in the chapter where, having referred to the way in which Christ, "the head", has so wonderfully provided for His "body" (v.15-16), Paul continues, "This I say **therefore**, and testify in the Lord, that ye henceforth walk not as other Gentiles walk ..." (v.17).

- Paul writes to them as **"the prisoner of the Lord"** ('*in* the Lord', JND), having already described himself as "Paul, the prisoner *of* Jesus Christ ('Christ Jesus', RV) for you Gentiles" (3: 1). In referring to himself in this way, Paul is emphasising his deep concern for his beloved brethren. He was, as we have seen, "the apostle of the Gentiles" (Rom. 11: 13) and his

God-given work was to "preach among the Gentiles the unsearchable riches of Christ" (Eph. 3: 8). His love for the Lord, and his love for the Gentiles meant imprisonment, and the man who was willing to endure such hardship expresses his deep concern for their spiritual welfare.

Paul, an imprisoned Jew on behalf of his Gentile brethren was, himself, diligently keeping "the unity of Spirit" in writing to them in this way! It has been nicely said that the man who is exhorting others to function, was functioning himself – in prison!

- Having prayed for them, Paul now beseeches them. Rather than commanding them, Paul says, "I ... **beseech** you that ye walk worthy of the vocation wherewith ye are called". The word "beseech" (*parakaleo*) means 'to call some one alongside'. Compare Mark 1 verse 40 ("And there came a leper to him, **beseeching** him, and saying unto him, if thou wilt, thou canst make me clean"); Mark 5 verse 18 ("He that had been possessed with the devil **prayed** - *parakaleo* - him that he might be with him"); Mark 5 verse 23 (And he Jairus, "**besought** him greatly, saying, My little daughter lieth at the point of death"). The word signifies, not merely asking, but asking with a sense of great urgency.

- Paul's deep desire was that they might "**walk worthy** of the vocation wherewith ye are called". That is, to "adorn the doctrine of God our Saviour" (Titus 2: 10). If in Chapters 1-3, we are **seated,** then in Chapters 4-6 we are **walking.** While we are to "walk **worthy** of the vocation wherewith we are called", we are deeply conscious that the 'prodigal son' speaks for us all in saying "I ... am **no more worthy** to be called thy son" (Luke 15: 21). See also Luke 3 verse 16 and Chapter 7 verses 6 & 7; in the latter case (Luke 7: 6, 7), we should notice that the centurion was deeply conscious of his unworthiness to **receive** the Lord (v.6), and of his unworthiness to **be received** by the Lord (v.7).

Do notice, in passing, that the New Testament speaks of our "high calling" (Phil. 3: 14), our "holy calling" (2 Tim. 1: 9), and our "heavenly calling" (Heb. 3: 1).

b) The way in which they were to walk, v.2

What is involved in walking "worthy of the vocation wherewith ye are called"? The answer follows: "Walk worthy of the vocation wherewith ye are called, **with all lowliness and meekness, with longsuffering, forbearing one another in love**".

- ***"With all lowliness."*** Not 'with lowliness', but "with ***all*** lowliness". That is, in complete lowliness, and at all times - not just when it suits us. The word translated "lowliness" (*tapeinophrosune*), meaning 'lowliness of mind, humbleness' (W.E.Vine), occurs in Acts 20 verse 19 ("serving the Lord with all humility of mind"); Philippians 2 verse 3 ("but in lowliness of mind let each esteem other better than themselves"). There was certainly no 'lowliness of mind' on the part of Jews to Gentiles. See Ephesians 2 verses 11-12.

- ***"With all ... meekness."*** Meekness has been defined as 'power under control'. It is often said that 'meekness is not weakness'. It describes inner self-control which does not give way to self-assertion and resistance. Moses was "very meek, above all the men which were upon the face of the earth" (Num. 12: 3). The Lord Jesus said, "Take my yoke upon you, and learn of me; for I am meek and lowly in heart: and ye shall find rest unto your souls" (Matt.11: 29).

- ***"With ... longsuffering."*** This translates *makrothumia* meaning 'long-tempered'. James calls it "slow to wrath" (James 1:19). That is, acting with self-restraint in the face of provocation.

- ***"Forbearing one another in love."*** The word translated "forbearing" (*anecho*) means 'a holding back - bearing with - enduring'. But, note, not with an aggrieved spirit, rather "***in love***".

c) The diligence they were to display, v.3

"Endeavouring to keep the unity of the Spirit in the bond of peace" or "Using diligence to keep the unity of the Spirit in the uniting bond of peace" (JND). The word rendered "endeavouring" (*spoudazo*) means 'to make haste, to be zealous, and hence, to be diligent' (W.E.Vine). The word is used in 2 Timothy 4 verse 9 ("Do thy ***diligence*** to come shortly unto me"); 2 Timothy 4 verse 21 ("Do thy ***diligence*** to come before winter"); 2 Peter 1 verse 10 ("Give ***diligence*** to make your calling and election sure", that is, secure in its objective); 2 Timothy 2 verse 15 ("***Study*** - *spoudazo* - to shew thyself approved unto God"). This is therefore something to which we must give careful heed.

- Diligence is required in ***keeping*** "the unity of the Spirit in the bond of peace". The word rendered "keeping" (*tereo*) is variously translated – for example 'keep' or 'hold fast'. See, for example, Acts 24 verse 23 ("he commanded the centurion to ***keep*** Paul"); Acts 16 verse 23 ("they cast them into prison, charging the jailor to **keep** them safely"); 2 Timothy 4 verse 7 ("I have **kept** the faith").

- Diligence is required in keeping "***the unity of the Spirit*** in the bond of peace". The word rendered "unity" (*henotes,* from *hen,* meaning 'one') occurs only here and in verse 13. It refers, not so much to the indwelling of the Spirit which, of course, unites all Christians, but the practical result of that indwelling. The former can never be disrupted but here is something that evidently *can* be disrupted. Hence, we are enjoined 'to keep' it. Sowing of "discord among brethren" (the opposite of keeping the unity of the Spirit) is an abomination to God. See Proverbs 6 verse 19.

- Diligence is required in keeping "the unity of the Spirit in ***the bond of peace"***. The "bond of peace", that which binds together (*sundesmos*), is largely explained by Colossians 3 verse 14, "And above all these things, put on love, which is the bond of perfectness". See also Colossians 2 verse 19, "The head, from which all the body by joints and bonds having nourishment ministered, and knit together, increaseth with the increase of God". It is often said that while we cannot create "the unity of the Spirit", we can keep it. We must therefore "Follow after the things which make for peace, and things wherewith one may edify another" (Rom. 14: 19). There can be little doubt that "the 'peace' mentioned here refers primarily to "the peace having been made between converted Jews and Gentiles" (Albert Leckie). See Ephesians 2 verses 14, 15 and 17.

This brings us to:

2) THE PROVISION FOR UNITY, vv.4-16

Provision for unity has been made, *(a)* through the unity of the faith (vv.4-6) and *(b)* through the diversity of the gifts (vv.7-16).

a) Through the unity of the faith, vv.4-6

In these verses "there are seven doctrinal unities to be observed in the endeavour to keep the unity of the Spirit. These are related to the three persons in the Godhead" (A.Leckie). Hence, "There is one body, and **one Spirit**, even as ye are called in one hope of your calling; **one Lord**, one faith, one baptism, **one God and Father** of all, who is above all, and through all, and in you all". As F.F.Bruce observes, "We may compare the mention of 'the same Spirit ... the same Lord ... the same God' in 1 Corinthians 12 verses 4-6".

Put differently, but helpfully, it has been said that "the first triad centres on the work of the Spirit, whereas the next triad centres on Christ. The third triad focuses entirely on God as Father. This shows that although the different Persons in the Godhead have differing roles, they are completely unified in every aspect of the divine nature and plan". (Supplied by Justin Waldron).

The seven "doctrinal unities" are these:

i) "One body", v.4

This is clearly stated earlier in the epistle: Christ "is our peace, who hath made both (converted Jews and Gentiles) one", having reconciled "both unto God in *one body* by the cross ..." (2: 13-16). Compare Colossians 3 verse 15, "And let the peace of God rule in your hearts, to the which also ye are called in *one body*". "One body" conveys "the unique character of the church, and in its oneness there is included converted Jew and Gentile" (A.Leckie).

ii) "One Spirit", v.4

This is also clearly stated earlier in the epistle: "For through him (Christ) we both have access by *one Spirit* unto the Father" (2: 18). See also 1 Corinthians 12 verse 13, "For by *one Spirit* are (were) we all baptized into one body, whether we be Jews or Gentiles, whether we be bond or free, and have been all made to drink into *one Spirit*". The 'baptism of the Spirit' refers to the church corporately, and took place once. That is, on the day of Pentecost. Believer's baptism signifies that something has ended and something has begun, and so does the 'baptism of the Spirit'. It signifies the end of old divisions (Jew and Gentile), and the beginning of an entirely new relationship – "one body".

iii) "One hope of your calling", v.4

Paul prayed that the believers at Ephesus might know "what is the hope of his calling" (1: 18), that is, "the redemption of the purchased possession, unto the praise of his glory" (1: 14). The Jew had an earthly hope; the Gentile was without hope (2: 12); now both have one hope of their calling – not an earthly hope for converted Jews and a heavenly for converted Gentiles, but '*one hope*'" (A.Leckie). Titus 2 verse 13 refers to "that blessed hope".

iv) "One Lord", v.5

"There is 'one Lord' whom Jew and Gentile must confess" (A.Leckie). Paul reminded the believers at Rome that "the scripture saith, Whosoever believeth on him (the Lord Jesus) shall not be ashamed. For there is no difference between the Jew and the Greek: for the same Lord over all is rich unto all that call upon him. For whosoever shall call on the name of the Lord shall be saved" (Rom. 10: 11-13).

"Acknowledging the Lordship of Christ is a giant step towards spiritual unity. It is difficult for two believers to claim to obey the same Lord, and yet not walk together in unity. See Romans 10 verse 9" (Supplied by Justin Waldron).

v) "One faith", v.5

"One faith" evidently refers to "the Christian faith" (A.Leckie) and therefore to "the faith which was once delivered unto the saints" (Jude v.3), that is, to the 'body of faith' - what is believed. The local assembly should be "the pillar and ground of the truth" (1 Tim. 3: 15). The doctrines of the faith are to be communicated by one generation to the next. See 2 Timothy 2 verse 2.

vi) "One baptism", v.5

If Paul had in mind here the 'baptism of the Spirit', he would doubtless have associated it with "one Spirit" (v.4) rather than with "one Lord". He makes the point here that "Jewish and Gentile believers alike acknowledge one Lord ... and had undergone one baptism in His name" (F.F.Bruce). Compare Acts 19 verses 1-5.

vii) "One God and Father of all", v.6

Paul reaches the zenith of his seven 'doctrinal unities' here: "One God and Father of **all**, who is above **all**, and through **all**, and in you **all**". In the words of F.F.Bruce, "Here Paul echoes the language of an Old Testament prophet: 'Have we not all one father? Hath not one God created us?' (Mal. 2: 10). But thanks to the Son of God, who came to show us the Father Himself, our appreciation of the Fatherhood of God is deeper than it could have been before Christ came. Now Gentiles as well as Jews have come, through Christ, to know this one God as their Father. It was to former pagans, worshippers of many gods, that Paul wrote in 1 Corinthians. 8 verse 6: 'Yet to us there is one

God, the Father; of whom are all things, and we unto him' (RV)".

Once, Gentiles were "without God in the world" (Eph. 2:12). Now, with believing Jews, believing Gentiles are "an habitation of God through the Spirit" (Eph. 2: 22). Once, God dwelt only amongst Israel. Now, He dwells in His church. Compare 2 Corinthians 6 verse 16.

The statements here merit closer attention.

- **He is the Creator of all**: "One God and Father of all". Paul is evidently not referring only to believers here. The best explanation comes from Paul himself whilst preaching on Mars' Hill: "God that made the world ... hath made of one blood all nations of men ... for in him we live, and move, and have our being ... Forasmuch then as we are **the offspring of God**, we ought not to think that the Godhead is like unto gold, or silver, or stone, graven by art and man's device" (Acts 17: 24-29).

- **He is transcendent over all**: "above all". He is so transcendent that He "humbleth himself to behold the things that are in heaven, and in the earth!" (Psalm 113: 6).

- **He is pervasive throughout all:** "through all". That is, His "sovereignty, providence and government" (A.Leckie) are everywhere.

- **He is immanent in all**: "and in you all". This indicates His unique relationship with believers. Only here does Paul say, "in **you** all", indicating His permanent indwelling (his 'immanence'). This is staggering, to put it mildly: the Creator of all, who is transcendent over all and pervasive throughout all, indwells His people! That is, **all** His people, whether of Jewish or Gentile ancestry.

This brings us to the second way in which provision has been made for unity, namely:

b) Through the diversity of the gifts, vv.7-16

The first thing we should say is that diversity does not mean division! If in verses 4-6 we have things in which **all** believers share, then in verses 7-16 we have things which are bestowed individually: "But unto **every one** of us is given grace according to the gift of Christ" (v.7).

We will address these verses in our next study.

THE EPISTLE TO THE EPHESIANS

"He ... gave gifts unto men"

Read Chapter 4: 7-16

In our previous study, we noted that Ephesians 4 brings us to the second major division of the epistle, and that each section may be summarised in one word - **Belief** (chs. 1-3) and **Behaviour** (chs. 4-6). The first refers to our position "in Christ", and the second to our practice "in the Lord".

In this connection we also noted that Chapters 4-6 commence with an appropriate introduction: "I therefore, the prisoner of the Lord, beseech you that ye walk worthy of the vocation (*klesis*, 'a calling') wherewith ye are called" (4: 1), and that the epistle stresses, first of all, that this means walking in unity, referring particularly to the "one new man" and the "one body" (2: 15, 16) comprising Jew and Gentile. We then went further and suggested that having made *(1)* a *plea for unity* (vv.1-3), "endeavouring to keep the unity of the Spirit in the bond of peace" (v.3), Paul then describes *(2)* the *provision for unity* (vv.4-16) and, with the latter in mind, he proceeds to discuss *(a)* the unity of the faith (vv.4-6); *(b)* the diversity of the gifts (vv.7-16).

1) THE PLEA FOR UNITY, vv.1-3

Bearing in mind that while "the unity of the Spirit" cannot be broken 'vitally' (A. Leckie), it can certainly be disturbed in practice. W.W.Wiersbe had this in mind in saying, "Paul is quite concerned that Christians do not break the unity of the Spirit by agreeing with false doctrine (Rom. 16: 17-20), and the apostle John echoes this warning (2 John vv.6-11). The local church cannot believe in peace at any price, for God's wisdom is 'first pure then peaceable' (James 3: 17). Purity of doctrine of itself does not produce spiritual unity, for there are churches that are sound in faith, but unsound when it comes to love. This is why Paul joins the two: 'speaking the truth in love' (Eph. 4: 15)".

Ephesians

This brought us to:

2) THE PROVISION FOR UNITY, vv.4-16

As stated above, we noted that in these verses, Paul draws our attention to *(A)* the unity of the faith (vv.4-6) and *(B)* the diversity of the gifts (vv.7-16). Provision for unity has been made:

A) Through the unity of the faith, vv.4-6

In these verses "there are seven doctrinal unities to be observed in the endeavour to keep the unity of the Spirit. These are related to the three persons in the Godhead" (A.Leckie). Hence, "There is one body, and **one Spirit**, even as ye are called in one hope of your calling; **one Lord**, one faith, one baptism, **one God and Father** of all, who is above all, and through all, and in you all".

This brings us to the second way in which provision has been made for unity, namely:

B) Through the diversity of the gifts, vv.7-16

The first thing we should say is that diversity does not mean division! If in verses 4-6 we have things in which **all** believers share, then in verses 7-16 we have things which are bestowed **individually**: "But unto **every one** of us is given grace according to the gift of Christ" (v.7).

We must notice the following: *(a)* the origin of the gifts (v.7); *(b)* the imparting of the gifts (vv.8-10); *(c)* the order of the gifts (v.11); *(d)* the purpose of the gifts (v.12-16).

Alternatively: *(a)* **Who** gave the gifts? (v.7); *(b)* **When** were the gifts given? (vv.8-10); *(c)* **What** are the gifts in question? (v.11); *(d)* **Why** were the gifts given? (vv.12-16).

a) The origin of the gifts, v.7

"But unto every one (*hekastos*, meaning 'each') of us is given grace according to the measure of the gift of Christ." The word "grace" (*charis*) has been defined as "the friendly disposition from which the kindly act proceeds, graciousness, lovingkindness, goodwill generally" (W.E.Vine). The word is once rendered "benefit" (2 Cor. 1: 15).

All the gifts are 'charismatic'. They are all gifts of grace. The word "gift" (*dorea*) means "a free gift, stressing its gratuitous character" (W.E.Vine).

The gifts are here described here as "the gift of Christ". In 1 Corinthians, gifts are associated with the Holy Spirit (1 Cor. 12: 4), and in Romans, with God (Rom. 12: 3). The bestowal of gifts and the ability to exercise them comes from the Godhead. What an honour! What a privilege!

Every believer is gifted. Compare 1 Corinthians 12 verse 7, "The manifestation of the Spirit is given to **every man** (as above, *hekastos*, meaning 'each', 'every' or 'everyone') to profit withal". It is unfortunate that the term 'gifted brother' is almost exclusively applied to men who excel in public preaching and teaching. We unwittingly convey the idea that such brethren are a class apart, and that their particular gift is the only one of any importance. On the contrary, every saint is gifted: "As every man hath received the gift ('a gift', JND), so minister the same one to another, as good stewards of the manifold grace of God" (1 Pet. 4: 10).

We should therefore notice:

- *That none are excepted.* "But unto **every one of us** is given grace according to the measure of the gift of Christ."

- *That none are excused*. "But unto every one of us **is given grace** according to the measure (*metron*) of the gift of Christ." The imparting of the gift is accompanied by ability to use it. We have more 'measurements' in verses 13 and 16.

- *That none can exult.* "But unto every one of us is given grace according to **the measure of the gift of Christ."** In the words of W.E.Vine, "Whatever the endowment, His is the bestowment and the adjustment". Compare verse 8, "**he ... gave gifts**"; verse 11, "And **he gave** some ..."

Paul emphasises elsewhere that none have any ground to exult in their ability. See, for example, Romans 12 verses 3-6, "For I say, through the grace that is given unto me, to every man that is among you, not to think of himself more highly then he ought; but to think soberly, according as God hath dealt to every man the measure of faith ... having then gifts differing according to the grace that is given unto us ..."; 1 Corinthians 4 verse 7, "What hast thou that thou didst not receive? Now if thou didst receive it, why dost thou glory, as if thou hadst not received it?"

b) *The imparting of the gifts, vv.8-10*

"Wherefore he saith, When he ascended up on high, he led captivity captive, and gave gifts unto men." The coming of the Holy Spirit, consequent on the Lord's ascension, was the occasion on which the Lord's gifts to His church (but not only to the church) were imparted, and the permanent presence of the Holy Spirit means that the gifts continue to be bestowed.

Paul refers here to Psalm 68 verse 18, "Thou hast ascended on high. Thou hast led captivity captive. Thou hast **received** gifts for men". It has been pointed out (F.F.Bruce) that under divine inspiration, Paul quotes an alternative reading – "**gave** gifts unto men", since this was more appropriate to his present purpose. Peter combines 'received' and 'gave' in saying, "Therefore being by the right hand of God exalted, and having **received** of the Father the promise of the Holy Ghost, he hath **shed forth** this which ye now see and hear" (Acts 2: 33). The connection with the Lord's ascension is explained by John as follows: "But this ('out of his belly shall flow rivers of living water') spake he (the Lord Jesus) of the Spirit, which they that believe on him should receive; for the Holy Ghost was not yet given; because that Jesus was not yet glorified" (John 7: 37-39).

Psalm 68 commences with, "Let God arise, let his enemies be scattered" (v.1), referring back to Judges 5 verse 12, "Lead thy captivity captive, thou son of Ahinoam". We should notice that in Judges 5, the very powers (Sisera, Jabin, the Canaanites) that held Israel captive, were themselves made captive. This is very important. As F.F.Bruce observes in connection with Ephesians 4, "there is little basis for the traditional view that the captives whom Christ led captive consisted here of the souls of men whom His victory liberated from the thraldom of death". There can be no doubt that the words, "when he ascended up on high, he led captivity captive, and gave gifts unto men", refer to His triumph over "the vanquished principalities and powers, whose attack upon Him had been signally frustrated" (F.F.Bruce). See Colossians 2 verse 15. In His ascension, the mighty Conqueror of satanic forces has given "gifts unto men". Sin held men in captivity, but Christ has bestowed blessings on them!

Chapter 4:7-16

We should note that the gifts have been given "unto **men**" generally, not only 'unto the church'. That is, men in general benefit from them. Hence the reference to "evangelists". They are not mentioned in 1 Corinthians 12 verse 28. But why the parenthesis in verses 9-10? "Now he that ascended, what is it but that he also descended first into the lower parts of the earth? He that descended is the same also that ascended up far above all heavens, that he might fill all things."

i) "He that ascended"

The statement points out that the Lord Jesus, having "***descended***" to earth in incarnation, has "***ascended up*** far above all heavens". Paul does not say that, like Enoch, the Lord Jesus was "translated" (Heb. 11: 5), because whereas Enoch was taken to a place he had never seen before, the disciples saw the Lord Jesus "ascend up ***where he was before***" (John 6: 62). The Saviour said, "***I came forth from the Father***, and am come into the world: again I leave the world, and ***go to the Father***" (John 16: 28). Paul puts it like this, "And without controversy great is the mystery of godliness: God was ***manifest in the flesh***, justified in the Spirit, seen of angels, preached unto the Gentiles, believed on in the world, ***received up into glory*** ('received up in glory', JND)" (1 Tim. 3: 16). We should notice:

- "***God was manifest in the flesh.***" This refers to His incarnation, and exhibits His humility. Through the Incarnation, we have ***Deity on earth***.

- "***Received up in glory***" (RV). This refers to His ascension, and exhibits His glory. Through the Ascension, we have ***humanity in heaven***. There is a man in heaven: an incarnate man.

The Lord Jesus ***"ascended up"*** (Eph. 4: 10; John 6: 62; John 20: 17). He was ***"received up"*** (Mark 16: 19; 1 Tim. 3: 16). He was ***"carried up"*** (Luke 24: 51). He was ***"taken up"*** (Acts 1: 9). He was ***welcomed up*** (Acts 3: 21), where the word "receive" (*dechomai*) means 'to receive readily and deliberately'. It carries the idea of a welcome, a ready reception. See Psalm 110 verse 1.

The fact that the Lord Jesus "ascended up far above all heavens" is perfectly clear - wonderfully clear! Psalm 113 verse 6 tells us just how "far above all heavens" this is: He "humbleth himself to behold the things that are in heaven ..." How about that!

Ephesians

But what about, "he also descended first into the *lower parts* of the earth? This brings us to

ii) "He that ... descended"

Since the Lord Jesus ascended from the place to which He descended, the "lower parts of the earth" cannot refer to some imagined subterranean regions, but to the earth itself in relation to heaven. See Isaiah 44 verse 23: "Sing, O ye heavens; for the Lord hath done it: shout, *ye lower parts of the earth* ..." See also Isaiah 55 verse 9, "For as the heavens are higher than the earth, so are my ways higher than your ways."

Paul refers here to the Lord's descent, in incarnation, from heaven to earth, and his ascent from earth to heaven. But do "the lower parts of the earth" refer to the imagined presence of the Lord in Hades? Psalm 16 verse 10 with Acts 3 verse 15 are usually cited in this connection. Does this mean that the Lord Jesus went to *Sheol* (New Testament, *Hades*) when He "yielded up the ghost"? One thing is perfectly clear, the Saviour went to a place of joy and peace: "Verily I say unto thee, Today shalt thou be *with me in paradise*". That is, to the place to which Paul refers in saying "caught up to the third heaven ... caught up into paradise" (2 Cor. 12: 2-4). Quite obviously, the Saviour did not go to the same place as the rich man in Luke 16: "And in hell he lift up his eyes, being in torment". To quote W.E.Vine: "Christ, at His death, having committed His spirit to the Father, went in spirit immediately into Heaven itself, the dwelling place of God (the Lord's mention of the place as Paradise must have been a great comfort to the malefactor; to the oriental mind it expressed the sum total of blessedness)".

But if this is so, how must we understand the words, "Thou wilt not *leave my soul in hell*"? Psalm 16 verse 10. The word "leave" is very strong, and means to leave behind, to forsake, to abandon. The Psalm itself supplies the answer: "*Their* sorrows shall be multiplied that hasten after another god ..." Psalm 16 verse 4. "Thou wilt not leave *my* soul in hell". The New Translation (JND) and RV render verse 10 as follows: 'For thou wilt not leave my soul *to* Sheol'. Others are rightly abandoned to *Sheol*: but not so the Lord Jesus. "The *wicked* shall be turned into hell (*Sheol*), and all the nations that forget God" (Psalm 9: 17).

In descending "into the lower parts of the earth" the Lord Jesus could not conceivably come *lower*. It involved "the death of the cross" (Phil. 2: 6-8). In ascending, He could not possibly have gone *higher.* He "ascended up far above all heavens, that he might fill all things". Compare Ephesians 1 verses 20-21. In the words of F.F.Bruce, "That is to say that He might pervade the whole universe with His presence from the lowest depths to the highest heights". "To fill all things with Himself is the glorious end of His descent and ascension – this could not otherwise have been realised" (A Leckie). The reconciliation of "all things unto himself" rests on "the blood of his cross" (Col. 1: 20).

This brings us to:

c) The order of the gifts, v.11

"And he gave some ('to be', italicised, RV), apostles; and some, prophets; and some, evangelists; and some, pastors and teachers." The gifts here are evidently the men themselves.

Bearing in mind that Paul tells us here that the Lord Jesus "gave gifts unto men" (*anthropos,* men in general, mankind), evangelists are included. Compare 1 Corinthians 12 verse 28 where, as already noted, evangelists are not mentioned: "And God hath set some in the church, first apostles, secondarily prophets, thirdly teachers ..." In this case, Paul is referring to the local assembly. The statement in this verse covers two periods:

- **Apostles and prophets** "formed the Lord's foundation-gifts to His church" (F.F.Bruce). See Ephesians 2 verse 20. The late Mr. Percy Parsons (speaking at Eastbrook Hall, Waltham Abbey in the 1950s) likened these gifts, and others, to the scaffolding swathing a building in course of construction, but that once the building was complete, scaffolding was no longer necessary. Similarly, with the advent of "that which is perfect" (the completed Scriptures, 1 Cor. 13:10), apostles and prophets were no longer necessary. Neither are in existence today, and the teaching of people who state otherwise must be given the 'blue pencil' treatment.

- **Evangelists and pastor-teachers** "are required in each generation" (F.F.Bruce). He continues: "The church can never dispense with men who preach the gospel and bring men and women to the knowledge of the truth, nor yet with men who can teach and guide in the way of truth those who have been evangelised and converted". While not all who preach the gospel could be described evangelists - in New Testament times, an evangelist was

Ephesians

essentially a pioneer - nevertheless every believer ought to be engaged in the business of making known the gospel.

d) The purpose of the gifts, vv.12-16

This may be summarised as follows: *(i)* maturity (vv.12-13); *(ii)* stability (vv.14-15); *(iii)* harmony (v.16).

i) Maturity, vv.12-13

"For the perfecting of the saints, for the work of the ministry, for the edifying of the body of Christ: till we all come in the unity of the faith, and of the knowledge of the Son of God, unto a perfect man, unto the measure of the stature of the fulness of Christ." The gifts have been given:

- **"For (pros) the perfecting of the saints."** The Greek preposition (*pros*) is important: it means 'towards'. In this case, towards 'perfecting (*katartismos*). Perfecting, that is, in the sense of "*mending (katartizo)* their nets" (Matt. 4: 21; Mark 1: 19). That is "to render fit, complete" (W.E.Vine) . See also Galatians 6 verse 1, "restore (*katartizo*) such an one". The gifts have been given, not as an end in themselves, but with a view to the spiritual fitness of the saints. So that they might be equipped for (*eis* – with a view to):

- **"The work of the ministry"** or **'the work of service'.** In this connection it has been said that the gifts have been given to "get everybody working!"

Once again, the Greek preposition here (*eis*) is important: it means 'unto' or 'with a view to'. In this case, with a view to "the work (*ergon*) of the ministry (*diakonia*)".

- **"The edifying of the body of Christ."** Paul uses the preposition *eis* again. The "work of the ministry" has in view the building up (*oikodome*) of the body of Christ (the church) which W.E.Vine defines as "the strengthening effect of teaching", adding "the idea conveyed is progress resulting from patient effort".

As F.F.Bruce nicely observes, "The healthy growth of the believing community is the aim in view in all the ministries which the Lord has entrusted to His people". He notes a remark made by E.K.Simpson that "In the theocracy of grace there is in fact no laity".

We have an example of all this at work in the help given to Apollos by Aquila and Priscilla who "expounded" (set out in its parts) unto him the way of God more perfectly (accurately)". With the result that on arriving at Corinth, Apollos "helped them much which had believed through grace" (Acts 18: 24-28).

The "perfecting of the saints ... the work of the ministry ... the edifying of the body of Christ" is **ongoing**: "Till we all come in the unity of the faith, and of the knowledge of the Son of God, unto a perfect man, unto the measure of the stature of the fulness of Christ" (v.13). While, at first glance, this might seem to look on to the coming of the Lord when, most certainly, there will completeness as never seen before, nevertheless Paul evidently has in mind the attainment of such maturity here and now. The force of "Till we **all** come" is, it seems, not so much 'Till we all – believers past, present and future - come together at one time, that is, at the coming of the Lord', but 'Till we come **now**' in fellowship with each other "in the unity of the faith, and of the knowledge of the Son of God, unto a perfect man, unto the measure of the stature of the fulness of Christ".

This is something attainable **now.** The "unity of the faith" can and should be enjoyed now. We have already been reminded of the necessity to "keep the unity of the Spirit in the bond of peace" (v.3). The words, "Till we **all** come ..." remind us that spiritual growth takes place in context of fellowship with each other (3: 18). We have already been reminded of the "one faith" (v.5), that is, "the faith which was once delivered unto the saints" (Jude v.3). The "knowledge (*epignosis*)of the Son of God" reminds us that Paul prayed that the Ephesian believers might "know (*ginosko*) the love of Christ that passeth knowledge (*gnosis*)". In both cases, the Paul refers to "an increasing personal acquaintance with Him in corporate as well individual experience" (F.F.Bruce). We have already learnt that "the church ... is his body (Christ's body), the fulness ('the complement') of him that filleth all in all" (1: 23). "Now she is to attain that 'fulness' in the spiritual growth and life of her members" F.F.Bruce). W.E.Vine puts it like this, "The standard of spiritual stature which is essentially Christ's".

All this – **now.** This will lead to

ii) Stability, vv.14-15

"That we henceforth be no more children ('babes', JND), tossed to and fro, and carried about with every wind of doctrine, by the sleight of men, and cunning craftiness, whereby they lay in wait to deceive; but, speaking the truth in love, may grow up into him in all things, which is the head, even Christ." The contrast is clear:

- **"No longer babes"** (JND), verse 14. That is *(i)* **unstable**: "tossed to and fro ..."; *(ii)* **gullible**: subject to the "the sleight (*kubia*, a cube) of men", sly (W.E.Vine): a reference to dice-playing; *(iii)* **subject to "cunning craftiness**" (*panourgia*, meaning 'all-working'), or 'sticking at nothing to gain its ends' (compare 2 Cor. 4: 2); *(iv)* **in danger from deception:** from people lying "in wait to deceive" or, "after the wiles of error" (RV), deceit of various kinds.

- **"May grow up"**, verse 15. This will mean "speaking the **truth** in love" ('dealing truly', RV margin), as opposed to being "tossed to and fro, and carried about with **every wind of doctrine**". It has been said that "the exhortation is not simply to speak (or tell the truth), but instinctively to recognise the truth, hold it and live it. The speaking must be 'in love': truth without love engenders legality, love without truth engenders licence" (A.Leckie). But it is more than that: "May grow up **into him** in all things, which is the head, even Christ". He was never "carried about with every wind of doctrine" - whether from Pharisees or Sadducees. He was never caught unawares by "**the sleight of men**", by "**cunning craftiness**", or by men lying "**in wait to deceive**". To "grow up into him in all things" means the body will match the head in speaking "the truth in love", and in overcoming the devices of Satan.

Growing up into Him "in all things" will mean

iii) Harmony, v.16

"But speaking the truth in love, may grow into him in all things, which is the head, even Christ: from whom the whole body fitly joined together, and compacted by that which every joint supplieth, according to the effectual working (translating one word - *energeia*) in the measure of every part ('the due measure of every part') maketh increase (*auxesis*, growth, increase) of the body unto the edifying of itself in love" (vv.15-16). Paul refers here to "the head, even Christ" and then to "the whole body". The head is the source of growth; each member is a channel of growth.

Chapter 4:7-16

- **"The head, even Christ."** F.F.Bruce explains this most helpfully: "Each part of the body will function as it ought while it is under the control of the head; if it escapes from this control and tries to act independently, the result is very distressing. So it is under the control of Christ that the members of His Church function harmoniously together, sharing His life and attaining maturity under His fostering care..."

- **"The whole body ..."** F.F.Bruce continues: "The members of His Church function harmoniously together ... supplied with nourishment and fitted together by means of the joints and ligaments (cf. Col. 2: 19). The phrase 'fitly framed' is a rendering of the Greek verb *synarmologeo*, which we have already noted in Ephesians 2 verse 21 (its only other New Testament occurrence), where it is used of the harmonious construction of the Church as 'a holy temple in the Lord'. The phrase 'knit together' represents the Greek *symbibazo* ('to put together'), which has this same sense in Colossians 2 verses 2 and 19. The word rendered 'joints' (Greek *haphe*) probably denotes the ligaments by which the various parts of the body are connected".

"The Lord Jesus is the source of growth" and "every member is exactly designed for their own place and function, and perfectly joined to every other member so as to make a complete living organism" (supplied by Justin Waldron). The words "compacted by that which every joint supplieth" emphasise "the indispensability of every member. In the human body, each joint and ligament fulfils a role in the growth and usefulness of the body. So it is in the body of Christ. No member is superficial, every member is necessary" (supplied by Justin Waldron).

In the body of Christ, the church, all this will be ineffective unless it is implemented in love. "But speaking the truth *in love*, may grow into him in all things, which is the head, even Christ: from whom the whole body fitly joined together, and compacted by that which every joint supplieth, according to the effectual working in the measure of every part, maketh increase of the body unto the edifying of itself *in love*".

THE EPISTLE TO THE EPHESIANS

"Walk not as other Gentiles walk"

Read Chapter 4: 17-19

As we have already noted, more than once, Ephesians 4 brings us to the second major division of the epistle, and each section may be summarised in one word - **Belief** (chs. 1-3) and **Behaviour** (chs. 4-6). The first refers to our position "in Christ", and the second to our practice "in the Lord".

As we have also noted, The 'second half' of the Epistle (chs.4-6) commences with an appropriate introduction: "I therefore, the prisoner of the Lord, beseech you that ye walk worthy of the vocation (*klesis*, 'a calling') wherewith ye are called" (4: 1). Paul does not leave it there – far from it: having said "walk worthy of the vocation wherewith ye are called", he continues by telling us what this means in practice. In the words of W.W.Wiersbe, it means walking in unity (4: 1-16), walking in purity (4: 17 - 5: 21), walking in harmony (5: 22 – 6: 9) and walking in victory (6: 10-20). The word "walk" occurs five times in this part of the epistle.

A) WALKING IN UNITY, vv.1-16

This has particular reference to the unique constitution of the church, which Paul calls the "one new man" and the "one body" (2: 15, 16) comprising Jew and Gentile. After noting *(1)* his ***plea for unity*** (vv.1-3), "endeavouring to keep the unity of the Spirit in the bond of peace" (v.3), he then describes *(2)* the ***provision for unity*** (vv.4-16) and, with the latter in mind, he proceeds to discuss *(a)* the unity of the faith (vv.4-6); *(b)* the diversity of the gifts (vv.7-16).

1) THE PLEA FOR UNITY, vv.1-3

This flows out of the fact that while "the unity of the Spirit" cannot be broken 'vitally' (A. Leckie), it can certainly be disturbed in practice.

2) THE PROVISION FOR UNITY, vv.4-16

Provision for unity has been made, *(a)* through the unity of the faith (vv.4-6) and *(b)* through the diversity of the gifts (vv.7-16).

a) The unity of the faith, vv.4-6

In these verses "there are seven doctrinal unities to be observed in the endeavour to keep the unity of the Spirit. These are related to the three persons in the Godhead" (A.Leckie). Hence, "There is one body, and **one Spirit**, even as ye are called in one hope of your calling; **one Lord**, one faith, one baptism, **one God and Father** of all, who is above all, and through all, and in you all". The 'unity of the faith' ("**one** Spirit ... **one** Lord, **one** faith, **one** baptism, **one** God and Father of all") is accompanied by

b) The diversity of the gifts, vv.7-16

In our previous study, we observed that diversity does not mean division! If in verses 4-6 we have things in which *all* believers share, then in verses 7-16 we have things which are bestowed *individually*: "But unto **every one** of us is given grace according to the gift of Christ" (v.7). In this connection, we noted:

- **The origin of the gifts** (v.7). They are described as "the gift of Christ". We noted that Paul is evidently referring here, not so much to the 'gift' or 'gifts' which a man possesses, but rather to the man himself.

- **The imparting of the gifts** (vv.8-10). They were bestowed in association with the ascension of the Lord Jesus, and therefore in association with the bestowal of the Holy Spirit. Compare verse 8 with Acts 2 verses 33-34.

- **The order of the gifts** (v.11). They fall into two categories. *(i)* **Apostles and prophets.** These "formed the Lord's foundation-gifts to His church" (F.F.Bruce). See Ephesians 2 verse 20. *(ii)* **Evangelists and pastor-teachers.** These "are required in each generation" (F.F.Bruce).

- **The purpose of the gifts** (vv.12-16). This may be summarised as follows: *(i)* maturity (vv.12-13); *(ii)* stability (vv.14-15); *(iii)* harmony (v.16). The reader is referred to the previous study for details. This brings us to:

B) WALKING IN PURITY, 4: 17 - 5: 21

With verse 17, Paul begins to develop other aspects of the overall theme, "walk worthy of the vocation wherewith ye are called" (4: 1). Hence: "This I say therefore (in view of the wonderful provision made for us as described in the previous verses), and testify in the Lord, that ye henceforth walk not as other Gentiles walk ..." Later, the apostle stresses the necessity to "walk in love" (5: 2), "walk as children of light" (5: 8) and "walk circumspectly ('accuracy which is the outcome of carefulness', W.E.Vine)" (5: 15).

In this connection, Paul contrasts the way in which *(1)* the Gentiles walk (vv.17-19) and *(2)* the way in which the Lord's people are to walk (vv.20-32).

1) HOW THE GENTILES WALK, vv.17-19

"This I say **therefore** (with all this resource), and testify in the Lord, that ye henceforth walk not as other Gentiles walk, in the vanity of their mind" (v.17). According to J.N.Darby (*The New Translation*), some texts omit "other" or 'the rest of' (JND).

We should notice that Paul invokes the authority of the Lord in relation to the 'walk' of the believer. He is not expressing his own opinion in the matter (nor, of course, on any other matter). The word rendered "testify" (*marturomai*) occurs in Acts 20 verse 26 ("I take you to record this day") and Galatians 5 verse 3 ("testify"). In the words of Albert Leckie "These three occasions ... indicate a solemn enunciation. The words "'in the Lord' give added weight. Having entered upon the practical section of the epistle, the reference to 'Lord' (*kurios*) should now be observed. A change of life on the part of these Gentiles was vital, of the utmost importance". F.F.Bruce writes similarly, "He emphasises, too, that the following injunctions are not his own; in laying them down he is bearing witness with authority, as the apostle of the Lord, to those who belong to the same Lord" that "it is **the Lord's will** that they should cease to live the old pagan life".

Well, how do pagans live? The answer follows as Paul draws attention *(a)* to the root cause of Gentile behaviour (vv.17-18), and then **(b)** to the resulting fruit in Gentile behaviour.

a) The cause of Gentile behaviour, vv.17-18

"Walk not as other Gentiles walk, in the vanity of their mind, having the understanding darkened, being alienated from the life of God through the ignorance that is in them, because of the blindness of their heart: who being past feeling, have given themselves over unto lasciviousness, to work all uncleanness with greediness." We should notice:

- **"The vanity of their mind"** (v.17) . Paul commences with the mind (*nous*), "in the vanity (*mataiotes*) of their mind (compare v. 23)", and thus traces the state described in verse 19 to its source. Romans 1 verse 21 tells us all we need to know: "Because that, when they knew God, they glorified him not as God, neither were thankful; but became vain (*mataioo*) in their imaginations, and their foolish heart was darkened". Vanity in the New Testament is sometimes closely associated with idolatry. See, for example, Acts 14 verse 15.

The word "vanity" means 'producing nothing profitable ... emptiness as to result.' The word "mind" (Greek *nous*) refers to the seat of reflective consciousness. But why are they possessed of vanity of their mind? It is because -

- **"Having the understanding darkened"** (v.18). These people cannot say, "Thy word is a lamp unto my feet, and a light unto my path" (Ps.119: 105). The word "understanding" (*dianoia*) means 'a thinking through, or over: a meditation, reflecting' (W.E.Vine). The word "darkened" is used of physical darkness in the New Testament (Rev. 9: 2; 16: 10), but here it is used in the same way as in Romans 1 verse 21, "their foolish heart was darkened". As F.F.Bruce observes, "How could it be otherwise, when men turn their backs on the true Light?" But why is the "understanding darkened"? It is because -

- **"Being alienated from the life of God through the ignorance that is in them"** (v.18). The word "alienated (*apallotrioo*) occurs again in Colossians 1 verse 21 (And you, that were sometimes alienated, and enemies in your mind by wicked works, yet now hath he reconciled ..."). Being "alienated from the life of God" means "dead in trespasses and sins" (2: 1).

"Paul ascribes this estrangement from God to men's innate ignorance, but an ignorance which is not excusable, because it stems from the fact that 'they refused to have God in their knowledge' (Rom 1: 28)" (F.F.Bruce). But why is this so? It is because of –

- **"The blindness of their heart"** (v.18) or **"the hardness of their hearts"** (RV/JND). The word translated "blindness" (*porosis*) means 'a hardening'. See also Mark 3 verse 5; Romans 11 verse 25. It is said that "this ancient Greek word is used medically to denote the callus formed when a bone has been fractured and reset. Such a callus is even harder than the bone itself" (supplied by Justin Waldron).

Attention is drawn to the following:

- **"Being past feeling."** Literally, 'ceasing to feel pain' (*apalgeo*)'. According to W.E.Vine, our English word 'neuralgia' derives from this Greek word! If you have neuralgia you certainly feel pain!! However, the connection is the word *algos*, which means pain: here the prefix (*apo*) means something you don't feel. So "being past feeling" means incapable of sensing the difference between right and wrong; insensible to good and evil, honour and shame, corruption and purity. In summary, no sense of shame. Compare 1 Timothy 4 verse 2, "having their conscience seared with a hot iron" or "cauterised as to their own conscience" (JND).

- **"Have given themselves."** What follows ("unto laciviousness") was something that they did deliberately. They 'gave themselves up' to unrestrained impurity and covetousness. In consequence, as F.F.Bruce points out, God gave them up (or 'over') ... "to just this way of life" (Rom. 1: 24, 26, 28).

- **"Unto lasciviousness."** W.E.Vine defines this (*aselgeia*) as "excess, licentiousness, indecency, wantonness". It has been said that "the bad man usually tries to hide his sin; but the man who has *aselgeia* in his soul does not care how much he shocks public opinion so long as he can gratify his desires" (supplied by Justin Waldron).

- **"To work all uncleanness with greediness."** "Uncleanness" (*akatharsia*) means impurity as in Ephesians 5 verses 3 and 5. See also Galatians 5 verse 19, and Colossians 3 verse 5. It refers to moral impurity. "Greediness" (*pleonexia*) means 'covetousness'. That is, a continuous lust for more. In Ephesians 5 verse 3 and Colossians 3 verse 5, it is used in connection with sensuality. In the latter passage, Paul makes it clear that sensuality can be an idol.

Now let's read the verse again: the following 'analysis' was contributed at the Eastbourne Bible Readings in May 2002. "Who being past feeling (they are *insensitive*) have given themselves over (they are *intemperate*) unto lasciviousness (they are *indecent*) to work (they are *industrious*) all uncleanness (they are *ingenious*) with greediness (they are *insatiable*)". As noted above, "greediness" means covetousness – a desire to have more. This brings us to:

2) HOW THE LORD'S PEOPLE ARE TO WALK, vv.20-32

In this section Paul discusses how the saints are to walk *(a)* generally, verses 20-24, and *(b)* particularly, verses 25-32. We will consider these verses in our next study.

However, we cannot conclude without noting that these verses begin with the words, "But ye have not so learned Christ" (v.20). If verses 17-19, we see how unregenerate *men* walk, then in verses 20-21, we see how *the perfect Man* walked.

If we have enjoyed the "but" of divine intervention: we "were by nature the children of wrath, even as others, *but God* ..." (2: 4), and the "but" of divine reconciliation: we "were without Christ, being aliens from the commonwealth of Israel ... having no hope, and without God in the world: *but now* ..." (2: 13), then we also enjoy the "but" of divine perfection. Having described the ugly behaviour of the Gentiles, Paul says "*But* ye have not so learned Christ ..." (4: 20).

THE EPISTLE TO THE EPHESIANS

"Put off ... put on"

Read Chapter 4: 20-32

In previous studies we have noted that having said, "I therefore, the prisoner of the Lord, beseech you that ye walk worthy of the vocation, wherewith ye are called" (4: 1), Paul continues by telling us what this means in practice. In the words of W.W.Wiersbe, it means walking in unity (4: 1-16), walking in purity (4: 17 - 5: 21), walking in harmony (5: 22 – 6: 9) and walking in victory (6: 10-20). The word "walk" occurs five times in this part of the epistle.

Confining ourselves, at the moment, to Chapter 4 verses 17-32, we have also already noticed that Paul contrasts the way in which *(1)* the Gentiles walk (vv.17-19) and *(2)* the way in which the Lord's people are to walk (vv.20-32).

1) HOW THE GENTILES WALK, vv.17-19

In this connection, Paul draws attention *(a)* to the root cause of Gentile behaviour (vv.17-18), and then *(b)* to the resulting fruit in Gentile behaviour (v.19).

a) The cause of Gentile behaviour, vv.17-18

"Walk not as other Gentiles walk, in the vanity of their mind, having the understanding darkened, being alienated from the life of God through the ignorance that is in them, because of the blindness of their heart …"

b) The fruit in Gentile behaviour, v.19

"Who being past feeling have given themselves over unto lasciviousness, to work all uncleanness with greediness."

This brings us to:

2) HOW THE LORD'S PEOPLE ARE TO WALK, vv.20-32

In concluding our previous study, we noticed that having described ugly Gentile behaviour, Paul says, "But ye have not so learned Christ" (v.20). If verses 17-19, we see how unregenerate **men** walk, then in verses 20-21, we see how **the perfect Man** walked.

In this section (vv.20-32) Paul discusses how the Lord's people are to walk **(a)** generally, verses 22-24, and **(b)** particularly, verses 25-32.

a) Generally, vv.20-24

As already noted, the section begins with the words, "But ye have not so learned Christ" (v.20). The word "learned" (*manthano* akin to *mathetes*, a disciple) does not simply refer to "the doctrine of Christ, but to Christ Himself, a process not merely of getting to know the Person, but of so applying the knowledge as to walk differently from the rest of the Gentiles" (W.E.Vine). It means to learn as a disciple.

What Paul describes in verses 17-19 was totally absent in their Saviour. "In him is no sin" (1 John 3: 5).

The words which follow – "***If so be*** that ye have heard him, and been taught by him ('in him', JND)" (v.21) – are not words of doubt, but of argument. The words, "If so be that **ye have heard him** …" refer to their conversion (see John 5: 24), and the following words - "and **been taught by him ('in him')**" - refer to the teaching they had received. Paul emphasises that the men who taught them did so, not on their own authority, but as led and directed by the Lord Jesus. Their teaching was **'in him'**. Compare 1 Thessalonians 4 verse 2; 1 Peter 4 verse 11.

As F.F.Bruce points out: "The use of the name Jesus by itself ('as truth is in Jesus') is so rare in the Pauline letters that when it occurs we look for some special significance in it, some emphasis on our Lord's incarnation and earthly life". The Lord Jesus exhibited moral truth in His life as a perfect man. Hence "as truth is in **Jesus**". Thus, as we have already said, in verses 17-19, we see how unregenerate **men** walk, but in verses 20-21, we see how **the perfect Man** walked.

Paul now applies the "truth ... in Jesus" which they had "been taught", namely that they were to be in practice what they were by divine calling. Paul emphasises this in Colossians 3 verses 8-14: "But now ye also **put off** all these; anger, wrath, malice ... seeing that ye **have put off** the old man with his deeds; and **have put on** the new man which is renewed in knowledge after the image of him that created him ... **Put on** therefore, as the elect of God, holy and beloved, bowels of mercy, kindness ..."

Here, in Ephesians, Paul emphasises the latter, although J.N.Darby's *New Translation* reads differently, a variation that arises from the "tension between the indicative and imperative" moods (F.F.Bruce) - something which need not detain us now since the practical thrust of the passage is abundantly clear.

Following, then, the AV/RV translation, we must concentrate on the injunctions "put off" (v.22) and "put on" (v.24). We are to "put off ... the old man". It is "**corrupt** according to the deceitful lusts". We are to "put on ... the new man". It is "**created** in righteousness and true holiness". It has been put like this: "Think of a prisoner who is released from prison, but still wears his prison clothes and acts like a prisoner, not a free man. The first thing you would tell him is 'put on some new clothes'". (Supplied by Justin Waldron)

i) "Put off", vv.22-23

"That ye put off concerning the former conversation the old man, which is corrupt according to the deceitful lusts; and be renewed in the spirit of your mind."

The expression, "the old man" (Rom. 6: 6; Col. 3: 9) occurs only in Paul's epistles. Our "old man", that is, the man that we were in Adam, was crucified at Calvary (Rom. 6: 6). This is proclaimed in believer's baptism when the brother or sister being baptised is, in figure, 'buried' with Christ, and thus "united with him by the likeness of his death, by affirming that their old man was crucified with him" (F.F.Bruce).

We should emphasise, again, that "the old man" is 'the man we once were in Adam'. It is not 'the old nature', but the 'man I once was'. To "put off concerning the former conversation (*anastrophe*, mode of life) the old man" is to "henceforth walk not as other Gentiles walk" (v.17). That "old man" is "corrupt according to the deceitful lusts". The word "corrupt" (*phtheiro*) means 'waxing corrupt' (W.E.Vine) or "morally decaying on the way to final ruin" (Moule). "Deceitful lusts" are 'lusts of deceit', that is, lusts excited by deceit: deceitful desires in our nature.

Having referred to "the vanity of their mind" (v.17), Paul now refers to "the spirit of your mind", that is, not the mind itself, but the power which directs the mind. F.F.Bruce observes that the injunction, "And be renewed (*ananeoo*) in the spirit of your mind" echoes Romans 12 verse 2, "Be ye transformed by the renewing of your mind", and that this inward renewal can only come about by obedience to the apostle's next injunction". "If the 'old man' goes on corrupting itself, the child of God goes on being renewed in the spirit of his mind" (A.Leckie). This "renewal" is brought about by the Holy Spirit as we read and practise the word of God. See Psalm 119 verses 9-11.

ii) "Put on", v.24

"And that ye put on the new man, which after God is created in righteousness (manward) and true holiness" or "holiness of truth" (RV), that is, Godward. Compare Romans 13: 13, "put ye on the Lord Jesus Christ ..."

The "new man" is "new" in respect of character. If the "old man" refers to 'the type of person we were in Adam' then the "new man" refers to 'the type of person we are to be in Christ', having "learned Christ" (v.20), having "heard him" (v.21), that is, having heard His voice in conversion, and having been "taught by him ('taught in him').

The "new man" is "after God". That is, like God Himself. The word "after" (*kata*) means 'according to'. So 'according to' means to be "in harmony with His will" (A.Leckie). "Adam, having neither the knowledge of good nor evil, was created in innocence; the new man, created according to God, is characterised by truth - which truth, whether it be in relation to God or man, is regarded not only as right, but sacred (*hosiotes*, true holiness: the word only occurs here and in Luke 1: 75)" (A.Leckie).

But what does this mean in terms of everyday conduct? This follows in verses 25-32 where the visible effect of "put ye on the new man" is demonstrated. Having spoken about the subject generally (vv.20-24), Paul now speaks about it –

b) Particularly, v.25-32

Let's look at it like this:

i) "Wherefore putting away lying, speak every man truth with his neighbour: for we are members one of another" (v.25).

This involves *'putting off'* and *'putting on'*. So **put off** "lying", and **put on** "truth": "speak every man truth with his neighbour". Paul cites Zechariah 8 verse 16, here: "These are the things that ye shall do: speak ye every man truth to his neighbour; execute the judgment of peace and truth in your gates". The passage refers to the conduct of God's earthly people in their coming regeneration: "And I will bring them, and they shall dwell in the midst of Jerusalem: and they shall be my people, and I will be their God, in truth and in righteousness" (Zech. 8: 8).

Perhaps Paul refers to lying first since Satan opened his offensive against Adam in this way (Gen. 3: 4-5). He is the 'father of lies' (John 8:44).

Instead of practising "lying" *(pseudos)* or 'falsehood', the Lord's people are to "put on the "holiness of truth" (v.24, RV). "Lying" is a feature of "the old man, which is corrupt according to the deceitful lusts" (v.22). This includes hypocrisy, false impressions, half truths, being 'economical with the truth'. Ananias and Sapphira lied by creating a false impression (Acts 5: 1-4).

The word "neighbour" has a wider connotation than the English word conveys. It is evidently used here with particular reference to the Lord's people: "for we are members one of another", which emphasises that we ourselves are affected, and fellowship is affected as well. Our personal conduct affects our fellow-believers.

ii) "Be ye angry, and sin not: let not the sun go down upon your wrath: neither give place to the devil" (vv.26-27).

This also involves *'putting off'* and *'putting on'*. So **put off** smouldering anger: "Be ye angry and sin not", and **put on** constraint: "Let not the sun go down upon your wrath: neither give place to the devil". The word "angry" *(orgizo)* indicates a more settled anger than *thumos*, meaning "wrath". Anger in itself is not sinful. In the temple, the Lord Jesus "looked round about on them with anger, being grieved for the hardness of their hearts" (Mark. 3: 5).

Paul is saying that if we must be angry, justly so, then we are 'to be angry without sinning'. That is, by exercising a firm constraint over the duration of our anger: "let not the sun go down upon your wrath (*parorgismos*)". The word "wrath" here (a strengthened form of *orge,* meaning 'anger') "points especially to that which provokes wrath, and suggests a less continued state than *orge*" (W.E.Vine). Hence, "let not the sun go down on your (sense, feeling of) provocation". The sun 'goes down' at 6 p.m. in the Middle East!

We must not forget that it can be a sin to **take** offence, as well as to **give** it. There should be no brooding over wrongs inflicted. See Psalm 4 verse 4, "Stand in awe, and sin not (the Hebrew word means 'to quiver with strong emotion'): commune with your own heart upon your bed, and be still". Compare, 1 Corinthians 14 verse 20, "in malice be ye children". All this is extended with the words, "neither give place to the devil". "By letting the sun go down upon our wrath, our communion is disturbed, and in this we sin; and we give the devil the territory in which he can operate" (A.Leckie).

iii) "Let him that stole steal no more: but rather let him labour, working with his hands the thing that is good, that he may have to give to him that needeth" (v.28).

This also involves **'putting off'** and **'putting on'.** So **put off** stealing: "Let him that stole steal no more", and **put on** sharing: "but rather let him labour ... that he may have to give ..." The 'old man' steals: the 'new man' shares. We must now read Titus 2 verse 10.

Paul was certainly an example of his own ministry. See Acts 20 verses 34-35. This is far more than: "Thou shalt not steal". Quite clearly, the Lord's people are not to steal. Quite the opposite: they are to put themselves in a position where they 'have **to give**'. Grace gives far more than the law demands. Grace abounds!

The word "labour" (*kopiao*) means 'to toil to the point of weariness' and the word "good" (*agathos*) means 'beneficial in its effect'. That is, the reverse of stealing! Compare Romans 12 verse 13, "Distributing to the necessity of the saints". The 'old man' is interested in 'getting', while the 'new man' is interested in 'giving'.

iv) "Let no corrupt communication proceed out of your mouth, but that which is good to the use of edifying, that it may minister grace

unto the hearers. And grieve not the holy Spirit of God, whereby ye are sealed unto the day of redemption" (vv.29-30).

This also involves ***'putting off'*** and ***'putting on'***. So ***put off*** "corrupt communication", and ***put on*** "that which is good to the use of edifying, that it may minister grace to the hearers". "If in verse 28 the work of our hands must be good and be used to help the needy, then in verse 29 the words of our mouth must be good so as to edify the hearer" (A.Leckie).

- Our speech (*logos*) is not to be ***harmful.*** It must not be "corrupt (*saphros*)", meaning 'unfit for use, putrid, rotten'.

- Our speech, rather, is to be ***helpful:*** "that which is good (*agathos*) to the use of edifying (building up, as in vv.12, 16), that it may minister (*didomi*, give) grace (*charis*, benefit) unto the hearers" or "such as is good for edifying as the need may be, that it may give grace to them that hear" (RV). Compare Colossians 4 verse 6, "Let your speech be always with grace, seasoned with salt, that ye may know how ye ought to answer every man".

"Corrupt speech is one sure way of grieving the Holy Spirit of God" (A.Leckie). The implication is that unedifying conversation is grievous to Him. We should notice His character - "Holy"; His deity - "of God"; His personality - "grieve not": an influence cannot be grieved! No true believer, surely, would wish to cause the indwelling Holy Spirit pain and distress. "The full title, the Holy Spirit of God, is in sharp contrast to speech that is bad or putrid" (A.Leckie). See also 1 Thessalonians 4 verse 8.

We should also notice His work: "whereby ye are sealed unto the day of redemption". The word "sealed" indicates ratification of ownership. For further recommended reading on the subject, see, for example, Jeremiah 32 verses 6-15. Believers are sealed by the Holy Spirit, thus signifying that they are in divine ownership, "unto the day of redemption". See Romans 8 verse 23; Ephesians 1 verse 14.

"Let all bitterness, and wrath, and anger, and clamour, and evil speaking, be put away from you, with all malice: and be ye kind one to another, tenderhearted, forgiving one another, even as God for Christ's sake hath forgiven you" (vv.31-32).

This also involves ***'putting off'*** and ***'putting on'***. So ***put off*** "all bitterness, and wrath, and anger, and clamour, and evil speaking ... with all malice", and **put on** kindness, tenderheartedness and forgiveness, "even as God for Christ's sake hath forgiven you".

F.F.Bruce points out the connection with the previous verse (v.30): "So, **lest the Spirit be grieved,** let everything be put away which menaces unity of heart and purpose among believers". While "bitterness" (*pikria*) could mean "annoying pinpricks" (the root *pik* means 'to cut or prick: to use a sharply pointed instrument'), it is far more likely to mean a "bitterness of spirit" that, for example, "harbours grudges" and "seeks revenge" (A.Leckie). Compare Acts 8 verse 23; Romans 3 verse 14; Hebrews 12 verse 15. Bitterness of spirit and "wrath" (*thumos,* 'flaring outbursts of rage' or hot anger/passion), are not far apart. It is often said that "anger" (*orge*), which follows "wrath" on Paul's list, is ill-will **suppressed**, whereas "wrath" is ill-will **expressed.**

The word "clamour" (*krauge*) means 'outcry ... controversy ... public quarrelling', and "evil speaking" *(blasphemia)* means "injurious speech" ('railing'). F.F.Bruce calls them "public quarrelling and slanderous whispers". "Malice" (*kakia*), denotes badness in quality. According to W.E.Vine *kakia* is the opposite of *arete,* meaning 'excellence'.

F.F.Bruce connects the "vices" listed in verse 31 with the "graces" described in verse 32 as follows: "Such catalogues of vices are not infrequent in the New Testament writings; ugly as they are, they help to throw into clearer relief the corresponding graces, such as Paul lists in the following verse". Here they are:

"Be ye kind (*chrestos*, 'gentle, gracious, helpful') one to another, tenderhearted (*eusplanchnos*, 'compassionate, good-hearted': rendered 'pitiful' in 1 Pet. 3: 8), forgiving (*charizomai*) one another, even as God for Christ's sake hath forgiven (*charizomai*) you" (v32). "Mutual kindness, compassion, and a readiness to forgive are the qualities which should characterise Christians. Most appropriately so; for they were the qualities which characterised Christ. Moreover, He ascribed these same qualities to God, and made that fact the chief reason why the children of God should exhibit them. By the exercise of love and forgiveness, He told His disciples 'ye shall be the sons of the Most High: for he is kind toward the unthankful and evil. Be ye merciful, even as your Father is merciful' (Luke 6: 35-36, RV)".

The word twice rendered "forgiving ... forgiven" (*charizomai*) is translated "frankly forgave" in Luke 7 verse 42. Its primary meaning is 'to grant as a free gift'. We are to forgive one another after the divine example: "even as God for Christ's sake hath forgiven you". "God was the source of forgiveness, Christ the cause and occasion" (A.Leckie).

"Let us never forget God's loving-kindness towards us, in that He has provided for us a righteous means of forgiveness, through Christ's atoning death. Equally, we must remember that God's intervention on our behalf has established both a pattern and a standard, to regulate our behaviour. How do I react when my brother hurts me, or sins against me? Surely my attitude must be coloured by this – God has forgiven me" (George Hall). (Extracted from *Choice Gleanings*, 14th November, 2008.)

THE EPISTLE TO THE EPHESIANS

"Walk in love ... but"

Read Chapter 5: 1-7

At this advanced stage in our Ephesian studies we hardly need to be reminded that Chapters 1-3 deal with our **position** and Chapters 4-6 with our **practice** as believers. As we noted in introducing the epistle, it is often said that the letter may be summarised as dealing with the wealth, wisdom, walk and warfare of God's people but that, on reflection and in order to obtain a better overall picture, it might be better to adopt a revised version, *viz:* the wealth (1: 1 - 3: 21), walk (4: 1 - 5: 21), relationships (5: 22 - 6: 9) and warfare (6: 10-20) of God's people. Exit the neat alliteration (!) but enter something, hopefully, rather more in keeping with the text.

Now let's readdress the 'walk' of God's people (4: 1 – 5: 21). Having said, "I therefore, the prisoner of the Lord, beseech you that ye **walk** worthy of the vocation wherewith ye are called" (4: 1), Paul continues by telling us what this means in practice, namely, that believers must walk in unity (4: 1-16), and then in purity (4: 17 - 5: 21). The latter is stressed in four ways:

- "This I say therefore, and testify in the Lord, that ye henceforth **walk not as other Gentiles walk** ..." (4: 17).

- "**Walk in love**, as Christ also hath loved us, and hath given himself for us, an offering and a sacrifice to God for a sweet smelling savour" (5: 2).

- "For ye were sometimes darkness, but now are ye light in the Lord: **walk as children of light**" (5: 8).

- "See then that ye **walk circumspectly**, not as fools, but as wise, redeeming the time, because the days are evil" (5: 15-16).

All this calls for a definition, and W.E.Vine, as always, is most helpful. He tells us that *peripateo* means "the whole round of the activities of individual life". That nicely says it all.

1) "WALK NOT AS OTHER GENTILES WALK", 4: 17-32

We have already noticed that in these verses, Paul contrasts the way in which the Gentiles walk (vv.17-19) with the way in which the Lord's people are to walk (vv.20-32).

a) How other Gentiles walk, vv.17-19

"This I say therefore, and testify in the Lord, that ye henceforth **walk not** as other Gentiles **walk**, in the vanity of their mind, having the understanding darkened, being alienated from the life of God through the ignorance that is in them, because of the blindness of their heart: who being past feeling, have given themselves over unto lasciviousness, to work all uncleanness with greediness."

b) How the Lord's people are to walk, vv.20-32

If unregenerate Gentiles have "the understanding darkened, being **alienated** from the life of God ..." (vv.17-19), then the conduct of the Lord's people must reflect the fact that they **possess** "the life of God". As already noted, the section begins with the words, "But ye have not so learned Christ" (v.20). The word "learned" (*manthano* akin to *mathetes*, a disciple) does not simply refer to "the doctrine of Christ, but to Christ Himself, a process not merely of getting to know the Person, but of so applying the knowledge as to walk differently from the rest of the Gentiles" (W.E.Vine). It means to learn as a disciple.

In the words of F.F.Bruce, also already noted, "The use of the name Jesus by itself ('as truth is in Jesus') is so rare in the Pauline letters that when it occurs we look for some special significance in it, some emphasis on our Lord's incarnation and earthly life". The Lord Jesus exhibited moral truth in His life as a perfect man. Hence "as truth is in **Jesus**". Thus, as we have already said, in verses 17-19, we see how unregenerate **men** walk, but in verses 20-21, we see how **the perfect Man** walked.

There is no need to restate the teaching of verses 22-32, except to remind ourselves that we are to "put off ... the old man" which is "**corrupt** according to the deceitful lusts" (v.22), and to "put on ... the new man" which after God is **created** in righteousness and true holiness" (v.24). What this involves can be seen from the following table:

"put off"	*"put on"*
v.25 "Wherefore putting away lying"	"speak ... truth with his neighbour"
v.26 "Be ye angry, and sin not"	"let not the sun go down ... wrath"
v.28 "steal no more"	"give to him that needeth"
v.29 "Let no corrupt communication ..."	"but that which is good"
vv.31, 32 "Let all bitterness ... be put away"	"be ye kind one to another ..."

The last of these is developed in Chapter 5 verses 1-2, "Let all bitterness, and wrath, and anger, and clamour, and evil speaking, be put away from you, with all malice: and be ye kind to one another, tenderhearted, forgiving one another, even as God for Christ's sake hath forgiven you. **Be ye therefore followers of God, as dear children; and walk in love".**

We now meet the first of the next three injunctions: "Walk **in love**" (v.2), to be followed by "walk **as children of light**" (v.8) and "walk **circumspectly**" (v.15). (See also "walk in wisdom", Col. 4: 5).

John the Baptist, "looking upon Jesus as he **walked**", said, "Behold the Lamb of God" (John 1: 36). The Lord Jesus exemplified every "walk" described in Ephesians! 1 John 2 verse 6 now becomes compulsory reading, "He that saith he abideth in him, ought himself also so to walk, even as **he walked**". This brings us to:

2) "WALK IN LOVE", vv.1-2

We are to "walk in love" **(a)** in view of the love of God (v.1) and **(b)** in view of the love of Christ (v.2).

a) In view of the love of God, v.1

"Be ye therefore followers (*mimetes*, meaning 'imitators') of God, as dear (*agapetos,* meaning 'beloved') children (*tekna*)." It is worth noticing that Paul refers here to "dear **children**", rather than 'dear sons'. The difference is important. The word "children" implies **family likeness**.

For other occurrences of *mimetes* (imitators: AV 'followers'), see 1 Corinthians 4 verse 16 ("Be ye followers of me"), Chapter 11 verse 1 ("Be ye followers of me, even as I also am of Christ"). See also Hebrews 6 verse 12 (*mimetes*) and Hebrews 13 verse 7 (*meomai*). W.E.Vine points out that the verb (*meomai*) "is always used in exhortations, and always in the continuous tense, suggesting a constant habit or practice". He says something similar in connection with the noun (*mimetes*). See his *Expository Dictionary*. The English words 'mime' and 'mimic' come from the Greek word here.

In passing, the word *huioi* meaning sons is used in Matthew 5 verses 44-48: "But I say unto you, Love your enemies ... that ye may be the children (*huioi*) of your Father which is in heaven ... Be ye therefore perfect, even as your Father which is in heaven is perfect".

To be "kind one to another, tenderhearted, forgiving one another, even as God for Christ's sake hath forgiven you" (4: 32), makes us 'imitators of God'. He has been, and remains, "kind ... tenderhearted ... forgiving" toward us. Do we imitate God in our attitude to fellow-believers? It is often said that:

>   *To err is human:*
>   *To forgive is divine.*

It is also said that

>   *He little knows of God or heaven*
>   *Who never breathes the word 'Forgiven'.*

b) In view of the love of Christ, v.2

"And walk in love, as Christ also hath loved us, and hath given himself for us, an offering and a sacrifice to God for a sweetsmelling savour." While verse 1 emphasises our relationship with **fellow-believers,** verse 2 emphasises our **acceptance with God.** We follow the Lord Jesus in His acceptance with God. Most certainly, verse 2 refers to our relationship with fellow-believers, but it is the fragrance of that relationship to God which is emphasised here. Note:

*i)   **The practical reality of His sacrifice.*** The love of the Lord Jesus for us was not a mere attitude or theory - it was a practical reality. "And walk in love, as Christ also hath **loved us**, and hath **given himself for us** ..." He displayed His love for us at immense personal cost, reminding us that there is a cost to us in following Him in this way. See, for example, 1 John 3 verses 16-18: "Hereby perceive we the love of God ('hereby we have known love', JND), because he laid down his life for us: and we ought to lay down our lives for the brethren. But whoso hath this world's good, and seeth his brother have need, and shutteth up his bowels of compassion from him, how dwelleth the love of God in him? My little children, let us not love in word, neither in tongue; but in deed and in truth".

*ii)   **The voluntary nature of His sacrifice.*** "Christ also hath loved us, and hath **given** himself for us."

*iii)   **The fragrance to God of His sacrifice.*** "An offering and a sacrifice to God for a sweet smelling savour." While the words "offering" (*prosphora*) and "sacrifice" (*thusia*) are said to be the Greek equivalents of the Hebrew *minchah* (referring to the meal offering) and *zebach* (referring to the peace offering) respectively, it seems better, in the interests of clarity, to confine ourselves to the actual meaning of the two words here. They are not technically differentiated in this passage.

-   "An offering." This, as noted above, translates *prosphora,* meaning 'to carry to' (Wuest) or 'to bring to' (Vine). The word emphasises **how** the Lord Jesus displayed His love for us: He acted on our behalf voluntarily. The word *prophora* is also used, for example, in Hebrews 10 verses 10 and 14.

-   "A sacrifice." This, as also noted above, translates *thusia* from *thuo,* meaning "to kill a sacrificial victim, to immolate, to sacrifice" (Wuest), emphasising **what** the Lord Jesus actually did in displaying His love towards us. The word *thusia* is also used, for example, in Hebrews 9 verse 26; Hebrews 10 verses 12, 26.

In passing, the burnt, meal and peace offerings (Leviticus 1-3) were all burnt as incense, and this is reflected in Ephesians 5 verse 2: "a **sweet smelling** (*euodia*) **savour** (*osme*)". Compare Philippians 4 verse 18: "But I have all, and abound; I am full, having received of Epaphroditus the things that were sent from you, an **odour** (*osme*) of a **sweet smell** (*euodia*), a sacrifice acceptable, wellpleasing to God". See also 2 Corinthians 2 verses

15-16: "For we are unto God a *sweet savour* (*euodia*) of Christ, in them that are saved, and in them that perish: to the one we are the *savour* (*osme*) of death unto death; and to the other the *savour* (*osme*) of life unto life".

This is far more than an exercise in Greek vocabulary. By linking the three passages, we conclude that the fellowship shown to Paul by the assembly at Philippi, and the preaching of the Gospel by Paul and his colleagues, was permeated by the fragrance of Christ! This gives our stewardship and our preaching a very elevated character. But it is not licence for evil behaviour, for believers are to:

3) "WALK AS CHILDREN OF LIGHT", vv.3-14

This paragraph is governed by the words, "For ye were sometimes darkness, but now are ye light in the Lord: walk as children of light" (v.8). These verses may be divided as follows: *(a)* "Ye were sometimes darkness (vv.3-7); *(b)* "Now are ye light in the Lord", vv.8-14.

a) "Ye were sometimes darkness", vv.3-7

We now move from love (vv.1-2) to lust (vv.3-7); from a "sweet smelling savour" to a vile stench. Do notice that Paul does not say that we were 'in darkness', but 'darkness' - not having the character of God. In these verses Paul describes that "darkness" (vv.3-4), together with its implications (vv.5-7). In passing, Paul refers elsewhere to "the power of darkness" (Col. 1: 13), "the rulers of the darkness ..." (Eph. 6: 12), and asks the question, "What communion hath light with darkness?" (2 Cor. 6: 14).

i) The character of the "darkness", vv.3-4

Paul calls this "the unfruitful works of darkness" (v.11). We should notice that he speaks first about our *morality* (v.3): "But fornication, and all uncleanness, or covetousness, let it not be once named among you, as becometh saints". In other words, he refers to our *walk*. Then he speaks about our *mouths* (v.4): "Neither filthiness, nor foolish talking, nor jesting, which are not convenient; but rather giving of thanks". In other words, he refers to *talk.*

- *Morality, v.3.* In this connection, Paul refers to "*fornication*" (*porneia*), that is, to illicit sexual intercourse. See 1 Thessalonians 4 verse 3: "This is the will of God, even your sanctification, that ye should abstain from *fornication*".

Chapter 5:1-7

The Thessalonian believers "turned to God from idols" (1 Thess. 1: 9): they were also to turn from what was associated with idolatry, that is, harlotry. They were now to behave "*not* in the lust of concupiscence (desire), even as the Gentiles which know not God" (1 Thess. 4: 5).

Paul then refers to *"uncleanness"* (*akatharsia*). That is, all uncleanness - in thought, word and deed: moral uncleanness. Compare Ephesians 4 verse 19, "Who being past feeling, have given themselves over unto lasciviousness, to work all uncleanness with greediness". "Fornication" and "uncleanness" are linked in Colossians 3 verse 5. Bearing in mind that in 1 Thessalonians 4 verses 1-8, Paul deals with immoral behaviour, he writes, "For God hath not called us unto uncleanness, but unto holiness" (v.7).

Finally, Paul refers to "*covetousness*" (*pleonexia*). In context, Paul is again referring to immoral behaviour. As F.F.Bruce observes, "We may think it strange to see covetousness so closely associated with these vices, but Paul is simply moving from outward manifestations of sin to their inner springs in the cravings of the heart". See Exodus 20 verse 17. Compare 1 Thessalonians 4 verse 6, "that no man go beyond and defraud his brother (*pleonekteo*, to act covetously against him) in any matter (in *the* matter)". That is, in the matter of moral conduct. Covetousness refers to desire in the heart. See Matthew 5 verse 28.

These things are to "not be once named among you as becometh *saints*". We are not to talk or speak about them, but reprove them. There are, obviously and sadly, occasions when these things necessitate assembly discipline, but they are not to be the subject of general conversation. They are not fit subjects for discussion amongst the Lord's people.

- Mouth, v.4. "Neither filthiness, nor foolish talking, nor jesting, which are not convenient (becoming, suitable); but rather giving of thanks." We are not to be given to lightness and jocular reference to the subjects mentioned in verse 3.

Paul now refers to "*filthiness*" (*aischrotes*), meaning what is obscene and indecent. Compare "filthy communication (*aischrologia*)" (Col. 3: 8). This is followed by "*foolish talking*", that is, indecent talking. "Foolish talking" translates *morologia* from *moros*, meaning 'foolish, dull, stupid' (W.E.Vine). But it is more than idle talk. W.E.Vine quotes Trench here: 'that talk of fools which is foolishness and sin together'. Finally, Paul refers to *"jesting"* (*eutrapelia*), meaning ribaldry - buffoonery - flippancy - coarse vulgarity.

Quite the opposite to the 'good medicine' of a 'merry heart' (Proverbs 17: 22). The mouths of believers are to be filled with thanksgiving. Compare Colossians 4 verse 6, "Let your speech be alway with grace, seasoned with salt", not with "jesting", which, according to F.F.Bruce, Aristotle defined as 'cultured insolence!'

ii) The implications of the "darkness", vv.5-7.

In summary, we are told that people who practise "the unfruitful works of darkness" (v.11) are unsaved (v.5), and will be judged (v.6-7).

a) People who do these things are unsaved, v5

"For this ye know, that no whoremonger, nor unclean person, nor covetous man, who is an idolater, hath any inheritance in the kingdom of Christ and of God." If in verse 3, we have **actions and deeds**, now, in verse 5, we have **the actors and the doers.**

First of all, the "**whoremonger**" (*pornos*), the person who commits "fornication" (*porneia*) in verse 3. Secondly, the "**unclean person**" *(akathartos),* the person who commits "uncleanness" (*akatharsia*) in verse 3. Thirdly the "**covetous man**" (*pleonektes*), the person who is motivated by covetousness (*pleonexia*) in verse 3.

The three words describe those who are characterised by these things, rather than believers who might temporarily fall into sin, serious as that is in itself. Compare John's word, "he that **practiseth** sin (AV, 'whosoever committeth sin')" (1 John 3: 4, JND). See also 1 John 3 verses 8 and 9. The words, "nor covetous man, **who is an idolater**", refer to someone who sets their affection on earthly things (see Col. 3: 2). The 'earthly things' follow, and the list begins with "fornication" and "uncleanness" (Col. 3: 5). Such people are unsaved, and have no "inheritance in the kingdom of Christ and of God". The "kingdom of Christ and of God" is populated by people who are 'imitators of God' (v.1) and who walk acceptably to God as Christ did (v.2). For the term "kingdom of Christ and of God", compare Revelation 11 verse 15. It is, of course, one kingdom. In the present passage (note this), the kingdom is, perhaps described as the 'kingdom of Christ' mediatorially, and as the 'kingdom of God' ultimately, in its consummation (1 Cor. 15: 28).

The kingdom has present and future aspects. Those characterised by the conduct described in the passage cannot possibly be members of that kingdom now, or at any time in the future. The word "kingdom" implies **rule:** it refers to men and women subject to divine authority. Compare Romans 14 verse 17, "For the kingdom of God is not meat and drink, but righteousness and peace and joy in the Holy Ghost".

b) People who do these things will be judged, v.6

"Let no man deceive you with vain words: for because of these things cometh the wrath of God upon the **children (huios, sons) of disobedience.**" It has been pointed out that since the apostle is thinking of character, the word is 'sons' and not 'children'" (A. Leckie). Compare Ephesians 2 verse 2, JND.

The New Testament warns elsewhere against the assertion that "freedom from the law implies freedom to sin" (F.F.Bruce). See, for example, Romans 6 verse 1; Jude verse 4. As F.F.Bruce points out, Paul "characterises all such sophistries as 'empty words'", and continues: "It is precisely this sort of behaviour ... that brings down the wrath of God on the 'sons of disobedience' ... This is a theme which he elaborates especially in Romans 1 verse 18ff, where he shows the successive stages in which 'the wrath of God is revealed from heaven against all ungodliness and unrighteousness of men'". We should notice that according to Romans 1 verse 18, the "wrath of God" is already "revealed from heaven".

We were once "the children of wrath (*orge,* meaning 'anger'), even as others" (Eph. 2: 3), but "God hath not appointed us to wrath (*orge*) ..." (I Thess. 5: 9): the Lord Jesus is "our deliverer from the coming wrath (*orge*)" (1 Thess. 1: 10, JND). That is, the "wrath" of the coming tribulation.

Paul's conclusion is clear: "Be not ye therefore partakers (*summetochos*) with them" (v.7). He uses the same noun, meaning joint-partaker, in Ephesians 3 verse 6, where it refers to "Gentile believers who are joint-sharers with Jewish believers in the body of Christ; here, contrariwise, it is used of partnership in iniquity" (F.F.Bruce).

Having considered verses 3-7 under the heading "were sometimes darkness", we must next turn our attention, to verses 8-14 under the heading, "now ... light in the Lord".

THE EPISTLE TO THE EPHESIANS

"Walk as chidren of light"

Read Chapter 5: 8-21

As we have noticed in recent studies, having urged his readers to "**walk** (*peripateo*) worthy of the vocation wherewith ye are called" (4: 1), Paul continues by telling them what this means in practice, namely, that believers must walk in unity (4: 1-16), and then in purity (4: 17 - 5: 21). The latter is stressed in four ways:

- "This I say therefore, and testify in the Lord, that ye henceforth **walk not as other Gentiles walk** ..." (4: 17).

- "**Walk in love**, as Christ also hath loved us, and hath given himself for us, an offering and a sacrifice to God for a sweet smelling savour" (5: 2).

- "For ye were sometimes darkness, but now are ye light in the Lord: **walk as children of light**" (5: 8).

- "See then that ye **walk circumspectly**, not as fools, but as wise, redeeming the time, because the days are evil" (5: 15-16).

1) "WALK NOT AS OTHER GENTILES WALK", 4: 17-32

In summary, these verses describe, firstly, how unregenerate Gentiles walk (vv.17-19) and, secondly, how the Lord's people are to walk (vv.20-32). The latter requires us to "put off ... the old man" which is "**corrupt** according to the deceitful lusts" (v.22), and to "put on ... the new man" which is "**created** in righteousness and true holiness" (v.24).

2) "WALK IN LOVE", 5: 2

Having said, effectively, "**put off**... all bitterness ... wrath ... anger ...clamour ... evil speaking ... malice", and "**put on**" kindness, tenderheartedness and forgiveness - "even as God for Christ's sake hath forgiven you" (4: 31-32) - Paul urges us to "be ... therefore followers of God, as dear children; and walk in love" (5: 1-2). To be "kind one to another, tenderhearted, forgiving one another, even as God for Christ's sake hath forgiven you" (4: 32), makes us 'imitators of God' (5: 1). He has been, and remains, "kind ... tenderhearted ... forgiving" toward us. But this is not licence for evil behaviour, for believers are to -

3) "WALK AS CHILDREN OF LIGHT", vv.3-14

The paragraph takes its structure from the words, "For ye were sometimes darkness, but now are ye light in the Lord: walk as children of light" (v.8), and may be divided as follows: **(A)** "Ye were sometimes darkness" (vv.3-7); **(B)** "Now are ye light in the Lord", vv.8-14.

A) "Ye were sometimes darkness", vv.3-7

Having described the character of the darkness (vv.3-4), and the implications of the darkness (vv.5-6), that is, that people who practise "the unfruitful works of darkness" (v.11) are unsaved (v.5), and will be judged (v.6), there can only be one piece of advice: "Be *not* ye therefore partakers (*summetochos*) with them" (v.7).

In this connection, verses 3-6 each give a reason why we should not be "partakers with them": we are "**saints**" (v.3); we are to be **thankful** (v.4); we have an "**inheritance in the kingdom of Christ and of God**" (v.5); we are delivered from "**the wrath of God**" (v.6).

We should notice that Paul does not say 'For ye were in darkness', but "For ye were **sometimes darkness** ..." (v.8). Not 'in darkness', but 'darkness', that is, not having the character of God. This brings us to:

B) "Now are ye light in the Lord", vv.8-14

Having said, emphatically, "Be not ye therefore partakers with them" (v.7), that is, with "the sons of disobedience" (v.6, JND), Paul now reinforces the point". We are not to be "partakers with them", because a fundamental change has taken place in our position: we "were sometimes ('once', JND) darkness, but now ... light in the Lord".

Paul is making the same point as before, but instead of stating what we ***must not do*** - "Be not ye therefore partakers with them" – he now states what we ***must do*** – "walk as children of light".

With this in mind, we should now notice what Paul has to say *(a)* about our position (v.8a) and *(b)* about our practice (vv.8b-14).

a) Our position, v.8a

The 'fundamental change' is as basic as the difference between light and darkness. "For ye were sometimes darkness, but now are ye light in the Lord: walk as children of light." Compare Ephesians 4 verses 18-20: once "having the understanding ***darkened***, being alienated from the life of God through the ignorance that is in them, because of the blindness of their heart ... But ye have not so learned Christ".

F.F.Bruce points out that "The opposing themes of light and darkness are frequently used in the New Testament to denote the divine kingdom as against all that is contrary to it ... The basic principle of this opposition is stated most succinctly in 1 John 1 verse 5, 'God is ***light***, and in him is ***no darkness*** at all'". Light and darkness are polar opposites. Darkness cannot be light, and light cannot be darkness. "Woe unto them that call evil good, and good evil; that put darkness for light, and light for darkness ..." (Isa. 5: 20).

Referring now to the 'opposing themes of light and darkness', we should note, for example, the following.

- Paul refers back to the beginning of Creation in saying, "God, who commanded the ***light*** to shine out of ***darkness***, hath shined in our hearts, to give the ***light*** of the knowledge of the glory of God in the face of Jesus Christ" (2 Cor. 4: 6; Gen. 1: 2-3).

- The Lord Jesus, "The Eternal Word, agent of God in the first creation" (F.F.Bruce) said, "I am the ***light*** of the world: he that followeth me shall not walk in ***darkness***, but shall have the ***light*** of life" (John 8: 12). Compare John 3 verses 19-21, "And this is the condemnation, that ***light*** is come into the world, and men loved *darkness* rather than *light*, because their deeds were evil. For every one that doeth evil hateth the *light,* neither cometh to the *light*, lest his deeds should be reproved. But he that doeth truth cometh to the *light*, that his deeds may be manifest, that they are wrought in God".

- Believers are thankful, with Paul, that God has "made us meet ('fit') to be partakers of the inheritance of the saints in *light*: who hath delivered us from the power of *darkness*, and hath translated us into the kingdom of his dear Son" (Col. 1: 12-13).

b) Our practice, vv.8b-14

We are to "***walk as children of light***" (v.8b). Compare 1 Thessalonians 5 verse 5, "Ye are all the children (sons) of *light*, and the children (sons) of the day: we are not of the night, nor of *darkness*". It has been said that we are to walk as 'those whose souls have been penetrated and gripped by the truth of God'.

To "walk as children of light" is explained in the verses which follow (vv.9-14). A brief perusal of the passage leads us to the conclusion that to "walk as children of light" means *(i)* the production of spiritual fruit in our lives (vv.9-10), *(ii)* the avoidance of unfruitful practices in our lives (vv.11-13), *(iii)* the need for constant alertness in our lives (v.14).

i) The production of spiritual fruit in our lives, vv.9-10.

The words, "For the fruit of the Spirit is in all goodness and righteousness and truth" (AV) certainly look perfectly acceptable as they stand, that is, until you look elsewhere. It comes as 'a bit of a shock' to read, "for the fruit of the *light* [is] in all goodness and righteousness and truth" (JND). The RV says the same. The RSV, ESV and NEB all have "the fruit of light", but not La Sainte Bible - "Car le fruit *de l'Esprit* consiste en toute sorte de bonté, de justice et de vérité". (You just can't trust the European Union!) It looks rather confusing, doesn't it? What is more, none of us are textual critics! Perhaps, therefore, we ought to listen to Prof. F. F. Bruce M.A. (Cantab), D.D. (Aberdeen):

"The 'Received Text' reads 'the fruit of the Spirit' (so A.V.), under the influence of Galatians 5 verse 22; but, although it has the unusually strong support of Papyrus 46, it must be regarded as inferior to the reading 'the fruit of the light'. This latter reading is confirmed not only by the weight of the evidence, but also by the context, in view both of the general theme of light in these verses and of the counterbalancing reference to 'the unfruitful works of darkness in verse 11. The fruit of the light is simply the manner of life produced in believers by the true light which dwells within them – a manner of life marked by 'goodness and righteousness and truth'".

We should note that Paul does say, "in *all* goodness and righteousness and truth". These are absolute requirements.

- **"Goodness"** (*agathosune*), from *agathos,* signifies "that which being good in its character and constitution, is beneficial in its effect" (W.E.Vine).

- **"Righteousness"** (*dikaisosune*), means 'what is right or just'- 'rectitude'.

- **"Truth"** (*aletheuo*) meaning 'veracity' or 'sincerity and integrity'. See also Ephesians 4 verse 21 ("even as truth is in Jesus", RV), meaning "not merely ethical truth, but truth in all its fullness and scope, as embodied in Him; He was the perfect expression of the truth" (W.E.Vine).

The attaching words, **"Proving** (*dokimazo*) what is acceptable unto the Lord" (v.10) means approving or recognising what is well-pleasing to Him. It carries the idea of testing with the expectation of approving. See also Romans 12 verse 2, "That ye may prove (*dokimazo*) what is that good, and acceptable, and perfect, will of God". The daily renewing of our minds will enable us to recognise "what is that good, and acceptable, and perfect, will of God". Handley C. G. Moule puts it nicely in saying that through the renewing of his mind, the Christian "can discern, in conflicting cases, the will of God from the will of self or of the world".

The word "acceptable" (*euarestos*) means 'well pleasing', as in 2 Corinthians 5 verse 9, "Wherefore we labour ('make it our aim') that, whether present or absent, we may be accepted of him ('well-pleasing to him')". So, walking as children of light, we put all matters to the test as to whether or not they are well pleasing the Lord.

ii) *The avoidance of unfruitful practices in our lives, vv.11-13.*

Attention is drawn to three things in particular here. The "unfruitful works of darkness" have already been described: see verses 3-5.

- We are to have "no **fellowship** with the **unfruitful** works of darkness" (v.11). These stand in direct contrast to "the **fruit** of the light" (v.9, JND). Compare 2 Corinthians 6 verse 14.

- We are to "**reprove** (*elencho*: 'expose', JND margin) the unfruitful works of darkness" (v.11). But how are we to do this? After all,

- We are not even to "**speak** of those things which are done of them in secret" (v.12). How then can we 'reprove' or 'expose' them? We should say, in the first place, that the words, "for the things that are done by them in secret it is shameful even to say" (JND) cannot mean that we must never make reference to them. Paul did so in Romans 1 verses 24-32, and the Lord Jesus said, "If I had not come and **spoken** unto them, they had not had sin, but now they have no cloak for their sin" (John 15: 22).

There is, however, a vast difference between referring to "the things that are done by them in secret", and dwelling on the details. W.W.Wiersbe points out that "the motto today seems to be 'Tell it like it is!'", and continues, "And yet that can be a dangerous policy when it comes to exposing the filthy things of darkness, lest we unconsciously advertise and promote sin".

The greatest and most effective exposure of sin is accomplished by the lives of men and women who "walk as children of light". As W.W.Wiersbe observes, when the Lord Jesus "was here on earth, the perfection of His character and conduct exposed the sinfulness of those around Him. This is one reason why the religious leaders hated Him and sought to destroy Him". See, again, John 3 verses 19-21. In Paul's words, "But all things that are reproved ('discovered' or 'exposed') are made manifest by the light: for whatsoever doth make manifest is light" (v.13). We should notice his reference to the exposure ("made **manifest**, v.13) of things "in **secret**", (v.12). Compare Luke 8 verse 17 ("For nothing is secret that shall not be made manifest ...").

By walking "as children of light", our lives will expose the darkness of others. What the light does in the natural world, the life of the believer does in the spiritual world. This leads to -

iii) The need for constant alertness in our lives, v.14

"Wherefore he saith, Awake thou that sleepest, and arise from the dead (a plural word - 'dead ones'), and Christ shall give thee light." Paul evidently refers here to Isaiah 60 verse 1, "Arise, shine, for thy light is come, and the glory of the LORD is risen upon thee", a passage describing the glory of the Millennial kingdom.

Paul's words here - "Awake thou that sleepest, and arise from the dead" - are tantamount to saying: "Be not ye therefore partakers with them" (the children - sons - of disobedience), or "have no fellowship with the unfruitful works of darkness" (vv.7, 11). Albert Leckie puts it like this: "To those who stir themselves from indifference and lethargy and stand up from among those who are spiritually dead, Christ shines upon them as the sun. Not as a light to expose, but to enlighten, to give warmth and to transform".

So, in summary: "Be not ye ... partakers with them" (v.7); "And have no fellowship with the unfruitful works of darkness" (v.11); and, now, "arise from the dead" (v.14). That is, 'don't be asleep - indifferent to your position'; 'don't be identified with those who are "dead" ('the dead ones'), that is, the unregenerate'. Compare Romans 13 verses 11-13, "It is high time to wake out of **sleep**. Let us cast off the works of **darkness**. Let us put on the armour of **light**". Verse 14 may be summarised as 'Sleep - stir - shine'.

This means that we will:

3) "WALK CIRCUMSPECTLY", vv15-21

"See then that ye walk circumspectly (*akribos*, meaning 'accurately ... exactly ... carefully'), not as fools (*asophos*), but as wise (*sophos*)." Instead of walking foolishly, as identified with the unregenerate in verse 14 - "as if ignorant of spiritual and eternal verities", we must walk wisely - as "intelligent as to spiritual and eternal verities" (A.Leckie). This involves the following:

a) Good stewardship of time, v.16

"Redeeming the time, because the days are evil." That is, "not redeeming time, as usually understood, but seizing every good and favourable opportunity" (JND margin). Compare 1 Corinthians 7 verses 29-30, "But this I say, brethren, **the** time is short (not, 'time is short')" and this fact is to govern us domestically ("they that have wives be as though they had none"), emotionally ("they that weep, as though they wept not; and they that rejoice, as though they rejoiced not"), commercially ("and they that buy, as though they possessed not"). Ephesians 5 verse 16 is often rendered, 'buying up the opportunities'. See, for example, Barzillai and his friends who brought "beds, and basins, and earthen vessels, and wheat, and barley ..." for David and his men prior to the battle in the wood of Ephraim (2 Sam. 17: 27-29). See, again, for example, Mary of Bethany. She 'bought up the opportunity' to anoint the Lord. There was no other opportunity. She was like a bright gem against a dark background. 'Buying up the opportunities' often involves "a word in season to him that is weary" (Isa. 50: 4).

b) Understanding the Lord's will, v.17

"Wherefore be ye not unwise, but **understanding** what the will of the Lord is." In context, this refers to His will for us in evil days, the need for clear perception: the word rendered "understanding" (*suniemi*) means 'to bring or set together'(W.E.Vine). Such 'clear perception' is acquired by reading the Scriptures. It is there that we obtain divine guidance. The will of God is found in the Word of God: the rest – understanding - will follow. It is a case of "***doing*** the will of God from the heart" (Eph. 6: 6). We all need to be like "the children of Issachar, which were men that had understanding of the times, to know what Israel ought to do" (1 Chron. 12: 32). That is men with the ability to use their discernment. Men who could assess a situation, and give good advice. Albert Leckie points out that it is not 'the will of God' here, but rather 'the will of the ***Lord'***, that is, as related to daily living.

c) Being filled with the Spirit, v.18

"And be not drunk with wine, wherein is excess; but be filled with the Spirit." A warning here: being "drunk with wine" brings to mind men like Nabal (1 Sam. 25: 36) and Belshazzar (Dan. 5: 4), and even Lot (Gen. 19: 30-38). But what about Noah! (Gen. 9: 20-21). We would hardly expected it of him! We should now read Proverbs 23 verses 19-21.

To be "filled with the Spirit" (compare Acts 2: 13-21) means to be controlled and directed by Him. The Scriptures speak of being filled with, for example, "wrath" (Luke 4: 28), with "indignation"(Acts 5: 17) and with "envy" (Acts 13: 45). We are told that the command involves the present tense – 'keep on being filled'. This is not a sovereign act of God for special occasions, as at certain times in the book of Acts. Neither is there any thought of ecstatic experience. The results of being "filled with the Spirit" are seen on either side of the verse!

d) Rejoicing in spirit, v.19

"Speaking to yourselves in psalms and hymns and spiritual songs, singing and making melody in your heart (with your heart', JND) to the Lord." This, as opposed to the "song of the drunkard" (Psalm 69: 12). To 'make melody in our hearts to the Lord' is certainly evidence of being "filled with the Spirit".

While the word "yourselves" could admit the meaning 'one another'', it more likely refers to personal, rather than public, devotion. It is our personal devotion to the Lord: hence "singing and making melody in (with) your heart **to the Lord**". It has been suggested that "psalms" express personal experience, that "hymns" are an ascription of praise to God, and that "spiritual songs" express spiritual truths.

e) Giving thanks always, v.20

"Giving thanks always for all things unto God and the Father in the Name of our Lord Jesus Christ" or "Giving thanks at all times for all things to him [who is] God and [the] Father in the name of our Lord Jesus Christ" (JND).

Both the joy in our hearts (v.19) and the thanksgiving with our lips (here) are evidence of being "filled with the Spirit".

As Paul says elsewhere, "Rejoice evermore … in every thing give thanks; for this is the will of God in Christ Jesus concerning you" (1 Thess. 5: 16, 18).

f) Submitting yourselves one to one another, v.21

"Submitting yourselves one to another in the fear of God." Since this is "mutual and reciprocal, there is no thought of superiority or inferiority here" (A.Leckie).

F.F.Bruce concludes his commentary on this section of the Epistle as follows: "It is easier to pay lip-service to the duty of mutual submission than to practise it, but when it is undertaken in a spirit of reverence for Christ it can be achieved. When Peter enjoins this same attitude, he does so in words which recall Christ's own example in girding Himself with a towel to perform a lowly service for His disciples: 'Yea, all of you gird yourselves with humility, to serve one another' (1 Pet. 5: 5; cf. John 13: 4f)".

Chapter 5:8-21

"Submitting yourselves one to another in the fear of God" is a most suitable introduction to the next section of the Epistle. Having considered the wealth (1: 1 - 3: 21), and walk (4: 1 - 5: 21) of God's people, we must now consider the relationships of God's people (5: 22 - 6: 9), where "pre-eminently should mutual consideration and deference be shown, between husbands and wives, between parents and children, between masters and servants" (F.F.Bruce).

THE EPISTLE TO THE EPHESIANS

"Christ also loved the church"

Read Chapter 5: 22-33

We have noticed that in the earlier verses of this chapter, Paul addresses God's people generally. The instruction is applicable to all. There are no categories. Believers are described in general terms: "dear children" ('beloved children', JND" (v.1); "saints" (v.3) "children of light" (v.8). As believers, we are to submit ourselves "one to another in the fear of God" verse 21. The four exhortations in connection with our "walk": "walk not as other Gentiles walk …" (4: 17); "walk in love" (5: 2); "walk as children of light" (5: 8); "walk circumspectly" (5: 15), are addressed to all.

Having considered the wealth (1: 1 - 3: 21), and walk (4: 1 - 5: 21) of God's people, we must now consider the relationships of God's people (5: 22 - 6: 9), where "pre-eminently should mutual consideration and deference be shown …" (F.F.Bruce). We come, then, to a section in the epistle which addresses particular believers. Whereas Ephesians 5 verses 1-21, not to mention Chapter 4, have addressed all believers in connection with their common relationship with God, Paul now deals with specified categories of believers in their relationships with each other. These are: *(A)* wives and husbands (5: 22-33); *(B)* children and parents (6: 1-4); *(C)* servants and masters (6: 5-9). We should notice the order: wives before husbands, children before parents, and servants before masters. "Grace puts the weaker first each time" (A.Swanson). We should also notice that these mutual relationships are set in the context of our relationship with the Lord. Hence, of wives and husbands, we read, "Wives, submit yourselves unto your own husbands, *as unto the Lord*" (5: 22); of children and parents, "Children, obey your parents *in the Lord*" (6: 1); of servants and masters, "Servants, be obedient to them that are your masters … *as unto Christ*" (6: 5-6).

Very clearly, 'Christianity' is all-embracing. No part of life is exempt from the influence and guidance of God's Word, which must impact every relationship. This brings us to –

A) WIVES AND HUSBANDS, 5: 22-33

The section commences with wives and husbands (v.22), and continues in the reverse order (v.25), ending with both: "let every one of you ... so love his wife even as himself; and the wife see that she reverence her husband" (v.33). Perhaps this is to emphasise their equality.

We must notice that the relationship between wives and husbands (following Paul's first order of mention) is elevated to the very highest level. It is to be patterned on the relationship between Christ and the church. Hence the thrice-repeated expression, "even as": "For the husband is head of the wife, *even as* Christ is head of the church" (v.23); "Husbands, love your wives, *even as* Christ also loved the church" (v.25); "For no man ever yet hated his own flesh; but nourisheth and cherisheth it, *even as* the Lord the church" (v.29).

What an honour, in our married lives, to reflect the beauty of the relationship between Christ and the church! The teaching given here is totally opposed to the dictates of the 'feminist movement' and other ideologies, which regard this as both radical and retrograde. However, the believer should gladly conform to the will of God, rather than to modern thinking.

Notice, too, that there is nothing arbitrary about these instructions. Reasons are given. "Wives, submit yourselves unto your own husbands, as unto the Lord. *For* the husband is the head of the wife" (v.23); *"Therefore* as the church is subject unto Christ, so let the wives be subject to their own husbands in everything" (v.24); "He that loveth his wife loveth himself, *for* no man ever hated his own flesh; but nourisheth and cherisheth it, *even as* the Lord the church: *for* we are are members of his body ... *For this cause* shall a man leave his father and mother, and shall be joined unto his wife, and they two shall be one flesh" (vv.28-31).

The section may be divided as follows: *(1)* wives and their submission (vv.22-24); *(2)* husbands and their devotion (vv.25-30); *(3)* marriage and its inception (vv.31-32); *(4)* the concluding exhortation (v.33).

1) WIVES AND THEIR SUBMISSION, vv.22-24

We must notice three things here: *(a)* the nature of the submission (v.22); *(b)* the reason for the submission (v.23); *(c)* the practice of the submission (v.24).

A) The nature of the submission, v.22

"Wives, submit yourselves unto your own husbands, as unto the Lord." While the words rendered "wives" (*gune*) and "husbands" (*aner*) could be rendered 'women' and 'men', the context clearly decides! Just as the context decides in 1 Corinthians 11 verse 5 onwards.

This injunction emphasises the ***willing and joyful*** nature of the submission. It is "as unto the Lord". Attention is drawn to the following:

i) "Wives, submit yourselves ..." The nature of this submission must be rightly understood. It is not an involuntary submission. Let it also be said that submission does not infer inferiority! Eve was to be "an help meet" for Adam (Gen. 2: 18). This does not mean that wives become slaves. The words "meet for him" mean 'to match him' (Basil Atkinson). In all that God intended her to be and to do, she was his counterpart. She was not in any way inferior to him. She too was created "in the image of God" (Gen. 1: 27).

ii) "Unto their own husbands ..." See also verse 24. Quite obviously, this is not a warning against an illicit relationship, although such a warning might not be inappropriate. The expression, "own husbands", emphasises the unique relationship between husband and wife, that is "the particular and special and binding relationship of marriage" (Albert Leckie, (*What the Bible Teaches – Ephesians*).

iii) "As unto the Lord." If we take this to mean that she is to submit to her husband in exactly the same way that she submits to the Lord, this might imply that wives must give unqualified submission to their husbands, even when something wrong is involved. But, as Albert Leckie points out, "there is no thought of unqualified submission ... her submission must not conflict with supreme loyalty to her Lord". In the words of F.F.Bruce, "The phrase 'as unto the Lord' does not mean that they should yield to their husbands the same deference as they would yield to Christ Himself, but that deference to their husbands is a duty which they owe to the Lord". Compare Colossians 3 verse 18, "Wives, submit yourselves unto your own husbands, as *it is fit* in the Lord". "When the Christian wife submits herself to Christ, she will have no difficulty in submitting to her husband" (W.W.Wiersbe). She will then defer to him, notwithstanding his defects, and notwithstanding her superiority, if this is the case, intellectually and even spiritually.

B) The reason for the submission, v.23

Verse 23 advances the second of two reasons for her submission. We already noted the first (v.22), *viz*, the Lordship of Christ. Paul now (v.23) draws our attention to the husband's headship in Christ. "For the husband is head of the wife, even as Christ is head of the church: and he is the saviour (*soter*) of the body." While there is strong support for saying that Paul refers here to Christ as the "saviour of the body" in that He "nourisheth and cherisheth" the church (v.29), a stronger case can be made for suggesting that this actually refers to the husband.

In the words of R.C.H.Lenski, Paul here "lifts Christian marriage ('as unto the Lord') to a plane that is so high that we are astounded". He continues: "If it is obvious that the church can only have one head, then in marriage, which is a miniature of this, there can only be one head. Two heads would not only cause a duality, it would produce a monstrosity".

Headship is not dictatorship. In dealing with the subject, Albert Leckie observes that while "Sarah called Abraham 'lord' (1 Pet. 3:6), the husband is never referred to as lord of his wife but head of his wife. Lordship can involve abject subjection; headship is rather affectionate subjection". As we will see, as Head of the church (see Eph. 1: 22-23), the Lord Jesus provides for His body: see Chapter 4 verse 12. Just as the church receives from the Head guidance, provision, and care, so every Christian wife should look to her husband for the same things, gladly recognising that this is a divine order.

C) The practice of the submission, v.24

"Therefore as the church is subject unto Christ, so let the wives be to their own husbands in every thing." How is the church "subject unto Christ"? Not, as noted above, with "abject subjection", but with "affectionate subjection" (A.Leckie). Christianity restores creatorial order. "In the state of innocence, the husband was the head, and the wife subjected herself to him as the head. God made marriage so ideal, lovely, blessed, perfect. Sin entered and disturbed this relation. Eve fell, Adam followed, God's order was subverted. In the state of sin the divine and blessed order is disturbed in two directions: wives seek to rule their husbands" and "husbands tyrannise their wives often to the point of enslaving them. Endless woe results" (R.C.H.Lenski).

The expression, "in every thing" means as, again, noted above, "in every relationship and interest that does not conflict with her supreme loyalty to her Lord" (A.Leckie).

2) HUSBANDS AND THEIR DEVOTION, vv.25-30

"Husbands, love your wives, even as Christ also loved the church ..." Love here has the meaning of 'keep on loving'. It is *agape* (selfless love) not *phileo*. The love now described is of such a kind that makes it a delight for the wife to subject herself to such a loving husband. This reminds us, beautifully, of the marriage of Rebekah to Isaac: "And Isaac ... took Rebekah, and she became his wife; and he loved her" (Gen. 24: 67).

The words, "even as" denotes likeness of manner. It cannot mean, obviously, to the same degree, but rather after the same pattern. There are two major matters in this section:

- The pattern of Christ's love in its accomplishments (vv.25-27). This emphasises what Christ in love has accomplished, and will accomplish for the church. The teaching is introduced with the words, "Husbands, *love* your wives, even as Christ also loved the church ..." (v.25).

- The pattern of Christ's love in its intimacy (vv.28-29). This goes further and emphasises, not now what Christ has accomplished for the church, but what the church has become to Him. The teaching is introduced with the words, "*So* ought men to *love* their wives as their own bodies ... for we are members of his body".

a) The pattern of Christ's love in its accomplishments, vv.25-27

The love of the Lord Jesus for the church covers: *(i)* a past act (v.25); *(ii)* the present condition (v.26); *(iii)* the prospective glory (v.27).

Chapter 5:22-33

i) A past act, v.25

"Christ also loved the church, and gave himself for it." The words, "gave himself", emphasise the supreme act of Christ's love: His death on the cross. This evidently stresses His love in *acquiring* the church. He gave Himself. His love was sacrificial.

"For it" does not imply limited atonement: it does not negate the universality of His work and death.

So, following the pattern, husbands are to give themselves for their wives. "Husbands, love your wives, **even as** Christ also loved the church." Husbands must give themselves in love. Not just the housekeeping, but themselves! It means not being possessed by self-interest and self-centredness. The husband must have his wife's interests and welfare and well-being constantly in mind. Compare, in a different context, Philippians 2 verses 3-4; Ephesians 5 verse 2.

ii) The present condition, v.26

"That he might sanctify and cleanse it with the washing of water by the word." We notice that both verb and participle are aorists, which in this case means that the act of sanctifying and the act of cleansing are synonymous. It is quite obvious to us, but not to all commentators, that this does not refer to baptism, but to the new birth. The verse refers, not to a process, but to one act. Compare Titus 3 verse 5. This initial sanctifying, cleansing, has been accomplished "by the word (*rhema*)": The *spoken* word, not the written word (*logos*). Since this is the case, we have to ask, 'the spoken word **by whom**?' The answer is found in John 5 verses 25-26; John 15 verse 3. It is the spoken word of the Son of God.

The work is **positive**: "sanctify". He has put us "into a state corresponding to the divine nature" (A.Leckie). The work is **negative**: "cleanse". We should note the words here: "sanctify" (*hagiazo*, to make holy); "cleanse" (*katharizo*, to be free from impure admixture).

But what is the application? That love has secured a **holy** relationship. Love desires a **holy** relationship.

iii) The prospective glory, v.27

"That he might present it to himself a glorious church, not having spot or wrinkle, or any such thing: but that it should be holy and without blemish." The third aspect of His love for the church is both final and future.

On the natural level, a bride will endeavour to make herself as beautiful and attractive as possible – and rightly so. But in this case, the church, the bride of Christ, can do nothing of herself. It is *His* work. She owes it all to Him. Compare 2 Corinthians 11 verse 2. We should note the following:

- The church will be *presented by Christ to Himself.* In describing, the coming glory of the church, Paul tells us that Christ will present "her to Himself, making her stand forth by His side enfolded in glory, beautiful in sanctity, as the spotless Bride of the Lamb. The aorist points to the one great act of Christ. After all that Paul has said on the oneness and unity, the church now appears as one glorious person" (R.C.H.Lenski). The word rendered "present" *(paristemi)* means 'to cause to stand beside or near'. See also 2 Corinthians 4 verse 14; Chapter 11 verse 2; Colossians 1 verses 22 and 28.

- The church will be *"glorious"*. This is *positive*. The word rendered "glorious" *(exdoxos)* means 'honoured, splendid, gorgeous' (W.E.Vine).

- The church will be *"without spot, or wrinkle, or any such thing: but that it should be holy and without blemish"*. This is *negative*; what the church is not. Note the words employed: "*without spot* (*spilos*)", meaning without stain or defilement. That is, from without. No trace of the influence of this sinful world. Then "*without wrinkle*". That is, from within: due to faults in the body: particularly age! Perhaps we could say, 'no trace of the flesh'.

The world about the church causes the stains, and the flesh still in her causes the wrinkles. In glory, the church will be pure and ageless! She will be "holy" (*hagios*), pure and unpolluted, and "without blemish" (*amomos*), "without blame, shame or stain (1 Pet. 1: 19) visibly attached" (A.Leckie). The negative terms "spot" and "wrinkle" are figurative, and the corresponding terms ("holy and without blemish") are literal. Compare Ephesians 1 verse 14; 1 Peter 1 verse 19.

Divine love has secured, not only a pure bride (v.26), but a beautiful bride (v.27). This brings us to:

b) The pattern of Christ's love in its intimacy, vv.28-29

Paul now adds another perspective. If in verses 25-27, it is husband and wife, then in verses 28-29, it is "one flesh" (v.31). If in the first case, husbands should love their wives, because she is his wife then, in the second place, a husband should love his wife because she is himself. Both sections are introduced with "love ... wives" (vv.25, 28).

Hence we now read, "So ought men to love their wives as their own bodies. He that loveth his wife loveth himself" (v.28) or "So ought men also to love their **own** wives as their **own** bodies: he that loves his own wife loves himself" (JND). Attention is drawn to the following:

- The word "ought" (v.28) means to owe a debt, to be obligated (*opheilo*). It could be rendered 'one must'.

- The words "own wives ... own bodies ... own wife" (v.28, JND/RV) clearly indicate that wives are not possessions. A man's wife is himself. So it is not a case of a husband loving his wife *as* if she was his own body, he should love his wife because she actually *is* his own body.

- The plural is followed by the singular (v.28, JND/RV). This emphasises the general principle and the personal responsibility.

- This counteracts practices among the Jews and in the pagan world. In the first case (the Jewish world), according to certain rabbis, any husband could dismiss his wife for the most trivial cause, or for no cause at all, and she had no recourse. In the second case (the pagan world), it was worse, reminding us that the early church, particularly, comprised converts from Judaism and from the pagan world.

Since "he that loveth his wife loveth himself" (v.28), it follows that he will nourish and cherish her. We must notice *(i)* the practice (vv.28-29a), and *(ii)* the pattern (vv.29b-30).

i) The practice, vv.28-29a

What does a husband's wife's body require? It requires food and it requires warmth. Therefore a husband, regarding his wife as his own body, will attend to her needs. He will care for her. Compare Matthew 6 verse 25; James 2 verse 16.

In saying, "he that loveth his wife loveth himself", Paul is not exhorting the husband to love his wife as an extension of self-love, or because it is to his own advantage. Again, the word *agapao* used here for love (selfless love) shows that this is not the cause. A man should seek his own highest spiritual welfare, and so the highest good of his wife in every way, as united to him in the marriage bond.

ii) The pattern, vv.29b-30

The intimate care and love that a husband owes and should give his wife reflects the perfect and more wonderful care and love that the Lord now bestows on the church, His bride: "For no man ever yet hated his own flesh; but nourisheth and cherisheth it, **even as the Lord the church**" (v.29). This raises two questions -

- How does the Lord "nourish" (*ektrepho*, to nurture) the church? A husband 'nourishes' his wife by providing food. "He nourishes his wife by the labour of his hands", and the Lord Jesus nourishes His church "by the teacher" (A.Leckie).

- How does the Lord 'cherish' (*thalpo*, to keep warm) the church? A husband 'cherishes' his wife, by providing warmth and protection. "He cherishes his wife with the love of his heart", and the Lord Jesus cherishes His church "by the pastor" (A.Leckie). Compare Ephesians 4 verse 11; 1 Thessalonians 2 verse 7.

Albert Leckie sums it up like this: "Our Lord said "take no (anxious) thought for your life, what ye shall eat, or what ye shall drink; nor yet for your body, what ye shall put on" (Matt. 6:25). Nourishing requires eating and drinking, cherishing putting on of garments. To be warmed and filled are things needful to the body (James 2: 16)". As noted above, in the marriage bond the husband "nourishes his wife by the labour of his hands and cherishes her with the love of his heart. Thus the Lord (*christos*, Christ, JND) cares for His church: He nourishes by the teacher and cherishes by the pastor".

This is extended in verse 30. Note the connection: "So ought men to love their wives as **their own** bodies" (v.28) and "we are members of **his body**" (v.30). It is often said that Eve was not taken from Adam's head – to rule over him, nor from his feet – to be trampled on, but from under his arm – to be protected: near to his heart – to be loved.

For the record, JND omit the words "his flesh ... bones" (v.30). F.F.Bruce wants us to know that this is not a terrible problem: The addition ("flesh ... bones), while not original, is quite in keeping with the argument of the passage, especially as the apostle goes on immediately to quote Genesis 2 verse 24".

"The members are part of Him, as the branches are part of the vine in the teaching of John 15. As in the divine purpose the wife becomes part of the very life of her husband, and he nourishes and cherishes her, even so the Lord does to us as members of Himself, part of His own life that He has joined to Himself" (Francis Foulkes, *Tyndale New Testament Commentaries*).

We come now to another aspect of the subject. If in verses 22-24, we have the duties of wives, and in verses 25-32, we have the duties of husbands, then in verses 31-32, we have the unity of husband and wife in marriage. Paul goes back to the beginning. So:

3) MARRIAGE AND ITS INCEPTION, vv.31-32

"For this cause shall a man leave his father and mother, and shall be joined (*proskollao*, 'to be glued to') unto his wife, and they two shall be one flesh. This is a great mystery; but I speak concerning Christ and the church."

We must now listen again to Francis Foulkes: "This statement from the creation story is the most profound and fundamental statement in the whole of Scripture concerning God's plan for marriage. It is the ultimate bulwark against polygamy ... It is the ultimate argument against promiscuity; It is the ultimate reason against the dissolution of marriage by divorce. When our Lord was questioned concerning the legal permission given to divorce, He gave the answer that must still be given. In an imperfect society, in need of such laws, and for the 'hardness of men's hearts', divorce may be allowed, but it is a declension from the divine purpose, and can never be seen in any other light. The Lord Jesus gave no new teaching on the matter, but directed His appeal back to this verse (Matthew 19: 3-9, Mark 10: 2-12). Prior to marriage, a man or woman had his or her closest bond with parents, and to them owed the greatest obligation. The new bond and obligation that marriage involves transcends the old. Filial duty does not cease, but the most intimate relationship now, and the highest loyalty, is that between husband and wife, and parents only impair that relationship by trying in any way to come between. There must be a leaving of parents on the part of husband and wife, and a corresponding renouncing of rights on the part of the parents". Note: Adam did not leave "father and mother": he had none to leave!

It may seem hardly necessary to add, but present practices do make it important, that marriage involves one man and one woman – not two men, or two women, or, for that matter, one man and two or more women, or one woman and two or more men.

The complete union of husband and wife is expressed in the words "one flesh". See 1 Corinthians 6 verses 16-17. We should carefully note the expressions: "one body", that is, in relation to a harlot; "one flesh", that is, in relation to marriage; "one spirit", that is, in relation to the Lord.

There was a mystery about the relationship between Adam and Eve: "This is a great mystery" or "This mystery is great" (JND). Why did God apparently deviate in creation, and *not* make Eve out of the earth, as He had made Adam? The mystery is now revealed! It was prophetic! "When God made the woman there was a secret in His heart - that one day He would have an help meet for His own Son, a bride, a wife that would be His body!" (A. Leckie). Paul reveals the "mystery" in saying, "I speak concerning Christ and the church" (v.32).

4) THE CONCLUDING EXHORTATIONS, v.33

Paul concludes by returning to the practical implications of the marriage bond. He addresses husbands and wives:

a) Husbands

"Nevertheless, let every one of you in particular, so love his wife even as himself ..." F.F.Bruce says it all: "each husband must treat his wife no worse than he would treat himself; her welfare is indissolubly bound up with his own". It has been said that "Love, pure and simple, but transcendent, the truly Christian love *(agape)* that embraces what is pure in every other love, is the husband's duty".

b) Wives

"And the wife see that she reverence (*phobeomai*, to fear) her husband." Albert Leckie points out that this must be understood as respect, and F.F.Bruce uses the word 'deference', adding that "It need hardly be said that if the wife is to reverence her husband, he has an obligation to deserve her reverence".

THE EPISTLE TO THE EPHESIANS

"Children obey ... Servants be obedient"

Read Chapter 6: 1-9

As we noticed, in our previous study, Chapter 5 verses 22-33 ("Wives, submit yourselves unto your own husbands as unto the Lord ... Husbands, love your wives ...") bring us to a new section of the Epistle. In the earlier verses of Chapter 5, Paul addresses God's people generally. The instruction is applicable to all. There are no categories. Believers are described in general terms: "dear children" ('beloved children', JND" (v.1); "saints" (v.2) "children of light" (v.8). As believers, we are to submit ourselves "one to another in the fear of God". The four exhortations in connection with our "walk": "walk not as other Gentiles walk ..." (4: 17); "walk in love" (5: 2); "walk as children of light" (5: 8); "walk circumspectly" (5: 15), are addressed to all.

We also said that having considered the wealth (1: 1 - 3: 21), and walk (4: 1 - 5: 21) of God's people, we must now consider the relationships between God's people (5: 22 - 6: 9), where "pre-eminently should mutual consideration and deference be shown ..." (F.F.Bruce). Whereas Ephesians 5 verses 1-21, not to mention Chapter 4, have addressed all believers in connection with their common relationship with God, Paul now deals with specified categories of believers in their relationships with each other. These are: *(A)* wives and husbands (5: 22-33); *(B)* children and parents (6: 1-4); *(C)* servants and masters (6: 5-9).

In this connection, we have already noted the order: wives before husbands, children before parents, and servants before masters. "Grace puts the weaker first each time" (A.Swanson). We also noted that these mutual relationships are set in the context of our relationship with the Lord. Hence, of wives and husbands we read, "Wives, submit yourselves unto your own husbands, *as unto the Lord*" (5: 22); of children and parents, "Children, obey your parents *in the Lord*" (6: 1); of servants and masters, "Servants, be obedient to them that are your masters ... *as unto Christ*" (6: 5-6).

Very clearly, 'Christianity' is all-embracing. No part of life is exempt from the influence and guidance of God's Word which must impact every relationship. We should add that if no part of life is exempt from the influence and guidance of God's Word, then it follows that no part of life will be exempt from the direction and guidance of the Holy Spirit. The three godly relationships discussed here, with other things, all flow from being "filled with the Spirit" (5: 18).

Perhaps we should take the opportunity to say that being "filled with the Spirit" is not marked by 'charismatic' utterances, and extravagant behaviour, but, rather, by submission to the will of God. It has been observed that John the Baptist was filled "with the Holy Ghost, even from his mother's womb" (Luke 1: 15), but "John did no miracle". On the other hand, we must notice what else people said, "John did no miracle: *but all things that John spake of this man (the Lord Jesus) were true*" (John 10: 41). What a testimony!

Amongst other things, being "filled with the Spirit" regulates attitudes: in this case, as noted, the attitudes of wives and husbands, children and parents, servants and masters.

1) WIVES AND HUSBANDS, 5: 22-33

We dealt with this important subject in our previous study, noting in passing that the section commences with wives and husbands (v.22), continues in the reverse order (v.25), and ends with both: "let every one of you ... so love his wife even as himself; and the wife see that she reverence her husband" (v.33).

This brings us to

2) CHILDREN AND PARENTS, 6: 1-4

"Children, obey your parents in the Lord: for this is right. Honour thy father and mother, which is the first commandment with promise, that it may be well with thee, and thou mayest live long on the earth. And, ye fathers, provoke not your children to wrath: but bring them up in the nurture and admonition of the Lord." Paul refers, first of all, to children, and then to fathers.

a) Children, vv.1-3

Paul advances three reasons why children should obey their parents: *(i)* it is "right" (v.1); *(ii)* it is commanded (v.2); *(iii)* it has a happy result (v.3).

i) It is "right", v.1. "Children, obey your parents in the Lord: for this is right." According to Kenneth Wuest, the phrase "in the Lord" is to be construed with "obey". In other words, the words "in the Lord" refer to the children, rather than the parents. Albert Leckie concurs: "That the children are *addressed directly* ... means that the writer is thinking of Christian children". Obedience to their parents is obedience to *the Lord.* Quite clearly, Paul is thinking here of a 'Christian home'. Here, then is the pattern for Christian children: "obey your parents in all things; for this is well-pleasing unto the Lord" (Col. 3: 20).

The Lord Jesus "went down with them ... (Mary and Joseph), and was subject (*hupatasso*, meaning, 'to place under') unto them" (Luke 2: 51). The Lord's own example is the pattern for Christian children:

For He is our childhood's pattern,
Day by day like us He grew.

God's Word expresses His displeasure over disobedience to parents (Rom. 1: 30; 2 Tim. 3: 2).

While Paul evidently has in mind a Christian home where Christian principles prevail, Christian children in non-Christian homes could face a crisis of conscience if parents require their children to do something contrary to Bible teaching. If it becomes necessary to invoke Acts 5 verse 29, this must be done with courtesy and respect.

The command is followed by the **reason**: "obey your parents in the Lord: **for this is right".** While this is probably best explained by what follows (obedience to parents was required by the law), W.W.Wiersbe observes that there "is an order in nature, ordained of God, that argues for the rightness of an action. Since the parents brought the child into the world, and since they have more knowledge and wisdom than the child, it is right that the child should obey his parents".

ii) It is commanded, v.2. "Honour thy father and mother; which is the first

Chapter 6:1-9

commandment with promise ..." So obedience to parents is not only right, it is a divine commandment.

The word translated "honour" (*timao*) involves respect, and is **an advance** on "obey". The way in which the Lord Jesus referred to the fifth commandment (see Mark 7: 9-13), emphasises that the command: "***Honour*** thy father and mother" is not limited to childhood.   See Addendum.

iii) It has a happy result, v.3. "Honour thy father and mother, which is the first commandment **with promise, that it may be well with thee, and thou mayest live long on the earth.**"

The fifth commandment, cited here, is called "the first commandment with promise" (perhaps meaning the first commandment of this nature in the Old Testament). "Honour thy father and thy mother; that thy days may be long upon the land which the LORD thy God giveth thee" (Exod. 20: 12); "Honour thy father and thy mother ... that thy days may be prolonged, and that it may go well with thee, in the land which the LORD thy God giveth thee" (Deut. 5: 16).

We should notice that in referring to the fifth commandment, Paul makes no reference, for obvious reasons, to "the ***land*** which the LORD thy God giveth thee". He substitutes the word "***earth***" for land. But what about his reason for the injunction, "that it may be well with thee, and thou mayest live long upon the earth"?

The answer lies not in the idea that all obedient children are guaranteed long life, but in the fact that disobedience to parents will bring disaster.

For this reason Solomon gave a vast amount of instruction to his son: "My son, forget not my law; but let thine heart keep my commandments: for length of days, and long life, and peace, shall they add to thee" (Prov. 3: 1-2). Solomon's instructions were intended to preserve his son from harm. See, for example, Proverbs 7 verses 1-5, "My son, keep my words, and lay up my commandments with thee. Keep my commandments, and live; and my law as the apple of thine eye. Bind them upon thy fingers, write them upon the table of thine heart. Say unto wisdom, Thou art my sister; and call understanding thy kinswoman: that they may keep thee from the strange woman, from the stranger which flattereth with her words". Following her is likened to an ox "going to the slaughter", or a fool "to the correction of the stocks" (v.22). The remaining verses (vv.23-27) describe the ensuing disaster, and it certainly seems that the days of the young man described by Solomon would *not* be "prolonged in the land".

Disobedience to parents indicates an undisciplined life – leading to vice and dissipation. In which case, it will *not* "be well with thee"!

b) Fathers, v.4

"And, ye fathers, provoke not your children to wrath ('provoke ... to wrath' is one word: *parorgizo,* as in Eph. 4: 26) but bring them up in the nurture and admonition of the Lord." The word translated "fathers" (*pateres)* may be rendered 'parents', but it would appear that Paul is thinking particularly of the responsibility of fathers here.

It has been pointed out that in verse 1 the word "parents" translates *goneusin*, and in verse 2 "father and mother" translates *pater metera*. From this it does seem that Paul is thinking here "not only of the particular responsibility of the father, but of a peculiar danger: 'provoke not your children to wrath'" (A.Leckie).

One thing is clear: "Parents (according to F.F.Bruce) have an obligation to their children as well as children to their parents; if children must obey their parents, parents should deserve their children's obedience". He continues, "It is possible even for Christian parents, to be so unreasonable in their demands on their children that the children are irritated beyond measure and wonder whether it does any good to try to please their parents and do what they say". Albert Leckie concurs: "Children obey; fathers exercise necessary self-control so that by not continually looking for faults, nor showing relish and hastiness in correction, nor personal bad example, they do not provoke to anger. A clash of personalities must be avoided; and discipline must be just, never harsh, but exercised in love".

Paul writes similarly in Colossians 3 verse 21, "Fathers, provoke not your children to anger, lest they be discouraged". Children can be provoked by over-protection, favouritism, discouragement, failure to make allowances, neglect, bitter words, cruelty. Need we say more?

Rather than 'provoking them to wrath', the Christian father should bring up his children in "the nurture and admonition of the Lord".

- The words rendered "***bring them up***" (*ektrephete,* from *trepto,* to rear, feed, nourish) mean to promote health and strength. Compare Ephesians 5 verse 29, "no man ever yet hated his own flesh; but ***nourisheth*** (*ektrepho*) and cherisheth it, even as the Lord the church". Compare also Acts 7 verses 20-21, "Moses ... was exceeding fair, and ***nourished up*** *(anatrepho)* in his father's house three months: and when he was cast out, Pharaoh's daughter took him up, and ***nourished*** (*anatrepho*) him as her own son". See also 1 Timothy 4 verse 6, "***nourished up*** (*entrephomai*) in the words of faith and of good doctrine".

- The word rendered "***nurture***" (*paideia*) means training, education, discipline, correction (Heb. 12: 5, 7, 8, 11). In Albert Leckie's words, "the father who brings up his child for the Lord will not encourage nor sympathise with faults, but with kindness, yet strictness, correct". According to the late Duke of Windsor (Edward VIII), "Everything in the American home is controlled by switches, **except the children!**" (quoted by W.W.Wiersbe).

- The word rendered "***admonition***" (*nouthesia*) means instruction or warning. "As the failures of Israel have been recorded for our admonition (1 Cor. 10: 11), and the heretic must be admonished twice (Titus 3:10), so fathers cannot omit the warning aspect of instruction (Deut. 6: 7, 20; 11: 18, 19; Prov. 13: 24; 29: 15)" (A. Leckie). It should be said that parental discipline must always be explained. The father who just says: 'This hurts me more than it hurts you' as he wallops his misbehaving child, isn't likely to achieve a great deal.

In it all, Paul is referring here to "the nurture and admonition **of the Lord**". Everything is to be undertaken with reference to His will and authority. It has been nicely said (F.F.Bruce) that "since children are a "heritage of the LORD" (Psalm 127: 3), their "training" should be undertaken with a sense of responsibility to Him, so that from their early days they may learn to worship and love Him". Hence the instructions in Deuteronomy 6: 6-9, "And these words, which I command thee this day, shall be in thine heart: and thou shalt teach them diligently unto thy children, and shalt talk of them when thou sittest in thine house, and when thou walkest by the way, and when thou liest down, and when thou risest up".

Eli failed here: he reproved Hophni and Phinehas (1 Sam 2: 22-25) but that was all, and God had to say to him: "Thou ... honourest thy sons above me" (1 Sam 2: 29). David failed here with Adonijah: his father "had not displeased him at any time in saying, Why hast thou done so?" (1 Kings 1: 6). But what of children who do not respond to teaching and instruction, and who choose to go their own way? We do know that in these sad circumstances the **Lord** does understand parental grief. See Isaiah 1 verse 2, "I have nourished and brought up children, and they have rebelled against me; the ox knoweth his owner, and the ass his master's crib: but Israel doth not know, my people do not consider". This brings us to:

2) SERVANTS AND MASTERS, vv.5-9

We are now out of the home, and in the workplace where Paul discusses employee/employer relationships. The apostle addresses servants (*doulo*i, bondservants) in verses 5-8, and masters (*kurioi*) in verse 9. As Albert Leckie points out: "Both the Christian slave and the Christian master had been set free from their spiritual slavery and had now the same Master in heaven. The Christian slave served with good will 'as to the Lord (*kurios*)' (v.7), while the Christian master recognised that he too had responsibilities as a slave to the same Master (*kurios*) in heaven" (v.9).

a) Servants, vv.5-8

"Servants, be obedient to them that are your masters according to the flesh, with fear and trembling, in singleness of heart, as unto Christ; not with eyeservice, as men-pleasers; but as the servants of Christ, doing the will of God from the heart; with good will doing service, as to the Lord, and not to men; knowing that whatsoever good thing any man doeth, the same shall he receive of the Lord, whether he be bond or free." We should notice the following:

i) **The sphere of their service, v.5.** They served their masters only in temporal things. Their service was "according to the flesh". Where Christian slaves served Christian masters, the master's authority did not include the spiritual realm. Christian slaves and masters alike were fellow-servants of one Lord, Jesus Christ" (F.F.Bruce). This leads to:

ii) **The respect in their service, v.5.** "Servants, be obedient to them that are your masters according to the flesh, with fear and trembling, in singleness of your heart, as unto Christ." Compare Colossians 3 verses 22 and 24: "Servants, obey in all things your masters according to the flesh ... ye serve the Lord Christ". The fact that they might serve a Christian master did not mean that they could do so with lesser obedience and fidelity, and if "the

Christian slave had an unbelieving master, he would serve him the more faithfully now because the honour of Christ and the gospel was bound up with the quality of his service" (F.F.Bruce). F.F.Bruce continues, "Paul refers here, not to a servile fear, but to the fear of God. The collocation of 'fear and trembling' in the service of God appears in 1 Corinthians 2 verse 3 with reference to Paul himself, and in 2 Corinthians 7 verse 15 and Philippians 2 verse 12 with reference to Christians. For Christian slaves the service of their earthly masters was a special form of the service of God, to be discharged in a spirit of reverence towards Him". We should add that there should be "fear and trembling" lest they should bring discredit **upon Him.**

The expression "singleness" ("singleness of heart") translates *haplotes* from *haplous* meaning 'simple' or 'single', with "the thought of sincerity present in Romans 12 verse 8; 2 Corinthians 11 verse 3, Ephesians 6 verse 5; Colossians 3 verse 22" (W.E.Vine). This excludes grudging obedience or 'a fit of the sulks'. It is translated "bountifulness" or 'liberality' (RV) in 2 Corinthians 9 verse 11. This leads to:

iii) **The genuineness of their service, v.6.** "Not with eyeservice, as men-pleasers; but as the servants of Christ, doing the will of God from the heart (*ek psuches,* 'from soul')." So they are to serve with heart (v.5) and soul (v.6): "not reluctantly nor grudgingly, but with keenness and enthusiasm" (A.Leckie). Paul censures deception. In this case the deception of only "working hard when the master's eye, or the foreman's, is on him" (F.F.Bruce). The Lord's eye is upon us at all times! Compare Colossians 3 verse 23, "Whatsoever ye do, do it heartily, as to the Lord, and not to men". As servants in employment, we are as much "servants of Christ" as we are servants of the company or the proprietor.

iv) **The willingness in their service, v.7** "With good will doing service, as to the Lord, and not to men." Here it is again: "as **unto Christ**" (v.5); "as the **servants of Christ**" (v.6); "as to **the Lord**" (v.7). As Albert Leckie points out, "while men benefit from prompt and hearty service, this is because of a higher accountability – 'as to the Lord'"

Peter points out that this should hold good even if a "froward" master was involved: "Servants, be subject to your masters with all fear; not only to the good and gentle, but also to the froward" (1 Pet. 2: 18). The word "froward" (*skolios*) means 'crooked' and is used here to describe "tyrannical or unjust masters" (W.E.Vine).

v) The reward for their service, v.8.

"Knowing (*oida*, knowing assuredly) that whatsoever good thing any man doeth, the same shall he receive of the Lord, whether he be bond or free." We must listen again to F.F.Bruce: "It is Christ, and not one's earthly master, who is the final arbiter and rewarder of work well done. This would encourage a Christian slave to work cheerfully and zestfully, even for a master who was unreasonable and impossible to please: he knew that it was from Christ that his thanks would come".

W.W.Wiersbe relates the story of the old missionary who was returning home after many years of sacrificial service in Africa. On the same ship was President Theodore Roosevelt, returning to the States after a big-game hunt in Africa. When the ship docked at New York, great crowds greeted the President, and the press was there to cover the story. The old missionary and his wife walked off the ship unnoticed and made their way to a cheap hotel to spend the night, before travelling west.

"It just doesn't seem right!" the missionary said to his wife in a rather bitter tone. "We give our lives in Africa to win souls for Christ, and when we arrive home, there's nobody to meet us and there's no reward. The President shoots some animals and gets a royal welcome!"

As they were praying before retiring, it seemed that the Lord spoke to them and said: "Do you know why you haven't received your reward yet, My children? It's because you aren't home yet!"

b) Masters, v.9

If Christian slaves have their duties, so do Christian masters. Paul is not one-sided. "And, ye masters, do the same things unto them, forbearing threatening: knowing that your Master also is in heaven; neither is there respect of persons with him."

This was so in the Old Testament: "Thou shalt not rule over him (a brother in employment as a 'hired servant') with rigour; but shalt fear thy God" (Lev. 25: 43). The word "forbearing" (*aniemi*) means 'to desist from' (W.E.Vine). In saying, "forbearing threatening" (*apeile*), Paul reminds masters that they must not "adopt a hectoring or browbeating attitude towards their slaves, but treat them fairly, rendering to them 'that which is just and equal', Colossians 4 verse 1" (F.F.Bruce). We are reminded that the Lord Jesus "threatened not" (1 Pet. 2: 23).

For good 'industrial relations' in the Old Testament, see Ruth 2 verse 4, "Boaz came from Bethlehem, and said unto the reapers, The LORD be with you" (Boaz). And they answered him, The LORD bless thee". For good 'industrial relations' in the New Testament, see Luke 7 verses 1-10, "And a certain centurion's servant, who was **dear** unto him, was sick ..." At the same time, the servant was a good employee: "I say ... to my servant, Do this, and he doeth it". His soldiers were simply "**under**" him.

Paul concludes the section by saying, "knowing that both their and your Master is in heaven, and there is no acceptance of persons with him" (v.9, JND). He does not differentiate – or show favouritism.

We cannot leave the passage without remembering that the perfect Master washed the feet of His disciples: "If I then, your Lord and Master, have washed your feet; ye also ought to wash one another's feet" (John 13: 14).

Addendum

"Honour thy father and mother"

The Pharisees taught that if people wished to avoid their responsibilities for supporting parents, all they had to do was to say that the finance which should have been used in this way was going to be offered to God: "it is Corban, that is to say, a gift, by whatsoever thou mightest be profited by me". (The word "Corban" means an offering, and was "the Hebrew term for any sacrifice", W.E.Vine). The Lord Jesus said that this was "making the word of God of none effect". The Pharisees had a whole range of devices for avoiding the plain teaching of God's Word. We must make sure that we do not do the same.

THE EPISTLE TO THE EPHESIANS

"The whole armour of God"

Read Chapter 6: 10-17

As we have noted from time to time in our Ephesian studies, it is often said that the Epistle covers the wealth, wisdom, walk and warfare of God's people. However, on reflection, we felt that in order to obtain a better overall picture, this needed some amendment, and suggested the following: the wealth (1: 1 - 3: 21), walk (4: 1 - 5: 21), relationships (5: 22 - 6: 9) and warfare (6: 10-24) of God's people. While this destroys the neat alliteration (!), it is, hopefully, rather more in keeping with the text.

However, alliteration refuses 'to wave the white flag' when faced with Ephesians 6 verses 10-24. Enter W.W.Wiersbe (*Ephesians - Be Rich*), with the following (plus an editorial addition): *(1)* The Enabling (vv.10-11); *(2)* The Enemy (v.12); *(3)* The Equipment (vv.13-17); *(4)* The Energy (vv.18-20); *(5)* The Encouragement (vv.21-24). No, this isn't 'plagiarism' – a 'plagiarist' is someone who passes off someone else's writing as his own. In Mill Lane Bible Studies, we do endeavour to name our sources where appropriate. (Sometimes, however, we just can't remember them!)

It is not without significance that Paul deals with the warfare of God's people at the *end* of the Epistle. Amongst other things, all that has gone before prepares us for conflict. For example, we have learnt a great deal about the "truth" with which we are to be 'girded' in battling with "principalities ... powers ... the rulers of the darkness of this world" (v.12).

As we have noticed, Paul deals in Chapters 4-6 for example, with assembly life (4: 1-16), personal life (4: 17 – 5: 21), married life (5: 22-33), family life (6: 1- 4), and business life (6: 5-9). If we are faithful to God here and, of course, in any sphere of life – *expect conflict!*

Let's listen, again, to Warren Wiersbe: "Sooner or later every believer discovers that the Christian life is a battleground, not a playground, and that he faces an enemy who is much stronger than he is – apart from the Lord. That Paul should use the military to illustrate the believer's conflict with Satan is reasonable. He himself was chained to a Roman soldier (v.20), and his readers were certainly familiar with soldiers and the equipment they used".

Conflict should be followed, not by defeat, but by conquest. Paul puts it like this: "Wherefore take unto you the whole armour of God, that ye may be able to withstand in the evil day (that is, in any 'evil day'), and having done all, to stand. Stand therefore …" (vv.13-14). We are to stand before attack (v.11), during attack (v.13) and after attack (v.13).

This will make us "a good soldier of Jesus Christ" (2 Tim. 2: 3) along with others – our 'fellowsoldiers' (Phil. 2: 25). We are to "Fight the good fight of faith (or 'the good fight of the faith', JND margin)" (1 Tim. 6: 12). The word twice rendered 'fight' here, one being a verb (*agonizomai*) and the other a noun (*agon*), makes it very clear indeed that this is far more than a passing brush with the enemy.

This brings us to:

1) THE ENABLING, v.10-11

"Finally, my brethren, be strong in the Lord, and in the power of his might. Put on the whole armour of God, that ye may be able to stand against the wiles of the devil." Paul goes on to explain why we need God's power and God's armour: "For we wrestle not against flesh and blood, but against principalities, against powers, against the rulers of the darkness of this world, against spiritual wickedness in high places" (v.12).

If all this looks daunting - and it does - and our foes seem implacable - then we must remember that "greater is he that is in you, than he that is in the world" (1 John 4: 4).

Paul deals with the enemy in the same order as John. First of all, he deals with the provision made for us in the conflict – the enabling (vv.10-11), and then with the opposition encountered in the conflict – the enemy (v.12).

In connection with the provision made for us in the conflict, Paul refers *(a)* to the power available (v.10); *(b)* to the provision made (v.11); *(c)* to the potential for victory (v.11).

i) **He refers to the power available**. "Finally, my brethren, be strong in the Lord, and in the power of his might" (v.10). Amongst other things, they were his "brethren" in conflict.

The power to overcome lies in the "recognition of the Lordship of Christ" (A.Leckie). This is of paramount importance. The Old Testament furnishes us with an excellent illustration. With the battle for Jericho before him, Joshua "fell on his face before "the captain of the host of the LORD", saying "What saith my lord unto his servant?" (Josh 5: 13-15). "Thus with the children of God today: there must be submission to the Lordship of Christ, and a recognition that He is the arch-strategist, and is for us. And what resource is available: 'the power of His might': 'Power' (*kratos*) is force superior to all opposition, and 'might' (*ischus*) inherent vital power!" (A.Leckie).

It is well worth remembering that Paul's two words here (*kratos* and *ischus*) occur in Ephesians 1 verse 19 when Paul is describing the resurrection and ascension of the Lord Jesus. It has been said (A.Leckie) that in Ephesians 1 verse 19, Paul refers to divine power towards us; in Chapter 3 verse 16 to divine power in us; in Chapter 6 verse 10 to divine power for us. In each case, reference is made to the occurrence of words from the root *dunamis*.

Joshua was to be "strong and of a good courage" in connection with the task before him, the teaching of God's Word, and the trials that lay ahead (Joshua 1: 6, 7, 9).

ii) **He refers to the provision made**. "Put on the whole armour of God" (v.11). It is "the whole armour of **God**". He provides the armour – we put it on. All of it! We need it all. Nothing must be missing. The word "armour" translates *panoplia,* hence our English word 'panoply' meaning 'a full suit of armour: any complete protection' (*Nuttall's Standard Dictionary*).

Compare: "the armour of light" (Rom. 13: 12); "the armour of righteousness" (2 Cor. 6: 7). In these two instances, the word "armour" translates *hoplon*, meaning the actual weapons. The verb 'to arm oneself' (*hoplizo*) occurs in 1 Peter 4 verse 1 ("**arm** yourselves likewise with the same mind"), and a strengthened form of the verb (*kathoplizo*) is used in Luke 11 verse 21 ("When a strong man **armed** keepeth his palace ...").

Chapter 6:10-17

The armour is available and is to be donned **before** the conflict. Joshua was in the enjoyment of divine power before it was actually demonstrated in the fall of Jericho. Hence, as noted above, we are to stand before attack (v.11), during attack (v.13) and after attack (v.13).

iii) He refers to the potential for victory. "That ye may **be able to stand** (meaning 'stand firm') **against the wiles of the devil**" (v.11). That is, for the third time (!), to 'stand firm' before (v.11), during (v.11) and after (v.13) attack.

The word translated "wiles" (*methodia* or *methodeia*, W.E.Vine) also occurs in Ephesians 4 verse 14, "cunning craftiness, whereby they lie in wait to deceive (*methodia,* literally, 'unto circumvention of deceit')". Satan is here called "the devil", meaning 'the accuser' or 'slanderer'.

We need the "whole armour of God" because the enemy could use any tactic/ruse at any time in any place, including demeaning, falsely accusing and misrepresenting God's people. See, for example, Acts 21 verses 28-29.

This brings us to:

2) THE ENEMY, v.12

"For we wrestle not against flesh and blood, but against principalities, against powers, against the rulers of the darkness of this world, against spiritual wickedness in high places."

In this connection, we should notice the following: *(a)* how we contend with the enemy; *(b)* the enemy with whom we contend.

a) How we contend with the enemy

"We wrestle …" According to W.E.Vine, the word translated "wrestle" (*pale*) is "akin to *pallo*, to sway, vibrate". Used here metaphorically, it describes the ongoing spiritual conflict in which believers are engaged. The word emphasises the close personal combat involved. We should notice that the word "against" is used five times in the verse.

b) The enemy with whom we contend

Paul looks beyond men to the spiritual powers that control them. They use human agencies, but "flesh and blood" are not the real foe. Paul makes the point earlier in the epistle: "In time past ye walked according to the course of this world, according to **the prince of the power of the air, the spirit that now worketh in the children of disobedience**" (2: 2).

For examples, see John 14 verse 30 where the Lord Jesus says, not 'Judas' or 'the soldiers', but "**the prince of this world cometh**", and 1 Thessalonians 2 verse 18, where Paul says, not 'evil men hindered us', but "**Satan hindered us**". See also Revelation 2 verse 13.

We have already noticed that our arch-enemy is "the devil" (v.11). He is "the god of this world ('age')" (2 Cor. 4: 4). But he has an unseen army at his command which Warren Wiersbe calls 'Satan's helpers'. Paul tells us *(i)* what they are called ("principalities" and "powers"); *(ii)* what they do (they keep men in darkness); *(iii)* where they are located ("in the heavenlies", JND).

i)   **What they are called.**   Paul calls them "principalities" and "powers". The word "principalities" translates *arche,* meaning 'government, rule' (W.E.Vine). Daniel was told about the activities of "the prince of the kingdom of Persia" and "the prince of Grecia" (Dan. 10: 13, 20). Both of them were in contention with "Michael, one of the chief princes ... your prince" (Dan. 10: 13, 21). The word "powers" translates *exousia,* meaning "the ability or strength with which one is endued", leading "to the power of authority, the right to exercise power" (W.E.Vine).

It has been said that "principality" is dignity of position, and "power" is executive authority (Albert Leckie). We should also point out that Scripture refers to good principalities and powers (see Eph. 1: 21; 3: 10; Col. 2: 10), and to evil principalities and powers (Eph. 6: 12; Col. 2: 15), suggesting that the latter represent Satanic rivalry against the former.

We should add that the "principalities and powers" were created by the Lord Jesus (perhaps on the "fourth day"), see Colossians 1 verse 16. The existence of evil "principalities and powers" must be one result of the fall of Satan. They have no power to separate believers from "the love of God which is in Christ Jesus our Lord" (Rom. 8: 39).

ii)   **What they do.**   They rule. Paul calls them "the rulers of the darkness of this world", or "the world rulers of this darkness" (RV), or "the universal lords of this darkness" (JND). The words "world rulers" (RV) translate one word (*kosmokrator*), and refers to "unseen forces of immense power who rule men and keep them in darkness (see Luke 22: 53, 'this is your hour and the power of darkness'; Colossians 1: 12-13, 'the Father ... who hath delivered us from the power of darkness')" (A.Leckie).

iii) Where they are located. They are located "in the heavenlies" (JND). The expression "in the heavenlies" first occurs at the beginning of the Epistle: God has "blessed us with all spiritual blessings in heavenly places in Christ ('in the heavenlies in Christ', JND)" (1: 3), emphasising that unlike the Jew whose blessings are located in Canaan or 'Immanuel's land' (Isa. 8: 8), our blessings have an entirely different setting. It is a characteristic phrase. It is where Christ sits, Chapter 1 verse 20. It is where we sit with Him, Chapter 2 verse 6. It is where the principalities and powers see the wonder of the church, Chapter 3 verse 10. It is where the emissaries of Satan are active, Chapter 6 verse 12. "The heavenlies" is a general term, not referring directly to heaven itself, but to what is heavenly in nature as opposed to what is earthly in nature.

The word translated 'heavenlies' (*epouranios*) is used in John 3 verse 12: "If I have told you earthly things, and ye believed not, how shall ye believe if I tell you of heavenly things?"

Satan and his hosts are busy, not only in the world around us, but in the world above us. We have an example in the attempts of Balak to have Israel cursed by God, only to be told by Balaam, "Surely there is no enchantment against Jacob, neither is there any divination against Israel (Num. 23: 23). Satan is called the "accuser of our brethren" (Rev. 12: 10). He accused Joshua, the high priest, only to be told by the Lord, "The LORD rebuke thee, O Satan ...." (Zech. 3: 1-2). Satan has not changed one little bit since then. At the end-time, he will be ejected from the heavens, when it will be said, "the accuser of our brethren is cast down, which accused them before our God day and night" (Rev. 12: 10).

We must remember that Satan is not omnipotent, omnipresent or omniscient. He is a creature. He is a defeated being. See Hebrews 2 verses 14-15. We must remember, too, that the Lord Jesus is "far above all" (Eph. 1: 21; Col. 2: 10).

Ephesians

This brings us to:

3) THE EQUIPMENT, vv.13-17

"Wherefore take unto you the whole armour of God, that ye may be able to withstand in the evil day, and, having done all, to stand. Stand therefore, having your loins girt about with truth ..." (vv.13-14). Paul tells us elsewhere that "the weapons of our warfare are not carnal, but mighty through God to the pulling down of strongholds" (2 Cor. 10: 4). (In passing, this is evidently a reference to the conquest of Jericho.) At the risk of repeating ourselves, we should notice what Paul emphasises in verse 13.

- **The necessity for the armour.** "Wherefore", that is, in view of the might of the enemy –

> *Principalities and powers,*
> *Mustering their unseen array,*
> *Watch for thine unguarded hours*
> *Watch and pray.*

- **The necessity for all the armour.** "Wherefore take unto you the **whole** armour of God." Not 'part': the 'whole'.

- **The provision of the armour.** "Wherefore take unto you the whole armour of **God**." It is divinely provided. We just 'put it on'. This is so important: "**take unto** you the whole armour of God". We must make a conscious decision to put on the armour. It doesn't 'just happen'.

- **The effect of the armour:** "that ye may be able to withstand in the evil day." It is true, of course, that in a general sense, "the days are evil" (Eph. 5: 16). But here, "**the** evil day" is a particular day, when an individual, assembly, family, place, is attacked. It is not then a case of hastily donning the armour when "the evil day" arrives. After all, we do not know when it's coming! Rather, then, we must wear it at all times, so as to be ready. We must be in a constant state of readiness. Sometimes, of course, like the Jews, we have "a good day" (Esther 8: 17). Not every day is an "evil day"!

The armour will enable us to "withstand (*anthistemi*, 'to set against')". For "resist" (*anthistemi*) see, for example, Galatians 2 verse 11; James 4 verse 7 and 1 Peter 5 verse 9 - all 'evil days'. It was an "evil day" for Nehemiah when he was told, "Let us shut the doors of the temple: for they will come to slay thee; yea, in the night will they come to slay thee". But just listen to his reply: "Should such a man as I flee?" (Neh. 6: 10-11). It was an "evil day" for Peter's first readers (see 1 Pet. 4: 12) and for the church at Smyrna (see Rev. 2: 10).

It has been said that "we cannot advance against the devil and his hosts with equipment from our own arsenal". Like David, we have to say, "I cannot go with these (Saul's armour and sword); for I have not proved them" (1 Sam. 17: 39).

- **The permanence of the armour.** "Having done all, to stand." Else the enemy might regroup and attack again! Note, yet again: stand before (v.11), during (v.13) and after (v.13) the engagement. It has been nicely said that we do not fight **for** victory, but **from** victory!

We now come to the armour itself: "Stand therefore, having your loins girt about with truth, and having on the breastplate of righteousness; and your feet shod with the preparation of the gospel of peace; above all, taking the shield of faith, wherewith ye shall be able to quench all the fiery darts of the wicked. And take the helmet of salvation, and the sword of the Spirit, which is the word of God" (vv.14-17).

a) "Loins girt about with truth", v.14

"Stand therefore, having your loins girt about with truth." We have to decide whether Paul refers here to "truth" in the sense of 'truthfulness' or "truth" in the sense of divine truth, that is, the doctrines which comprise 'the truth'.

The former is certainly the case in Isaiah 11 verse 5: "righteousness shall be the girdle of his loins" and faithfulness the girdle of his reins". But since Paul is dealing here with "the armour of God", something divinely provided, it does seem that he is referring to "truth revealed, the truth of this epistle, 'the word of truth' (1: 13); and 'as the truth is in Jesus' (4: 21), gripping and strengthening so as to be able to stand - the truth holding the person rather than the person holding the truth" (A.Leckie). We are to 'gird on' truth (*perizonnumi,* to bind round about with a girdle). To gird your loins also means to get rid of any encumbrances (like a long flapping garment) and therefore be ready for action.

But why "loins"? The loins are connected with strength, whether in connection with, for example, "behemoth" (Job 40: 16) or the 'virtuous woman' (Prov. 31: 17) (How's that for a mixture!). According to M.R.Vincent, "To strike through the loins (see Deut. 33: 11) is to strike a fatal blow. To lay affliction on our loins (Psalm 66: 11) is to afflict heavily. Here was the point of junction for the main parts of body armour, so that the girdle formed the common bond of the whole". The "belt" with which the loins were girded was the "foundational piece of armour for a Roman soldier" and had "latches" to which other pieces of armour were attached. The "belt" effectively bound other pieces of armour together "into one cohesive piece" (quoted by Justin Waldron).

b) "The breastplate of righteousness" v.14

"Having on the breastplate of righteousness." Once again, we have to make a decision. Is Paul referring to practical righteousness, or the fact that we have been "made the righteousness of God" in Christ? (2 Cor. 5: 21). The answer must be the same as before. The "righteousness" here is part of "the armour of God", and since this is a divine provision, it is not practical righteousness. As Albert Leckie observes, if it were practical righteousness, then "the enemy could easily shoot through that!" He adds, "It is the person resting on what they are in Christ". In the battle it is so important to have the breastplate in place – to have the assurance that we are right with God, and "Therefore being justified by faith, we have peace with God through our Lord Jesus Christ" (Rom. 5: 1). The breastplate covered vital organs. According to Warren Wiersbe, it was made of "metal plates or chains, covering the body from the neck to the waist, both front and back". The believer can sing:

> *What though the accuser roar*
> *Of things that I have done.*
> *I know them all, and thousands more –*
> *Jehovah findeth none.*

c) "Feet shod with the preparation of the gospel of peace", v.15

"And your feet shod with the preparation of the gospel of peace." Compare Isaiah 52 verse 7, "How beautiful upon the mountains are the feet of him that bringeth good tidings, that publisheth peace ..."

Bearing in mind that Paul is still describing the Christian soldier, readiness to preach the gospel is an essential part of spiritual warfare. Engagement with an enemy bent on our destruction should not lessen our evangelism, whether corporate or personal. Feet "shod" implies readiness. The word (*hupodeo*) means, literally, 'to bind underneath', and was "used of binding of sandals" (W.E.Vine). Compare Acts 12 verse 8, "Gird thyself, and bind on thy sandals". God's people in Egypt were to keep the Passover with 'their loins girded and their shoes on their feet' (Exod. 12: 11). They were to be ready to leave. While, according to W.E.Vine, "feet shod with the **preparation** (*hetoimasia*) of the gospel of peace" denotes readiness, it also has the meaning of 'firm footing', perhaps reminding us that we must not be "moved away from the hope of the gospel" (Col. 1: 23). We need to have "a secure footing on the gospel of peace" (A Leckie).

d) "Taking the shield of faith", v.16

"Above all ('in all'), taking the shield of faith ('withal taking up the shield of faith' RV), wherewith ye shall be able to quench all the fiery darts of the wicked ('the wicked one', JND)."

The large shield (*thureos*), from *thura*, a door) envisaged by Paul here measured 4 ft x 2 ½ ft., and was sometimes curved on the inner side. It covered the whole body.

The necessity for such a shield may be illustrated by the attempt of Potiphar's wife to seduce Joseph (Gen. 39: 7-21) and the evil intentions of Joseph's brothers (Gen. 37: 18-20), of whom Jacob said, "The archers have sorely grieved him, and shot at him, and hated him", adding, "but his bow abode in strength ..." (Gen. 49: 23-24). In both cases, Joseph had to contend with "the fiery darts of the wicked". The "fiery darts" refers to ancient fire darts. "Darts and similar missiles were dipped in pitch or some other combustible material, which was then set alight so that the missiles, once released, might serve the purpose of the incendiary bombs of our own day. But Satan's darts, says Paul, are not only stopped but extinguished when met by resolute faith" (F.F.Bruce). It has been said that 'self-confidence is combustible!'

But is it the 'shield of *our* faith'? Is it not what we believe rather than the faith with which we believe it? The "fiery darts" may well be "thoughts of disbelief and distrust that can become a fire in the soul" (A Leckie). The Lord told His people "I have loved you", but they said, "Wherein hast thou loved us?" They did not take "the shield of faith" to counteract their doubts about the goodness and love of God. God had told them that He loved them: this should have been sufficient for them. The word of God would have shielded them.

e) "The helmet of salvation", v.17

"And take the helmet of salvation ..." Compare Isaiah 59 verse 17: in dealing with Israel's wickedness, the Lord will "put on righteousness as a breastplate, and an helmet of salvation upon his head" and "the garments of vengeance for clothing". He will be "clad with zeal as a cloke". See also 1 Thessalonians 5 verse 8, "But let us, who are of the day, be sober, putting on the breastplate of faith and love; and for an helmet, the hope of salvation (that is, that the Lord's coming will bring deliverance from coming wrath: see 2 Thess. 2: 1-2)".

The word translated "take" here (*dechomai)* differs from "take" (*analambano*) in verses 13 and 16. According to W.E.Vine, the word *dechomai* means 'to receive', whereas *analambano* means 'to take to oneself'. W.E.Vine suggests that in the case of *dechomai* (here) there is "a heartiness in the taking". However, we will have to leave this to the grammarians!

What is perfectly clear is that "the helmet (*perikephalaia*) is cover for the head" (A. Leckie). He continues: "The believer's mind is under constant attack: doubts about salvation assail, and the only protection is to rest on what one is by grace!" Our protection against insidious attack in this way is to stand firmly in our minds on the doctrine of salvation. In doing this, we rest on the words of the Lord Jesus: "Verily, verily, I say unto you, He that heareth my word, and believeth on him that sent me, hath everlasting life, and shall not come into condemnation; but is passed from death unto life" (John 5: 24).

f) "The sword of the Spirit", v.17

"And take ... the sword of the Spirit, which is the word of God." Bearing in mind that Paul uses *rhema* here (referring to the spoken word, as opposed to *logos*, referring to the word of God in general), the "sword of the Spirit" is "that word given by the Spirit appropriate to the occasion". (A.Leckie). F.F.Bruce concurs: "The 'word' (*rhema*, as in Eph. 5: 26) is that utterance of God appropriate to the occasion which the Spirit, so to speak, puts into the believer's hand to be wielded as a sword which will put his spiritual assailants to flight. Our Lord's threefold use of this sword when tempted in the wilderness may serve as an example and encouragement to all His followers. This is the one weapon of attack in the panoply of God; against it there is no defence, "for the word (*logos*) of God is living, and active, and sharper than any two-edged sword' (Heb. 4: 12)". (See also Psalm 149: 6.) It was certainly effective in Acts 7 verse 54 when wielded by Stephen: his hearers were "cut to the heart".

We will consider, the final two paragraphs, *(4)* The Energy (vv.18-20) and *(5)* The Encouragement (vv.21-24) in our next and final 'Ephesian' study.

THE EPISTLE TO THE EPHESIANS

"Praying always ... and watching thereunto"

Read Chapter 6: 18-24

In our previous study we adopted, with one small 'home-grown' amendment, W.W.Wiersbe's analysis of Chapter 6 verses 10-24, viz: *(1)* The Enabling (vv.10-11); *(2)* The Enemy (v.12); *(3)* The Equipment (vv.13-17); *(4)* The Energy (vv.18-20); *(5)* The Encouragement (vv.21-24).

1) THE ENABLING, vv.10-11

"Finally, my brethren, be strong **in the Lord**, and in **the power of his might**. Put on the whole **armour of God**, that ye may be able to stand against the wiles of the devil."

2) THE ENEMY, vv.12

"For we wrestle not against flesh and blood, but **against principalities, against powers, against the rulers of the darkness of this world, against spiritual wickedness in high places**". There is no pleasant compromise: it is "against ... against ... against ..."

3) THE EQUIPMENT, vv.13-17

"Wherefore take unto you the **whole armour of God**, that ye may be able to withstand in the evil day, and, having done all, to stand. Stand therefore, having your loins girt about with truth ..."

This brings us to:

4) THE ENERGY, vv.18-20

In engaging with the enemy, the Christian soldier must be energised by prayer. Hence we read: "Praying always with all prayer and supplication in the Spirit, and watching thereunto with all perseverance and supplication for all saints. And for me, that utterance may be given unto me, that I may open my mouth boldly, to make known the mystery of the gospel, for which I am an ambassador in bonds: that therein I may speak boldly, as I ought to speak".

We should notice that Paul deals, firstly, with prayer generally (v.18), and then with prayer particularly (vv.19-20).

a) Praying generally, v.18

"Praying (*proseuchomai*) always with all prayer (*proseuche*) and supplication (*deesis*) in the Spirit, and watching thereunto with all perseverance and supplication (*deesis*) for all saints." We cannot fail to notice: "*all* prayer ... *all* perseverance ... *all* saints".

Preachers today often talk about 'unpacking a verse', and while we might – just 'might' - query the expression, we will agree that every word counts!

i) **"Praying always"** or "praying at all seasons" (JND), that is, at every opportunity and in all circumstances. Paul makes the same point differently in saying elsewhere, "Pray without ceasing" (1 Thess. 5: 17). W.E.Vine illustrates this with reference to a papyrus discovered in Egypt: "An old papyrus letter, lately discovered in Egypt (he was writing in 1914) but written as far back as the Apostles' days, speaks of an 'incessant cough'. Thus not uninterrupted prayer, but constantly recurring prayer is the thought here".

Paul urged the Colossian believers to "Continue (*proskartereo*, 'persevere', JND) in prayer, and watch in the same with thanksgiving" (Col. 4: 2).

ii) **"With all prayer and supplication."** "All prayer" means every kind of prayer - formal, silent, vocal, secret, public, petitionary, ejaculatory.

- **"Prayer."** This is the general word for prayer (*proseuche*) and may be distinguished from "supplications" in its coverage of on-going and regular prayers.

- **"Supplication."** The word (*deesis*) means 'an asking' or 'an entreaty' and often occurs in circumstances of particular need. See, for example, Luke 1 verse 13: "Fear not Zacharias: for thy **prayer** (*deesis*) is heard"; Romans 10 verse 1: "My heart's desire and **prayer** (*deesis*) to God for Israel is, that they might be saved"; James 5 verse 16, "The effectual fervent **prayer** (*deesis*) of a righteous man availeth much". So "supplications" covers special matters. Often in the assembly prayer meetings there are requests for special prayer.

Since Paul refers to four aspects of prayer in 1 Timothy 2 verse 1, we'll take the opportunity to add the remaining two:

- **"Intercession."** This emphasises a further aspect of prayer, that is, representation on behalf of others. Its only other occurrence as a noun is in 1 Timothy 4 verse 5, but the verb form occurs in Romans 11 verse 2, "Elias ... maketh intercession against Israel".

- **"Giving of thanks."** This speaks for itself. One mark of unsaved people is absence of thankfulness. See Romans 1 verse 21. Paul elsewhere urges us to: "Continue (persevere) in prayer, and watch in the same with **thanksgiving**" (Col. 4: 2). See also Philippians 4 verse 6, which employs three of the words in 1 Timothy 2 verse 1 "Be careful for nothing; but in everything by **prayer** and **supplication,** with **thanksgiving,** let your requests be made known unto God".

iii) "In the Spirit." That is, "in the power of the indwelling Spirit" (A. Leckie, *What the Bible Teaches – Ephesians*) meaning, directed by the Spirit. Prayer must therefore be spiritual and biblical. It will not be an empty practice – a case of just 'going through the motions'. It will be marked by concern, conviction and relevance. When the indwelling Holy Spirit is not grieved (Eph. 4: 30), our prayers will not be hindered. We must never forget that "If I regard iniquity in my heart, the Lord will not hear me" (Psalm 66: 18).

iv) "Watching thereunto." The word rendered "watching" (*agrupneo*) means "to be sleepless (from *agreuo*, to chase, and *hupnos*, sleep), and is used metaphorically, to be watchful in Mark 13 verse 33, Luke 21 verse 36 and Hebrews 13 verse 17. The word expresses not mere wakefulness, but the watchfulness of those who are intent upon a thing" (W.E. Vine). We must be intent upon prayer. It must claim absolute attention.

v) **"With all perseverance."** The word rendered "perseverance" (*proskarteresis*) means to "continue stedfastly in a thing and give unremitting care to it" (W.E.Vine). The word *proskartereo*, literally, 'to be strong towards', is found, for example in Acts 2 verse 42 ("they continued stedfastly ..."), Acts 2 verse 46 ("continuing daily ...") and, as already noted, Colossians 4 verse 2 ("Continue in prayer ...").

vi) **"And supplication for all saints."** As Albert Leckie observes, this "'persevering constancy' is 'for all saints' – because none are without need". Prayer is to be made "for *all* saints", and for "*all* men" (1 Tim 2: 1).

The Lord Jesus told His disciples that "men ought always to pray, and not to faint" (Luke 18: 1) and, as always, He was the perfect exemplar of His own ministry. See, for example, "And in the morning, rising up a great while before day, he went out, and departed into a solitary place, and there prayed" (Mark 1: 35), reminding us of David's words: "My voice shalt thou hear in the morning, O LORD; in the morning will I direct my prayer unto thee, and will look up" (Psalm 5: 3).

Luke emphasises the Lord's 'prayer life': He prayed at His baptism (3: 21). He "continued all night in prayer to God" before choosing the apostles (6: 12-13). Luke tells us that "he was alone praying" (9: 18), that He prayed on the Mount of Transfiguration (9: 28-29), that "he was praying in a certain place" (11: 1). He prayed in the Garden of Gethsemane (22: 41).

This brings us to:

b) Praying particularly, vv.19-20

"And for me, that utterance may be given unto me, that I may open my mouth boldly, to make known the mystery of the gospel, for which I am an ambassador in bonds: that therein I may speak boldly, as I ought to speak." As Albert Leckie observes, "Though an apostle, he set a value on the prayers of others for him".

We should note the following: *(i)* Paul's objective (v.19); *(ii)* Paul's ministry (v.19); *(iii)* Paul's role (v.20); *(iv)* Paul's circumstances (v.20).

Ephesians

i) Paul's objective, v.19

"And for me, that utterance may be given unto me, that I may open my mouth boldly, to make known the mystery of the gospel" or "to make known with boldness the mystery of the glad tidings" (JND).

Paul now asks for prayer for himself. But in doing so, he is not thinking about his own welfare, but of the progress of the gospel. In asking the believers at Ephesus to pray for him, Paul did not say: 'Pray that the Lord will deliver me *from* prison', but rather, 'Pray that the Lord will keep me faithful *in* prison'.

Compare 2 Thessalonians 3 verses 1-2, "Finally, brethren, pray for us, that the word of the Lord may have free course, and be glorified, even as it is with you". Only then does he add: "And that we may be delivered from unreasonable and wicked men: for all men have not faith".

The word translated "utterance" (*logos*) means 'speech', the thing uttered. In requesting prayer by the believers in Colosse, Paul asks not only for himself, as here, but also that "a door of utterance" (Col. 4: 3) ('a door of the word', JND) might be opened, suggesting opportunity to speak (Col. 4: 3). Here, in Ephesians 6 verse 19, Paul refers to the *ability* to speak, whereas there, in Colossians 4 verse 3, he refers to the *opportunity* to speak. It is noteworthy that whether Paul is speaking about the ability to speak or the opportunity to speak, he is reliant on God-given help. Here, in writing to the Ephesians, he asks them to pray "that utterance may be *given* unto me, that I may open my mouth boldly, to make known the mystery of the gospel".

In this connection, Albert Leckie suggests that the words "open my mouth" carry the idea of public utterance with gravity and dignity. Compare Acts 10 verse 34, "Then Peter opened his mouth, and said, Of a truth I perceive that God is no respecter of persons". W.E.Vine explains that the word "boldness" *(parrhesia)* means "the absence of fear in speaking boldly; hence confidence, cheerful courage ..." See also verse 20. The same boldness is found in Hebrews 4 verse 16 and Chapter 10 verse 19.

ii) Paul's ministry, v.19

"And for me, that utterance may be given unto me, that I may open my mouth boldly, to make known *the mystery of the gospel* ..." Paul refers here to "the *mystery* ... which in other ages was not made known unto the sons of men, as it is now revealed unto his holy apostles and prophets by the Spirit; that the Gentiles should be fellow-heirs, and of the same body, and partakers of his promise in Christ by the gospel" (Eph. 3: 1-12).

Paul is not referring here to **the terms** of the gospel - these **are** revealed in the Old Testament - but to the blessing of Jew and Gentile without distinction. Compare Romans 16 verses 25-26: "Now to him that is of power to stablish you according to my gospel, and the preaching of Jesus Christ, according to the revelation of the **mystery,** which was kept secret since the world began, but now is made manifest, and by the scriptures of the prophets, according to the commandment of the everlasting God, made known **to all nations** for the obedience of faith ..."

iii) Paul's role, v.20

"For which I am **an ambassador** in bonds, that therein I may speak boldly, as I ought to speak" or "for which I am an ambassador [bound] with a chain (singular)" (JND). Interestingly enough the word rendered "ambassador" (*presbeuo*) is translated "aged" in Philemon verse 9, leading W.E.Vine to say that "Elder men were chosen as ambassadors".

Paul tells us more about his role as an ambassador in 2 Corinthians 5 verse 20. In undertaking the "ministry of reconciliation" and in conveying the "word of reconciliation", Paul and his companions acted as ambassadors. "Now then we are ambassadors for Christ, as though God did beseech (you) by us: we pray (you) in Christ's stead, be ye reconciled to God" or 'We are ambassadors therefore on behalf of Christ, as though God were intreating by us ..." (RV). See Proverbs 13 verse 17, "A wicked messenger falleth into mischief but a faithful ambassador is health".

An ambassador acts and speaks, not only on behalf of, but also in the place of, the sovereign from whom he receives his commission. An ambassador is a representative of another country and another monarch. He is a citizen of another country. He promotes the interests of another country. He seeks to enhance the reputation of another country. He knows the mind and will of that country.

There is therefore a need for faithfulness and precision. This is not a figure of speech or an analogy, but quite factual. God speaks through Christ's ambassadors.

> *I am a stranger here within a foreign land:*
> *My home is far away up on a golden strand.*
> *Ambassador to be, of realms beyond the sea:*
> *I'm here on business for my King.*
>
> *This is the message that I bring,*
> *A message angels fain would sing,*
> *'Oh be ye reconciled',*
> *Thus saith my Lord and King,*
> *'O be ye reconciled to God'.*

iv) Paul's circumstances, v.20

But in the Epistle to the Ephesians, Paul is an "ambassador in bonds": strictly speaking, 'in a chain' (singular). As the RV margin points out, this refers to "the chain (*halusis*) around his wrist by which he was handcuffed to the soldier who guarded him" (F.F.Bruce). Compare 2 Timothy 2 verse 9, "Wherein (referring the gospel) I suffer trouble, as an evil-doer, even unto bonds: but the word of God is not bound". The messenger may be in bonds – but not the message! Someone has described Paul's "bonds" (or 'bond') as his 'chain of office'!

Even so, he asks his brethren at Ephesus to pray that, despite his chain, in his own words, "therein I might speak boldly, as I ought to speak". Let this resonate **with us** too: "I ought to speak". We ought to **pray to God** (Luke 18: 1), and we ought to **speak to men** (Eph. 6: 20). "Ought to speak" means 'It is necessary to speak'.

In passing, "Many people have wondered from time to time what it must have meant for a Roman soldier to be handcuffed (for some four hours at a time) to a man like Paul! A prisoner? Which of the two was the prisoner?!" (F.F.Bruce).

F.F.Bruce asks the question, "Were their prayers answered?" and continues, "Let Luke, Paul's companion, bear his testimony: 'he abode two whole years in his own hired dwelling, and received all that went in unto him, preaching the kingdom of God, and teaching the things concerning the Lord Jesus Christ with all boldness (*parrhesia*), none forbidding' (Acts 28: 20)".

This brings us to:

5) THE ENCOURAGEMENT, vv.21-24

"But that ye also may know my affairs, and how I do, Tychicus, a beloved brother and faithful minister in the Lord, shall make known unto you all things: whom I have sent unto you for the same purpose, that ye might know our affairs, and that he might comfort your hearts" (vv.21-22).

The word translated "comfort" (*parakaleo*) can certainly mean 'consolation', but equally, it so often means 'encouragement'. Just think about it – a man in a chain thinks of encouraging others! Tychicus was coming to update them on Paul's situation and well-being.

According to J.N.Darby, Tychicus was "**the** beloved brother and faithful minister in the Lord". Timothy is similarly described: "**the** brother Timothy" (2 Cor. 1: 1). Paul, seemingly, uses the definite article here to emphasise that Tychicus embodied all that would be expected of a "beloved brother". Tychicus was a well-balanced man. Paul says the same thing about him in Colossians 4 verse 7, adding "and fellowservant in the Lord" or, as F.F.Bruce puts it, "his fellow-slave (*syndoulos*)".

The way in which Paul describes him speaks volumes. Tychicus was not only respected for his loyalty to the truth: he was 'esteemed very highly in love' (1 Thess. 5: 13). His faithful ministry had not made him a hard dogmatist who stood alone and aloof. There was a warmth and attractiveness in his character which drew the love and affection of those who knew him. Tychicus too must have been a tonic to other Christians: "whom I have sent unto you ... that ye may know our estate, and that he may comfort your hearts" (Col. 4: 7-8, RV). How much of a tonic are we to each other: or are we more like 'wet blankets'? Do remember what happened at Kadesh-barnea (Deut. 1: 28).

The Epistle concludes with Paul's benediction: "Peace be to the brethren, and love with faith, from God the Father, and the Lord Jesus Christ. Grace be with all them that love our Lord Jesus Christ in sincerity. Amen" (vv.23-24).

Albert Leckie points out that the benediction here differs "in many ways from that in his other epistles and it must be seen as a summing up of the epistle". We must note the following:

- ***"Peace to the brethren."*** "As brethren the former enmity between Jew and Gentiles has now gone (2: 14, 15, 17)) and they have been called upon to give diligence to keep the unity of the Spirit in the bond of peace (4: 3)" (A.Leckie). As F.F.Bruce observes, "The peace which he bespeaks for them is no conventional salutation, but the enjoyment of peace which comes from God the Father and the Lord Jesus Christ".

- *"Love with faith."* F.F.Bruce continues: "From that source, too, comes the love combined with faith which he desires to abound among them". Albert Leckie notes that "faith is pre-supposed and must be accompanied with love to all the saints (1: 15); converted Jew and Gentile would bear with one another in love (4: 2); and as members of the same body would enjoy self-edification in love (4: 16). This love is from 'God the Father and the Lord Jesus Christ', conjointly as source and channel and in perfect equality".

- *"Grace."* "Grace be with all them that love our Lord Jesus Christ in sincerity, Amen." While this may well express the apostle's desire that they would enjoy "a sense of divine favour, both in salvation (2: 5, 8) and service (4: 7)" (A.Leckie), it is worth considering that Paul uses the word grace here in the sense of the immense benefit bestowed upon God's people: see 2 Corinthians 1 verse 15. It is something to be enjoyed by "all them that love our Lord Jesus Christ in sincerity (*aphtharsia*, incorruption)". M.R.Vincent calls this "imperishable and incorruptible love", and F.F.Bruce adds that "where such love for Christ is present, the grace of God can never be absent". It is not present with those who "love not the Lord Jesus Christ" (1 Cor. 16: 22).